Minsky, Crisis and Development

Minsky, Crisis and Development

Edited by

Daniela Tavasci

and

Jan Toporowski

palgrave
macmillan

First published 2010 by
PALGRAVE MACMILLAN

Palgrave Macmillan in the UK is an imprint of Macmillan Publishers Limited, registered in England, company number 785998, of Houndmills, Basingstoke, Hampshire RG21 6XS.

Palgrave Macmillan in the US is a division of St Martin's Press LLC, 175 Fifth Avenue, New York, NY 10010.

Palgrave Macmillan is the global academic imprint of the above companies and has companies and representatives throughout the world.

Palgrave® and Macmillan® are registered trademarks in the United States, the United Kingdom, Europe and other countries.

ISBN-13: 978–0–230–23507–6 hardback

This book is printed on paper suitable for recycling and made from fully managed and sustained forest sources. Logging, pulping and manufacturing processes are expected to conform to the environmental regulations of the country of origin.

A catalogue record for this book is available from the British Library.

A catalog record for this book is available from the Library of Congress.

10 9 8 7 6 5 4 3 2 1
19 18 17 16 15 14 13 12 11 10

Printed and bound in Great Britain by
CPI Antony Rowe, Chippenham and Eastbourne

Contents

Part II Minsky and Development

Part III Minsky and Crises in the Emerging Markets

List of Tables

List of Figures

List of Acronyms

ABBank	An Binh Bank
APIC	Additional Paid-in Capital
ARM	Adjustable Rate Mortgage
BCRA	Banco Central de la República Argentina
BIS	Bank of International Settlements
Cataco	Can Tho Agricultural and Animal Products Company
CDO	Collateralised Debt Obligation
CDS	Credit Default Swap
CIEM	Central Institute for Economic Management
CS	Common Stock
DFID	Department for International Development
DSCR	Debt Service Cover Ratio
EBIT	Earnings Before Interest and Tax
EBITDA	Earnings Before Interest and Tax, Depreciation and Amortisation
ECLAC	Economic Commission for Latin America and the Caribbean
ENGE	Encuesta Nacional a Grandes Empresas
INDEC	Instituto Nacional de Estatistica y Censo de la República Argentina
EVN	Electricity of Vietnam Group
FIH	Financial Instability Hypothesis
Garco 10	Garment Company No. 10
GC	General Corporation
GP Bank	Global Petrol Bank
Geruco	Vietnam Rubber Group
Habeco	Hanoi Beer and Alcohol Corporation
Habubank	Hanoi Building Bank
Handico	Hanoi Housing Development and Investment Corporation
HCMC	Ho Chi Minh City
IFS	International Financial Statistics
IMF	International Monetary Fund
LA&C	Latin America and Caribbean
Lilama	Vietnam Machinery Erection Corporation
Mobifone	Vietnam Mobile Telecom Services Company
MBAs	Mortgage-Backed Assets
MBSs	Mortgage-Backed Securities
MSB	Maritime Bank

Navibank	Nam Viet Bank
Nhabeco	Nha Be Garments Company
NIAS	Nordic Institute of Asian Studies
OECD	Organisation for Economic Cooperation and Development
Petrolimex	Vietnam Petroleum Corporation
Petrovietnam	Vietnam Oil and Gas Group
PG Bank	Petrolimex Group Bank
PJICO	Petrolimex Insurance Company
PLS	Profit and Loss Share
PVFC	Petrovietnam Finance Corporation
PVI	Petrovietnam Insurance Company
PV Power	Petrovietnam Power Corporation
RFC	Rubber Finance Company
Sasco	Southern Airport Services Company
Satra	Saigon Trading Corporation
SBV	State Bank of Vietnam
Seaprodex	Vietnam Sea Products Corporation
SHB	Saigon Hanoi Bank
SOCB	State-Owned Commercial Bank
SOE	State-Owned Enterprise
Tacombank	Tan Viet Joint Stock Commercial Bank
Tamexco	Tan Binh Production Service Trading and Export Company
UNDP	United Nations Development Programme
VCCI	Vietnam Chamber of Commerce and Industry
Vinachem	Vietnam Chemical Corporation
Vinacoal	Vietnam Coal Corporation
Vinacomin	Vietnam Coal and Mineral Industries Group
Vinapaco	Vietnam Paper Corporation
Vinaphone	Vietnam Telecom Services Company
Vinapimex	Vietnam Paper Corporation
Vinashin	Vietnam Shipbuilding Industry Group
Vinatex	Vietnam Textile and Garment Group
VMS	Vietnam Mobile Telecom Services Company
VNCC	Vietnam Cement Corporation
VNPT	Vietnam Post and Telecommunications Group
Vtec	Viet Tien Garments Corporation
WC	Washington Consensus
WTO	World Trade Organisation

Notes on Contributors

Editors

Daniela Tavasci is completing her PhD in Economics and is Teaching Fellow at the School of Oriental and African Studies, University of London. She has 7 years of experience in the financial sector – asset management. She studied in Bologna, faculty of Economics and faculty of Political Science and in Buenos Aires, Facultad Latinoamericana de Ciencias Sociales – Unesco.

Jan Toporowski is Reader in Economics and Chair of the Economics Department at the School of Oriental and African Studies, University of London; Research Associate in the Research Centre for the History and Methodology of Economics of the University of Amsterdam; and Senior Member, Wolfson College, University of Cambridge. In 2005 he was Visiting Research Fellow at the Bank of Finland in Helsinki.

Contributors

Valeria Arza is Researcher at the Argentinean National Research Council (CONICET) and at CENIT-Argentina, and Lecturer at the University of Buenos Aires (UBA). She has completed a postdoctoral study on University–Industry interactions at Matisse at the Centre d'Economie de la Sorbonne. She holds a PhD from SPRU, University of Sussex, and she has published papers and book chapters on the determinants of firms' innovative and investment behaviour in developing countries.

Riccardo Bellofiore is Professor of Political Economy at the Hyman P. Minsky Department of Economics at University of Bergamo, where he teaches Monetary Economics, History of Economic Thought and Theories of Knowledge. He is also research associate at the History and Methodology of Economics Group at the University of Amsterdam. He edited (with Piero Ferri) two volumes on the *Economic Legacy of Minsky* for Edward Elgar in 2001 and wrote the introduction for the reprint of the Italian translation of Minsky's book on John Maynard Keynes (Bollati Boringhieri, 2009). In 2009 he edited *Rosa Luxemburg and the Critique of Political Economy* (Routledge) and (with Roberto Fineschi) *Re-reading Marx. New Perspectives after the Critical Edition* (Palgrave).

Dirk Bezemer holds a PhD degree in economics from the University of Amsterdam (2001). For several years he worked in academia, consulting and government positions in London before taking up a position at the University of Groningen. His research and teaching are in the economics of development and transition and in monetary economics.

Scott Cheshier is completing his PhD in Business and Management at Queen Mary, University of London, and teaching at the Fulbright Economics Teaching Program in Ho Chi Minh City. Previously at the United Nations Development Programme in Hanoi, he has published several research papers on the Vietnamese economy.

Victoria Chick is Emeritus Professor of Economics at University College London. She studied Economics at the University of California, Berkeley, where she was taught by Hyman P. Minsky, and at LSE. She has published widely on monetary theory and policy, the economics of Keynes and methodology, including a reappraisal of Keynes's *General Theory: Macroeconomics After Keynes* (MIT Press). She has been a visiting scholar at several universities in Europe and the Americas. Her current project is a book, *The Economics of Enough: Steps toward Sustainability*.

Moritz Cruz holds a PhD in economics from University of Manchester. Currently he works as a researcher and lecturer at the Instituto de Investigaciones Económicas of the Universidad Nacional Autónoma de México. His research interests are post-Keynesian macroeconomics and development economics.

Gary A. Dymski is Professor of economics at the University of California, Riverside. From 2003 to 2009, he was founding director of the University of California Center Sacramento. His most recent books are *Capture and Exclude: Developing Nations and the Poor in Global Finance* (Tulika Books, New Delhi, 2007), co-edited with Amiya Bagchi, and *Reimagining Growth: Toward a Renewal of the Idea of Development*, co-edited with Silvana DePaula (Zed, London, 2005). Gary has published articles and chapters on banking, financial fragility, urban development, credit-market discrimination, the Latin American and Asian financial crises, economic exploitation, housing finance and the subprime lending crisis.

Paula Español is Director of the Centre for Studies on Production (CEP) dependent of the Ministry of Production of Argentina. She is Lecturer for undergraduate and graduate students at the University of Buenos Aires (UBA). She holds a PhD from L'ecole des hautes etudes en sciences sociales (EHESS), Paris, France. Her research interests are on topics related to sectoral production structure and firms' innovative and investment behaviour in developing countries.

Joseph Halevi was born in Israel and lived in Italy, studying at the University of Rome. He has taught at the New School for Social Research in New York and at Rutgers University, New Jersey. He currently teaches in the Political Economy Department of the University of Sydney and is associated with the Université de Picardie in France and with the International University College in Turin. His research deals with the history and theories of monopolistic capitalism. Since 1990 he is a regular contributor to the Italian daily *Il manifesto*.

Michael Hudson is Distinguished Professor of Economics at the University of Missouri (Kansas City) and the author of *Trade, Development and Foreign Debt* (new edition, 2009). He has edited four colloquia volumes for the International Scholars Conference on Ancient Near Eastern Economies (ISCANEE) published by the Peabody Museum (Harvard) and CDL Press, as well as many articles on the history of money and books on modern international finance. With Professor Wunsch he has co-edited *Creating Economic Order: Record-Keeping, Standardization and the Development of Accounting in the Ancient Near East* (CDL Press, Bethesda, 2004).

Ewa Karwowski studied international relations at the Technical University Dresden as well as the Panthéon-Assass/Paris II and economics at the School of Oriental and African Studies. She has experience working in (inter-) governmental institutions in Germany, Poland, the European Union and Malaysia. Currently she is an Overseas Development Institute fellow and works as a senior economist in South Africa.

Noemi Levy-Orlik is Professor of Economics at Universidad Nacional Autónoma de México (UNAM). Her research interests include macroeconomics, economic development, monetary economics and the analysis of financial institutions in third world countries. She has written two books and edited six books (in collaboration with Guadalupe Mántey). The last two are: *Cincuenta Años de Políticas Financieras para el Desarrollo. Asociación estratégica para la gobernabilidad y la inclusión social* (50 years of financial policies for economic development) and *Políticas Macroeconómicas para Países en Desarrollo*, (Macroeconomic policies for developing economies).

Richard Marshall is a final year doctoral student at the University of Manchester. Prior to registering for a PhD, he worked on poverty reduction issues and economic policy for the United Nations Development Programme, serving in Mongolia and in Bosnia and Herzegovina. He has also undertaken assignments for the Asian Development Bank and the United Nations Conference on Trade and Development.

Yasuyuki Matsumoto is Head of Asia and Emerging Markets and Global Co-Head of Credit and Alternative Investments of The Norinchukin Bank

(Japan). He received his PhD in economics from SOAS, University of London. His academic objectives are financial economics and political economy of Asian business and his publications include Financial Fragility and Instability in Indonesia (Routledge, 2007).

Yeva Nersisyan is an iPhD student in Economics/Mathematics and Statistics at University of Missouri-Kansas city. She has received a BA with honours in Economics from Yerevan State University, Armenia. Her research interests include Macroeconomics, Monetary and Financial Economics, Monetary and Fiscal Policy and Job Guarantee Programs.

Anastasia Nesvetailova is a Senior Lecturer in International Political Economy at City University. She is the author of *Fragile Finance: Debt, Speculation and Crisis in the Age of Global Credit* (2007, Palgrave) and *Financial Alchemy in Crisis: The Great Liquidity Illusion* (2010, Pluto).

Juan Pablo Painceira is completing his PhD at the School of Oriental and African Studies, University of London. He has worked for 15 years at the Banco Central do Brasil.

Julia S. Loe works as a journalist in the leading independent Scandinavian think-thank 'Mandag Morgen'. Previously she worked in the regional newspaper *Bergens Tidende* and the national Norwegian business newspaper *Dagens Næringsliv* (Norwegian Business Daily).

Jonathan Pincus is Dean of the Fulbright Economics Teaching Program, a collaborative effort of the Economics University of Ho Chi Minh City and the Harvard Kennedy School. A specialist in the political economy of Southeast Asia, he has completed numerous research, teaching and policy assignments in Vietnam, Indonesia and beyond.

Jeffrey Sommers is Associate Professor at the University of Wisconsin-Milwaukee and visiting faculty at the Stockholm School of Economics in Riga (SSE Riga). He is the co-director of the Silk Roads Project and creator and curator of the Andre Gunder Frank Memorial Library at SSE Riga. His research centres on economic history, global studies, global governance and hegemonic transitions. Embedded within this work is research on European Studies, with emphasis on labour migration in Europe within the framework of a wider political economy and regulatory regimes. Recent empirical studies have been on Baltic labour migration from new EU Member States in the context of European integration. He has held two Fulbrights in Latvia.

Luigi Ventimiglia is completing his PhD in Economics and teaching Quantitative Methods for Economics at the School of Oriental and African Studies, University of London. He has 10 years of experience in the financial sector as trader and fund manager. His research interest is in monetary policy and international economics.

Alessandro Vercelli is Professor of Economics at Siena University, Italy. He has been Vice-President of the International Economic Association. He is author and editor of several works in economic policy, cycle theory, environmental economics, development and economic methodology. He has published *Methodological Foundations of Macroeconomics: Keynes and Lucas*, Cambridge, 1991, Cambridge University Press); *Macroeconomics: A Survey of research Strategies* (edited with N. Dimitri, Oxford, Oxford University Press, 1992); *Psychology, Rationality and Economic Behaviour: Challenging Standard Assumption* (edited with B. Agarwal, 2005, London, Palgrave (IEA series)); *Global Sustainability. Social and Environmental conditions* (co-authored with S. Borghesi).

Bernard Walters is Senior Lecturer in Economics at the University of Manchester. He is interested in the macroeconomics of development, particularly in the context of the transition economies. His has co-authored numerous publications: with Moritz Cruz, 'Is the Accumulation of International Reserves good for Development?', *Cambridge Journal of Economics*; with Marshall R. and Nixson F.I. 'Privatisation and Regulation in an Asian Transitional Economy: The Case of Mongolia?', *Public Administration and Development*; with Nixson F.I. 'Privatization, Income Distribution and Poverty: the Mongolian Experience' *World Development*; with Moritz Cruz and A.E. Amman 'Expectations, the Business Cycle and the Mexican Peso Crisis', *Cambridge Journal of Economics*.

Charles J. Whalen is Executive Director and Professor of Business and Economics at Utica College and visiting fellow in the School of Industrial and Labour Relations at Cornell University. His research interests include macroeconomics, labour and employment relations, and the history of economic thought. He is editor of three books, *Political Economy for the 21st Century* (M.E. Sharpe, 1996), *New Directions in the Study of Work and Employment* (Edward Elgar, 2008) and *Human Resource Economics and Public Policy* (W.E. Upjohn Institute for Employment Research, 2010).

L. Randall Wray is Professor of Economics and Research Director of the Center for Full Employment and Price Stability at the University of Missouri, Kansas City. His current research focuses on providing a critique of orthodox monetary policy, and the development of an alternative approach. He also publishes extensively in the areas of full employment policy and the monetary theory of production. With Levy Institute President Dimitri B. Papadimitriou, he is working to publish, or republish, the work of the late financial economist Hyman P. Minsky; and he is using Minsky's approach to analyse the current global financial crisis.

Introduction

Daniela Tavasci and Jan Toporowski

> Some have dubbed this a 'Minsky moment', but the observation belittles the range and depth of Minsky's work. Now it is time to take seriously the insights of Hyman Minsky and build upon his groundbreaking work in order to find ways of putting our financial system on a more solid footing.
>
> (Henry Kaufman, 2008, Foreword to new edition of *Stabilizing an Unstable Economy*)

This edited volume arises out of a seminar series at the School of Oriental and African Studies on developing countries, the ideas of Hyman Minsky and his critique of neoclassical economics. As the financial crisis evolved, however, the discussions came to focus much more on the impact of the current downturn and on the ways in which financial development progressed in the main financial centres now in difficulty. As the contributions to this volume came in, it became apparent that this was the worst recession since the 1930s. This was accompanied by much fashionable commentary on Minsky's work whose analytical value is here open to doubt. Voguish references to 'Minsky Moments', in particular, generally trivialise his insights. The premise of this volume of collected essays is that it is necessary to adapt and refine the original vision of Minsky in order to use his insights to shed light on a number of different contexts. These essays present 'interpretations of Minsky rather than detailed exegesis of his ideas. Minsky always avoided arguments over "what the great man really said", preferring, instead, to present an interpretation. This... [volume] follows the practice of "standing on the shoulders of giants" which Minsky prefers' (Wray, 1992: p. 162).

However, any adaptation must be consistent with his conception of how market economies with sophisticated financing mechanisms operate. First and foremost, this means that any analysis that relies on the actual existence of General Equilibrium would be unacceptable from the Minskyan point of view.

This Introduction deals with the three main ideas that underpin the 18 chapters in this volume inspired by the vision that Minsky had of a capitalist economy with developed financial institutions. As Minsky himself fought against the 'banalisation' of the General Theory, this collection firstly seeks to challenge the trivialisation of the Financial Instability Hypothesis (FIH). This corresponds to Part I, Minsky Today. Our second key idea is to reflect on the distance between neoclassical theory, which was able to absorb some of the insights of J.M. Keynes, and the Minskyan vision of the economy, including his understanding of the state and the market. Part II, Minsky and Development, expands on this. Finally, the book is intended to remind readers that Minsky thought deeply about the development of the capitalist economy. His reflections on that evolution provide particularly fruitful ideas for understanding the specific dynamics of rapidly evolving and vulnerable economies of developing countries and their crises (Part III).

I.1 Reducing the Financial Instability Hypothesis to banality: Hedge-Speculative-Ponzi and Minsky Moments

There are at least two reasons why the global financial crisis seems to have spawned an upsurge of interest in the ideas of Minsky, otherwise so systematically ignored in mainstream discourse. First, the analysis put forward by the neoclassical synthesis, and its New Classical and New Keynesian successors, of the antecedents and transmission mechanisms of the increasingly frequent financial crises, turns out to be very limited (see, for example, Chapters 2–7 with respect to accounts of the recent global crisis). Secondly, it is likely that this recent interest in the work of Minsky comes from the fact that '"Keynesianism" is associated, in the public mind, with "government intervention" and "demand management"' (Chick, 1992: p. 25). Today that government intervention is desperately required and since economics lends legitimacy to economic policy (Minsky, 1986) the FIH seems to be what is needed.

In Chapter 6 of *Stabilising an Unstable Economy* Minsky entitled the last section 'The Reduction of the Keynesian Revolution to Banality' (Minsky, 1986: p. 156). Similarly, this introduction opens a polemic against General Equilibrium considerations and the way in which the neoclassical synthesis had interpreted the revolutionary insight of J.M. Keynes. More specifically, Keynes had uncovered 'essential flaws in capitalist modes of organising accumulation and how policy can cope with these flaws' (ibid.). However, these essential insights were put aside by the neoclassical synthesis and by its 'banal proposition that all would be well if a proper mix of monetary and fiscal policies can be achieved' (ibid.).

Likewise today, the three financial postures of hedge, speculative and Ponzi presented in the FIH and the concept of Minsky Moment have recently become slogans, especially in the media and in the commentaries circulated within the financial sectors. These media and academic publications have disseminated concepts with no explanation or contextualisation within the critique that Minsky advanced of a capitalist economy with developed financial institutions, or within his evolutionary approach and the importance he places on the relation between innovation and regulation, the role he assigns to institutions and so on. The general discussion on the credit crunch has selected only fragments of the taxonomy of the FIH. There is a real risk that the FIH may be stripped of its underlying logic and reduced to mere taxonomy. As a consequence, every period of financial crisis, regardless of its characteristics, would be simply indicated as a Minsky Moment, ignoring the dynamics described in the FIH (see, for example, Chapters 5 and 6).

However, the very term 'Minsky Moment' has recently been used with different meanings. The first one indicates Minsky's current popularity; as the Minsky moment 'has become a fashionable catch phrase on Wall Street' (Lahart, 2007: p. 1). In reality, Minsky never used the expression 'Minsky Moment'. He concentrated on explaining the endogenous dynamic that makes a capitalist economy with financial institutions so unstable. This raises the question of why academics and practitioners realise only now the value of his insights and why he was ignored for such a long time, even during periods of crisis.

In its current usage, the term 'Minsky Moment' is a label pinned to brief periods of time when the markets evolve in accordance with Minskyan theory. This is opposed to the 'normal' (Magnus, 2007) functioning of the market which is determined by internal self-equilibrating forces. But for Minsky, 'The instability and incoherence exhibited from time to time is related to the development of fragile financial structures that occur *normally* within capitalist economics in the course of financing capital assets ownership and investment' (Minsky, 1986: p. 101, italics added). Incoherence and instability are then not exceptional features ultimately posing as exogenous shocks or due to human nature. They are, for Minsky, inherently inescapable features of a capitalist economy with financially developed institutions. As a result, to say that we have an economics for 'normal' times, and an alternative economics that works only during specific times, times of crisis, is inconsistent with Minsky's central idea that crises evolve from periods of tranquillity.

However, 'Minsky Moment' is also interpreted in a different way. Borrowed from physics, a moment indicates a turning effect produced by a force on an object, or like a snapshot taken out of a dynamic process. Other examples in development economics are the turning points of Lewis and Kuznets. They are critical points in a wider process or dynamic. This is applied with the idea of contextualising 'the moment' within a wider dynamic mechanism. Chapters 1, 5 and 6 expand on this idea.

I.2 Minsky and the development of economics

Minsky was disappointed with the way in which economics developed as a discipline. He took every opportunity to draw attention to the inadequacy of neoclassical economics in terms of both its theoretical posture and the technical apparatus that relied upon it (the forecasting models).

Firstly, he was particularly concerned that the neoclassical synthesis was inconsistent with Keynes' General Theory. He showed how the neoclassical synthesis was achieved successively from Hansen-Klein to Hicksian IS-LM and finally to the Patinkin resolution, ending up being a theory which was not able to provide insights to economic policy (Minsky, 1986). '*The neoclassical synthesis became the economics of capitalism without capitalists, capital assets, and financial markets*' (Minsky, 1986: p. 120, italics in original). But he went further in criticising the way economics had evolved. He labelled the debate between monetarists and Keynesians as 'academic nit-picking' (Minsky, 1986: p. 102). 'Both schools argue that the business cycle can be banished from the capitalist world;...at most they are critical of some institutional or policy details.... Neither are troubled by the possibility that there are serious flaws in a market economy that has private property and sophisticated financial usages. The view that the dynamics of capitalism lead to business cycles that may be thoroughly destructive is foreign to their economic theory...that is...the neoclassical synthesis.' (Minsky, 1986: p. 102).

Secondly then, mainstream economics increasingly relied on the efficiency of the market mechanism. Minsky's view about the capacity of the market to reach 'satisfactory performance' was impressively critical. 'While the market mechanism is a good enough device for making social decisions about unimportant matters such as the mix of colors and the production of frock, the length of skirts, or the flavor of ice cream, it cannot and should not be relied upon for important, big matters such as the distribution of income, the maintenance of economic stability, the capital development of the economy, and the education and training of the young' (Minsky, 1986: p. 101). This view then has to be considered, today, within a paradigm that is completely different from neoclassical theory and its successors. Moreover, Minsky's view rejects the notion that markets may exhibit some failures which can be fixed with appropriate regulatory adjustments.

Thirdly, and as a consequence, Minsky allocated a very specific role to economic policy. He described a dynamics in which the state played a role with its regulatory power that would set boundaries to economic activities. These boundaries, nonetheless, were overcome by innovations. 'The evolution from financial robustness to financial fragility did not take place in a vacuum. The sources of the change can be traced to profit opportunities open to financial innovators *within a given set of institutions and rules*; a drive to innovate financing practices by profit-seeking households, businesses and bankers; *and legislative and administrative interventions by governments and central bankers*' (Minsky, 1986: p. 197, italics added). Chapter 11 expands on the 'institutional Minsky' in a context of a transition economy. Therefore, within this vision, there is scope for an essential positive role of state institutions. These can set limits to the downturn so that the instability would not cause depression, so that 'it' would not happen again.[1] This position is essentially different from other supporters of state intervention, amongst the successors of the neoclassical synthesis, who see it as necessary to fix the market, to make it work smoothly. On the contrary, for Minsky, the economy will never be smooth, and the role of the state is to prevent depression from arising out of the inevitable instability.

I.3 Minsky and economic development

Minsky developed his FIH in the context of a closed economy, using, as his model, an economy with developed financial institutions such as the United States. To what extent his theory may be applied to developing countries depends on a number of 'adaptations'. Recently, especially after the Asian Crisis, the idea of applying Minskyan elements to developing countries has been extremely successful (see, for example, Bezemer, 2001; Arestis and Glickman, 2002; Cruz *et al.*, 2006; Martinez, 2006; Arza and Español, 2008, to name just a few). The reason for this success does not depend on the nature of the Minskyan theory as a theory of crisis, confinable to moments, exclusively applicable to non-'normal' brief periods of time. The fundamental reason of this success, rather, lies in the description of a dynamics of the real-world economy (Papadimitriou and Wray, 2003: p. xiii) that is missing in standard economic theory.

The economics of Minsky is dynamic because its object of study is capital accumulation in an environment in which the development of the capitalist financial institutions and relations is fundamental. Not only does he describe the dynamic of the business cycle, which is today the reason why he is so famous, but he also had in mind a longer run perspective on the development of capitalism (see, for example, Chapters 2, 4, 6, 10 and 18). His joke that there are 'as many varieties of capitalism as Heinz has pickles' (Minsky, 1991: p. 10) inspired Chapters 11, 13 and 14 on transition economies. These varieties could be also identified in terms of the evolution of the relation that finance has with the real economy. An example of such analysis, employing the flows of funds methodology, is Chapter 12.

However, today, we live in money manager capitalism: 'The emergence of return and capital-gains-oriented blocks of managed money resulted in financial markets once again being a major influence in determining the performance of the economy. However, unlike the earlier epoch of finance capitalism, the emphasis was not upon the capital development of the economy but rather upon the quick turn of the speculator, upon trading profits...' (Minsky, 1993: p. 113). Today's money manager capitalism sets the stage for the analysis of the 'financialised' derivatives on primary commodities as a new asset class in Chapter 10. Money manager capitalism (see Chapter 2) is characterised by a context of limited safety nets for the unemployed, privatised pension and social security systems and a general retreat of the big government that had operated during the previous phase of capitalism in developed countries.

Nonetheless, the vision of Minsky is also suitable for analysing economic development in contexts of rapidly changing financial relations and institutions such as many emerging economies since the beginning of the 1990s. In fact, increasingly, new generations of scholars analyse crises in emerging countries in the Minskyan tradition. They show how developing economies have also exhibited vulnerability to the dynamics of the global economy. This vulnerability has been captured thanks to adaptations of Minsky expanding his original framework to account for new dimensions. This expansion was made possible especially because of Minsky's dynamic vision of capitalist development.

'The Schumpeter-Keynes vision of the economy as evolving under the stimulus of perceived profit possibilities remains valid. However, we must recognize that evolution is not necessarily a progressive process: the financing evolution of the past decade may well have been retrograde' (Minsky, 1993: p. 113). Minsky thought in a complex manner about the way in which a market economy operated with sophisticated financing mechanisms. These complexities frequently exceeded the formal categories and mathematics in which he tried to express his ideas. The intricacy of his ideas was exacerbated by his attempts to incorporate in his analysis not entirely consistent influences from such disparate authorities as Marshall and Schumpeter (Toporowski, 2008). It is this complexity that makes Minsky's analysis so difficult to present in reduced form, but makes that analysis such a fruitful source of insights into the many different economies that are being integrated not just by trade between themselves, as postulated by the classical political economists, but also by financial relationships operating through a global financial system. Finance, rather than the standard textbook dilemma of allocating scarce resources to competing uses, has become *par excellence* the common problem of countries at different stages of economic development. Minsky's importance for contemporary economics lies in the fact that he, more than any other economist, entered his economic analysis through finance, rather than through some abstracted or exogenous human desire to exchange natural endowments for some preferred pattern of consumption. His ideas may have been limited by his preoccupation with American patterns of financing. But those ideas have achieved global significance because those market systems of financing came to dominate international finance. This volume offers up some of the insights that his ideas can provide in the un-American setting of emerging markets.

I.4 Structure of the book

In the first part of this edited volume, 'Minsky Today', Chapter 1 gives an original adaptation of the financing units while the following chapters give different accounts of the recent crisis using various elements in Minsky's work. The remaining chapters in Part I assess critically much of the commentary about the recent crisis based on partial readings of Minsky.

In 'Minsky Moments, Russell Chickens and Grey Swans: the Methodological Puzzles of the Financial Instability Hypothesis', Alessandro Vercelli highlights the inability of orthodox theory to account for recurrent financial crises. This inadequacy is due, he maintains, to the postulate of *regularity*, considered an indispensable condition for economics to be regarded as a science. The chapter introduces a new classification of the financial units according to the interaction between liquidity and solvency conditions, in accordance with Minsky's view of a monetary economy, and providing an analytical update and adaptation of his insights.

Chapter 2, from Yeva Nersisyan and L. Randall Wray, sees the present crisis as the result of a long-term evolution towards fragility in a context of deregulation and de-supervision started in the 1970s. The effects of the crisis are analysed in terms of further concentration of the financial system which increasingly complicates the problem of policy dealing with 'too big to fail' institutions.

An adaptation of Minsky's balance sheet approach to understand the case of agents with diverse wealth and income characteristics is the core of Chapter 3 by Gary Dymski. The interaction between financial exclusion and the opening up of financial markets, which expanded opportunities to create new products for the excluded, increases the financial fragility of the economy. The effects, given the involvement of those who would have been excluded without these new products, provide a deeper social content to Minsky's analysis.

However, Minsky had also a vision about the evolution of capitalism in a long-term perspective. The next chapter, by Riccardo Bellofiore and Joseph Halevi, highlights how, in order to give a full account of the 2007–2008 crisis, it is necessary to integrate the rise of debt and financial innovation of the 1980s, linked with the deficiency of profitable effective demand of Magdoff-Sweezy and Minsky, with two new elements. They incorporate, firstly, the role of capital market inflation (Toporowski, 2000) and, secondly, the bond between 'traumatised workers' and 'manic depressive savers-plus-indebted consumers'.

In Chapter 5, Anastasia Nesvetailova expands upon political economy aspects of Minsky's vision. Nesvetailova argues that, recently, many mainstream commentators have rehabilitated Minsky only partially with respect to the cyclical nature of financialised capitalism with its financial fragility and the role of leverage. These elements have, in fact, challenged the scaffolding of orthodox finance theory. Nevertheless, she shows how this recent commentary has rather neglected the illusionary liquidity-creating function of innovation.

Similarly, Chapter 6, by Charles Whalen, criticises the use of expressions such as 'Minsky moments' and 'meltdowns' which have been recently used to identify specific incidents rather than the evolutionary path of economic activity at the core of the Minskyan system of thought. The account offered by this chapter draws from two amongst the most important intellectual influence on Minsky, Keynes and Schumpeter. The chapter concentrates on policy proposals and compares them with the policies recently undertaken by the US government.

Chapter 7, by Julia Loe, concludes the first part of this edited volume with an account of the international context of the recent crisis. Originating in the United States, the most externally indebted country today, the present financial instability is related to the macroeconomic imbalances and financial inflation in that country. Those imbalances, in turn, transmit instability to other countries.

The second part of this collection of essays is entitled 'Minsky and Development' and it is dedicated to the economic dynamics present in developing countries. This part is introduced by Chapter 8, authored by Victoria Chick. The chapter illustrates the main outline of Minsky's theory of finance. Rather than his theory of crisis, it concentrates on the structural relationships that Minsky posits by contrasting Minsky's framework with Keynes' more familiar framework. The implications of his framework are discussed for transition economies and for developing economies.

Chapter 9 is authored by Noemi Levy-Orlik. Following Toporowski (2000), the chapter argues that financial inflation is due to speculation activities, undermining investment spending and increasing consumption ratios, till financial bubbles burst. For developing countries, financial inflation and deflation are to be seen mainly in relation with external capital movements that, despite low investment expenditures, have relatively low impacts on consumption. In Latin America, the industrial recession of the 1980s was partially reversed by the globalisation of capital markets which, attracting capital, inflated stock index prices, overvalued domestic currencies and generated volatile, economic recoveries.

However, fragility comes in many forms in developing countries. In Chapter 10, Luigi Ventimiglia and Daniela Tavasci focus on the problems faced by primary commodity-dependent developing countries. They show, in a Minskyan perspective, that within a money manager capitalism setting, the financialisation of many markets increases the fragility of countries whose export revenues and exchange rates are mainly dependent on one commodity.

The next chapter, by Scott Cheshier and Jonathan Pincus, focussing on the only article Minsky wrote on transition economies, offers an original account of the recent evolution of the Vietnamese economy. Within an evolutionary approach, the emphasis on the evolution of institutions is central. Institutional innovation increases the tendency towards financial instability undermining the capacity of policymakers to control macroeconomic variables.

Chapter 12 concentrates on a more 'technical' method to describe Islamic banking in Malaysia. Using a flow of funds analysis, Ewa Karwowski shows how credit is used by households for housing purchases, inflating asset prices, encouraging speculation and hence increasing fragility. Through financial inflation and over-capitalisation, banking reproduces the typical features of the Minskyan instability.

Jeffrey Sommers, Dirk Bezemer and Michael Hudson close this second part with Chapter 13 on Latvia, using a political economy perspective. They interpret the present situation of Latvia in terms of Minskyan debt dynamics, deregulation and privatisation, by way of polemic against the 'small' government advocated by the Washington Consensus and the EU policy, thanks to which, they argue, Latvia went from being a model student of the International Monetary Fund (IMF) to represent another collapsed country.

Part III is dedicated to a number of crises interpreted along the Minskyan dynamics. These tend to focus on specific countries and concentrate on particular aspects which are all relevant for the unfolding of the present global crisis. Ordered in inverse chronological order, they describe a number of crises that have characterised the increased financial instability of the recent period, from the Asian crisis to Latin America.

Chapter 14 opens this last part with an account of Mongolia by Richard Marshall and Bernard Walters contextualising the Minskyan approach within a central Asia transition economy. It provides a review of banking and financial liberalisation in a small open economy in transition.

Along similar lines, against financial liberalisation, Valeria Arza and Paula Español describe the Argentinean crisis in 2001. They discuss how financial liberalisation started in 1992, gave rise to a Minskyan cycle of optimistic expectation during the upward phase of the business cycle triggering speculative behaviour which contributed to macroeconomic financial fragility which eventually erupted in the 2001 collapse.

Chapter 16 deals instead with Minskyan policy prescriptions and the roles of fiscal and monetary policies during the downside of the business cycle. Moritz Cruz and Bernard Walters show, however, how in deregulated contexts such as those of Argentina, Mexico and Brazil during the second half of the 1990s, there is scope for these kinds of policies but the possibilities for a government to pre-empt a crisis are, in fact, limited.

Finally, the last two chapters deal with re-visiting two of the Asian financial crises of 1996–1997. In Chapter 17, Juan Pablo Painceira describes the fundamental role of banking in the Korean crisis. The Minskyan theoretical approach is used through banks' liquidity preferences determining the credit supply during the business cycle.

In Chapter 18, Yasuyuki Matsumoto gives an account of the Indonesian crisis using a financial accounting framework to measure the financial instability of economic units and to aggregate micro activities into macro financial structures.

In addition to the authors of these chapters, we would like to thank participants in the Money and Development Seminars at the School of Oriental and African Studies of the University of London during the academic year 2007–2008 for the contributions that they made to the discussion of some of the papers and many of the ideas that appear in this volume. In particular we would like to thank the Research Committee of the School's Faculty of Law and Social Sciences for generously supporting the seminars out of which this book has grown.

Note

1. 'Can "it" Happen Again'? (Minsky, 1982) is a famous essay in which 'it' is the Great Depression of the 1930s.

References

Arestis, P. and M. Glickman (2002) 'Financial crisis in Southeast Asia: dispelling illusion the Minskyan way', *Cambridge Journal of Economics*, vol. 26.

Arza, V. and P. Español (2008) 'Les Liaisons dangereuses: a Minskyan approach to the relation of credit and investment in Argentina during the 1990s', *Cambridge Journal of Economics*, vol. 32.

Bezemer, D.J. (2001) 'Post-socialist financial fragility: the case of Albania', *Cambridge Journal of Economics*, vol. 25.

Chick, V. (1983) 'A question of relevance: the *General Theory* in Keynes's time and ours', *South African Journal of Economics*, vol. 51: 3 reprinted in (1992) *On Money, Method and Keynes: Selected Essays by Victoria Chick*, P. Arestis and S.C. Dow (eds) (London: Macmillan).

Cruz, M., E. Amann and B. Walters (2006) 'Expectations, the business cycle and the Mexican peso crisis', *Cambridge Journal of Economics*, vol. 30.

Kaufman, H. (2008) Foreword to the new edition of Minsky H.P. (1986) *Stabilizing an Unstable Economy* (New Haven, CT: Yale University Press).

Lahart, J. (2007) 'In time of tumult, obscure economist gains currency,' *The Wall Street Journal*, 8th August.

Magnus, G. (2007) 'The credit cycle and liquidity: have we arrived at a Minsky moment?' UBS Research, March 2007.

Martinez, G.X. (2006) 'The political economy of the Ecuadorian financial crisis', *Cambridge Journal of Economics*, vol. 30.

Minsky, H.P. (1982) *Can 'It' Happen Again? Essays on Instability and Finance* (New York: Sharp).

Minsky, H.P. (1986) *Stabilizing an Unstable Economy* (New Haven, CT: Yale University Press).

Minsky, H.P. (1991) 'The transition to a market economy', *Working Paper no. 66, The Jerome Levy Economics Institute*, November.

Minsky, H.P. (1993) 'Schumpeter and finance' in *From Market and Institutions in Economic Development: Essays in Honour of Paulo Sylos Labini*, Biasco, S., A. Roncaglia, M. Salvati, and P. Sylos-Labini (eds) (London: Palgrave Macmillan).

Papadimitriou, D.B. and R.L. Wray (2003) In Preface to the new edition of *Stabilizing an Unstable Economy* (New Haven, CT: Yale University Press).

Toporowski, J. (2000) *The End of Finance, Capital Market Inflation, Financial Derivatives and Pension Fund Capitalism* (London: Routledge Frontiers of Political Economy).

Toporowski, J. (2008) 'Minsky's "induced investment and business cycles" ', *Cambridge Journal of Economics*, vol. 32.

Wray, R.L. (1992) 'Financial conditions and macroeconomic performance' in *Essays in Honor of Hyman P. Minsky*, Minsky, H.P., S.M. Fazzari, and D.B. Papadimitriou (eds) (Armonk, NY: M.E. Sharpe).

Part I
Minsky Today

1
Minsky Moments, Russell Chickens and Grey Swans: The Methodological Puzzles of Financial Instability Analysis

Alessandro Vercelli

1.1 Introduction

Although Minsky's FIH has been discussed and extended by many scholars since its inception, it is not yet a full-fledged theory as a precise specification of the relationship between some of the crucial variables is still missing or remains largely implicit (a critical survey of much of the literature may be found in Tymoigne, 2006). For that reason Minsky has been often accused of 'implicit theorising' (see in particular Tobin, 1989). In this view the theoretical axioms are not clearly spelled out and their implications for explanation and prediction are insufficiently argued (Toporowski, 2005, 2008). For that reason most academic economists dismissed the FIH, although a few high-level practitioners continued to consider it quite relevant for their choices. In our opinion this is a *non sequitur*. We have to take seriously the criticism of implicit theorising but from it we should draw conclusions quite different from those of many Minsky's critics. Implicit theorising is typical of new revolutionary theories (in the sense of Kuhn, 1970).

After the first intuition of a new paradigm, the underlying theory is made fully rigorous and explicit only through the systematic work of generations of scholars. The invisible hand argument put forward by Adam Smith is a case of implicit theorising. Walras and Pareto made a crucial step towards explicit theorising about the working of a competitive market model one century later, but only with Arrow and Debreu has the theory been fully axiomatised after almost two centuries of efforts on the part of generations of economists.[1] Therefore, in the case that we believe – as we do – that in Minsky's contributions there are important insights which we should not ignore, we have to invest in their development and clarification in order to make them more explicit and operational.

What Schumpeter calls 'pre-analytic vision' (Schumpeter, 1954) plays a crucial role in science, even in hard scientific disciplines such as physics (Kuhn, 1970). This role is particularly important in a discipline as economics that has to deal with the complexity of human motivations. What is really important in Minsky's original version of the FIH is the powerful pre-analytic vision of the working of a sophisticated financial economy, rather than the fragments of economic analysis in which he tried to translate it (see, in particular, Minsky, 1975, 1982, 1986). We believe that Minsky's vision proved to be increasingly relevant for an economy in which finance has been playing a growing role.

The structure of the chapter is as follows. In the second section we discuss why Minsky's 'vision' is so badly needed today. In the third section we develop a constructive criticism of Minsky classification of financial units that underlies his approach. This leads us to suggest a more general and operational classification. In the light of this revised classification, in the fourth section we express in qualitative terms an elementary model that aims to express the core of FIH, that is, its strictly financial part. In the light of this model, we are in a position to discuss in the fifth section some of the most controversial methodological issues underlying the FIH in the conviction that the future of the FIH depends on their constructive solution. The sixth session concludes.

1.2 Minsky moments, Russell chickens and grey swans

The sudden popularity enjoyed by Minsky's FIH during the last financial crisis (and in other similar episodes before) reveals a widespread dissatisfaction with received economic wisdom, at least as far as financial crises are concerned. The prevailing point of view is that while orthodox theory is good enough in normal conditions (believed to apply most of the time) it is unsatisfactory in abnormal times characterised by severe financial instability (Minsky moments). Conventional theory is believed to be incapable of forecasting, avoiding or mitigating a generalised and particularly deep financial crisis such as the subprime one. We contend that in order to understand financial crises and learn how to avoid or mitigate them, we need an approach much more general than that of mainstream economics. The inadequacy of orthodox theory in times of financial crisis does not depend on details that can be easily added or mended, but on its vision of the working of a monetary economy, and in particular on a fundamental assumption that underlies its approach. This is the postulate of *regularity* of economic phenomena that is considered by many orthodox economists as a necessary requisite for economics as a 'science'.[2] The most lucid and uncompromising statement of this position may be found in Lucas (1981). In his opinion economics as a 'science' has to be based on the equilibrium method that applies only to stationary stochastic processes:

> insofar as business cycles can be viewed as repeated instances of essentially similar events, it will be reasonable to treat agents as reacting to cyclical fluctuations as 'risk' or to assume their expectations are *rational*, that they have fairly stable arrangements for collecting and processing information, and that they utilise this information in forecasting the future in a stable way, free of systematic and easily correctable biases.
> (Lucas, 1981: p. 224)

Lucas does not deny that economic phenomena may be irregular, that is, characterised by uncertainty (in the Knightian sense), disequilibrium, instability, non-stationarity, bounded rationality and thus less-than-rational expectations. He mentions in particular the Great Depression that 'remains a formidable barrier to a completely unbending application of the view that business cycles are all alike' (Lucas, 1981: p. 273). He claims, however, that the analysis of irregular phenomena has to remain outside the scope of economic science. In Lucas's opinion this is not a serious problem since the Great Depression is the only significant example of deep and persistent irregularity in economic phenomena. He believes, however, that this historical episode has been an exception and that its weight in secular trends has been vanishing with time:

> If the Depression continues, in some respects, to defy explanation by existing economic analysis (as I believe it does) perhaps it is gradually succumbing to the law of Large Numbers.
> (Lucas, ibid.: p. 284)

This assertion betrays the conviction that 'it', a severe and persistent financial and economic crisis comparable to the Great Depression, cannot happen again and that the period of serious financial crises is over. This conviction proved to be just wishful thinking since starting from the early 1980s we had financial crises of increasing severity and scope up to the grave subprime financial crisis that many observers likened to the Great Depression. In recent crises there has been a revival of Minsky's contributions that, however, have been rapidly dismissed and denigrated in periods of apparent calm. Many mass-media economists, practitioners (both in management and government) and even academic economists often speak, write and act as if orthodox economics were the true theory in most moments, with the only exceptions of Minsky moments considered as extremely rare states of affairs (that, as Greenspan said, 'happen once in a century'). They reason as if the laws of economics were temporarily and locally suspended in proximity of Minsky meltdowns.[3]

We may wonder if this schizophrenic attitude is justified. Minsky is typically rediscovered when it is too late to avoid or thwart the crisis, since the seeds of the following ones, as he often emphasised, are sowed in periods of tranquillity (Minsky, 1975). We claim that we have to adopt a pre-analytic vision that is valid both in calm and stormy periods. It is here where Minsky's FIH is still inspiring. Its contributions apply in both situations and account for the transition from normal to troubled times. Of course, it is much more difficult to translate such a general vision in explicit analytic models. In our opinion, however, a good economic theory is much more than 'a set of instructions for building' economic models (Lucas, 1981). The pre-analytic vision (in the sense of Schumpeter, 1954) must be general enough to help us choose the right approach for the circumstances (Vercelli, 2005).

The practical implications of the regularist approach and the need of a more general point of view may be expressed through a parable freely inspired by a famous remark of the philosopher Bertrand Russell:[4]

> In the animals farm there was a flock of rational chickens [rational in the sense of Lucas] that were more than happy to run to the farmer every morning to be fed. Only one eccentric chicken was increasingly nervous as he had noticed that older chickens had periodically disappeared. One day he expressed the fear that the benevolent farmer was fatting them for the slaughterhouse. The other chickens did not take him seriously. They protested that he was a lugubrious troublemaker and that if some chickens had disappeared this depended on a fox occasionally perturbing the farm's tranquillity. They claimed, however, that no one should worry for the future as the farmer had promised to strengthen the fence the day after. That night the eccentric chicken escaped from the farm before a stronger fence would prevent it and saved himself. The following morning all the other chickens were put on a lorry and brought to the slaughterhouse.

The moral of this parable is that the rational chickens behaved according to a 'science' based on empirical regularities (the farmer fed them every morning): their empirical regularity was apparently wrong only on a particular morning but that moment was the most important one. The eccentric chicken saved himself because he had a more general point of view than his fellow 'rational' chickens.

A popular metaphor likens the subprime crisis to a different bird: a black swan. When in the new-discovered Australia the explorers found black swans, this surprise started to be used as a criticism of induction from empirical regularities to universal laws such as 'all the swans are white'. Since then, the expression *black swan* has been used to indicate an event having a very small probability (in the light of past empirical evidence) that cannot be excluded from the set of possible events. Regularism, however, may still be defended on practical terms. According to the pragmatic version of the regularist view, such as that suggested by Lucas, if we live in Europe we may be fairly confident that swans are white and this empirical regularity may be good enough to guide our choices in most circumstances. A landscape painter, for example, could safely decide to use the colour white and not black to portray a swan swimming in a European lake. Such an attitude, however, would be wrongly applied to financial crises for two basic reasons. First, although the probability of meeting a black swan in Europe is low, its effects (in our case the consequences of a Minsky moment or, worse, a Minsky meltdown) are huge so that we have to take this possibility very seriously.[5] Second, even European swans are not always white: young swans are dark grey and become white only when they are adult. Thus we need a theory of the vital cycle of swans in order to understand and forecast their colour. Financial crises are grey rather than black swans because they are cyclically recurring. We need a theory that accounts for the whole life cycle of financial conditions to explain how they periodically change colour and, under given circumstances, may become dark black. This is what Minsky did with his FIH.

1.3 A suggested classification of financial conditions

Minsky often started his numerous restatements of the FIH by a classification of the financial units according to their financial conditions (see, for example, Minsky, 1982, 1986). We follow the same strategy in this chapter as we need this sort of microeconomic foundations to be in a position to pursue the aggregate analysis of financial fluctuations. The main reason for this is that, contrary to what is often assumed in mainstream economics, financial conditions matter as they influence in a crucial way the behaviour of economic units. As is well known, Minsky distinguishes between hedge and non-hedge financial units (speculative and Ponzi). Hedge financial units are characterised by realised financial outflows not exceeding realised financial inflows and therefore do not have liquidity problems in the current period, and expect that this will happen also in each of the future periods within the decision time horizon. Speculative and Ponzi financial units, on the contrary, have problems of liquidity in the current period as their financial outflows exceed their financial inflows. Speculative financial units expect that these liquidity problems will characterise only the early periods of their decision time horizon while they expect a surplus of outflows in subsequent periods assuring their solvency. Ponzi units expect instead that their liquidity problems will last longer so that only a huge expected surplus in the final period of their time horizon will assure *in extremis* their solvency. The Ponzi units are characterised also by a second criterion: while the speculative units expect to be always able to pay the interest due, this is not true of Ponzi units that have thus a much more urgent need to roll-over their debt.

Minsky uses this threefold classification in a very suggestive way and applies it with a wealth of illuminating institutional and policy details. However, his taxonomy is not fully satisfactory for theoretical and empirical analysis, being a discontinuous measure applicable only to solvent units.

We adopt a different classification that allows a continuous measure in a two-dimensional space and applies also to virtually insolvent units. The dimensions we choose are closely related to the two basic dimensions considered by Minsky in his classification: an index of liquidity in the period t, k_{it}, that measures the ratio between the current realised outflows e_{it} and the current realised inflows y_{it} in a certain period, and an index of solvency k^*_{it} which measures the capitalisation of expected k_{it} for all the future periods within the time horizon m. The current financial ratio is thus given by $k_{\text{it}} = e_{\text{it}}/y_{\text{it}}$. Such a ratio may assume a value greater than 1, that implies a financial deficit, and sustain it for many periods provided that it is properly financed; this implies a corresponding reduction in the stock of cash balances or an increase in the stock of debt or a mix of the two, and this affects the financial constraints faced by the unit in the future.

The crucial variable that defines the financial viability of an economic unit may be expressed in a very simple way by an index of solvency, or net worth, of the unit obtained by capitalising the expected k_{it}. We may thus define the following condition of financial sustainability:

$$k^*_{\text{it}} \leq 1.$$

We can understand this condition in intuitive terms by observing that when $k^*_{\text{it}} > 1$ the 'net worth' of the financial unit is negative. In this case the unit is virtually insolvent unless it succeeds to promptly realise a radical financial restructuring or to be bailed out by other units or the state.

These liquidity and solvency indexes are expressed as ratios, rather than differences as in Minsky, because in this way we can represent all the units within a box 1×1 or in the immediate proximity of its borders. In principle, there are infinite financial conditions that can be represented in such a Cartesian space and in our opinion this may be a significant advantage over Minsky's ternary classification for the dynamic analysis of financial fluctuations. However, we may keep in touch with Minsky's taxonomy: if we consider the space to the left of the solvency barrier, we can easily verify that the units underneath the horizontal line are hedge units in the language of Minsky, while the units above are speculative or Ponzi units. Minsky does not explicitly consider in his classification the units beyond the vertical line that are virtually insolvent. We believe that this is a crucial shortcoming of Minsky's classification. A virtually insolvent financial unit does not necessarily go broke since it may save itself through a radical restructuring or downsizing of its activity, or it may be bailed out by the state or other firms. The destiny of such *distressed* financial units, as we are going to call them, is crucial to describe, explain and forecast financial crises and in order to choose the best possible policy to keep them under control. Therefore, the suggested continuous measurement of units' financial conditions allows a ternary classification that is similar, but not identical, to Minsky's classification: hedge, speculative (and Ponzi) and distressed units.

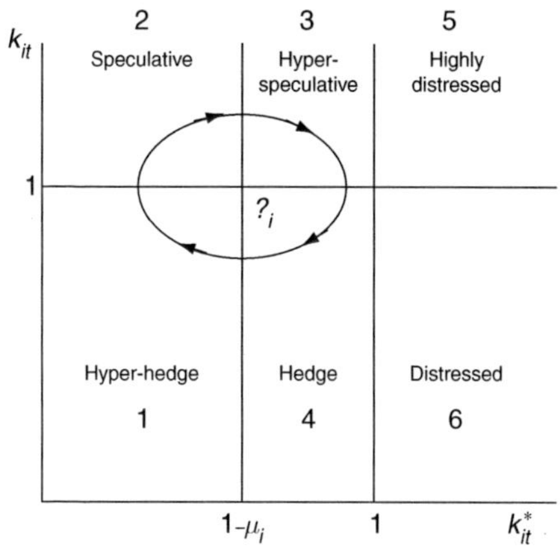

Figure 1.1 Classification of financial units and the cycle of financial conditions.

In order to use this Cartesian space for the study of financial fluctuations, we need a further essential ingredient. We assume that units, in order to minimise the risk of bankruptcy, choose a margin of safety, that is, a maximum value of the solvency ratio sufficiently lower than 1; a threshold beyond which a unit does not want to go. Let's call the safety margin $1-\mu$ and let's assume that $0,5 < 1-\mu < 1$. So we have to introduce a further vertical line at the left of the solvency barrier and this allows a refinement of the classification in six financial postures (see Figure 1.1). Units in field 1 may be called hyper-hedge as they do not have problems neither from the liquidity point of view nor from the solvency point of view. Units in field 2 are speculative as they have liquidity problems but do not perceive solvency problems. Units in field 3 are hyper-speculative as they have both liquidity problems and solvency problems. Units in field 4 are hedge units because they do not have liquidity problems but perceive that they may incur solvency problems in the future as their safety margin is too small. Finally we have to consider the units in financial distress. We can distinguish between highly distressed financial units being both illiquid and virtually insolvent (in field 5), and distressed units that are virtually insolvent but have managed in the current period to obtain financial inflows in excess of financial outflows raising hopes of survival (in field 6). This six-fold classification of financial conditions of economic units keeps a bridge with Minsky's classification while trying to eliminate some of its shortcomings.

1.4 The core of financial instability hypothesis revisited

The modified classification of financial units suggested in the preceding section allows a reformulation of the FIH's core through a very simple model of financial fluctuations in the space defined by k_{it} and k^*_{it}. We contend that the basic building block of the FIH is the interaction between liquidity and solvency conditions (respectively k_{it} *and* k^*_{it}). We refer the analysis to all economic units (financial and non financial firms and households) as their financial behaviour became in the last decades increasingly integrated. This approach is sometimes followed also by Minsky (see Arestis and Glickman, 2002: p. 240). Of course, after this first stage of analysis, we should specify it for different categories of units. In this chapter, however, we keep the analysis at a high level of abstraction.

The feedback between k_{it} and k^*_{it} may be described in the following way (see Vercelli, 2009 for a more detailed elaboration). As soon as a unit perceives to be beyond the safety margin $1 - \mu_i$, it reacts by reducing its current illiquidity margin $(1 - k_{it})$ in order to decrease k^*_{it}. On the other hand, whenever it is within the safe zone $(k^*_{it} < 1 - \mu_i)$ the unit is pushed by competition to increase the financial outflows more than the inflows, and thus k_{it}, in order to increase utility or returns. An increase of k_{it} beyond the liquidity line $(k_{it} > 1)$ in principle deteriorates k^*_{it} by increasing debt while worsening expectations, and vice versa (see Figure 1.1).

The feedback between k_{it} and k^*_{it} may be represented by a very simple continuous-time model which aims to help an intuitive perception of the main causal relations:

$$\frac{k^{*}{}_{it}}{k_{it}} = -\alpha_i \left[k^*_{it} - (1 - \mu_i)\right]$$

$$\frac{\dot{k}^*_{it}}{k^*_{it}} = \beta_i (k_{it} - 1)$$

where $\alpha_i, \beta_i > 0$ represent speeds of adjustment of the unit i and a dot over a variable indicates the derivative with respect to time.[6]

The phase diagram of this Lotka-Volterra model shows that financial units tend to fluctuate in a clockwise direction around the equilibrium point ω_i (see Figure 1.1). The equilibrium ω_i is here a centre, while a shock shifts the representative point on a different orbit that may be external or internal to the original orbit (see, for example, Gandolfo, 1997).

In order to understand the financial behaviour of economic units, we have to introduce a further variable: financial fragility. This variable plays a crucial role in Minsky's approach but its meaning has been so far quite controversial (see, for example, Goldsmith, 1982). We define the financial fragility of a unit as the minimal size of the shock that produces its virtual bankruptcy. In geometric terms, the degree of financial fragility is given by the distance between the representative point and the insolvency line (plus an infinitesimal magnitude). A different, but equivalent phrasing for the same concept could be the following: the financial fragility of a unit is given by the minimal size of the shock that would make negative the net worth of the unit. Both definitions lead us to interpret financial fragility in terms of structural Instability (Vercelli, 1991).

By aggregating inflows and outflows of the single units we obtain aggregate outflows e_t, aggregate inflows y_t, an aggregate liquidity ratio k_t and an aggregate solvency ratio k_t^*. We interpret this process of aggregation not only as a statistical device but as the counterpart of a real phenomenon. The dynamic behaviour of units is fairly synchronised along the financial cycle for two reasons determining their herd-like behaviour. First, the pressure of the market pushes comparable economic units to accept a similar risk-taking position to obtain returns not inferior to those of the other units. Second, mass psychology spreads waves of optimism and pessimism that affect most units; in consequence, the perception of risk becomes insufficient in the boom and excessive in depression. By aggregating the financial conditions of all private units we obtain a model with the same qualitative characteristics of the micro model.

The aggregate model so obtained explains why in a monetary economy there is a tendency to persistent financial fluctuations. This is sufficient to account for the periodic increase of financial fragility when the representative point moves clockwise in fields 2 and 3 (see Figure 1.2). When the economy gets close to the solvency line, a shock may push the most fragile units beyond the solvency line determining their virtual bankruptcy. Their outflows are thus drastically cut reducing by the same amount the inflows of other units so that many of them are pushed in turn beyond the solvency line. This chain reaction triggers the acute phase of a financial crisis. When the contagion affects many units and triggers a recession we have a *Minsky meltdown*.

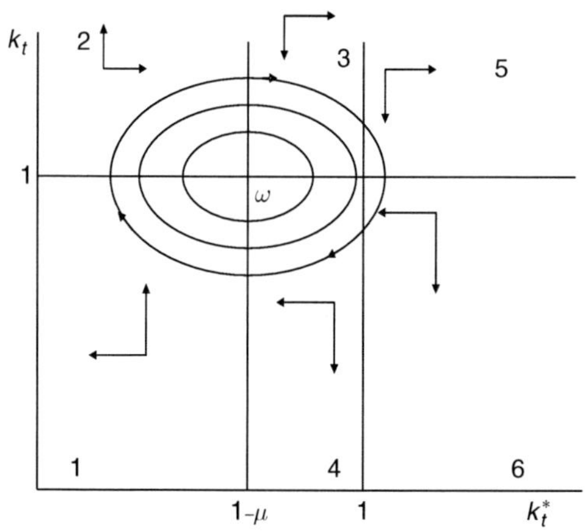

Figure 1.2 Aggregate financial fluctuations.

This core of FIH has to be developed in different directions. In a companion paper we develop in some more detail the analytical features of the model and its policy implications (Vercelli, 2009). In this chapter we only discuss a few methodological aspects of the approach here outlined.

1.5 Methodological implications

Although the heuristic model briefly discussed in the preceding section is extremely simple, it may be a useful reference to discuss a few methodological issues that have hindered so far a much-needed development of Minsky's research programme.

Let me first observe that Minsky's vision is much less reductionist than most other research programmes in economics. The economic system is seen as an open evolutionary system characterised by irreversible time. The system is thus characterised by complex dynamics so that periods of regular behaviour cannot be light-heartedly projected into the future. This basic viewpoint has wide-ranging methodological implications (Vercelli, 2005, 2009). We tried to capture some of them in the simplest possible way through the model sketched above. Although the feedback between k_t and k_t^* is expressed by two elementary equations, this model may be sufficient to represent in a stylised way the crucial self-referential loop, typical of a monetary economy, between part and whole (as k_t^* is nothing but the capitalisation of expected k_t), and between present (realised k_t) and future (expected k_t^*). It is well-known that a self-referential loop of this kind easily leads to complex dynamics and chaos (an example with a similar model may be found in Dieci *et al.*, 2006). The analysis cannot thus be restricted to stationary processes, equilibrium states or steady paths as in conventional economics without missing the most important part of the story and giving a misleading account of the rest.

Equilibrium has a role but only as a benchmark and reference point for analysing the complex dynamics of the system. For example, in the first figure, the point ω_i is an equilibrium in the dynamic sense of the term, but this does not entail the normative overtones of conventional equilibrium modelling. In particular, there is no reason to believe that the objective function of a unit is maximised at this point. On the contrary, it seems reasonable to assume that a higher point on the vertical passing through ω_i may imply higher utility or returns with the same margin of safety. However, a unit set on ω_i cannot reach such a point without triggering a cycle characterised by a persistent disequilibrium. In fact, according to the dynamic equations of the model, an exogenous shift towards a higher k_t would soon bring about a higher k_t^* beyond the safety margin and this would start to exert a downwards pressure on k_t. More in general, the higher points on the vertical describing the safety margin are transitory disequilibrium points.

We cannot thus assume that equilibrium states or paths are dynamically stable nor that the dynamic system is structurally stable. On the contrary, Minskyan financial instability is a combination of dynamic and structural instability. Weak dynamic stability would be sufficient to explain persistent financial fluctuations that periodically increase the financial fragility of units. As we have hinted at before, financial fragility should be interpreted instead as a measure of structural instability, that is, of the propensity of an economic unit to change radically the qualitative characteristics of its financial behaviour. Although we referred to the mathematical concept of structural instability to clarify the logical meaning of financial instability, in order to apply it consistently to our object we had to modify it substantially by introducing ε-structural instability (Vercelli, 1991, 2001). From the economic point of view the important point is that financial fragility cannot be interpreted correctly in terms of mere dynamic instability. It depends, however, on the dynamic instability of the cyclical path and affects it. We can infer from the model above that the less dynamically stable is the financial cycle the higher is the degree of financial fragility eventually reached by units; conversely, the higher the financial fragility of the system the worse is the contagion process enhancing the dynamic instability of the system during the acute phase of the crisis.

In the version here suggested of the FIH's core, as in that of Minsky, units' euphoria does not play a crucial role in explaining financial instability, both in its dynamic and structural sense, as the mechanism underlying financial fluctuations would produce financial instability and fragility even without euphoria. This is not to deny, however, that euphoria is typical of a sufficiently persistent boom and that its spreading encourages over-indebtedness and a more speculative stance of units, accelerating the inception of a financial crisis and aggravating its manifestations. By inserting in the model an endogenous mechanism of production of euphoria during the boom, we would make dynamically unstable the financial fluctuations of the representative point (Vercelli, 2009). We prefer, however, to keep separate these two building blocks of financial instability because they are characterised by a different degree of regularity. The dynamic behaviour of euphoria though correlated with that of cyclical fluctuations, like all psychological phenomena, is much more irregular and is subject to sudden changes that depend very much on a host of specific factors that may vary widely from country to country and from period to period.

We have to discuss at this point a possible objection to the specification of the model. The model's conservative nature (in the dynamic sense) has been considered in other contexts as quite implausible in economics because it implies structural instability in the strict mathematical sense: an infinitesimal perturbation would change the qualitative dynamics of the system (a case in point is Goodwin's model (1967) that has been criticised for this reason, for example, by Desai (1973), while a defence is found in Vercelli,

1983 and Veneziani-Mohun, 2006). In the model suggested in this chapter a possible justification is that this specification somehow captures structural instability observed in the real world. There is something in this answer: in fact a small perturbation may change in the real world the cyclical path from dynamically stable to unstable and vice versa. However, we believe, following Minsky, that the crucial factor of instability of a financial system is the periodic increase in financial fragility that gradually emerges in periods of tranquillity: '... success breeds daring, and over time the memory of past disaster is eroded. Stability – even of an expansion – is destabilising...' (Minsky, 1975: p. 127). For this to happen it is sufficient to assume that dynamic stability is too weak to thwart persistent fluctuations. In addition such a specification may be considered as a fit representation of what we believe to be a stylised fact: the interaction between liquidity and solvency conditions of financial units brings about persistent fluctuations that do not have an *intrinsic* tendency to change through time. It seems reasonable to argue that these changes – that no doubt are observed in the real world – depend on different factors that remain exogenous to this specification of the FIH core.

The specification chosen for our model may help us to clarify another controversial methodological issue: the role of shocks in a model of financial fluctuations.[7] In our suggested approach, as we believe in that of Minsky, the financial cycle is explained by the structural characteristics of the economy, as represented by the equations of the model, in sharp contrast with the conventional view prevailing in macroeconomics since the late 1970s. As is well-known, the latter is based upon the equilibrium approach worked out by Lucas in the 1970s (Lucas, 1981). In this view business cycles should not be interpreted as disequilibrium fluctuations around an equilibrium trend, as was usual before, but as the consequence of random shocks displacing equilibrium without disrupting it. As for the nature of relevant shocks, the prevailing view changed through time. In the first version of equilibrium business cycles Lucas considered relevant shocks as essentially monetary impulses brought about by discretionary decisions of monetary authorities. In the early 1980s the prevailing view shifted towards the 'real business cycles' approach (Kydland and Prescott, 1982) where fluctuations are produced by real shocks (mainly technological impulses). A bit later New Keynesian Economics struggled to reintroduce in the model Keynesian features such as asymmetric information (see, for a survey, Clarida *et al.*, 1999). The ensuing 'New Consensus' added real and nominal rigidities to the equilibrium approach but did not modify it in a substantial way (Woodford, 2003). On the contrary, in a model based on the FIH, shocks are not essential to explain neither persistent financial fluctuations nor a financial crisis. In particular we do not need shocks to explain the periodic increase of speculative attitudes, indebtedness and financial fragility of most units, and of the entire economy, culminating with a boom. This is not to say, however, that disturbances do not have any role to play in a FIH approach:

> A break in the boom occurs whenever ... reversals in present-value relations take place. Often this occurs after the increase in demand financed by speculative finance has raised interest rates, wages of labour, and prices of material.
>
> (Minsky, 1986: p. 220)

Reversals in present-value relations (that is, in our language, when k^*_{it} breaches the solvency barriers) are the more probable the higher is the fragility of units. In a fragile financial system, even a 'slight disturbance' may precipitate a crisis (Minsky, 1964). The concept of financial fragility is one of vulnerability to shocks that is periodically increased for endogenous reasons, as is shown also in our model. In addition, the triggering shocks are also typically endogenous in the sense that they are produced within the economic system. There is no reason, however, to exclude a role for exogenous shocks produced by forces not included in the theory (say, wars, natural catastrophes or foreign impulses; see Arestis and Glickman, 2002). This is particularly important if we use models in empiric analysis. Since models are bound to circumscribe the object of analysis, many factors, also economic factors, are condemned to remain exogenous to the model so that their impact on the endogenous variables has the logical nature of an exogenous shock, even if we rightly believe that these factors are in fact endogenous to the economic system. To avoid confusion between the two meanings of exogenous, we suggest distinguishing between *exogenous shock* in the usual meaning of factor not explicitly interacting with the endogenous variables of the model, and *uncorrelated shock* for a factor exogenous to the model that we believe to be also in the real world independent of endogenous variables. Summing up, disturbances have a role to play in the FIH; a role that, however, is very different from that played in conventional models of business cycle. In the conventional models shocks are essential and not easily identifiable:

> ... we are used to thinking of shocks as exogenous events, arising from "outside the model" so to speak. However, econometricians typically do not measure shocks directly but instead infer them from movements in macroeconomic variables that they cannot otherwise explain.
>
> (Bernanke, 2004)

In this view shocks are by definition the cause of fluctuations that economic fundamentals cannot explain, while in the FIH we would have fluctuations anyhow, while the relevant disturbances affecting them are sizeable, identifiable and have in principle an explanation.

Since the economic system is considered by the FIH as an open process characterised by irreversible time and complex dynamics, it is intrinsically unpredictable. This does not imply that we are left completely without compass in our decisions. We cannot rely on traditional probability and decision theories, unless we are in a period of tranquillity: even in this case, however, conventional probability and decision theories can be used, but only with the greatest caution. We have to resort in general to non-conventional probability theory (such as Choquet theory of capacities) or non-conventional decision theories in conditions of hard uncertainty. In particular we should expect the periodic emergence of financial fragility and the risk of recurrent financial crises, unless we take structural measures to mitigate them. In such a world, the economic agents cannot be rational in the usual sense. We cannot assume that agents succeed in converging instantaneously to the equilibrium position maximising their objective function. This, however, does not imply sheer irrationality. A rational agent may rely on rules of behavioural rationality adapting in the best possible way to a changing environment, taking account of the influence that may be exerted on the environment (Vercelli, 2005).

Finally, we emphasise that in the complex world of FIH the relationship between microeconomics and macroeconomics is much more complex than in conventional economics. The analysis of macroeconomic fluctuations is based on a previous analysis of units' financial conditions but is not derived from a simple linear aggregation of average behaviours. Aggregation is rooted in real-word processes that we mentioned above (Section 1.4). The behaviour of a financial unit, studied in isolation from the movement of other units, is unlikely to exhibit a very regular pattern because each unit is heavily conditioned by specific features: different risk aversion, technological impulses, regional constraints and so on. A certain degree of regularity and synchronisation is conferred to single units by the common influence exerted on them by aggregate financial fluctuations.

Summing up, a full-fledged behavioural analysis of units' dynamic behaviour requires macroeconomic foundations while the study of aggregate fluctuations has to rely on microeconomic foundations (analysis of single units' financial conditions). The interaction between micro and macro foundations does not involve a vicious logical circle as it is the consequence of a real process: the financial behaviour of each unit is heavily influenced by the behaviour of all the other units as expressed by aggregate indexes.

1.6 Conclusion

In this chapter we argued that Minsky's FIH initiated a research programme that is still worth pursuing to understand the working and evolution of financial capitalism and in particular the recurring episodes of financial instability. The vital feature of Minsky's contributions is the underlying vision concerning the working of a sophisticated monetary economy, rather than the analytical constructs in which he tried to translate it. We maintained in particular that the complex and well-articulated vision underlying the FIH did not lose its grip with the real world. On the contrary, its relevance for understanding, preventing or at least mitigating, financial crises has actually increased, provided that we update and develop its insights also from the analytical point of view. However, we cannot succeed in this task unless we understand the far-reaching methodological features of the approach designed and practiced by Minsky himself. This paper pursued this direction of analysis by suggesting a more general taxonomy of units' financial conditions. We argued that this alternative classification has the advantage of being continuous and considering explicitly also the units virtually broke. This allowed a study of units' fluctuations in the Cartesian space of financial conditions that has been used to clarify the core of FIH and Minsky's powerful methodological approach. We hope that the approach here advocated may be a starting point to update and develop the FIH in order to increase its theoretical and empirical scope.

Notes

1. The Arrow-Debreu model, however, lost much of the institutional, sociological and psychological insights that we find in Smith. More in general we should be aware that the process of making explicit a theory is almost never without costs, as it often relies on reductionist strategies.
2. This assumption is very similar to the postulate of 'uniformity of nature' claimed, among others, by Galileo, Hume, Kant and John Stuart Mill to lie at the very foundations of natural science. John Stuart Mill maintained that such a principle is a necessary foundation of inductive arguments. Inductivism has been subsequently rejected by philosophers of science such as Russell and Popper even in reference to natural sciences.
3. Similarly many physicists, even illustrious ones, believed that the laws of physics were distorted or 'suspended' in proximity of black holes. Oppenheimer for example maintained that time 'stopped' in the region characterized by a black hole (Oppenheimer and Volkoff, 1939). Physicists struggled to build a more general version of relativity theory able to account for the physics of black holes obtaining remarkable success in recent years (starting from Hawking and Penrose, 1970).
4. This is the remark: 'The man who has fed the chicken every day at last wrings its neck instead, showing that more refined views as to the uniformity of nature would have been useful to the chicken' (Russell, 1912, chap IV, *On induction*).
5. Taleb in his bestselling book *The Black Swan* uses the metaphor in a sense similar to that here suggested (Taleb, 2007). In his opinion, black swans have a crucial importance in Extremistan (although not so much in Mediocristan) while the world is becoming increasingly similar to Extremistan. This is particularly true with finance.
6. The specification of this model is based on Vercelli (2000) and Sordi and Vercelli (2006). The model here is expressed in continuous time while shocks are taken into consideration in qualitative terms and play a crucial, although accessory, role (see Section 1.5).
7. We define a shock as an impulse from a factor not considered explicitly in the model that impinges on the variables of the model.

References

Arestis, P. and M. Glickman (2002) 'Financial crisis in Southeast Asia: dispelling illusion the Minskyan way', *Cambridge Journal of Economics*, vol. 26.

Bernanke, B.S. (2004) 'The great moderation', Remarks by Governor B.S. Bernanke at the Meeting of the Eastern Economic Association, 20th February, Federal Reserve, Washington DC.

Clarida, R., J. Gali and M. Gertler (1999) 'The science of monetary policy: a New Keynesian perspective', *Journal of Economic Literature*, vol. 37: 4.

Desai, M. (1973) 'Growth cycles and inflation in a model of the class struggle', *Journal of Economic Theory*, vol. 6.

Dieci, R., S. Sordi and A. Vercelli (2006) 'Financial fragility and global dynamics', *Chaos, Solitons and Fractals*, vol. 29: 3.

Gandolfo, G. (1997) *Economic Dynamics – Study Edition*, 3rd edn (Berlin: Springer Verlag).

Goldsmith, R.W. (1982) 'Comment' in C.P. Kindleberger and J.P. Laffargue (eds) *Financial Crises: Theory, History, Policy* (Cambridge: Cambridge University Press).

Goodwin, R. (1967) 'A growth cycle' in C.H. Feinstein (ed.) *Socialism, Capitalism and Economic Growth* (Cambridge: Cambridge University Press).

Hawking, S.W. and R. Penrose (1970) 'The singularities of gravitational collapse and cosmology' in *Proceedings of the Royal Society of London, Series A, Mathematical and Physical Sciences*, vol. 314.

Kuhn, T.S. (1970) *The Structure of Scientific Revolutions*, 2nd edn (Chicago: Chicago University Press).

Kydland, F.E. and E.C. Prescott (1982) 'Time to build and aggregate fluctuations', *Econometrica*, vol. 50.

Lucas, R.E. (1981) *Studies in Business in Business Cycle Theory* (Oxford: Basil Blackwell).

Minsky, H.P. (1964) 'Financial crisis, financial system and the performance of the economy' in *Commission on Money and Credit* (Englewood Cliffs: Private Capital Markets, Prentice-Hall).

Minsky, H.P. (1975) *John Maynard Keynes* (New York: Columbia University Press).

Minsky, H.P. (1982) *Can 'It' Happen Again? Essays on Instability and Finance* (New York: Sharp).

Minsky, H.P. (1986) *Stabilizing an Unstable Economy* (New Haven, CT: Yale University Press).

Oppenheimer J.R. and G.M. Volkoff (1939) 'On massive neutron cores', *Physical Review*, vol. 55.

Russell, B. (1912) *The Problems of Philosophy* (London: Williams and Norgate).

Sordi, S. and A. Vercelli (2006) 'Financial fragility and economic fluctuations', *Journal of Economic Behaviour and Organization*, vol. 61: 4.

Schumpeter, J.A. (1954) *A History of Economic Analysis* (Oxford: Oxford University Press) reprinted by Allen and Unwin, London, 1982.

Tobin, J. (1989) 'Book review of "Stabilizing an Unstable Economy" by Hyman P. Minsky', *Journal of Economic Literature*, vol. 27.

Toporowski, J. (2005) *Theories of Financial Disturbance* (Cheltenham: Elgar).

Toporowski, J. (2008) 'Minsky's "induced investment and business cycles" ', *Cambridge Journal of Economics*, vol. 32.

Tymoigne, E. (2006) 'The Minskyan system', Part 1, 2, and 3, *Working papers* N°, *452, 453, 455 The Levy Economics Institute of Bard College.*

Veneziani, R. and Mohun, S. (2006) 'Structural stability and Goodwin's growth cycle', *Structural Change and Economic Dynamics*, vol. 17: 4.

Vercelli, A. (1983) 'Is instability enough to discredit a model?' in *Proceedings of the seminar on non-linear theory of fluctuating growth, Economic Notes*, vol. 3.

Vercelli, A. (1991) *Methodological Foundations of Macroeconomics. Keynes and Lucas* (Cambridge: Cambridge University).

Vercelli, A. (2000) 'Financial fragility and cyclical fluctuations', *Structural Change and Economic Dynamics*, vol. 1.

Vercelli, A. (2001) 'Minsky, Keynes and the structural instability of a sophisticated monetary economy', in R. Bellofiore and P. Ferri (eds) *Financial Fragility and Investment in the Capitalist Economy* (Cheltenham: Elgar).

Vercelli, A. (2005) 'Rationality, learning and complexity', in B. Agarwal and A. Vercelli (eds) *Psychology, Rationality and Economic Behaviour: Challenging Standard Assumptions* (London: Palgrave Macmillan).

Vercelli, A. (2009) 'A perspective on Minsky Moments: The core of the Financial Instability Hypothesis in light of the subprime crisis', Levy Working Paper, n. 579, The Levy Economics Institute of Bard College, Annandale-On-Hudson, 2009, forthcoming in *Review of Political Economy*.

Woodford, M. (2003) *Interest and Prices: Foundations of a Theory of Monetary Policy* (Princeton: Princeton University Press).

2
Transformation of the Financial System: Financialisation, Concentration and the Shift to Shadow Banking

Yeva Nersisyan and L. Randall Wray

2.1 Introduction

There is little doubt that the current crisis is the worst since the Great Depression. US real GDP fell by 5.4 per cent in the first quarter of 2009 alone and investment shrank by 50 per cent. The economy shed as many as 571,000 jobs from August to September, 2009 and November's official unemployment rate jumped to 10.2 per cent while the broader measure (U-6) rose to a post-depression record of 17.5 per cent (BLS). Yet despite all the dire statistics, most economists believe that the US economy is on the path to a recovery, albeit a jobless one. The conventional view points to the following as evidence: the Dow Jones Industrial Average crossed the 10,000 mark, the housing market is widely believed to have bottomed and credit is flowing again at least to some sectors.

Proffered explanations regarding the causes of the current debacle include: irrational exuberance, perverse incentives, greedy bankers and misguided policy. Some economists who follow Minsky, however, have argued that the current crisis was the expression of fundamental flaws of capitalism, and particularly of money manager capitalism (Wray, 2009). It was not unexpected, and came as a 'shock' only to the 'true believers' of free markets, like Alan Greenspan. The current crisis was not the result of greed, fraud or wrong incentives, although they all played a role. It was rather the ultimate outcome of a system that had evolved towards fragility over the past half century. As Minsky warned, stability is destabilising and it is not surprising that in the context of deregulation and de-supervision starting in 1970s the financial system had become prone to repetitive crises that became more frequent and longer-lasting.

Historically, major reforms that fundamentally change the structure of the system have taken place during major disturbances that create the necessary conditions by bringing together various groups interested in change. In the months that followed the failure of the Wall Street giant Lehman Brothers, which many believe triggered the crisis, there was a general consensus on the need for fundamental reforms. Even analysts pessimistic about the political will of the administration to reform Wall Street believed that change was inevitable to prevent the financial sector from undermining its own foundations. But today what's surprising is how little things have changed. There have been some superficial reforms but financial institutions are back to business as usual, booking imaginary profits and looking for another asset class to inflate.

Designing proper policies requires analyzing what really went wrong in the system and establishing regulations and institutions that would constrain the inherent instability of the system. So far, official policy propositions only tinker around the edges but leave the system's underlying structure largely unchanged. It seems that the most we can expect is an attempt to get the incentives right so that market discipline can start doing the job that it has so obviously failed to do. We believe this is doomed to failure. We face a systemic problem which can only be solved by modifying the system. As Minsky argued, the evolution of the financial system should be guided in a manner so as to reduce instability (Minsky, 1986/2008: p. 349). That requires fundamental change.

This chapter sheds light on the changes that have occurred in the financial structure of the US economy over the post-war period as it came to take an ever larger share of income flows. An examination of the shift of the relative weights of various types of financial institutions as well as other developments in the financial sector shows how the whole system evolved towards fragility. Increased concentration in the banking sector has created a few large 'too big to fail' institutions of 'systemic importance' – institutions we would prefer to designate as 'too big to save' because they are 'systemically dangerous'. This problem is exacerbated after each crisis as institutions that survive the crises become bigger and more powerful. Meanwhile, even though large portions of managed money have been wiped out during the crisis, it is obvious that it has made a comeback and is looking for another bubble. And policy is actually pursuing a strategy of increasing the size and importance of the most dangerous institutions.

Finally, we briefly discuss the reforms, or lack thereof, in the United States. Despite its anti-Wall Street rhetoric, the Obama administration has failed to bring any significant changes to the way finance operates. Rather, policy actions have not only failed to downsize the financial sector but have contributed to creating even larger institutions said to be too big to fail. And even Obama's timid proposals are facing major resistance from the financiers, thus, are unlikely to pass. As memories of the crisis fade away, the momentum for real change has been lost. Indeed, the policy response to date has sown the seeds for another crisis. We do not have the space to delineate specific alternatives, but argue that downsizing finance is a prerequisite to achieving any success at restoring stability to the financial system.

2.2 Financialisation of the US Economy

In his stages approach, Minsky called the current phase Money Manager Capitalism, characterised by 'highly levered profit-seeking organisations' such as money market mutual funds, mutual funds, sovereign wealth funds and private pension funds (Minsky, 1986/2008). A number of structural changes have contributed to creating a fragile financial system. The ultimate outcome is repetitive bubbles, which turn into financial crises after blowing up. It is ironic that after each crisis the financial sector 'recovers' first, leaving long lasting impacts on the real economy in terms of lost output and prolonged unemployment – and setting the stage for the next collapse.

Minsky rightly argued that relatively robust performance of the economy during the post-war period was not due to the private sector becoming more stable, it was rather the outcome of effective institutional constraints in the form of regulation, and creation of the Big Government and Big Bank. Another factor conducive to stability was that most debts had been wiped out during the depression leaving the private sector with little debt – simplifying balance sheets in Minsky's terms. Additionally, a large government deficit gave households and firms a safe financial asset in the form of government debt that was leveraged to produce robust growth (Wray, 2009).

Meanwhile, the New Deal Reforms ensured the financial sector's share of the economy remained fairly limited: it only performed a supporting role for the productive sector. A number of rules helped to restrict concentration in the financial sector and forestalled the emergence of large institutions of 'systemic importance' – especially the Glass-Steagall Act that separated commercial banks from investment banks ensuring a guaranteed profit for the former, as well as interstate banking rules that helped to limit the size of institutions and made regulating them easier.

The immediate post-war period, as Minsky argued, experienced long expansion with mild recessions but no financial crises. But stability is destabilising, and this long period of robust growth created the necessary conditions for financial crises to return. As financial innovations circumventing regulation flourished and New Deal regulations eroded, the system gradually transitioned to fragility making another debt deflation possible.

Over time, we saw an increasing role for the financial sector, the so-called financialisation of the economy. Unlike the early post-war period where finance played a peripheral role, largely supporting the industrial sector, in most developed countries it now dictated the rules of the game. Krippner defines financialisation as a 'pattern of accumulation in which profits accrue primarily through financial channels rather than through trade and commodity production' (Krippner, 2005). Indeed, the distinction between 'finance' and 'industry' disappeared as major manufacturers such as General Electric and General Motors constructed financial arms that were (at times) far more profitable than their manufacturing business. This made the real economy vulnerable to the instability in the financial sector.

Figure 2.1 shows how the financial sector's share of corporate profits has risen rapidly (especially since the 1970s) while its contribution to gross value added has remained relatively stable. In recent years, while the financial sector contributed just 20 per cent to GDP, it reaped 40 per cent of corporate profits.

The graph depicts the financial sector's outstanding credit market debt. From the mid-1970s outstanding debt has been growing rapidly – much

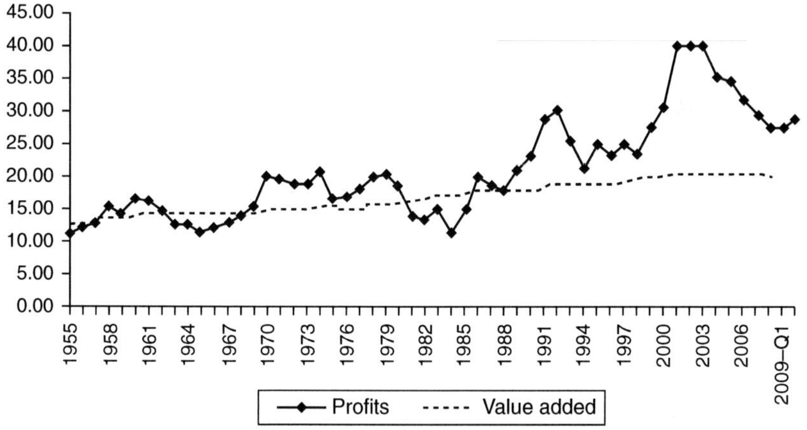

Figure 2.1 Share of the financial sector in corporate profits and value added.
Source: Bureau of Economic Analysis.

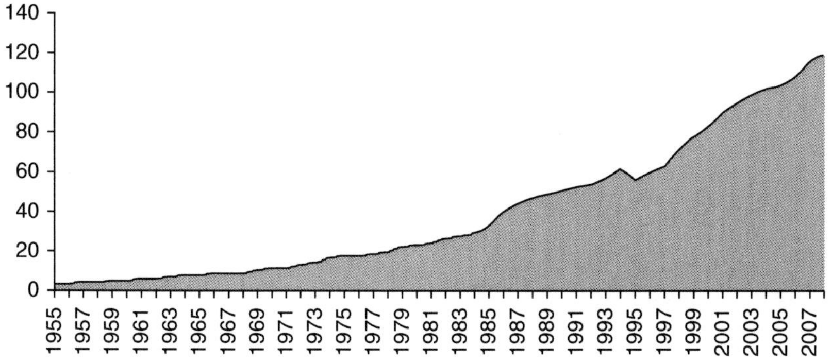

Figure 2.2 Financial sector credit market debt outstanding (percentage of GDP).
Source: Federal Reserve Flow of Funds Accounts.

more rapidly than GDP or the income flows necessary to service debt. This indicates that 'leverage' or 'layering' for the whole system has increased. Without the Big Bank and Big Government the graph would look very different: during each crisis the level of outstanding debt would decrease. But without a large-scale debt deflation, the financial sector has been allowed to expand outstanding debt to 120 per cent of US GDP (Figure 2.2).

2.3 Concentration and shift to the Shadow Financial Sector

The regulatory framework's dismantling since the 1970s boosted growing concentration in the financial system. US financial institutions grew in part because of the elimination of niche banking, allowing big banks to engage in a larger variety of financial activities. With globalisation and the rise of securitisation, many large domestic institutions became active participants in global financial markets thus growing even bigger. Each sector came to be dominated by a few large institutions with each institution being so large as to be able to bring down the whole system if it failed.

D'Arista argues that already by the 1980s the level of concentration was unacceptably high: 'Less than 1 percent of the total number of banks, securities firms and life insurers accounted for half of the total resources of those sectors. Property casualty insurers and thrifts were only slightly less concentrated with 2 percent of the former and 4 percent of the latter accounting for half of their sectors' resources. She also reports that as a result of a number of mergers and acquisitions in 1984 the top 10 securities firms (0.12 per cent of the firms in the sector) accounted for 41 per cent of the sector's capital and 47 per cent of total revenue (D'Arista, 2009). Today, of those top 10 securities firms, only one is left: Goldman Sachs. The rest have been merged or acquired by other institutions (Figure 2.3).

Another major transformation was the shift of the weight of the financial system away from banks and towards managed money. Commercial banks and saving institutions have become a much smaller share of the financial sector as seen from the relative shrinking of their assets. In 2007, institutional investors held about $24 trillion, or 38 per cent of total financial assets of the financial sector, compared to $12 trillion, or 19 per cent, held by banks (Flow of Funds Accounts). The rise of money managers has been accompanied by concentration of assets in each sector in the hands of very few institutions.

The graph below shows financial sector total credit market debt outstanding. Credit market debt owed by commercial banks, finance companies and savings institutions has decreased while borrowing by ABS issuers, Agency and Government-sponsored Enterprise (GSE)-backed mortgage pools as well as funding corporations has grown. A remarkable change is the increase of credit market borrowing by ABS issuers: from nothing in 1984 to more than 20 per cent of total credit market borrowing in 2008 (Figure 2.4).

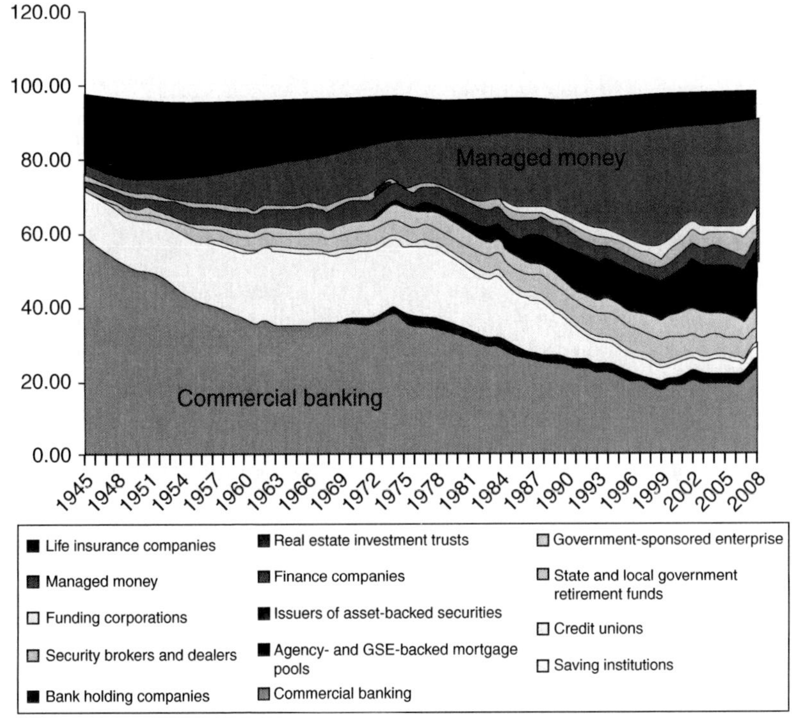

Figure 2.3 Shares of financial institutions (as percentage of total assets).
Source: Federal Reserve Flow of Funds Accounts.

2.4 The banking sector

Banks are central to the operation of a capitalist economy. Minsky argued that the assets and liabilities of banks largely determine the financial framework of the economy (Minsky, 1986/2008: p. 354). The fragility of the financial structure is based on the quality of loans made by bankers. If bankers finance risky operations, they become fragile. Before the invention of securitisation, banks were interested in granting loans only to creditworthy customers. As Minsky argued, a successful loan officer was considered to be 'a partner of a borrower' (Minsky, 1986/2008: pp. 260–261). Financial innovations such as securitisation and Credit Default Swaps (CDSs), however, have separated risk from responsibility, contributing to a deterioration of loan quality and hence greater fragility. Deregulation allowed banks to engage in all sorts of risky activities many of which are incompatible with the role banks are supposed to play. Many of the larger banks have changed so much that it is unclear whether they can be called banks.

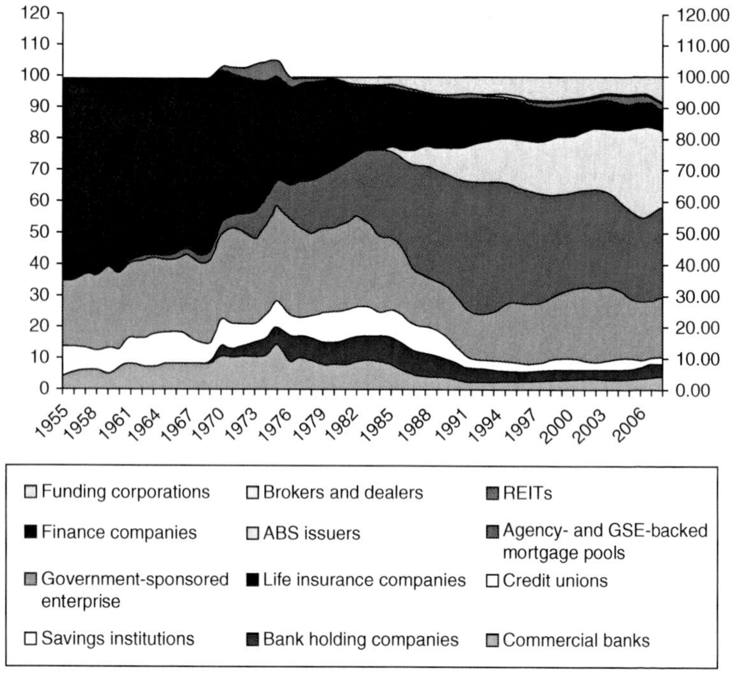

Figure 2.4 Credit market debt owed by financial institutions as percentage of total owed by the financial sector.
Source: Federal Reserve Flow of Funds Accounts.

Deregulation has also contributed to increased banking concentration, largely due to the elimination of Glass-Steagall as well as the outcome of the 'too big to fail' policy response during each crisis. Concentration has made the financial sector more fragile by creating a few large institutions that dominate more than half of the sector. The top 18 banks currently hold about 60 per cent of total assets with the top four holding about 40 per cent (this is even higher than pre-crisis levels) – compared with only 23 per cent of total bank assets in 1992 (Figure 2.5–2.7).

The income statements and the balance sheets of commercial banks reveal the changes that these institutions have undergone. In particular, non-interest income has become a larger share of income – see Figure 2.2. Much of this comes from 'off-balance sheet' activities; according to Mishkin non-interest income from off-balance sheet activities of banks increased from 7 per cent of total income in 1980 to 44 per cent in 2007 (Mishkin, 2007).

The largest US bank holding company is JPMorgan Chase. Unlike the smaller banks or banks as a whole, its non-interest income has exceeded

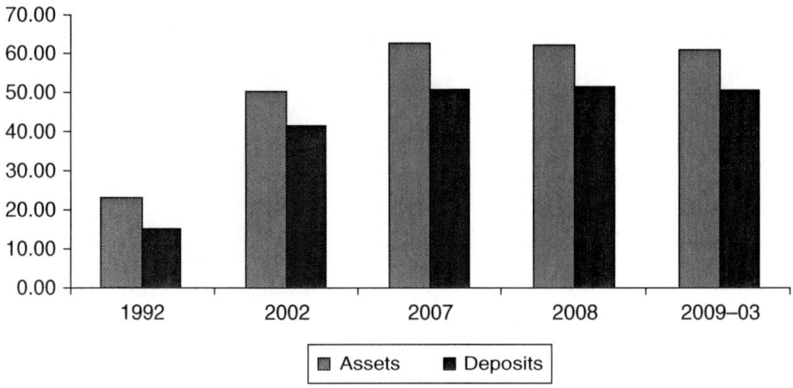

Figure 2.5 Total assets and deposits held by top 18 banks (as percentage of total).
Source: Federal Deposit Insurance Corporation.

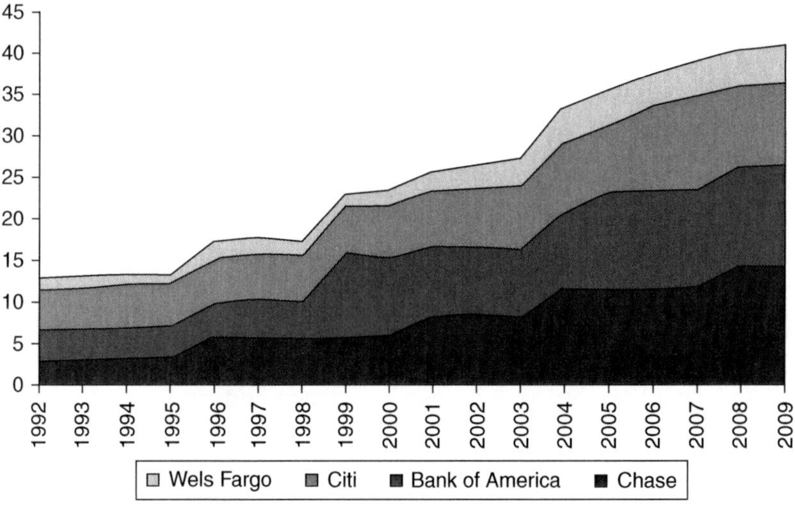

Figure 2.6 Share of total bank assets: four largest banks.
Source: Federal Reserve Flow of Funds Accounts.

interest income. The largest chunk of the non-interest income (about a quarter) comes from Trading Account gains and fees. The next biggest category is Net Securitisation Income and Servicing Fees, averaging nearly 15 per cent of non-interest income from 2002 to 2009. Investment banking, advisory, brokerage and underwriting fees and commissions have averaged at 13 per cent. Hence these three categories together have been the source of more than 50 per cent of non-interest income (Figure 2.8).

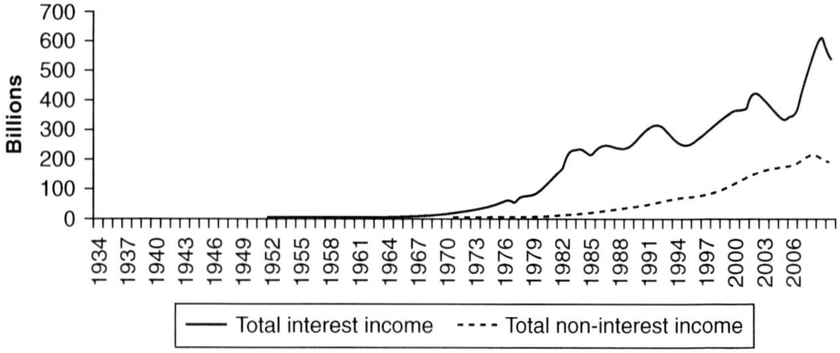

Figure 2.7 Interest vs. non-interest income. All FDIC insured banks.
Source: Federal Deposit Insurance Corporation.

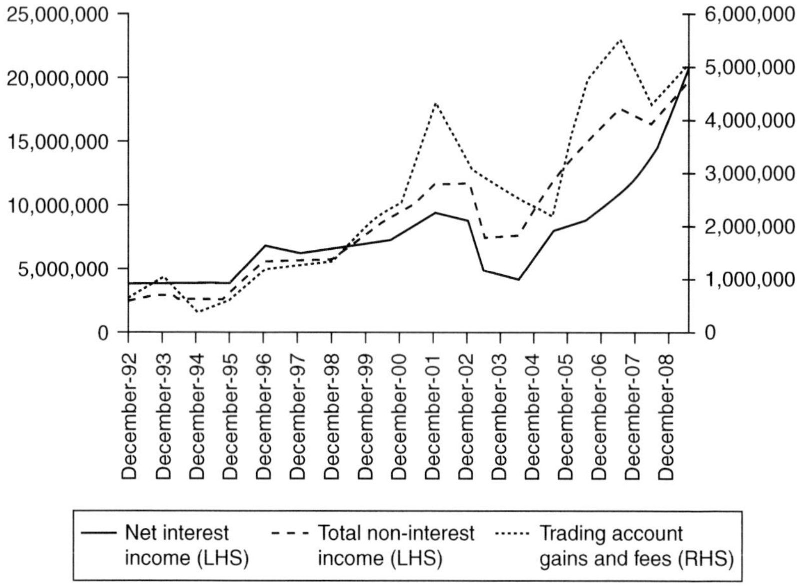

Figure 2.8 Chase: interest vs. non-interest income (in $ thousands).
Source: Federal Deposit Insurance Corporation.

As Minsky argued, if bankers put emphasis on the value of collateral rather than expected cash flows, a fragile financial system emerges because loan viability depends on expected market value of the assets pledged (Minsky, 2008: p. 261). This is precisely what has happened: banks originated mortgages which largely depended on the value of the collateral and especially on the bubble to maintain rising prices. Commercial and industrial loans, on the other hand, have decreased from 20 per cent of total assets to 10 per cent on average. This indicates that the larger banks aren't really in the business of making loans to businesses. Therefore, the rationale for bailouts – that capital injections into the larger banks will get credit flowing again – is fundamentally flawed (Table 2.1–2.3).

These tables show the loan composition of banks. We have divided the banks into three groups: the largest three, the largest 18 and all remaining banks. Larger banks are quite different from smaller banks in terms of the quantity as well as the type of loans. The largest three banks' loans and leases have decreased from 65 per cent of total assets to about 43 per cent in just over 15 years. Real estate loans have remained relatively stable at

Table 2.1 Top 18 banks (percentage of assets)

	1992	2002	2007	2008
Net loans and leases	59.58	54.26	56.40	47.50
All real estate loans	21.39	25.78	30.13	25.00
Commercial real estate	4.29	4.09	3.77	3.71
1–4 family residential	11.47	18.18	21.89	17.34
Commercial and industrial loans	20.67	13.11	11.80	10.91

Source: Federal Deposit Insurance Corporation.

Table 2.2 Top three banks (per cent of assets)

	1992	2002	2007	2008
Net loans and leases	65.72	49.32	47.37	43.03
All real estate loans	23.73	17.16	22.46	22.73
Commercial real estate	3.53	2.00	1.83	1.91
1–4 family residential	13.48	12.33	17.69	17.22
Commercial and industrial loans	21.58	13.84	11.68	10.28

Source: Federal Deposit Insurance Corporation.

Table 2.3 All other banks (per cent of assets)

	1992	2002	2007	2008
Net loans and leases	55.46	61.17	67.79	65.83
All real estate loans	25.79	32.81	40.85	41.78
Commercial real estate	8.28	11.77	15.35	14.66
1–4 family residential	13.75	14.54	13.06	16.05
Commercial and industrial loans	13.67	12.62	14.21	12.52

Source: Federal Deposit Insurance Corporation.

around 22 per cent; however, 1–4 family residential loans (which were the main product for securitisation) have risen. A very important change is the decrease in commercial and industrial loans – from about 22 per cent of total assets to 11 per cent in the last 15 years. The picture is fairly similar for the top 18 banks.

Commercial loans are granted with the expectation of future cash flows. Residential loans, on the other had, were increasingly made against the value of collateral. Reliance on residential mortgages made the banks vulnerable to changing conditions in the housing market thus giving rise to fragility.

Declining Net Loans and Leases has been accompanied by increasing trading. For example, at Chase trading has increased from 2.57 per cent in 1992 to about 21 per cent of assets in 2008 and for BoA from 2.43 per cent in 1992 to about 11 per cent of assets in 2008. A decrease in loans has also been compensated by holding more securities (rising from 5 per cent to 17 per cent of assets), and particularly asset-backed securities. At Citibank loans and leases have decreased to about 44 per cent of assets from over 64 per cent. Securities peaked at the end of 2006 at over 20 per cent and trading account assets at over 17 per cent of assets in 2007. In sum, these data show that the larger banks are different from traditional banks: for the most part, they are not in the business of making loans to the productive sector.

2.5 Innovations

Two 'innovations' played an especially important role in transforming the system towards fragility: securitisation and credit default swaps. The two developments went somewhat hand in hand with banks securitising every type of loan and the CDS issuers 'insuring' these securities. At the peak of the bubble mortgage-backed securities were about 70 per cent of total securities for the large banks and about 50 per cent for smaller banks. Larger banks securitised 40–60 per cent of 1–4 family residential loans, selling securities to managed money. AIG and other sellers of CDS were eager to 'insure' all these risks, enhancing credit (Table 2.4).

CDSs are marketed as insurance, or a way to hedge against risks, and therefore distribute risk to market participants who are most willing and able to bear it. However, as Lewis (2009) nicely explains, CDSs create risk out of thin air, essentially allowing holders to make bets on the death of assets, firms or even national governments. The data on derivatives is impressive. JPMorgan Chase, for example, held derivatives worth 6072 per cent of its assets at the peak of the bubble in 2007. The other two giants, Citigroup and Bank of America, although still far behind Chase, had 2022 per cent and 2486 per cent, respectively. Goldman Sachs, the other giant, had an astonishing amount of derivatives on its balance sheets: 25284 per cent of assets in 2008 and 33823 per cent as of June 2009. Citigroup and BoA now have more of this risk on their books than before the crisis (FDIC SDI database).

Table 2.4 Derivatives of three largest banks (percentage of assets)

Year	1992	1993	1994	1995	1996	1997	1998	1999	2000
BOA	28.57	149.13	330.55	567.61	770.94	622.39	743.81	975.41	1214.08
Citi	–	–	–	–	–	–	1017.19	930.50	1063.92
Chase	–	–	–	–	1769.43	2180.22	2904.64	3240.21	4003.92
Year	**2001**	**2002**	**2003**	**2004**	**2005**	**2006**	**2007**	**2008**	**30 June 2009**
BOA	1587.75	2061.91	2227.38	1655.10	1864.22	1950.14	2022.21	2111.35	2220.68
Citi	1083.17	1234.66	1420.55	1840.88	2177.27	2286.22	2485.69	2398.85	2526.96
Chase	3992.18	4363.33	5528.71	4236.34	4425.11	5185.53	6072.29	4744.24	4561.97

Source: Federal Deposit Insurance Corporation, SDI database.

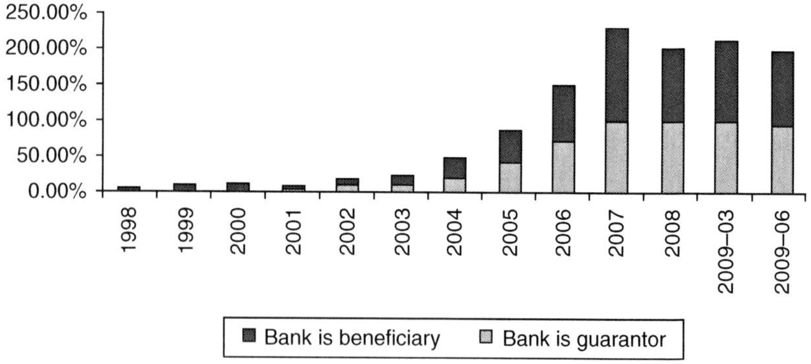

Figure 2.9 Citi: Notional amount of credit derivatives (percentage of total assets).
Source: Federal Deposit Insurance Corporation, SDI Database.

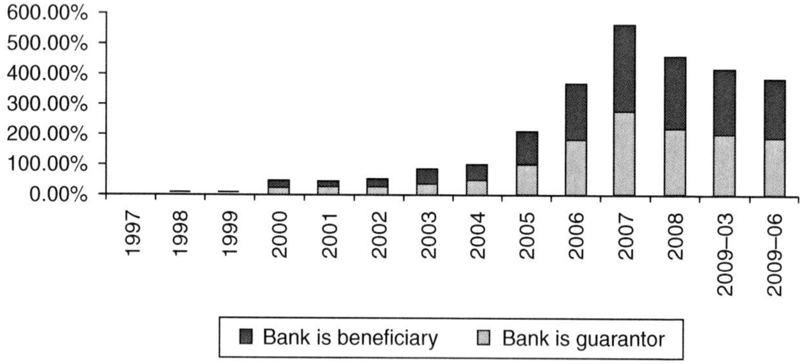

Figure 2.10 Chase: Notional amount of credit derivatives (percentage of total assets).
Source: Federal Deposit Insurance Corporation, SDI Database.

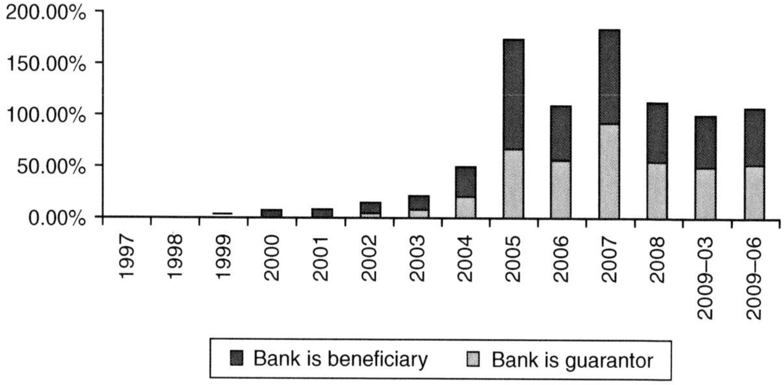

Figure 2.11 BoA: Notional amount of credit derivatives (percentage of total assets).
Source: Federal Deposit Insurance Corporation, SDI Database.

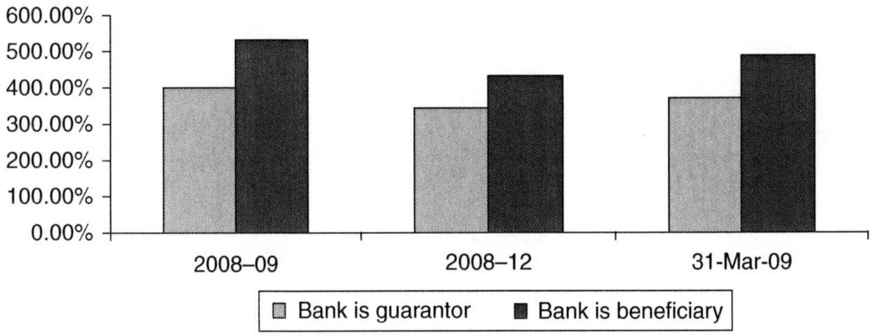

Figure 2.12 Goldman sachs: Notional amount of credit derivatives (percentage of total assets).
Source: Federal Deposit Insurance Corporation, SDI Database.

The largest chunk of these derivatives is interest rate swaps. It is still unknown how large the CDS market is as the derivatives market is mostly unregulated. The graphs below depict the level of Credit Derivatives (the notional amounts). The Federal Deposit Insurance Corporation (FDIC) doesn't break down this data any further, hence we can't know for sure how much of this is CDS (Figures 2.9–2.12).

2.6 Disparate effects of the crisis on financial institutions

There has been a major redistribution of wealth and power in the financial sector as a result of the crisis. Wall Street as a whole shrank but not all companies have been affected equally by the crisis. Citigroup, for example, has shrunk 55 per cent since the peak of the market and is still effectively on government support. Bank of America has also been hit severely by the crisis. Its market value has decreased by 37 per cent since the peak. It has, however, become bigger, in terms of asset size, by acquiring Merrill Lynch. JPMorgan Chase has been the largest beneficiary of the current crises, growing bigger and surpassing Citigroup and Bank of America as it became the largest bank in the United States. Unlike its peers, its value has increased 3.8 per cent from the peak of the market. Wells Fargo became the fourth largest bank in the United States, in terms of assets, after acquiring Wachovia. It has grown 3.3 per cent from the peak of the market. And note that peak was also the peak of the bubble (Figure 2.13).

As in every crisis, there have been losers and winners that have grown more powerful. What is different this time is the extent to which the 'predator state' – to use Galbraith's term – has been actively involved in determining which institutions will survive (Ferguson and Johnson, 2009). It has favoured some institutions over others by brokering a number of mergers, even fudging laws and regulations. By creating mega-institutions, it has given them immunity for future crises by labelling them 'too big to fail' and

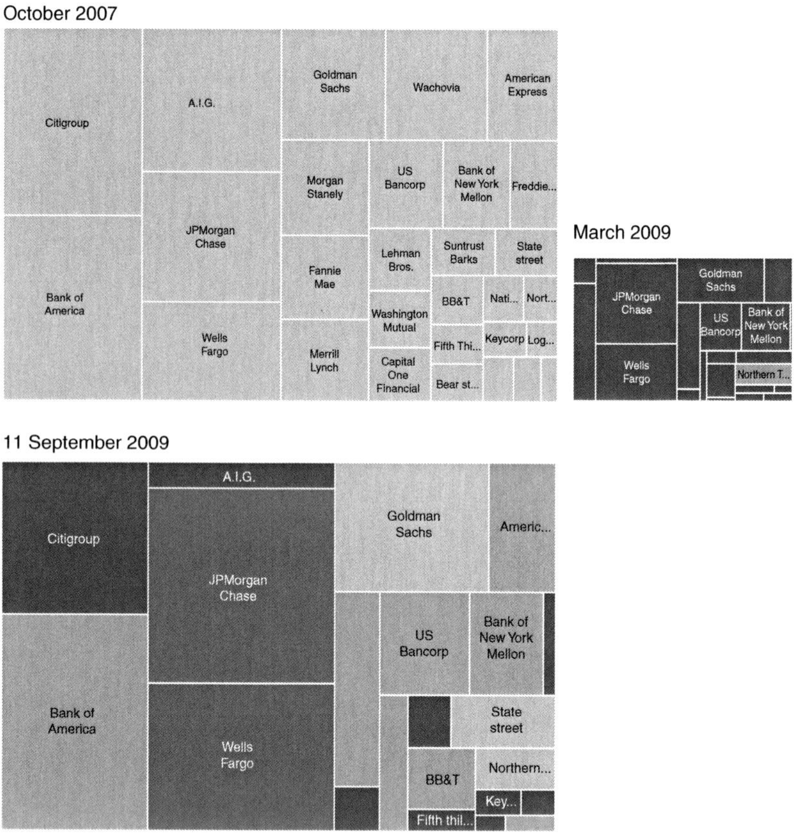

Figure 2.13 Absolute and relative size of largest institutions (*The New York Times*).

'systemically important' (while it refuses to provide a list naming its favoured institutions, the list certainly includes the top 20). Determining which institutions will be bailed out and which will go under, 'the predator state' has conducted a major redistribution of wealth and power.

2.7 Policy response

As the bursting of the housing bubble turned into a full-blown crisis after the collapse of Lehman Brothers, it seemed that there was a general consensus for meaningful reform. It was obvious that deregulation, de-supervision and self-regulation had failed and that real change was necessary to prevent the system from destroying itself. Additionally, reform was virtually required to attenuate public anger over the bailouts. In the eyes of many, the economy has survived the worst and is on a path to a recovery. Many economists now argue that it is time for the government to work out an exit strategy to downsize its share in the financial sector. Those fearing inflation have also argued that the Fed will soon need to start raising interest rates. Many on Wall Street, who were very eager to receive government support when their institutions were failing, are now arguing that government intrusions are unacceptable. In fact, despite major injections of bailout funds, the government has actually played a negligible role in the decision-making of those firms. One year after the collapse of the markets the government hasn't made any significant progress in reforming Wall Street.

There have been few criminal prosecutions of the financial geniuses who engineered the crisis. Executive pay is still at an all-time high with Goldman Sachs' 30,000 employees expected to get as much as $700,000 each in bonuses (Berenson, 2009). On top of everything else, large banks still reap government subsidies: the *Washington Post* reports that banks with more than $100 billion in assets are getting a competitive advantage by being able to borrow at interest rates 0.34 percentage points lower than rates charged to the rest of the industry (that advantage was only 0.08 per cent in 2007) (Cho, 2009).

Obama warned Wall Street that this is going to be 'the most ambitious overhaul of the financial system since the Great Depression', but he is not going to impose real change: 'Instead, we are calling on the financial industry to join us in a constructive effort to update the rules and regulatory structure to meet the challenges of this new century.... We have sought ideas and input from industry leaders, policy experts, academics, consumer advocates, and the broader public' (Obama, 2009). The government is looking at Wall Street with *naïveté*, hoping it will reform itself. However, if something can be learnt from the crisis, it is that we cannot rely on these institutions to self-regulate.

A progressive policy aimed at solving the issue of too big to fail institutions would break down every institution that is considered to be 'systemically important' into smaller functional pieces. Too big to fail institutions shouldn't be allowed to exist. They are too complex and too big to be safely managed and resolved if necessary. Allowing such institutions to exist gives too much power, both market and political, to behemoths. Instead, the FDIC should be allowed to determine which large banks are insolvent based on current market values. The balance sheets of the top 20 banks should be examined on a consolidated basis, with derivative positions netted (data indicates that most derivatives are held by the biggest banks, which serve as counterparties for one another). After netting positions the insolvent banks would be resolved following two principles: resolution at the least cost to the FDIC and with a view to downsizing institutions. The ultimate objective must be to minimise impacts on the rest of the banking system. It will be necessary to cover some uninsured losses to other financial institutions as well as to equity holders (such as pension funds) arising due to the resolution (Auerback and Wray, 2009).

This would help to simplify the financial system, reduce concentration and decrease its size relative to the economy. We will also need debt relief for households. This can include a package of policies that would replace unaffordable mortgages with better terms provided by strengthened GSEs. Some underwater mortgages should be foreclosed, with homeowners converted to renters with an option to repurchase the home later. Tax relief and job creation will help to boost ability to service debt, and will help to jump-start the economy so that firms can stop downsizing. The public retirement system will need strengthening and real health care reform is required.

The role of managed money must be reduced; this can be encouraged by eliminating various subsidies including tax-advantaged saving. Of course, all of this is a movement in the opposite direction to that currently envisioned by the Obama administration – which is actually trying to increase the financialisation of health care by forcing all individuals to purchase health 'insurance'. And managed money is looking to financialise death (through securitisation of 'death settlements', buying up life insurance policies of people with terminal illnesses) (Auerback and Wray, 2009). Managed money is searching for its next bubble which is probably in commodities futures (again) or carbon futures trading. Unless it is constrained, another boom and bust is inevitable.

Minsky argued that depressions play a useful role for capitalist economies: they simplify balance sheets by wiping out financial assets and liabilities. The result is a system where hedge units are a majority and which therefore is relatively stable. One reason why financial fragility built up over time in the post-war period was because there were no depressions. To be sure, there were financial crises that wiped out a significant proportion of debt in the economy. But because Big Government and Big Bank set floors and ceilings in the economy, each time the system recovered with still high levels of debt. Experience shows that this is not sustainable. While we are not advocating that the government allow a 1930s style debt deflation, we do argue that for any policy to be effective in the longer run, it needs to involve balance sheet simplification but without depression.

The government has all the powers necessary to re-regulate Wall Street. New Deal reforms were very successful in containing instability for a couple of decades. But innovations as well as deregulation rendered these ineffective. Minsky argued that the Fed and legislation can guide the evolution of the financial system to constrain instability by encouraging institutions and practices that reduce instability and constraining those that enhance it. He also argued that if the Fed can intervene to put a floor on the collapse it must also take initiative to 'prevent the development of practices conducive to financial instability' (Minsky, 1986/2008). The current crisis was a warning sign. The question is: will we take this warning seriously and reform the system or do we need another Great Depression to finally bring about real change.

> The profit-seeking bankers almost always win their game with the authorities, but, in winning, the banking community destabilises the economy; the true losers are those who are hurt by unemployment and inflation.
>
> (Minsky 1986/2008: p. 279)

As long as there are large pools of managed money looking for high returns, the question is where the next bubble will develop. The only hope is a substantial downsizing of managed money, which will help to reduce the influence of money managers on our economy and our political system.

References

Auerback, M. and Wray, L.R. (2009). 'Banks running wild: the subversion of insurance by "Life Settlements" and credit default swaps', *Policy Note, Levy Economics Institute*, 2009/9.

Berenson, A. (2009). 'A year after a cataclysm, little change on Wall St', *The New York Times*, 12 September.

Cho, D. (2009). '"Too big to fail" have grown even bigger: Behemoths born of the bailout reduce consumer choice, tempt corporate moral hazard', *Washington Post*, 28 August.

D'Arista, J. (2009). 'Financial concentration'. Working Paper No. 3. *Wall Street Watch*, August, available at www.wallstreetwatch.org

Ferguson, T. and Johnson, R. (2009). 'Too big to bail: the "Paulson Put", presidential politics and the global financial meltdown', Part 1: 'From shadow financial system to shadow bailout', *International Journal of Political Economy*, vol. 38, no. 1.

Flow of Funds Accounts of the United States, 1945–2008, Board of Governors of the Federal Reserve System, 11 June 2009.

Krippner, G. (2005). 'The financialization of the American economy', *Socio-Economic Review*, vol. 3, no. 2: p. 173.

Lewis, M. (2009). 'The man who crashed the world', *The Vanity Fair*, August.

Minsky, H.P. (2008) *Stabilizing an Unstable Economy* (New York: McGraw Hill).

Mishkin, F. (2007). *The Economics of Money, Banking and Financial Markets*, 8th ed. (Boston: Pearson Education).

Obama, B. (2009). 'Normalcy cannot lead to complacency', Speech delivered in New York, 14 September, available at http://www.whitehouse.gov/blog/Normalcy-Cannot-Lead-to-Complacency.

Wray, R.L. (2009). 'The rise and fall of money manager capitalism: a Minskyan approach', *Cambridge Journal of Economics*, vol. 33.

3

Linking Financial Globalisation with Financial Exclusion via a Minskyan Bridge

Gary A. Dymski

3.1 Introduction

In the past three decades the financial sectors in virtually every nation have been integrated into global finance, apparently expanding choice for domestic firms and residents from strictly local to global options. Paradoxically, however, this increasing openness has been paralleled by rising concerns among activists and social scientists about financial exclusion. Further, the period of financial globalisation has been accompanied by increasingly frequent, and ever more profound, financial crises. So the current period of financial globalisation has been linked with both more frequent financial crises and increasing levels of financial exclusion. The former occurs at the level of aggregates and nation-states, the latter at the level of regions and households. The link between financial globalisation and crisis has been extensively debated. But that between financial globalisation (and crisis) and financial exclusion has received virtually no attention. This can be traced to two factors. First, the dispute over financial globalisation and crisis has taken place almost exclusively among economists, on economists' theoretical turf. They have conducted a dense, sustained debate at the macro level without ever tapping the micro level at which financial exclusion occurs. Second, most studies of financial exclusion have been done in geography and urban sociology. Because of the virtual absence of exchanges between these fields and economics, opportunities for creative interdisciplinary cross-talk have been missed.[1]

This chapter suggests a bridge between processes of financial globalisation and crisis and the phenomenon of financial exclusion. To do this, we expand on Hyman Minsky's core concept of financial fragility. In his own writing, Minsky tended to work with representative firms and agents, as do most economic theorists. This is problematic for any study of financial exclusion, which necessarily involves at least two contrasting classes of agents, the financially included and the excluded. However, Minsky's balance-sheet approach is readily adapted to the case of agents with diverse wealth and income characteristics. This allows us to see how financial globalisation has expanded opportunities for the creation of financial products that can be adopted by economic units whose low levels of wealth and/or income would previously have left them outside of the formal financial system. These new products may generate or increase financial fragility for their adopters; and as such, they may make the financial system considered as a whole more crisis-prone. Thus, the interaction of financial exclusion and financial-market opening increases the extent of financial fragility in any economy. This makes financial crises more likely, and guarantees that the impact of episodes of financial crisis will be more extensive and socially destructive than they would be otherwise.[2]

We proceed as follows. The second section explores definitions of financial globalisation, crisis and exclusion. The third section then reviews three contemporary approaches to financial globalisation and crisis: those based on the efficient-markets, asymmetric-information and heterodox frameworks. The fourth section reflects on why economists' characterisations of financial globalisation and crisis have largely missed the emerging phenomenon of financial exclusion. The fifth section uses Minsky's balance-sheet approach to financial fragility to construct some notions about financial exclusion that are rooted in economic theory. The key notion here is that the extent of financial exclusion is greater, the more inequality in the distribution of wealth and income, in any society. The sixth section shows how the extent of financial exclusion and the character of financial fragility for economic systems depend, among other things, on two factors: the distribution of income and wealth, and the character of the national financial system. Shifts in the latter can dramatically alter the extent of financial exclusion, and in turn the level and depth of financial fragility. The seventh section examines how shifts in financial firms' strategies have affected the financial globalisation/exclusion linkage. Section 3.8 concludes.

3.2 Financial globalisation, financial crisis and financial exclusion: definitions

Whether financial globalisation is anything new is itself the subject of debate, largely because no one criterion for what constitutes financial globalisation has been established.[3] One approach measures the scale of cross-border financial flows relative to overall economic activity.[4] Some recent analyses using this measure suggest that cross-border financial flows have intensified substantially.[5] The evidence is not unambiguous, however; financial flows from global North to global South nations, always meagre, have accounted for a smaller proportion of overall cross-border lending after the late 1990s.[6] In any event, neoclassical economic theory presumes that capital should flow systematically from rich to poor countries (Lucas, 1990); but it does not. Papaioannou (2009) summarises the literature explaining this counter-theoretic result, and points out the importance of institutional development for capital flows.

Indeed, an alternative approach to financial globalisation precisely emphasises institutional development. Cerny (1994) suggests that financial globalisation can be measured by organisational changes: the development of both integrated world-wide market structures and of firms with the organisational capacity to centre their activities on these markets. Globalisation in this sense is well advanced: there now exists a set of globally mobile firms whose operations and strategies rely on, and help to extend, a set of integrated world financial markets.

Here we augment Cerny's micro behavioural definition, which emphasises the strategies of firms with global market reach, with another one: the notion of the global spread of standard sets of financial practices and products. To the extent that households and firms with given levels of financial resources and funding needs in any given country are able to obtain financial instruments that are closely similar – in terms of risks, contractual terms and costs – to households and firms in any other country, the global financial system can be said to be globalised. Examples of units 'with given levels of financial resources and funding needs' are wealth-owners with financial asset holdings totalling $50–100,000 and high-technology start-up companies seeking working capital. Financial globalisation in this sense involves the global homogenisation of financial products for similar classes of customer.

It is very important for our purpose to emphasise that homogenisation by customer class does not mean homogenisation across customer classes. On the contrary, customers of some types have an expanding set of investment and debt options, increasing their expected returns and lowering their transactions costs, while customers of other types have fewer savings options and higher costs.[7] This brings us to financial exclusion.

3.2.1 Social and financial exclusion

Social exclusion is a concept that has emerged jointly in the terrains of social theory and of civil society. It involves the idea that some members of society are denied full rights to participate in society. When applied to financial processes, social exclusion – that is, 'financial exclusion' – refers to the failure of the formal banking system to offer a full range of depository and credit services, at competitive prices, to all households and/or businesses. Because these households and/or businesses are systematically excluded – on the basis of race or ethnicity, geographic area, gender (or other common characteristic) – from 'financial citizenship', their ability to accumulate wealth is compromised.[8]

The concept of financial exclusion is one of the key concepts in the emerging geography of money and credit; this literature has been summarised as it has grown by Leyshon (1995, 1997) and by Martin (1999). The roots of this concept lie in the research traditions on racial discrimination and redlining in credit markets.[9] Geographers have, in effect, generalised the concepts of credit-market redlining and discrimination to encompass all banking services, and also to encompass customer classes other than those based on race and ethnicity *per se* (for example, rural households in northern or western portions of England might be considered a financially excluded class).

There are, in effect, two fundamental categories of financial exclusion: the absence of financial services, and the provision of financial services on an exploitative and/or super-risky basis. Financial intermediaries can generate financial exclusion *per se* – the absence of service provision – either by not locating their branches evenly over their service areas, or by not offering loans or other financial products on an equitable basis to some categories of customer. Research on the geography of money and finance has emphasised the importance of the distribution of credit and of banking services over space (Dymski, 1999; Lacker, 1995; Reibel, 2000) and the role of financial institutional structures and credit flows in creating and transforming urban places (Dymski and Veitch, 1992, 1996).

In turn, the failure to provide services may be categorical – for example, a refusal to offer deposit accounts to women. For those financial services for which customers must pass certain performance- and balance-sheet criteria, exclusion can be more subtle. For example, banks may be less likely to make loans to African American applicants than to other applicants with similar levels of creditworthiness. Determining whether such instances constitute systematic exclusion, purposeful or not, requires the use of empirical tests – the interpretation of which is often controversial (Dymski, 2006a).

A second category of financial exclusion involves the provision of financial services – especially credit – only on an exploitative and excessively risky basis. Activists have adopted the term 'predatory loans' to describe loans that often lead to loss of equity or foreclosure.[10] This category includes subprime loans – loans for prospective homeowners that involve higher-than-market-rate loan rates and penalty clauses, and which are made with little or no attention to borrowers' capacity to repay and/or to borrowers' equity in the homes they purchase.

3.3 Three contemporary approaches to financial globalisation and crisis

We turn now to the relationship between financial globalisation and financial crisis. As noted, this topic has generated a huge literature. At the risk of oversimplification, we divide this literature into three relatively distinct approaches. These approaches derive from theoretical disagreements about whether autonomous financial markets are efficient, and about whether the distribution of information among market participants can create incentive problems. These in turn lead to policy disagreements over the advisability of opening financial systems to cross-border entry.

Efficient-market theorists assert that barriers to the free flow of finance, and/or to opening markets for bank ownership and control, should be reduced or eliminated. Theorists focused on the implications of resource inequality and asymmetric information, by contrast, defend the need for autonomous national systems. Heterodox economists warn that financial relationships are inherently unstable due to uncertainty, and due to their interpenetration with the conflict-laden relationships inherent to capitalist accumulation processes.

3.3.1 Efficient-markets approach

The efficient-markets approach sees deregulation and openness to cross-border entry and financial flows as means of instilling market discipline in financial systems; the distortions that can be created by asymmetric information between borrowers and lenders are less important than those that subsidies (such as deposit insurance) and limitations on market participation can induce. Governments that insist on their own financial-market architectures not only are likely to stray from sound banking practices, but they are also standing in the way of economic modernisation.[11]

The reforms suggested by this approach are to free the interest rate and cut back government-sponsored enterprises (GSEs), thus encouraging savings and private-sector entrepreneurship. If government has artificially suppressed interest rates, this will increase the real return on financial assets. This should encourage savings, the creation of more enterprises, and entrepreneurship. In developing markets, proponents of the efficient-markets view regard financial consolidation and the entry of developing-nations' financial markets by larger and more sophisticated foreign financial firms as increasing the benefits of market liberalisation itself. Multinational banks' entry, in this view, will lead directly to greater efficiency and a broader range of financial services.[12]

Of course, many developing-country economies have experienced severe financial and economic crises after deregulating their financial systems and permitting large-scale cross-border lending. Proponents of the efficient-markets view do not think these recurrent crises condemn the fundamental premises of their approach; to the contrary, these crises are taken as evidence in support of their view.[13] For example, Knight (1998) argued that financial and banking-system instability primarily affected developing countries in this crisis because they lacked a fully developed set of financial instruments and institutions; the solution is tighter regulation and further financial-system development ('deepening') and opening.

Overall, World Bank and IMF economists have become more sceptical that the growth-enhancing benefits of financial globalisation and openness outweigh the enhanced risks that openness engenders. At the same time, these institutions' official 'line' vis-à-vis the benefits of financial liberalisation, cross-border financial flows and foreign-bank entry into developing-economy markets has not changed. Official economic reports of the IMF written since the Asian crisis affirm that when appropriately regulated, free international flows of capital will spur economic growth. The entry of larger developed-country banks into smaller developing countries can stabilise these nations' financial and banking markets (IMF, 2000, ch. 6).[14]

3.3.2 Asymmetric-information approach

This approach regards the key feature of credit markets as the asymmetric distribution of information between borrowers and lenders. Borrowers may have informational advantages of two kinds over lenders: information concerning their competency, which affects their probability of success (their 'type'); and their plans for using and repaying the loans they receive, which affect the likelihood of repayment (their 'effort'). Lenders' optimal response is to ration credit and when possible to use signalling mechanisms to screen borrowers.[15]

A 1981 article in the *American Economic Review* by Stiglitz and Weiss distilled and focused thinking about this approach. Numerous texts used the asymmetric-information model to assert that the debt crisis had arisen because of borrower nations' unwillingness to repay their debt (that is, because of realised moral hazard). Joseph Stiglitz himself co-authored an article taking this approach.[16]

This was not the endpoint of thinking about asymmetric information and credit markets in the South, however. The Latin American debt crisis of the 1980s spurred several comparisons of East Asian and Latin American economies (see, for example, Sachs, 1989). It became clear that principal-agent challenges of the sort captured in the asymmetric-information framework permeated the developing world. Some economists – Joseph Stiglitz prominently among them – argued that the Asian 'tiger' nations' high growth rates could be due in part to their use of success in using government-led arrangements to resolve asymmetric-information-related incentive problems.[17] When the Asian financial crisis of 1997–1998 occurred, Stiglitz (1996) and others defended developing nations' prerogative to regulate financial markets and their economies in non-neoliberal ways. Stiglitz deepened this view in subsequent writings (see Stiglitz, 2000, 2003).

3.3.3 Heterodox approach

Post Keynesians and structuralists have developed distinct heterodox views of financial globalisation. While there are several post-Keynesian approaches, here we focus on the ideas of Hyman Minsky and Paul Davidson. They both follow Keynes in emphasising the inescapability of uncertainty, as opposed to risk, on financing and portfolio decisions. Financial markets are notoriously prone to speculative bubbles and irrational shifts; when unchecked, market processes can generate speculative bubbles that can be burst only at a huge cost in business failures and job losses.

For post Keynesians, financial globalisation in the neoliberal period was definitively shaped by the 1971–1973 breakdown of the Bretton Woods system.[18] Financial globalisation in the absence of effective global governance of financial relations heightened speculative forces and led to the instability and crises of subsequent decades.[19] Advances in the sophistication of financial instruments and in market technology, by permitting more players to enter the market, widened unstable and unsustainable market flows and put market liquidity under ever more strain. And as globalisation-fuelled crises weakened national governments, regulators lost the ability to implement measures lessening exposure to financial crises and instability.

The structuralist approach, which has its roots in Lance Taylor's 1983 opus *Structuralist Macroeconomics*, shares with post Keynesians an appreciation of the centrality of financial fragility and instability in macro-dynamics. However, it highlights other factors as well: institutional development, market rigidities and government development policy. Some structuralists highlight international dynamics: for example, Eatwell and Taylor (2000) point out the inescapability in the post-Bretton Woods world of the 'trilemma', wherein liberalised capital markets, a fixed exchange rate and an independent monetary or fiscal policy are not mutually consistent. Other structuralist analyses focus on national dynamics: for example, Akyüz and Boratav's (2003) dissection of the 2000–2001 Turkish crisis includes attention to Turkey's structural macro problems, to the global macroeconomic environment and to the financial boom–bust cycle. Structuralists such as Chang (2002) and Singh (1998) have delineated the argument that Stiglitz has adopted in his most recent work: developing nations grow most rapidly when they can pursue autonomous developmental policies and dampen financial boom-bust cycles.

3.4 What economic theory misses: global trends and the US case

The previous section makes it clear that economists' views of financial globalisation and crisis diverge widely. All three approaches, however, have treated financial exclusion as a second-order phenomenon – that is, it emerges, as a micro-level phenomenon, as a consequence of macro level and structural factors (including the regulatory framework). The causality does not run the other way. The efficient-markets approach imagines that financial intermediaries competing for profits should, in the absence of regulatory distortions, provide credit and/or payments services to all customers capable of bearing the risk-adjustments and transaction costs their circumstances impose. There may be un-banked, but not financially exploited, customers.

The asymmetric-information view presumes that if sufficiently high barriers have been erected against influences from foreign financial firms and markets, then whether there are economic units without access to formal banks – and whether there are households that have access only to high-cost finance – depends on nation-state choices about which types of economic unit should have access to credit, and whether all economic units should have formal bank accounts. Inspired by the East Asian miracles of the 1970s–1990s, Stiglitz wants to preserve the ability of nations to choose national banking systems that channel credit supply to domestic industrial development. Typically, these East Asian financial systems provided basic formal banking services for all economic units, while providing very little consumer credit. That is, financial exclusion in terms of lack of access to the formal banking sector was not an issue due to public regulations that precluded it; and the problem of exploitative credit for low-income households did not arise because formal-sector banks did not lend to consumers. So Stiglitz' idealised scenario is the opposite of efficient-markets theorists' ideal: consumers cannot be financially exploited, and no one is un-banked.

The heterodox approach also envisioned that nation-states' welfare would be best served if financial globalisation processes could be stopped 'at the border'. The structuralist and post-Keynesian variants of heterodoxy both focused almost exclusively on 'the macro-foundations' of microeconomic phenomena such as financial exclusion. This is in part a methodological reaction to orthodox theorists' insistence that macroeconomic phenomena only exist if they can be traced to specific micro-market processes.[20] Many heterodox models leave micro-structures unspecified or make the assumption that workers neither save nor take on debt.[21] This means that financial exclusion in the sense of exploitative credit relations cannot arise. The question of whether some or all of the 'workers' in any such model are un-banked then never arises.

Structuralists and post Keynesians want to prevent unchecked external forces and market flows from further distorting and weakening the integrity of developing nations' macroeconomic structures. Only when macroeconomic safeguards are in place – from a Keynesian special-drawing right system to capital controls to a Tobin tax – should more liberalised flows be considered.

3.4.1 What economists have missed

What then do these approaches to financial globalisation and crisis miss? First, and most obviously, they pay no attention to the problem of unbanked people. Two-thirds of the population is outside the banking system in most of Latin America and Africa. There is a large overlap between the un-banked, unemployment and informalisation: according to a recent survey by First National Bank of South Africa, 79 per cent of the un-banked are unemployed, and have no recorded income.[22] In the United States, the 2004 and 2007 Surveys of Consumer Finances found that of the 20 per cent of the households with the lowest income levels, one quarter had no bank account; and 8 per cent of all households were un-banked (Bucks *et al.*, 2009).

Economists' discussions of financial globalisation and crisis also pay no attention to the behaviour of banking firms. So the possibility that behavioural or strategic shifts by domestic or foreign banks might impact economic dynamics is ruled out by assumption. The problem can perhaps be traced to the fact that economists' models of globalisation and crisis have focused on macro-structures and country-to-bank debt games. This said, it's clear that banks might make strategic shifts, if these will boost their expected profits. And these shifts can involve (and have involved) financially excluded populations: either reductions (or expansions) in the 'banked' proportion of the population, or increases (or decreases) in the volume of predatory and extremely risky loans. These shifts, in turn, could interact with changes in the degree of competition for markets, and in the availability of liquidity. There is no reason to rule out the possibility that such shifts might have feedback effects on macro-dynamics.

A third factor is missed in the approaches summarised above: the trend towards more income and wealth inequality, including nations that have historically been relatively equitable. Deepening inequality is a global phenomenon, whose consequences for the dynamics of financial globalisation should be explored. This is especially the case because income inequality leads to wealth polarisation.

Evidence from the United States neatly illustrates this phenomenon. Figure 3.1 presents some summary data from the last six Surveys of Consumer Finance conducted in the United States by the Federal Reserve. This

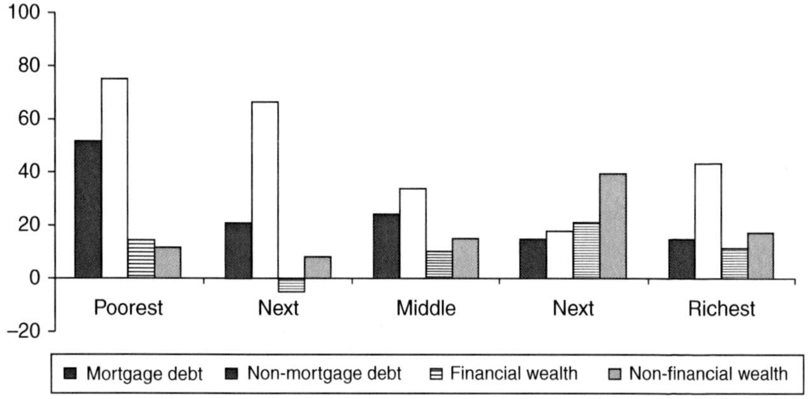

Figure 3.1 Average three-year growth rates, assets and debt, 1989–2004.
Source: Survey of Consumer Finances, FRB (by income quintiles).

figure illustrates the average percentage gains or losses in debt and wealth positions for households at different income levels, between 1989 and 2004. Lower-income households' debt levels grew by very large percentages, far outpacing the growth rates of their asset holdings. This pattern was moderated in the middle-income range: debt growth outdistanced asset growth by a smaller margin. Upper middle-income households' financial asset growth far exceeded their debt growth rates; and upper-income households' debt and asset growth rates were mixed.

While Figure 3.1 shows that the entire US class structure has been taking on more debt, it also shows that asset growth has systematically outpaced debt growth only at higher income levels. Data on US households' financial obligation ratios, collected by the Federal Reserve, amplify this point.[23] The debt obligations of renter households are systematically higher than those of homeowner households. Since renters earn systematically less income than homeowners, this means that lower-income households have heavier debt-financing obligations than upper-income households. The ratio of renter-to-homeowner financial obligations stood at 1.78 in 1980 when the series was first calculated, hit a peak at 1.95 in 2001, and has subsequently fallen to the 1.50 range. The fact that this ratio is consistently well over one signals the exposure of these households to predatory non-mortgage lending.

So, worsening wealth and income inequality matter at the micro-structural level. If banks react to it, this trend leads from uniform microstructures to diverse ones. And that emerging diversity will not be fixed by administrative design, but instead will be shaped by changing conditions in the supplier and customer markets which emerge to provide financial services to the financially excluded. Whether banks in one-size-fits-all banking systems *will* react depends on the pressures they may be under from competitors (including overseas banks) and from domestic wealthy households. The growing ranks of wealthier customers come to include many who want more aggressive return/risk options than are available through the plain-vanilla deposit and savings accounts tailored for the stable middle-class. The growing numbers of lower-income households with low and unstable balances mean, for banks, ever more customers whose accounts are being cross-subsidised, unless fees and charges are increased for low-balance accounts (a shift that will push some towards customers into the ranks of the un-banked).

Financial systems may shift, then, in the direction of differential access to financial assets and liabilities. And such shifts will be especially significant for Stiglitz's vision of an alternative, inclusive banking system focused on national growth, because it undercuts the viability of one-size-fits-all banking systems – like East Asia's in the 1980s. In effect, the battle between financial inclusion and exclusion, on one hand, and between equity-preserving and equity-reducing growth, on the other hand, is fought on dynamically shifting – and not static – ground.

3.5 A Minskyan balance-sheet approach to financial exclusion

Our intention here is to suggest how some of these missing links between financial globalisation and financial exclusion can be removed. We will do this via a Minskyan 'bridge'.

Minsky's vision of financial instability rests on the notion that economic units' balance-sheets evolved during the course of economic expansion in the direction of greater financial fragility.[24] This notion of the endogenous increase in financial fragility was captured in his depiction of three 'types' of unit: those characterised by robust, fragile and Ponzi financing structures. A unit has a robust financing structure when it is able to meet its interest obligations no matter what income draw it experiences. A fragile structure exists when an economic unit's expected income flow exceeds its debt obligations, but there are outcomes in which debt obligations exceed income. A Ponzi unit is one for which expected income will not suffice to meet repayment obligations.

Economic theory anticipates that a Ponzi unit is especially prone to speculate (shift towards riskier income-earning activities), since anticipated downside losses from low draws have no effect, whereas a high draw can pull the unit out of its financial trap.[25] However, there are more possibilities than this. A key move in making these other possibilities visible is to shift from the implicit concentration on firms, whether non-financial or financial, in Minsky's thinking, to a framework which also includes households. In financial theory, 'firms' (or portfolios) are constructed entities that unspecified economic agents use to seek gains. The agents in question stand apart from these entities. So an entrepreneur who chooses in a principal-agent lending situation whether to take on a riskier or safer project stands apart from that project; she will survive even if her project fails. This separation between project and agent disappears when we conceptualise households as financial units. For, households will survive as entities even if they have to take on crushing debts or sort out the implications of failed investment projects. If the implicit backdrop for theoretical models of firms' credit-market decisions is the casino, then that for households' credit-market decisions is the neighbourhood these households live in: and neighbourhoods vary widely across any city.

Here, we bring households into the Minskyan framework in two steps. First, let's think about units that 'do not save' systematically, but whose income levels may fluctuate around some normal consumption level. It is easy to imagine that 'banks' might provide 'income-smoothing' loans to facilitate these units' optimal (steady-state) consumption. It is easy to imagine a sustainability condition wherein, say, the interest rate a unit pays for a consumption-smoothing loan should be less than or equal to the discount rate used to evaluate the present value of consumption in two contiguous periods. In equilibrium, these rates will be equal.

Now, step two. What if there are two levels of incomes among 'workers' – one that is substantially lower than another. Then upper-income workers have bank accounts, but lower-income workers do not. Thus, only the former have access to income-smoothing loans from banks. The latter, if they are to borrow, must obtain loans from informal lenders, at substantially higher rates. This means that the interest load taken on to 'smooth' income will cause welfare losses. This implies that such liquidity-constrained households should reduce their expenditures rather than borrow. But this assumption is, in turn, heroic. Suppose the unit cannot, because it is too close to some subsistence level. This means, in Minskyan terms, that this unit shifts over time from fragile to Ponzi – not because of excessive risk-taking, but because of need. Note that adverse shifts in income for the lower-level unit would induce more such shifts towards Ponzi finance.

Section 3.2 pointed out that thinking of financial exclusion means thinking of units who may be un-banked, on one hand, and who are subject to financial exploitation, on the other. Both these possibilities are latent in step two above. Let us consider both categories of financial exclusion using this Minskyan lens.

The un-banked are quite likely to live on the very margin of reproduction, with few assets, and thus to be somewhere on the spectrum between fragile and Ponzi finance, as a normal state. Being behind on payments, acquiring tangible assets by financing them from rental-goods stores – these are normal conditions. Figure 3.2 illustrates the balance-sheet situation of an un-banked household. Assets and their corresponding liabilities are lined up opposite

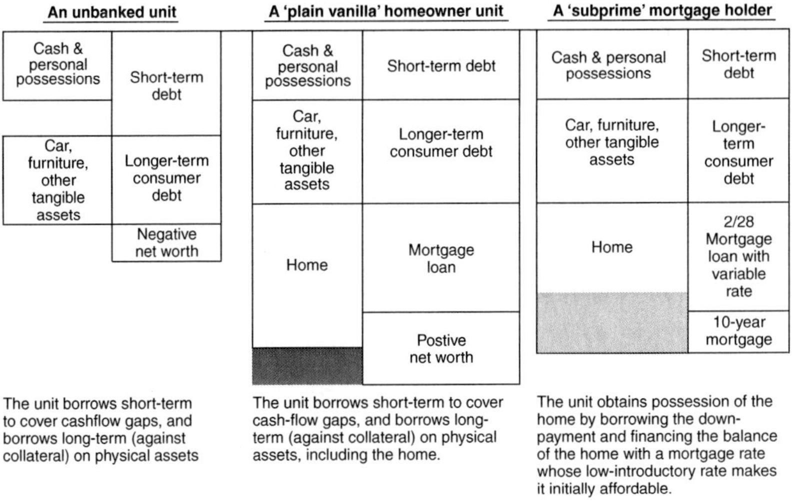

Figure 3.2 Three household balance-sheet types from a Minskyan perspective.

one another to highlight the sources of debt and, in the case shown, the existence of negative net worth. If this unit is unable to generate the cash-flow it needs to survive, it must either pawn whatever tangible assets it hasn't obtained by borrowing, or borrow more (in, say, a pay-day loan market). If it takes the latter course of action, it may be both un-banked and financially exploited.

The situation created by subprime lending is more complicated. To see it, we first consider a normal household unit – a household that acquires, in the normal course of events, a home and a home-mortgage loan to support it. Suppose the unit has a 20 per cent-down payment loan; and suppose again that the condition is such that the loan payment is a sustainable fraction of the household's income. Because the household's mortgage loan is less than the value of the housing asset acquired, shifts in asset-price will not generate insolvency.

The table depicts such a unit, which is also shown as having some cash and tangible assets, along with short-term and long-term consumer debt. This household has positive net worth. If the value of the home rises (shown via a dark-grey area), homeowner net worth will rise by a concomitant amount.

Now we consider the case of a household that has obtained a home by taking on subprime mortgage financing. As Wray (2007) points out, many different type of subprime loan have been marketed. Figure 3.2 shows a situation in which a household that was unable to make a down-payment against their home is given two mortgages: one, a 2/28 'variable rate' mortgage that has a below-market rate for 2 years, resetting thereafter to a fixed rate based on market conditions; second, a 10-year fixed-interest rate loan, which effectively substitutes for the home-buyer's down-payment. The term 'subprime lending' refers here to the fact that the home is obtained without any collateral margin in case of adverse home-value shifts; it may also be considered subprime insofar as a high rate is charged on the fixed-rate loan and high penalty rates for non-compliance are charged. If the home gains substantially in value, the homeowner can in principle unwind both mortgages (net of any penalties for pre-payment) and obtain a plain-vanilla mortgage loan. Otherwise, this unit's financial structure is unsustainable.

Another dimension of the balance-sheet depiction of financial exclusion should be highlighted. That is, financially included and excluded households are not randomly distributed across urban space. To the contrary, they cluster. Not only is this because upper- and lower-income households tend to live in near proximity: in addition, the line between financial exclusion and inclusion is racialised. Subprime mortgage loans initially targeted racial minorities, and the incidence of these loans is much higher in relatively segregated minority areas than elsewhere.[26]

So subprime loans are accentuating an established historical pattern, wherein homes and assets in areas with many minority residents grow in value more slowly than elsewhere, and wherein fewer households are homeowners in these areas than elsewhere. Thus, in neighbourhoods with primarily 'plain-vanilla' mortgages, people are in the normal course of things able to own homes at sustainable rates, thus gradually improving their capacities to own and to borrow at little risk, thus escaping debt dependence.

In neighbourhoods with many minorities, by contrast, many more homes are obtained without any collateral margin. In such neighbourhoods, fewer homes will be owned and home values will rise more slowly than elsewhere. There will be more un-banked households, engaged in predatory lending so as to survive. The relative paucity of households that are homeowners and have positive net worth means more neighbourhood exposure to short-term exploitation, making the situation of all asset-holders more precarious. So these two extremes co-exist in some portions of the city, typically those with disproportionate numbers of minorities: loans that are fragile and likely to fail, and people who are denied all but the most predatory loans, lacking wealth assets. The latter situation clearly creates a volatile, unsustainable mix.

So we have our Minskyan bridge. The upshot is once we replace the assumption that 'workers don't save (or borrow)' with a more realistic characterisation, and allow for different financial categories of household, the potential for a huge expansion of financial fragility among 'workers' becomes readily apparent. And it becomes obvious as well that this fragility will worsen as more households are financially exploited in precarious asset-value-growth environments. It is clear, then, that financial globalisation has, by loosening national controls over asset and liability acquisition, encouraged households to take on more, and more complex, financial obligations, opening new fronts of financial fragility. Can these class-exploitative (and race-differentiated) relations grow to such an extent that they are significant for the overall dynamics of accumulation? This question, debatable in 2005, no longer is.

The question that now confronts us is how the growth of this complex web of financial exclusion and exploitation might impact financial globalisation. This depends, in some sense, on how many financially excluded households there are, how they are distributed across space, and how the financially excluded are incorporated into banking/financial relations. The next two sections explore these dimensions in two steps: first, by examining national banking systems in this context; and second, by examining the implications of shifts in banking-firm strategy.

3.6 National banking systems, economic inequality and financial exclusion

So, financial globalisation leads to financial opening, and towards both the liberalisation and the bifurcation of financial markets, including the spread of financial exclusion and exploitation – that is, of micro-structural processes

	Is there effective state economic planning encompassing indirect or direct public guidance of credit flows?	
Are there large and efficient domestic economic groups?	Yes	No
Yes – including banks	Japan (pre-1990)	Chile, Japan (post-1990)
Yes – excluding banks	Korea (pre-1997), Brazil, South Africa, China	Korea (post-1997)
No	Taiwan	Many developing nations

Figure 3.3 National banking systems and developmental state structures.

which threaten the basis of macroeconomic reproduction. The pace at which globalisation-linked processes spread and the extent to which they threaten viable, nation-specific banking systems that have facilitated economic growth depend on several institutional preconditions.

One key is how deeply national banking systems have been embedded in national economic planning and development efforts. There are many different scenarios. Figure 3.3 depicts the starting points of some of the nations now caught up in financial globalisation processes. At one extreme are nations such as Japan before 1990, which enjoyed the benefits of coordinated state planning along with the orchestrated economic behaviour of large economic groups cooperating with the government. At the other extreme are nations that lack both large (domestic) economic groups and effective state planning. The case that Stiglitz' (1996) (and for that matter Zysman's (1984)) analysis emphasises is the shift from the two upper-left-hand boxes to any of the boxes on the right-hand side: the idea is that nationally autonomous banking systems can, if permitted to remain idiosyncratic and state-guided, serve as focal points for planning and thus as engines of growth. The situations of these nations are diverse: some have had large levels of foreign reserves (Taiwan), whereas some have not (Korea), which helps to explain which to speculative attack. But, of course, simply having an autonomous financial system is no guarantee of effective development, as the experiences of many nations in the extreme south-eastern corner of Figure 3.3 illustrates.

While comparative analysis of banking systems typically centres on the factors highlighted in Figure 3.3, the extent of income and wealth polarisation also affects the impact of national banking systems on growth and development, as Table 3.1 shows.

This figure suggests first that different nations vary widely in the ownership and size of their financial intermediaries. Some nations have networks of state development banks, postal banking systems or both; others have private banks, which can be small or large and domestic- or foreign-owned (or both).

Table 3.1 Banking structure and income/wealth polarisation

Network of state-owned developmental or postal banks?	**Degree of polarization of income and wealth**		
	Many poor, some middle, few rich or privileged	**Many middle class, few rich/poor**	**Polarized – many poor, many upper income**
Yes			
Without (private) domestic banks	China (pre-1991)		
With small domestic banks	West Africa, India	Taiwan, China (1990s)	
W/large domestic banks		Japan, Canada, Korea (pre-1998), UK (pre-1990), Germany, France	South Africa, Brazil, China (post-2000)
Domestic & foreign banks			Brazil (pre-1997), Mexico (pre-1994)
Level of financial exclusion?	Depends on state policies	Small or none	Depends on state policies
No			
With small domestic banks		USA (pre-1980s)	
Large domestic banks		USA (post-1980s), UK (post-1990), some EU states	South Africa, Brazil (post-1997)
Domestic & foreign banks		Korea (post-1998)	
Primarily foreign banks			Argentina, Mexico (post-1994)
Level of financial exclusion?	Vast majority	Small or none	Majority

These financial structures interact with different income-wealth structures among households. There are numerous possibilities, of which three are highlighted along Table 3.1's horizontal dimension. First come nations with a large number of poor households, some middle-income households and a small number of rich or privileged; among the ranks of such nations are China in its pre-liberalisation phase, the nations of West Africa and India, among many others. A second possibility consists of nations with a large number of middle-class households and relatively few poor or rich households. Nations with polarised or polarising income and wealth distributions (with many households that are very poor and a significant minority that are rich) constitute a third, and increasingly common, type.

Some historical situations are matched with the categorical possibilities in Table 3.1. Nations with primarily poor populations have generally had state-run banking systems, with only a rudimentary domestic private banking sector. If offices of large multinational banks are located in these nations, their purpose is primarily to service whatever multinational corporations have local trade or production operations. The People's Republic of China presents a special case. Prior to liberalisation, China had five functionally differentiated public banks; these institutions financed overall national priorities; but their regional branch offices served as regional development vehicles, especially in tandem with the now increasingly rare township and village enterprises (TVEs). This state-owned banking system was relatively efficient in spurring local production and service employment, albeit at the price of sporadic inflationary pressure and of the gradual build-up of bad debt. Arguably, China is now on a rapid two-fold transition, vis-à-vis Table 3.1, towards a situation of increasing income and wealth polarisation, with a rapidly growing domestic banking sector. In other places (such as West Africa and India), state public-sector banks have not been successful in spurring sustained growth.

Some nations, in turn, have had dominant middle-class populations, as well as developmental banks (and even postal-savings banking systems) – the middle/middle location in Table 3.1. The banking systems celebrated in Stiglitz' defence of the East Asian model are largely located here. Many already-developed nations – including the United States, the United Kingdom and many EU states – have also had dominant middle-class populations, though not developmental banks. The key point made by Table 3.1 is that most nations' banking/income structures have not stayed in the same cells. Nations that have started in the middle/middle positions of Table 3.1 have moved downward, as developmental and public postal-savings systems have been disbanded, and also rightward, as income and wealth distributions have become more polarised.

Taken together, Figures 3.3 and Table 3.1 suggest that banking systems differ widely in their functions and design and in the income/wealth contexts in which they operate. How robust these systems are in the face of market liberalisation and foreign-bank entry depends first and foremost on the structure and effectiveness of their credit supply and demand mechanisms. This in turn depends on the vibrancy of the flows of funds into these nations' banking systems, and on the way in which the demand for credit is accommodated. And this in turn depends on the distribution of income and wealth in society. When a nation's banking system draws in savings from a broad-based portion of the population, and is the sole (or nearly sole) channel for those savings, then it has substantial lending capacity – and is well positioned to serve domestic credit needs. But insofar as fewer households save domestically (because they are becoming un-banked or are unable to save because of rising living costs (or falling wages)), and insofar as more households are able to move their funds offshore or to divert them to outlets not in the national banking system, then the banking system's lending capacity will be weakened. Weakened lending capacity translates into changes in lending procedures. Banks that may in the past have been able to lend to small and moderate-size businesses may be forced to cut these lenders off in favour of larger and more credit-worthy businesses. Businesses not able to access credit through formal-sector banks must turn to 'curb' markets or informal arrangements, or forego credit arrangements.

It is readily seen that capacity loss in this sense can be triggered by a national drift towards heightened income/wealth inequality. Global economic trends, insofar as they are pushing nations towards greater income/wealth inequality, are simultaneously edging nations away from being able to successfully operate autonomous and economically functional banking systems. The rise in inequality, because it means increasing numbers of upper-income households, attracts multinational banks that are marketing savings and investment instruments in off-shore markets.

3.7 Financial strategic shifts, financial globalisation and financial exclusion

The key insight from Table 3.1 is that banking systems are shifting over time in a south-easterly direction. This movement towards ever more inequality and increasing private-sector involvement is pulling banking systems towards more financial exclusion and exploitation. This is generating strategic shifts by banking firms, which in turn hasten this gravitational pull.

With the growth of capitalist relations and of bourgeois life, systems of financial intermediation and circulation for middle-class households and for established firms also emerged. In some nations, large ('multinational') banks provided financial services for these middle-class and middle-firm markets; in other nations, these financial circuits were distinct. At the same time, financial crises have repeatedly occurred in these systems; so they have been remade several times over, and subjected to extensive public oversight.

The quarter-century after Second World War was marked, especially in Western Europe and North America, by the rise of the Fordist regime of accumulation (Amin, 1994). Fordism involved the creation of a relatively prosperous and secure working class; added together with the growing ranks of government workers and of business-owners, these institutional arrangements made possible a revolution of mass consumerism in upper-income nations. This consumer revolution was accompanied by a media revolution that transformed cultural aspirations in every corner of the globe: those who have the means to choose the commodities they consume increasingly want access to commodities that are globally understood as symbols of modernistic inclusion.

These shifts in household prosperity and consumption norms, combined with the institutional changes necessitated by the severe financial crises of the Great Depression, transformed the shape of financial intermediation. The 'public' had a demand for a growing range of financial products, including mortgages on real estate, savings accounts, educational and automobile loans and so on; at the same time, regulations and laws put into effect in the Depression created a financial system that was (most notably in the United States) segmented on a functional and even geographic basis. Private commercial banks collected household savings and made loans to businesses; mortgage companies and savings and loan associations emerged to collect savings and meet mortgage demands.

Meanwhile, the behaviour of the aggressive and globe-straddling multinational banks was moderated by heavy legislative and/or central bank oversight, by extensive public-bank involvement in core banking activities (in some nations) and by widespread governmental involvement in overseas lending and development efforts, and by the existence of the dollar-based Bretton Woods exchange rate system. Virtually all banks pursued largely conservative lending and deposit-market behaviour. For one thing, their hands were tied by extensive rules governing the markets they could serve, the products they could sell and the prices they could offer on those products; for another, the stable macroeconomic milieu of the immediate post-War period assured stable cash-flows from 'following the rules'. In the United States, consumer banking emerged as one component of the consumerist norms of the Fordist period.

The conjuncture of the breakdown of Bretton Woods, of extensive cross-border lending crises and of macroeconomic instability led to the gradual dissolution of Fordist-era banking structures. In the United States, the extensive body of government regulations that segmented financial product markets, limited banks' geographic expansion and governed financial prices was gradually eliminated in the 1980s and 1990s. An extensive wave of bank mergers was launched, as the remarkably fractionalised US banking system (a legacy of its settlement by frontier-expansion) was gradually reconfigured. In Europe, rapid advances towards monetary integration similarly led to the elimination of many idiosyncratic national rules governing financial product markets and the firms serving them. In the nations of the global South financial crises often led to the elimination or softening of restrictions on the entry and activities of overseas banking firms.

For a time, it appeared that technological change, recurrent overseas lending crises and the increasing ease of entry into financial activities would doom traditional banks, especially the large multinational entities. However, banks remade themselves strategically. Banks were once strategically timid, conducting familiar activities for well-defined customer bases in familiar markets without substantial change for long periods. This has changed. Banks now use information technologies and increasingly sophisticated communications strategies to both create new financial products and market these products to highly desired customers. Banks have never recaptured the core borrowing-and-lending business of the larger and more established businesses that began to escape their balance sheets in the late 1970s. Instead, large banks have found other services to provide their large corporate customers. These services involve the creation and marketing of securities, residual arrangements for credit and a variety of mechanisms for transforming, underwriting and off-loading risk. Indeed, sophisticated information technologies together with a growing number of liquid resale and derivatives markets have permitted banks to enter credit markets ever more deeply – to extend the range of credit markets – without concomitant increases in their risk-taking.

Banks have re-engineered consumer banking in response to the growing number of sophisticated, financially independent upper-income households. They have created specialty banking boutiques for the super-wealthy, as well as standardised, mass-market financial products that meet the needs of the merely prosperous, who often locate conveniently in near geographic proximity to one another in prosperous residential areas. Trying to foster brand loyalty, they cross-sell 'one size fits all' services to these upscale retail customers. Many mergers are undertaken with the aim of extending marketing reach and capturing depositors.

While the search in consumer banking is for more customers, not all customers are incorporated in the same way. Cross-subsidies within banking markets and across customer classes have been radically restricted, while cross subsidies within customer classes and across banking markets have become increasingly common. Potential customers that lack the potential to be stable, multi-product consumers of bank services are offered restrictive sets of services for which they must pay full price and bear risks. Bank cards, cheque-cashing and money-order services are increasingly being marketed to lower-income households not by independent suppliers or informal markets, but by subsidiaries of multinational banks. Because these households often are cash-short but have access to income flows (if more unstable and lower-level), they are targeted for short-term loans of several kinds, including payday loans. And because these lower-income households often lack competitive alternatives, the financial products they buy often build in substantial margins for the lenders. These loans are made to households in the left-most column of Figure 3.2.

Subprime mortgage lending is an example of a longer-term loan that is made on an exploitative basis: due to the absence of collateral, and the high level of risk, these loans are made at higher-than-market levels. This alone guarantees a higher-than-average rate of default. But the absence of any collateral margin for these loans makes these loans more financially fragile: any downturn in home market price will generate negative net worth for the mortgagee. As long as housing prices rise, the spread of financial fragility associated with the creation of more subprime loans will be relatively invisible. But once this dynamic reverses – amplified by reduced income flows for the financially excluded household holding these mortgages – there will be a cascading of financial instability from this hitherto-invisible source.

The search for financial customers then is quite different than in even the recent past. Where banks once pursued thick sets of somewhat heterogeneous borrowers and depositors in well-defined geographic markets, they now pursue thin sets of well-defined and homogeneous borrowers and depositors in shifting sets of geographic markets. An ever increasing array of standardised information, readily accessible through centralised computer databases, helps financial intermediaries slice potential customers into market segments. Upscale – 'default-proof' – customers are pursued fiercely, at home and abroad. But there are fewer (apparently) default-proof customers in a general population that has an ever-increasing proportion of lower-income households.

So banking firms' strategies have focused ever more attention on lower-income and socially excluded households. Credit markets in particular have seen increasing flexibility by banking firms. Methods of risk classification and risk neutralisation have been used to develop products that can be sold, directly or through subsidiaries, to the financially fragile as well as the financially robust. And borrowers are, on their side, not passive but active, as Vandenberg (2003) points out: they will do what they must to find credit, the question being at what price, and on what terms, and with what security and risk they will find it. Banks are not afraid to charge excessively high rates and penalty fees to their riskier customers. Indeed, practices that were once confined to the operations of informal lenders in shady corners have been normalised.

So, financial exploitation has gone mainstream. In ever more markets, potential borrowers break into two prototypical groups: one group whose assets and position are secure, and which both national and overseas lenders will regard as 'good risks' with whom they want long-term, sustained relationships; and a second group, whose wealth levels are so low that contracts are written with the hope of extracting sufficient returns in the short run to compensate for what will inevitably be (for most) longer-term insolvency problems. As Section 3.2.5 has shown, these two groups have very different financial-fragility profiles. So banking firms' efforts to differentiate customers and provide them with credit according to their risk profiles is likely to push a higher proportion of households in any nation into more financially fragile circumstances. The cumulative effect of these shifts is to increase aggregate financial fragility, and thus to accentuate the impact of financial instability (or to make this instability more likely).

The extent of financial inclusion and exclusion varies widely from country to country. In some nations, financial exclusion remains an unvarying component of social life, with only elites maintaining accounts in formal-sector banks. In other nations, financial exclusion for some households results from the process of financial stratification and homogenisation: the division of customers into ever-more-precisely defined segments, which are internally homogeneous but subject to vastly different terms and conditions in the loan market. There are other possibilities still. The principal points made in this section are these: changes in financial-firm strategies have increasingly fragmented credit markets; and financial exclusion and exploitation grow as do the wealth/income and security/insecurity divides.

3.8 Conclusion

This chapter has attempted to build a bridge between the literatures on financial globalisation and financial exclusion by adapting Minsky's balance-sheet approach to financial fragility. Existing theoretical approaches to financial globalisation focus on the efficiency implications of being open to or closed off from cross-border market forces, ignoring financial exclusion. In the efficient-markets view, any nationally idiosyncratic constraints on market forces in banking and finance are invariably ineffective, leading to rent-seeking and efficiency losses. In the asymmetric-information view, permitting nationally autonomous banking can generate efficiency gains. In the post-Keynesian/structuralist view, the key problem is recurrent financial crisis. In all these approaches, no analytical space is left open for financial exclusion.

This has created a large rift between the literature on financial globalisation and that on financial exclusion. The latter literature has pointed out the increasing importance of financial exclusion in both upper- and lower-income economies. The absence of any link between this micro-level phenomenon and the macro-dynamics of financial globalisation and crisis is thus surprising. This chapter attempts to create this link by showing how Minsky's balance-sheet approach to financial fragility can be extended to the household sector. Households with different levels of net worth and credit, in turn, have different degrees of financial fragility. In particular, borrowing by households that are financially excluded is especially likely to be a source of financial fragility for the economy as a whole. Households that borrow to compensate for inadequate income flows are likely to become Ponzi units; households that take on subprime mortgage loans to support home purchases are especially fragile, as any reduction in home prices or in borrower income can trigger insolvency. As the current global financial crisis demonstrates, small initial shifts in insolvency levels can generate a cascade effect that soon roils entire markets.

This analysis suggests that increasing financial exclusion may increase the likelihood of financial crisis, and hence the adverse impacts of financial globalisation. Of special importance are the rising levels of credit commitments that have been made to borrowers with low-level, risky incomes, and that have been made to homeowners that could afford homes only without making any down-payment. We have gone on to show that the sustainability of banking systems is linked to national levels of income and wealth inequality. Further, we have shown that financial firms' strategic reactions to shifting market opportunities in the neoliberal world, and to the increasing inequality of wealth and income, have affected the extent of financial exclusion and exploitation, and thus aggregate levels of financial fragility (and ultimately instability). In effect, the increasingly inter-related and globally active financial firms are both reacting to the increasingly polarised distribution of income and wealth around the world, and behaving in ways that worsen that divide.

Notes

1. On this problem of cross-talk, see Dymski (2006b).
2. Toporowski (2009) also explores the relationship between consumer borrowing and financial fragility.
3. See, for example, Bordo *et al.* (1998).
4. Dicken (2007) summarises empirical evidence on both macro and micro approaches to financial globalisation, and contrasts financial and non-financial globalisation processes.
5. See Lane and Milesi-Ferretti (2007).
6. For example, data for lenders reporting to the Bank for International Settlements indicate that while lending to global South nations increased from 1983 to 1996 (with the exception of lending to Latin America and the Caribbean, which decreased in the wake of the Latin American debt crisis), thereafter overall lending slowed. For example, in 1996, 12.9 per cent of the cross-border loans made by BIS-reporting banks were in developing countries; by 2004, this figure had slipped to 6.7 per cent, recovering slightly to 7.9 per cent in 2007 and then to 9.0 per cent in 2008. These figures, reported for the fourth quarter of each year, capture the crisis-related reduction in flows among global-North nations in 2008.
7. See Dymski (2009).
8. In the realm of social geography, this term was initially suggested by Leyshon and Thrift (1995). A representative volume that collects perspectives from civil society on financial exclusion, among other phenomena, is Social Watch (published

annually by the Third World Institute, Uruguay; see http://www.item.org.uy/eng/index.php).

9. Recent surveys of the literatures in this area are Austin Turner and Skidmore 1999 and Ladd 1998.
10. See, for example, http://www.acorn.org/index.php?id=2681.
11. Many IMF, World Bank and academic economists, led by Ross Levine and Asli Demirgüç-Kunt, have used econometric techniques to suggest links between financial structure and development; see Demirgüç-Kunt and Levine (2001).
12. All of these claims are assertions rooted in theory. Empirical studies have found few efficiency effects from financial consolidation. See Berger *et al.* (1999) and Dymski (1999, ch. 4).
13. For example, the World Bank's 1997 overview of developing-country financial systems reviews the 1980s Latin American debt crisis and 1994–1995 Mexican currency crisis. It admits that financial opening and cross-border financial flows entail the risks of financial instability and macroeconomic loss, but argues that these risks are outweighed by prospective efficiency and output gains. This volume offers a version of the 'there is no alternative' approach to financial liberalisation, according to which developing nations' governments can monitor and police their financial systems' solvency and risk, but not control their behaviour.
14. In fairness, many IMF economists have written studies sceptical of the efficient-markets line, especially after the subprime crisis exploded in late 2007.
15. In the efficient-markets approach, credit rationing does not occur because lenders can clearly differentiate between those borrowers who are, and are not, creditworthy at a given cost of funds.
16. See Eaton *et al.* (1986).
17. See, for example, Stiglitz *et al.* (1993), Stiglitz (1996) and Stiglitz and Uy (1996). Some political economists (among them Zysman, 1984) attributed the success of East Asian nations to their adoption of a government-led economic system, one element of which was a 'German-Japanese' financial system (in contrast to the 'Anglo-American' organisation of financial markets advocated in the efficient-markets approach).
18. See Davidson (1998) and Stretton (2000).
19. An exemplary example of a post-Keynesian analysis of financial crises is Kregel (1998) on the Asian crisis.
20. The proclivity to see micro-to-macro determination but not macro-to-micro influences is shared by both efficient-markets and asymmetric-information theorists. Stiglitz' differences with efficient-markets foes are rooted in disputes over mechanism design and the distribution of information.
21. Not all heterodox models do this; see Toporowski (2009).
22. Stovin-Bradford (2003) reports that efforts are under way to revise overall financial-charter law in South Africa in a manner that extends the umbrella of transaction banking services.
23. See http://www.federalreserve.gov/releases/housedebt/
24. For delineations of Minsky's core ideas about financial fragility, see Minsky (1975, 1986).
25. This stems from the limited liability of the borrower; her indifference to the greater likelihood of extreme losses (provided by the option of defaulting) makes increasingly high and unlikely outcomes more attractive. For explorations of this

problem, see Rothschild and Stiglitz (1970, 1971) and, more recently, Eeckhoudt and Hansen (1992).
26. See Dymski (2009).

References

Akyüz, Y. and K. Boratav (2003) 'The making of the Turkish financial crisis', *World Development*, vol. 31, no. 9.

Amin, A. (1994) (ed.), *Post-Fordism: A Reader* (London: Basil Blackwell).

Bordo M., B. Eichengreen, and J. Kim (1998) 'Was there really an earlier period of international financial integration comparable to today?', *National Bureau of Economic Research, Working Paper* No. 6738, Cambridge, MA.

Bucks B.K., A.B. Kennickell, T.L. Mach and K.B. Moore (2009) 'Changes in U.S. Family Finances from 2004 to 2007: Evidence from the Survey of Consumer Finances', *Federal Reserve Bulletin*, A1–A57.

Cerny P.G. (1994) 'The dynamics of financial globalisation: technology, market structure, and policy response', *Policy Sciences*, vol. 27.

Chang, Ha-Joon (2002) *Kicking Away the Ladder: Development Strategy in Historical Perspective* (London: Anthem Press).

Davidson, P. (1998). 'Post Keynesian employment analysis and the macroeconomics of OECD unemployment,' *Economic Journal, Royal Economic Society*, vol. 108, no. 448.

Demirgüç-Kunt, A. and R. Levine (eds) (2001) *Financial Structure and Economic Growth: A Cross-Country Comparison of Banks, Markets, and Development* (Cambridge: MIT Press).

Dicken, W. (2003) *Global Shift: Reshaping the Global Economic Map in the 21st Century* (Thousand Oaks: Sage Publications).

Dicken, P. (2007) *Global Shift: Mapping the Changing Contours of the World Economy* (London: Sage).

Dymski, G.A. (1999) *The Bank Merger Wave: The Economic Causes and Social Consequences of Financial Consolidation* (Armonk, NY: M.E. Sharpe).

Dymski, G.A. (2006a) 'Discrimination in the credit and housing markets: findings and challenges' in W. Rodgers (eds) *Handbook on the Economics of Discrimination* (Cheltenham, UK: Edward Elgar).

Dymski, G.A. (2006b) 'Targets of opportunity in two landscapes of financial globalisation', *Geoforum*, vol. 37.

Dymski, G.A. (2009) 'Racial exclusion and the political economy of the subprime crisis', *Historical Materialism*, vol. 17, no. 2.

Dymski, G.A. and J.M. Veitch (1992) 'Race and the financial dynamics of urban growth: LA as Fay Wray', in G. Riposa and C. Dersch (eds) *City of Angels* (Los Angeles: Kendall/Hunt Press).

Dymski, G.A. and J.M. Veitch (1996) 'Financial transformation and the metropolis: booms, busts, and banking in Los Angeles', *Environment and Planning A*, vol. 28.

Eatwell, J. and L. Taylor (2000) *Global Finance at Risk* (New York: New Press).

Eaton J., M. Gersovitz and J. Stiglitz (1986) 'The pure theory of country tisk', *European Economic Review*, vol. 30.

Eeckhoudt, L. and P. Hansen (1992) 'Mean-preserving changes in risk with tail-dominance', *Theory and Decision*, vol. 33.

International Monetary Fund (2000) *International Capital Markets: Developments, Prospects, and Key Policy Issues*. Washington, DC: International Monetary Fund, September.

Knight, M. (1998) 'Developing Countries and the Globalisation of Financial Markets', *Working Paper 98/105, Monetary and Exchange Affairs Department, International Monetary Fund*, Washington, DC.

Kregel, J. (1998) 'Yes, "it" did happen again: a Minsky crisis happened in Asia', *Working paper The Jerome Levy Economics Institute*, vol. 234.

Lacker, J. (1995) 'Neighborhoods and banking' Federal Reserve Bank of Richmond, *Economic Quarterly*, vol. 81, no. 2.

Ladd H.F. (1998) 'Evidence on discrimination in mortgage lending', *Journal of Economic Perspectives*, vol. 12, no. 2.

Lane, P.R. and G.M. Milesi-Ferretti (2007) 'The external wealth of nations mark II: revised and extended estimates of foreign assets and liabilities, 1970–2004', *Journal of International Economics*, vol. 73, no. 2.

Leyshon, A. (1995) 'Geographies of money and finance I', *Progress in Human Geography*, vol. 19, no. 4.

Leyshon, A. (1997) 'Geographies of money and finance II', *Progress in Human Geography*, vol. 21, no. 2.

Leyshon, A. and N. Thrift (1995) 'Geographies of financial exclusion: Financial abandonment in Britain and the United States', *Transactions of the Institute of British Geographers*, vol. 20, no. 3.

Lucas, R.E. (1990) 'Why doesn't capital flow from rich to poor countries?', *American Economic Review*, vol. 80, no. 2.

Martin, R.L. (1999) 'The new economic geography of money' in R.L. Martin (ed.) *Money and the Space Economy* (Chichester: Wiley).

Minsky, H.P. (1975) *John Maynard Keynes* (New York: Columbia University Press).

Minsky, H.P. (1986) *Stabilizing an Unstable Economy* (Yale: Yale University Press).

Papaioannou, E. (2009) 'What drives international financial flows? politics, institutions and other determinants', *Journal of Development Economics*, vol. 88.

Reibel, M. (2000) 'Geographic variation in mortgage discrimination: evidence from Los Angeles', *Urban Geography*, vol. 21, no. 1.

Rothschild, M. and J.E. Stiglitz (1970) 'Increasing risk: I. A definition', *Journal of Economic Theory*, vol. 2.

Rothschild, M. and J.E. Stiglitz (1971) 'Increasing risk: II. Its economic consequences', *Journal of Economic Theory*, vol. 3.

Sachs, J. (ed.) (1989) *Developing Country Debt and the World Economy* (Chicago: University of Chicago Press for the National Bureau of Economic Research).

Singh, A. (1998) 'Savings, investment and the corporation in the East Asian miracle', *Journal of Development Studies*, vol. 34, No. 6.

Stiglitz, J.E. (1996) 'Some lessons from the east Asian miracle', *World Bank Research Observer*, vol. 11, no. 2.

Stiglitz, J.E. (2000) 'Capital market liberalisation, economic growth, and instability', *World Development*, vol. 28, no. 6.

Stiglitz, J.E. (2003) *Globalisation and Its Discontents* (New York: W. W. Norton).

Stiglitz, J.E. and M. Uy (1996) 'Financial markets, public policy, and the East Asian miracle', *World Bank Research Observer*, vol. 11, no. 2.

Stiglitz, J.E. and A. Weiss (1981) 'Credit rationing in markets with imperfect information', *American Economic Review*, vol. 71.

Stovin-Bradford, R. (2003) 'It's a long walk to banking freedom', *Sunday Times (South Africa) Economics, Business & Finance*, 20 July.

Stretton, H. (2000) 'Neoclassical imagination and financial anarchy' *World Development*, vol. 28, no. 6.

Taylor, L. (1983) *Structural Macroeconomics* (New York: Basic Books).

Toporowski, J. (2009) 'The economics and culture of financial inflation', *Competition and Change*, vol. 13, no. 2.

Turner, M.A. and F. Skidmore (eds) (1999) *Mortgage Lending Discrimination: A Review of Existing Evidence* (Urban Institute: Washington, DC).

Vandenberg, P. (2003) 'Adapting to the financial landscape: Evidence from small firms in Nairobi', *World Development*, vol. 31, no. 11.

World Bank (1997) *Private Capital Flows to Developing Countries: The Road to Financial Integration* (Oxford: Published for the World Bank by Oxford University Press).

Wray, L.R. (2007) 'Lessons from the subprime meltdown', *Working paper no. 522, Levy Economics Institute of Bard College*, December.

Zysman, J. (1984) *Governments, Markets, and Growth: Financial Systems and Politics of Industrial Change* (Ithaca, NY: Cornell University Press, 1984).

4
Magdoff-Sweezy, Minsky and the Real Subsumption of Labour to Finance

Riccardo Bellofiore and Joseph Halevi

4.1 Monopoly capital and stagnation: the condition for the new forms of financial growth, Magdoff-Sweezy and Minsky

In the late 1970s a slim book was published containing the essays by Harry Magdoff and Paul Sweezy (1977) in the *Monthly Review*. The authors argued that US capitalism was characterised by stagnation and indebtedness, the latter overwhelmingly on the private side. The central issue was that banks were skating on thin ice and there was a connection running from monopoly capitalism to indebtedness. In a nutshell, the regime of oligopolistic capitalism generates a built in tendency towards unused capacity. The ensuing deficiency in effective demand relatively to the productive potential compels the private sector to rely on a growing debt. The central piece of that collection was a paper on the economics of banking which appears now remarkably far-sighted.

They showed how the expansion of lending was not the result of optimistic buoyancy regarding the economy, because growth rates had faltered. Rather, increased lending became the instrument to make money by gambling on the future capacity of the loans to be repaid despite liquidity constraints and the time lag needed to repay loans for investment in capital equipment. They identified a shift towards greater short-term borrowing. Shortly afterwards they pointed out an additional phenomenon, namely the systemic increase in the ratio of consumers' debt to disposable income. Both phenomena, they argued, stemmed from the underlying stagnationist tendency requiring an ever increasing indebtedness to keep the economy going (Magdoff and Sweezy, 1981).

Today there is a worldwide revival of Hyman Minsky's views about financial instability (Minsky, 1985), which may be connected to the Magdoff-Sweezy approach. In Minsky's case the burgeoning of credit happens when times are good and banks issue ever growing loans. A point is reached, however, where this process is not sustainable. Borrowers cannot meet interest payments, inducing a systemic tendency to a financial decelerator and debt deflation. Loans on which payments are due are called back and the whole system slides towards a credit crunch, which then becomes a financial crisis with real repercussions on the level of effective demand and employment.

In the Magdoff-Sweezy approach we must distinguish between different periods in the history of US capitalism. The dynamics of the overextension of credit must be put in the specific context. A systemic tendency to stagnation has been a structural feature of the American economy since the Great Depression, but countertendencies and original economic policies often made the system very dynamic. John F. Walker and Harold G. Vatter (1986) have shown that from 1933 to 1983, excluding Second World War, the US economy functioned above or at its potential for only 10 years: 3 during the Korean War and 5 during the Vietnam War. However, while before Second World War the system was prone to catastrophic collapses, after 1945 stagnation had been counteracted by institutional means such as military spending. This was the case not only in the United States. Charles Kindleberger (1970) stated that the Marshall Plan never ended as it just metamorphosed into the NATO military alliance, much of which was financed by Washington. Yet, Magdoff and Sweezy highlighted what had to become the main factor sustaining accumulation:

> Among the forces counteracting the tendency to stagnation, none has been more important or less understood by economic analysts than the growth, beginning in the 1960s and rapidly gaining momentum after the severe recession of the 1970s, of the country debt structure (government, corporate, and individual) at a pace far exceeding the sluggish expansion of the 'real' economy. The result has been the emergence of an unprecedentedly huge and fragile financial superstructure subject to stresses and strains that increasingly threaten the economy as a whole.
>
> (Magdoff and Sweezy, 1987: p. 13)

Debt growth in the 1960s is consistent with Minsky's views about banks' eagerness to lend in boom times. The long boom was followed by the stagnation of the 1970s, but, as Minsky said, this is what should be expected when 'Keynesian' economic policies intervene with the Big Bank and the Big Government: extension of debt goes together with a slowdown of growth and an increase in prices and wages. This also explains why the increase in debt in the 1960s, especially for households and corporations of all kinds, was much less than during the low growth decade of the 1970s. As Minsky and Magdoff-Sweezy would have expected, the financial system could not become more conservative, without risking another Great Crash like that of the 1930s. Moreover, with the negative real interest rates of 1973–1978, there was an incentive to borrow as much as to lend, since the real sector was likely to generate returns higher than the interest rates.

The 1980s signalled, however, the beginning of a turning point, so that the debt dynamics of the following decades cannot be fully explained by Minsky and/or Magdoff-Sweezy. Those were years of rather volatile and abrupt growth rates as exemplified by the sharp V shaped recession of 1981–1982, coupled with high interest rates and inflation. The US real growth rate in the 1980s rose only marginally above that of the previous decade. Why then did financial institutions launch into an unprecedented lending spree? The Magdoff-Sweezy and the Minsky dynamics, which link the rise of debt and the financial 'innovation' post 1980s with the deficiency of profitable effective demand, appear convincing as the starting conceptual framework for understanding the process that has led to the collapse of 2007–2008, but they must be developed and integrated. Only two elements of a new shape of capitalism can be underlined here: the role of capital market inflation; and the construction of a perverse connection between the 'traumatised' workers, on the one side, and the 'manic-depressive' savers-plus-indebted consumers, on the other.

4.2 Capital market inflation: Toporowski

Jan Toporowski (2000) has, rightly, highlighted capital asset inflation in many of his works. Contrary to Minsky's expectations, the indebtedness has been especially significant for financial businesses, and lately for households, rather than non-financial firms. Market for securities issued by financial intermediaries and bought by other financial intermediaries exploded. This does not represent a net expansion of credit. The building up of the capitalism of pension and institutional funds (beginning in the United States and the United Kingdom), and which corresponds to what Minsky would call money manager capitalism, had a direct impact on the balance sheet of corporations especially since the 1980s. Corporations issuing securities in the capital markets found that they could issue shares cheaply. The return on shares was mainly in the form of capital gains, and this was a crucial factor in originating systematic and disequilibrating capital assets inflation. Corporations issued capital in excess of their commercial and industrial needs.

A loop between financial inflation and overcapitalisation became embedded in the system, facilitated by the sole interest of fund managers in financial returns, shareholder value and also by new techniques of senior management remuneration and of debt management. Bank borrowing was substituted by cheaper long-term capital and excess capital. This latter was also reinvested in buying short-term financial assets. The merger and takeover mania and the balance-sheet restructuring completes Toporowski's argument. In this, he also explains why banks were forced to change their nature into fee-related businesses or originate-and-distribute activities, losing large corporations as costumers and then becoming more and more fragile.

As Toporowski argues, capital market inflation fuelled both long equity financing and housing market booms. Markets where the prospects of capital gains made disequilibrium feed on itself increased liquidity for a long while and improved the quality of collateral – Minsky's margin of safety endogenously improved in a self-justifying process. The rise in asset values was unconstrained because there was no automatic readjustment mechanism, no built-in tendency to equilibrium (of which both Neoclassicals and Neo-Ricardians are so fond).

Most interestingly, however, the non-financial companies' debt was reduced and the 'industrial capital' sector became more stable. This cannot be interpreted in line with the Minsky orthodoxy, but it was also not adequately appreciated by the Baran–Magdoff–Sweezy tradition. And the household debt not only increased, but supported consumption against stagnating if not declining individual personal incomes for most wage earners. The collapse of the saving propensity relative to personal income increased the multiplier and again stabilised the financial position of firms.

As Toporowski puts it, this mutually reinforcing combination of capital assets inflation and collateralised lending hedged speculative and Ponzi financing structures through capital gains, delaying the onset of the crisis. As long as asset inflation continued, asset markets remained liquid and made the building up of collateralised debt possible. Thus, it was not investments which caused over-indebtedness for non-financial companies. Rather, they were 'forced' into debt, initially, because of the capital asset inflation process on the rise and because of the behaviour of financial intermediaries; later, because of the downside effects on the same non-financial companies' cash inflows resulting from the breakdown in capital asset inflation.

4.3 The prices of capital assets

Before turning to the price of capital assets, it seems necessary to highlight a Minskyan conceptual segment that, once suitably modified, may help to explain the profit dynamics of a stagnation driven system. Minsky's first set of prices is that of current production and, in most cases, is set by standard mark-up procedures. His second set of prices is that of capital assets. Here it may be useful to refer to John Maynard Keynes.

In chapter 16 of the *General Theory* Keynes wrote:

> It is much preferable to speak of capital as having a yield over the course of its life in excess of its original cost, than as being *productive*. For the only reason why an asset offers a prospect of yielding during its life services having an aggregate value greater than its initial supply price is because it is *scarce*; and it is kept scarce because of the competition of the rate of interest on money. If capital becomes less scarce, the excess

> yield will diminish, without its having become less productive – at least in the physical sense.
>
> (Keynes, 1936: p. 213)

The thrust of the chapter is that the financial system allows capital assets to generate rent-like returns. The social formation of the scarcity of capital assets is not explained in Keynes. Minsky goes further arguing that the demand price of capital assets is largely disconnected from the costs of production. This second capital asset price is separate from the cost of production prices because it depends upon expectations and, according to Minsky, is tied to the values of stocks. The dependency upon expectations of the demand price for capital assets makes it volatile for the reasons outlined by Keynes in Chapter 12 of the *General Theory* which deals with the uncertain nature of long-term expectations.

The relation between the price of capital assets and the price of current production is, for Minsky, the pivotal relative price under capitalism. Favourable investment conditions rule whenever the former price rises relatively to the latter. The demand price for capital assets arises from within the sphere of finance, whereas the supply price of capital goods is determined within the sphere of production. In this context, the intersection of the rising supply curve for capital goods with the demand curve for capital assets determines the level of investment and its dynamics. By adding up all the firms Minsky obtains the aggregate level of investment, and then a tendency to an increasing leverage.

We shall not delve into the issue of whether this micro-foundation is sound. We just warn that both Keynes' socially constructed scarcity of capital assets and Minsky's two price system pertain not to supply and demand relations, but to the realm of capital as a social relation. This central aspect of the analysis of capitalism regularly eludes post-Keynesians, since they invariably veer off towards policy counselling which cannot possibly examine the question of capital as a social relation because policy must take the basic institutional framework as given. This central aspect, which was the distinguishing feature of Marx from the Classics, will loom in the remainder of this chapter.

4.4 From the tendency towards stagnation to the 'new capitalism'

We ought to view the present situation in a longer-run perspective. The crisis is not the outcome of reckless neoliberalism, as often is wrongly claimed. Many things have happened in the last four decades since the neoliberal turn of 1979–1980, except the retreat of the State in a general sense. Certainly the u-turn of 1979–1980 was accompanied by a drastic increase in nominal and real interest rates, the spread of uncertainty and the ensuing fall in investment. Social public expenditure was curtailed and wages as a proportion of national income fell, reducing wage earners' consumption.

Why then did the Great Effective Demand crisis not materialise in the 1980s? The quick answer is that there were political countertendencies. The most visible was Reagan's twin deficits which kept the United States and, through increased US imports, the rest of the industrialised world and Asian economies above water. The United States, along with the United Kingdom, Spain and Australia, acted as the market outlet of last resort both for the strong neo-mercantilisms of Germany and Japan and for the weak ones of, for example, Italy.

However, these were just countertendencies. As a direct consequence of the neoliberal u-turn, a new form of capitalism emerged in the 1990s. To be clear we do not think that this 'new' capitalism is the so-called 'globalisation', nor is it the alleged Empire dreamed by Antonio Negri and, finally, it is most definitely not the supposedly knowledge-centred capitalism based on immaterial production and crisis-free. This 'new capitalism' resurrects some aspects prevailing in the nineteenth century and is characterised by the three interconnected figures: traumatised workers, manic-depressive savers and indebted consumers. Its functioning is entirely based on the link between financialisation and the casualisation of work. This link interacts with the one highlighted by Toporowski.

4.5 Financial capitalism, traumatised workers, centralisation without concentration

Greenspan's traumatised workers are the product of the renewed supremacy of finance and its real effect on the organisation of production. This is shown by the impact on employment and employment contracts of junk bonds trading, of equity investment takeovers and the like.

The renewed supremacy of finance is not external to the system of productive and industrial firms. Sweezy observed, back in early 1970s, that the main focus of the large corporation has a financial character. The Minskyan money manager capitalism emanates from within the so-called industrial units of monopoly capital as corporate executives were interested in the financial side of the corporation's activities rather than in the productive and engineering side. This brought the rise of money managers by extending short-termism to the whole economic system. Stagnation helped to form a consensus among the ruling groups in favour of term financial gains.

Financial companies specialised in portfolio management formed from banks and/or other financial institutions. But portfolio managers became unable to study in depth the different companies in which they have their stakes. Furthermore, the design of financial instruments to disperse risk leads to ownership in several companies at once. The short-term horizon of financial management has been institutionalised by legislation which compels quarterly reporting on mark-to-market criteria. Only in early 2009, with the deepening financial crisis, has the United States reverted to annual reporting abandoning the mark-to-market method. In seeking short-term returns, money managers, who have vested interests in the short-term approach (stock options remunerations), exercise a significant influence over the organisation of production and work.

As a consequence, we have witnessed a process of centralisation without concentration, hand in hand with aggressive competition among capitals leading to systemic oversupply, a precondition for overproduction. Key sectors have gone through massive processes of acquisitions and mergers which required the mobilisation of money well above the needs of self-financing. Yet rather than large, vertically integrated, companies the outcome has been that of a productive structure oriented towards a network of plants and of productive units interacting through supply value chain networks. In other words, the centralisation of capital through mergers was not accompanied by its productive concentration. This means that that there is now a hierarchy of firms within the network system and the conditions of the employees depend upon the position of each firm in the supply value chain hierarchy. The tendency of centralisation without concentration helps to explain why the growth in production no longer entails the expansion of a homogeneous working class in a homogeneous territory (Sheffield till the late 1960s; Lille till the late 1970s; Turin till the late 1970s and Milan till the late 1980s; and so on) sharing the same material and juridical/legal conditions. The labour process is now fragmented. The degree of job casualisation may be limited in one pole and of devastating intensity in another, acting as threat on the more stable one. These outcomes have been brought about by the unleashing of capitalism to use the effective title of the last book by the late Andrew Glyn (2006).

4.6 The historical process leading to the subsumption of labour

The subsumption of labour by finance occurred in connection with the belief that the economic environment would stay relatively calm thanks to the means used to stave off stagnation. Since the European countries accepted and even nurtured stagnation in order to enforce wage deflation, the measures to fight stagnation came mostly from the United States and Japan. These are the largest and most globally connected economies in the world.

With the Wall Street crash in 1987, Japan very quickly reflated its economy by sharply reducing the Central Bank interest rate, thereby flooding with money both its and the American financial markets. That move turned out to be crucial to refuel liquidity in the starved US stock exchange but it also created a speculative bubble of gigantic proportions in Japan. But Tokyo increased interest rates in 1992 fearing a clash between the speculative overheating of the economy and its exports dynamics. Soon the economy collapsed into a state of deep stagnation with the yen rising till 1995. To avoid a depression, interest rates were cut to about zero and a large amount of money was pumped into the economy, expanding the budget deficit to nearly 10 per cent of GDP.

These hyper-Keynesian policies, while preventing Japan from sinking into a depression, did not restart growth. Instead, they opened up the way to the so-called yen carry trade. It became quite logical for both Japanese and foreign banks and financial companies to borrow in Japan in yen at insignificant interest rates, and 'invest' the money in higher yielding securities and stocks in the United States. The Japanese crisis and the US response to its own stagnation tendency became mutually compatible through the carry trade in yen.

The twin process of indebtedness and financialisation was the solution to stagnation in the United States. Throughout the 1980s and the 1990s, the productive branches servicing the financial sectors grew and absorbed an increasing share of real investment. In the late 1970s, this was driven mostly by company debts but became increasingly determined by households' debt (Magdoff and Sweezy, 1987; Chesnais, 2004). Terms like 'securitisation', describing offerings of titles to sustain private debt, or hedge funds, companies specialising in risk management, appear in the United States with increasing frequency from the late 1970s onward. For debt creation to offset the stagnationist deadlock, institutional space had to be created in the first place. In that decade, US capitalism was caught in a very serious stagnationist crisis determined by (a) the end of the Vietnam War; (b) the Start agreements with the USSR which capped the level of nuclear arsenals and of their vectors; and (c) the ousting of the Shah in Iran which dented another major source of military procurements and directly affected the US oil-finance network (Ferguson and Rogers, 1986). To put the matter into its historical perspective we must mention that, in the second half of the 1950s and throughout the 1960s, heavy fluctuations in the stock exchange affected neither policy decisions nor evaluations regarding future real investment. The Dow Jones index, for instance, was 700 in 1963 and just 750 in 1969 but with intermediate peaks around 1000 points (it displayed a volatility nearing 50 per cent). Yet these fluctuations were within a closed circuit as the banking system was insulated from the stock market because of the legislation of the Roosevelt era. The real economy and the profitability of both industry and finance were, instead, propelled by the spending policies induced by the Vietnam War. With the onset of stagnation in the 1970s the political and economic response gravitated towards the transformation of debt into a source of financial rents and of support to effective demand through household indebtedness. In this context, throughout the 1980s and 1990s the required institutional space was created by abolishing the safeguard provisions of the Roosevelt era and by changing pensions' financial flows from funds tied to specific entitlements into funds available for financial markets in which benefits came to depend upon capital market values.

The institutional expansion encouraged the belief that financial markets would show a systemic tendency towards the validation of expectations concerning future capitalisation. This 'confidence' was essentially the by-product of governmental activities centred on injecting liquidity internationally. Such policies began with the Wall Street crash of 1987, were expanded during the 1990s and acquired unprecedented proportions with the war in Afghanistan and in Iraq after 2001 and 2003. It is this kind of public money that sustained the fireworks of private moneys and the growth of the derivative markets. Without government created liquidity, the implementation of the large private financial operations of the last decade – from investments into junk bonds to private equity take-overs – would have been much more problematical, if at all possible.

This Ocean of state-injected liquidity had two effects. It has increased speculation and the volatility that goes with it. However, it seemed to have augmented the capacity to absorb this generated volatility: we witnessed the ingrained belief in the sustainability of an ever growing financialisation of the economy. Although there have been instances of financial bankruptcies with many victims, no chain event had occurred up to 2007 on a large scale, thanks to the continuing issuance of liquidity by the public authorities. The explosion of the dotcom bubble in 2000 began to shatter that belief but the swift transformation of American monetary policies into a new form of war financing in 2001 (De Cecco, 2007) created the conditions for the absorption of the many bankruptcies leading to the impression that the financial ocean would remain essentially calm.

4.7 The subsumption of labour by finance and monetary policies

By the mid-1990s capitalism was ripe for a different management of economic policies with a new dynamics of capital accumulation. This 'new' capitalism was not stagnationist, nor did it eschew, despite the declared deregulation of markets, an eminently political management of effective demand. In the new mode of regulation, wages were no longer a source of inflation (of a different kind from the one Minsky had in mind when elaborating on his Financial Instability Hypothesis in the 1970s). Statistically recorded unemployment can be reduced without a rise in wages, which in the United States have both been displaying a long-term decline, while in the Eurozone they are subjected to competitive deflation. The Phillips curve tends now to be flat. Indebted consumers are compelled to work more intensively thereby unifying an increase in the productive power of labour with longer working hours. In Marxian terminology the processes of extraction of relative and absolute surplus value were joined together.

The emergence of traumatised workers and indebted consumers has generated a real subsumption of labour by finance which transforms the conditions pertaining to the valorisation of production. Capitalism could now head anew towards full employment, which in reality means 'full underemployment' of a precariously employed flexible workforce. A full underemployment that could turn rapidly into mass unemployment of the kind we are witnessing today.

The new capitalist regulation of the 1990s was predicated upon the Central Bank issuing money and liquidity in amounts large enough to inflate stocks which become the preferred destination of private savings, at the detriment of government bonds. Traditional monetarism, based on the control of the supply of money, or on the wish to control that supply, is ditched in favour of the control of the rate of interest with reference to the so-called Taylor rule. The money supply curve becomes flat too: at the rate of interest set by the monetary authorities, the supply of money expands automatically by endogenously responding to demand. What matters in this context is the political management of the rate of interest.

4.8 Indebted consumers and manic-depressive savers

How did this system of regulation guarantee the dynamics of the system, albeit in a markedly uneven context? The two other figures of the indebted consumers and the savers in her or his manic-depressive state appear on the stage. They appear when asset price inflation becomes a full-blown speculative bubble, making greater consumption possible by means of additional credit. Saving out of disposable income falls and is almost annihilated. Consumption is, therefore, rendered autonomous from income; it is swelled by the wealth effect induced by the rise of stock or real estate prices.

The figure of the indebted consumer does not correspond to a situation of well-being, although it embodies a distortion towards opulent consumption skewed towards non-essential items. As the US case shows, middle class households had to increasingly depend on the work of at least two people in order to keep the same living standards. Elizabeth Warren has produced a definitive congressional testimony pointing out that US households have been spending a declining share of their incomes on consumption goods, thanks to the 'China price'. The rising part went to medical, education and insurance expenses. These are all sectors with strong financial rent elements. For many households, indebtedness has become a necessity and, at least, the only way to maintain an adequate standard of living in the face of falling real weekly earnings (Warren, 2007).

Thus the mechanism centred on the nexus between asset price inflation and monetary policies guaranteed for a relative long phase the monetary realisation of surplus value. However, it also doped the system. The indebted consumer has been the main factor sustaining the growth rate in the United States, while the latter has acted as the buyer of last resort for the neo-mercantilist economies of Japan, Korea, partly of Germany and to a larger extent of China. The model was, however, unsustainable as it set in motion a string of speculative bubbles leading to systemic crisis.

4.9 From bubbles to systemic crisis

After 2000, all stops were pulled in order to stave off the crisis and the strategy succeeded by combining a renewed Baran–Magdoff–Sweezy military Keynesianism with flooding the economy with liquidity in the wake of Greenspan's low rate of interest policy.

Asia's, and in particular China's and Japan's, dependency upon the US market helps. Asian countries have little alternative than to refinance US deficits by exporting capital to the US enabling, in this way, the Federal Reserve to pursue a low interest rate policy. The policy mix, if the ignition of two wars can be called policy, caused another round in the real estate price inflation which reproduced, in a modified way, the bubble mechanism of the *new economy*. Thus, while the dotcom bubble did require real investment in plant and equipment, the housing price inflation did not, so that, after 2003, investment lagged behind consumption.

The new bubble however, appeared wobbly from the start as it revealed itself very sensitive to a rise in interest rates. It is for this reason that it began to sputter in 2004, and by 2005, the decline in house prices commenced. The fragility of the new bubble meant that the Federal Reserve was losing control over monetary policies. In particular, the criterion of setting an inflation target became meaningless. The control of inflation became the instrument to enhance financial asset values. Insofar as these stimulated consumption-led-growth, they tended to rekindle inflation. However, whatever inflationary pressures existed, they came not from wages but from raw materials or from any possible degree of monopoly that business could attain. Wage deflation was also made to counterbalance those inflationary spurts. But if inflation were to be held in check far in advance of its actual appearance, interest rates would have to rise. Yet such a move was destabilising the process of asset price inflation, which the Fed was supposed to support.

It was believed that financial market efficiency would perform two connected miracles. The first miracle concerned securitisation's power to disperse risk. It was thought also that the effectiveness would be enhanced by increasing the complexity of financial instruments which would allow setting up a labyrinth of combined packages and sale sequences. But any warning to that effect was muzzled by government authorities.

The second miracle involved the magic of those phony products to direct surplus savings to the countries which were dis-saving, first and foremost to the United States. It did not happen because it could not happen. Securitisation is an opaque money making way to unload risk ad infinitum, whereas international imbalances cannot be corrected by the smooth transfers of savings, but rather by generating the real effective demand needed to correct them.

4.10 Neoliberalism and social liberalism

The model of the 'new capitalism' was certainly neoliberal but the State has never withdrawn. It has implemented neoliberal polices in relation to the welfare state, the labour market and the environment, but it has protected monopolies and large corporations' rent seeking property rights. It did not refrain from running large public deficits, and so on. Social liberalism is perhaps more free market oriented than neoliberalism.

Social-liberals are worried not only by State failures but also by market failures, and they claim to be in favour of more State together with more free market. Unlike the neoliberals they sincerely strive for more competition in markets for goods and services; in this way they are more for 'free competition' than the neoliberals are. They also advocate a greater regulatory role for the State ('liberalise in order to re-regulate' is their manifesto). They want a redistributive State in relation to the labour market and to welfare. For the former they do advocate labour flexibility, yet cushioned by a social protective network and by guarantees enforced through State regulations. They push for a form of universal welfare including guaranteed minimum incomes labelled with new terms such as *citizenship's income, basic unconditional income* and so on.

Social-liberals know that an indiscriminate attack on the Welfare State or on labour would impact negatively on the productivity of the latter. More than that: in a deep crisis, social-liberals do not reject the supporting role of State intervention as an essential provider of demand and the role of the Central Bank as a lender of last resort in a crisis. They would even worry and propose something against financial instability. In short, they are a bit Keynesian, according to circumstances. They claim to be in favour of strong industrial and credit policies with structural objectives through incentives and disincentives, while being at the same time strongly against any direct State intervention by means of even indicative plans, lest they stand accused of *étatism*. In general social-liberals talk about these issues when in opposition, while in office they focus on financial tightness as a prerequisite for more competitive policies.

In the above context today's truth is that social liberalism has been wiped out by far more than neoliberalism. The representatives of the latter have seen that the chains of bubbles were leading to a disaster, which actually materialised but perhaps less catastrophically than otherwise. They made central banks abandon inflation targeting rules, adopted indiscriminate moral hazard enhancing policies which are anathema for social-liberals. This when, with the world-wide fragmentation of labour, social movements are just about nonexistent and the hegemony is firmly with the people and classes who were in the driving seat all along.

References

Chesnais, F. (2004) *La finance mondialisée: racines sociales et politiques, configuration, conséquences*, F. Chesnais (ed.) (Paris: La Découverte).

De Cecco, M. (2007) *Gli anni dell'incertezza* (Bari: Laterza).

Ferguson, T. and N. Rogers (1986) *Right Turn: The Decline of the Democrats and the Future of American Politics* (New York: Hill and Wang).

Glyn, A. (2006) *Capitalism Unleashed* (Oxford: Oxford University Press).

Keynes, J.M. (1936) *The General Theory of Interest Employment and Money* (London: Macmillan).

Kindleberger, C. (1970) *Power and Money* (New York: Basic Books).

Magdoff, H. and P. Sweezy (1977) *The End of Prosperity: The American Economy in the 1970s* (New York: Monthly Review Press).

Magdoff, H. and P. Sweezy (1981) *The Deepening Crisis of U.S. Capitalism* (New York: Monthly Review Press).

Magdoff, H. and P. Sweezy (1987) *Stagnation and the Financial Explosion* (New York: Monthly Review Press).

Minsky, H.P. (1985) 'The financial instability hypothesis: a restatement' in P. Arestis and S. Thanos (eds) *Post Keynesian Economic Theory* (Armonk, N.Y.: M.E. Sharpe).

Toporowski, J. (2000) *The End of Finance: The Theory of Capital Market Inflation, Financial Derivatives, and Pension Fund Capitalism* (London: Routledge).

Walker, J.F. and H.G Vatter (1986) 'Stagnation – performance and policy: a comparison of the depression decade with 1973–1984', *Journal of Post Keynesian Economics*, vol. 8, no. 4.

Warren, E. (2007) *The New Economics of the Middle Class: Why Making Ends Meet Has Gotten Harder* (Testimony Before Senate Finance Committee).

5
Reclaimed by the Mainstream? Hyman Minsky and the Global Credit Crunch

Anastasia Nesvetailova

5.1 Introduction

Hyman Minsky had long been an outsider of mainstream finance and economics. A pessimistic theorist of financial capitalism, he did not fit into the increasingly technical, equilibrium-centred currents of economics. His timing as an institutionalist of Keynesian tradition was wrong too: the monetarism-dominated 1970s and the 1980s were not a friendly time for a post-Keynesian scholar. In this instance, it seems rather odd that an outcome of the continuing crisis has been to rehabilitate the name of Minsky – long an outsider of mainstream finance and economics – in the emergent analyses of the crisis. Commentators speak about a 'Minsky moment' in the financial system, repeat his wise observation that 'stability is always destabilising' and even note the element of Ponzi pyramids in the recent bout of securitisation. But which part of Minsky's vision of financial instability and economic reform do today's policymakers pick? And what precisely does a 'Minskyan' reading of finance suggest about the current state of the world financial markets?

This chapter aims to answer these questions by reviewing the emergent theorisations of the global credit crunch as in what can be considered as the 'mainstream' of crisis analytics and policy debate. Specifically, I focus on three Minskyan undertones in crisis theorising: (1) the notion of a 'Minsky moment' in the financial cycle; (2) the thesis about destabilising stability and (3) the crisis of Ponzi finance. To what extent have the current considerations of these issues moved beyond the analytical constraints of neoclassical economics and mainstream financial theory?

Analysing the usages of these concepts in the crisis commentary and conceptualisation of the credit crunch, and contrasting these with their wider meaning in the political economy of Minsky, I argue that despite appearances, the core of Minskyan theory of finance still sends a very inconvenient message to today's believers in financial innovation and competition. As a result, I found that a highly selective and fragmented version of Minsky's theory of finance is informing the emergent accounts of the credit crunch. Stylised as an end of the North Atlantic credit boom, in turn aggravated by the usages of specific products and techniques of securitisation the global crisis has not fundamentally compromised the intellectual edifice of efficient market theory of finance (EMT) and its central place in the formation of global policymaking. Minsky's political economy, with its critique of financial innovation in the deregulated credit system, thus remains as outside the 'mainstream' of finance as it was in his own time.

5.2 Hyman Minsky and financialised capitalism

Rather briefly, and unfairly crudely, Minsky's framework can be summarised as follows. Any capitalist system with an advanced financialised economy goes through cycles and institutional mutations. Regardless of the specific context of these transformations, there is an inherent, embedded conflict in this system – between shifts and rapid changes in the financial system and the state of the real economy (which includes economic stability generally and full employment). This basic conflict is centred on the process of financial innovation and the ability of private financial firms to raise and emit debt as their major form of financing: '... in a capitalist economy that is hospitable to financial innovation, full employment with stable prices cannot be sustained, for within any full-employment situation there are endogenous disequilibrating forces at work that assure the disruption of tranquillity' (Minsky, 2008: p. 199).

This ability to rely on debt and 'invent' money (even temporarily) in turn triggers a chain of transformations and leads conservative financial units (*hedge* financed unit, where existing obligations and debt commitments are consistently lower than the incoming profit flows) to become more risky (*speculative*, where not all profits flow can cover existing obligations) and, ultimately, *Ponzi* (where one can only repay old debt by borrowing anew).

This chain of debt-driven developments makes the financial system increasingly fragile, prompting the monetary authorities to intervene in order to prevent a structural economic collapse. Because capitalism is an incredibly diverse and constantly changing system, the resulting instability does not conform to any fixed model; the timing of the financial distress and crisis is almost impossible to identify in advance. Any policy response to financial instability, Minsky argued, should involve both monetary and fiscal measures, since on its own, monetary policy is ineffective: 'Monetary policy is of very limited effectiveness both in constraining inflation and in counteracting a depression' (Minsky, 1982: p. 173). Most controversially, Minsky showed that the mechanism that spreads fragility and crisis throughout the system centres on the complex chain of liquidity-stretching financial innovations that appear to enhance liquidity but in fact, by replacing state-backed money with privately created financial instruments, make the financial system progressively illiquid.

With his close focus on endogenous process of financial evolution and instability, for most of his own lifetime, Minsky remained a rather eccentric scholar, standing aside from the big intellectual armies of mainstream economics (Strange, 1998). It is only in heterodox political economy and, more recently, in International Political Economy that Minskyan analysis of financial instability has not only found a grateful audience, but also opened up a niche for a plethora of his intellectual successors. Yet heterodox political economists, however brilliant they might be, are still heterodox: rarely do you see their names on the pages of *Econometrica*, nor are they frequented by the journalists from the *Wall Street Journal* and the *Financial Times*. It is all the more striking, therefore, that one result of the global credit meltdown has been to rehabilitate the name of Minsky from the shadows of critical political economy, and place his work at the very centre of crisis commentary. The global credit crunch has been dubbed as a 'Minsky moment' in finance, or a crisis of 'Ponzi finance'. Does this suggest that the financial mainstream has finally realised its intellectual impotence in the face of systemic breakdowns? Has Minsky been rehabilitated completely? I suggest not.

5.3 From the 'Minsky moment' to a Minskyan crisis?

In the summer of 2007, George Magnus, chief economist of UBS, put the term 'Minsky moment'[1] at the centre of crisis analyses when he warned that a financial crisis might soon engulf the United States and international financial markets. According to Magnus, a 'Minsky moment' is 'the point where credit supply starts to dry up, systemic risk emerges and the central bank is obliged to intervene' (Magnus, 22 July 2007). Back in July 2007, Magnus and other observers believed that such a moment could be averted. We know that it was not.

As a result of the financial turmoil that has ensued, Minsky's theory of finance has attracted more attention, and references to the 'Minsky moment' recur on the pages of financial broadsheets, market commentary and research publications of some bodies responsible for financial governance. (Interestingly, these tend to be EU-based institutions, rather than their US counterparts.) Jean Claude Trichet, for instance, described a 'Minsky moment' as a situation 'whereby there is a sudden recognition and recoil from underlying credits whose quality was in fact worsening for years' (Trichet, 2008). Searching for explanations of the credit crunch, M. Knight, general manager of the BIS, stated: 'The explanation I find most persuasive focuses on... the key features of the recent turmoil: the lack of transparency in the originate-to-distribute model; the role played by credit rating agencies in the evaluation of structured products; and the covert reliance on special purpose vehicles to conduct off-balance sheet financial transactions on a large scale. The effect of all these influences was that when the "Minsky moment" came suddenly last summer, perceptions of risky exposures, both to credit losses and to liquidity shortages, rose sharply, as did uncertainty about where those exposures might materialise' (Knight, 2008: p. 1).

Thus, typically in these and similar accounts, a 'Minsky moment' describes a situation of a sudden collapse of the financial system, or a critical junction at which governments should intervene. This is not necessarily incorrect in capturing some of Minsky's message. In his theory of financial crisis, Minsky did argue that 'even after money market becomes unstable, the central bank, by monetising the vulnerable asset, can prevent widespread repercussions from occurring' (Minsky, 1982: p. 175). As governments world-wide have scoped up trillions of 'toxic' financial assets, and as the central banks have accepted privately issued debts as legitimate collateral in return for bailout lines, a 'Minsky moment' has arrived indeed.

At the same time, however, references to a 'Minsky moment' as a defining feature of the global credit meltdown are somewhat over-manufactured, for two reasons. First, Minsky himself never really focused on any precise 'moment'. Rather, he analysed the stages and mechanics of the financial cycle which, indeed, can encounter a period, or a factor, of distress that in turn sends a cascade of destabilising waves throughout the financial system. Second, a 'Minsky moment' is only the tip of a much bigger conceptualisation of financial crisis. The centre of his critique of financial capitalism was not a 'moment' or factor as such, but the actual processes and dynamics that are able to drive the financial system towards the critical state of fragility. Therefore, in what follows below I examine the place of the two other Minskyan concepts in emergent conceptualisations of the credit crunch: the paradox of stability and the role of Ponzi finance.

5.4 Destabilising stability: cyclical theories of the credit crunch

'Stability is always destabilising' Minsky famously stated in his financial instability hypothesis. It surely is. The global credit crunch came at the end of the more than a decade-long boom in the North Atlantic credit markets. That boom, in turn, paralleled a period of economic expansion, driven by consumption and unprecedented affordability of credit, which led many politicians to talk about 'new economy' – defined by a unique combination of low consumer price inflation and falling unemployment rates. Alan Greenspan has dubbed this period 'the new era of active credit management' (in Morris, 2008: p. 61). Amidst the ostensible rehabilitation of Minsky's work, it is this message about the paradox of stability that seems to dominate most commentaries on the credit crunch:

> The forward Minsky journey, this time around anyway, was the progression of risk-taking in the financial markets represented by the excess of

> subprime loans, structured investment vehicles (SIVs) and other shady characters inhabiting the shadow banking system. Their apparent stability begat ever-riskier debt arrangements, which begat asset price bubbles. And then the bubbles burst, in something I dubbed (years ago, in fact, when looking back on the Asian credit crisis) a 'Minsky Moment'.
>
> (McCulley, 2009: p. 1)

According to Minsky (and many others), 'good' times breed complacency, exuberance and optimism about one's position in the market, which leads to heavier reliance on leverage and underestimation of risks. Indeed, as stated famously by Citi's Chuck Norries in the wake of the subprime fiasco: 'When the music stops, in terms of liquidity, things will be complicated. But as long as the music is playing, you've got to get up and dance' (cited in Soros, 2008: p. 64). Most observers concur that the major factor in the global credit crisis has been the progressive underestimation, or misunderstanding, of risks by financial agents based, in turn, on the general sense of stability, economic prosperity and optimistic forecasts that had pervaded North Atlantic economies, creating bearish financial markets and what Soros has called a 'super-bubble' of credit.

> The creation of new securities facilitated the large capital inflows from abroad.... The trend towards the 'originate and distribute model'... ultimately led to a decline in lending standards. Financial innovation that had supposedly made the banking system more stable by transferring risk to those most able to bear it led to an unprecedented credit expansion that helped feed the boom in housing prices.
>
> (Brunnermeier *et al.*, 2009: p. 78)

However, politically the origins and longer-term implications of this trend to underestimate the risks have been viewed differently by different observers. Former US Treasury Secretary Henk Paulson, for instance, believes that the root cause of the credit bubble was the 'liquidity glut' coming from the emerging markets: 'Superabundant savings from fast-growing emerging nations... put downward pressure on risks and yield spreads everywhere.... This laid the seeds of the credit bubble that extends far beyond the US subprime mortgage market and now has burst with devastating consequences' (in Guha, 2009: p. 1). A UK-based policy reflection on the lessons of the credit crunch, the so-called Turner review, also stresses the destabilising link between global imbalances and financial advances in the North Atlantic economies: 'At the core of the crisis lay an interplay between macro-imbalances which had grown rapidly in the last ten years, and financial market developments and innovations which have been underway for about 30 years but which accelerated over the last 10 to 15, partly under the stimulus of the macro-imbalances' (FSA, 2009: p. 11). In this sense, many emergent theories that interpret the credit crisis in cyclical terms do appear to have strong undertone in Minsky's analysis of destabilising stability.

Indeed, optimistic expectations about the future of the economy have placated the senses of major economic and financial agents. Stability and good times, just as Minsky wrote, bred complacency, underestimation of true economic and financial risks, and outright greed and exuberance. According to cyclical theorisations then, the underlying cause of the continuing malaise is the markets' increasing tendency to under-price financial risks during the boom years of 2002–2007. As it is being argued, the booming housing market, the low-inflationary monetary policy (low-interest rates and the climate of cheap and easy credit), the constant competitive drive among banks and financial houses for commissions and aggressive techniques of investment, underpinned by expectations of unstoppable rises in the value of real estate, have numbed the financial sector's ability to estimate risks and rewards accurately. This, in turn, has pushed investors into acquiring riskier assets and techniques of trade:

> For almost a year and a half the global financial system has been under extraordinary stress – stress that has now decisively spilled over to the global economy more broadly. The proximate cause of the crisis was the turn of the housing cycle in the United States and the associated rise in delinquencies on subprime mortgages, which imposed substantial losses on many financial institutions and shook investor confidence in credit markets. However, although the subprime debacle triggered the crisis, the developments in the US mortgage market were only one aspect of a much larger and more encompassing credit boom.... Aspects of this broader credit boom included widespread declines in underwriting standards, breakdowns in lending oversight by investors and rating agencies, increased reliance on complex and opaque credit instruments that proved fragile under stress, and unusually low compensation for risk-taking.
>
> (Bernanke, 2009: 13 January)

Generally, therefore, ostensibly advancing Minsky's message about the paradox of financial stability, most mainstream commentators on the crisis tend to diagnose it as a behavioural problem of the market, specific to the most recent financial and economic cycle (2002–2007) and driven, fundamentally, by human failure. As stated in the Turner review, so far the most radical and critical policy reflection on the nature of the credit crunch, '... it seems likely that some and perhaps much of the structuring and trading activity involved in the complex version of securitised credit, was not required to deliver credit intermediation efficiently. Instead, it achieved an economic rent extraction made possible by the opacity of margins, the asymmetry of information and knowledge between end users of financial services and producers, and the structure of principal/agent relationships between investors and companies and between companies and individual employees. Wholesale financial services, and in particular that element devoted to securitised credit intermediation and the trading of securitised credit instruments, grew to a size unjustified by the value of its service to the real economy' (FSA, 2009: p. 49).

Interestingly in this instance, the actual diagnoses of why and how financial markets produce bubbles tend to draw on the Minsky-Kindleberger hypothesis of financial instability, sometimes going as far as to challenge the key assumptions of the EMT paradigm (IMF, 2008: p. 20; Trichet, 2008; FSA, 2009). As phrased in the 2009 Geneva Report: 'Most financial crises are preceded by asset price bubbles. Bubbles often emerge after financial liberalisations or innovations and can persist since even rational sophisticated investors find it more profitable to ride a bubble rather than to go against it. This is in sharp contrast to efficient market hypothesis, but supported by empirical findings.... Herding behaviour among financial institutions which are evaluated against the same benchmark are further contributing factors' (Brunnermeier *et al.*, 2009: p. 30).

To the extent that Minsky's original framework was a portrayal of a larger financial and business cycle, the theory of destabilising stability does indeed fit the consensus description of the global credit crunch (as, in fact, it fits any analysis of boom and bust waves in financial capitalism).

However, it is the nuances of interpretation of this cycle that make a difference. While Charles Kindleberger did indeed stress the element of irrationality in driving financial manias and panics, for Minsky, irrationality has little role to play in political economy. Rather, it is the internal mechanism within the liberalised credit system that precipitates fragility and crisis. In Minsky's analysis, fragility is an inherent feature of an advanced financialised economy. At the same time, according to Minsky, instability assumes many guises and is not caused by human behaviour as such but by the endogenous dynamics of the financial system driven by financial innovation and competition. It is this message that newly born Minskyans seem to overlook: emphasising the human factor in causing the crisis, they often view the global credit crunch as an extraordinary episode, or 'moment', in the otherwise smoothly functioning financial capitalism. In this sense, the crisis hits the markets as one extraordinary, exogenous shock.

Interestingly, protagonists of this view include lawyers who defended the fraudsters of Bear Sterns, politicians of different calibres on both sides of the Atlantic, as well as leading figures of economic policy such as Alan Greenspan. Facing accusations for his direct role in creating the bubble of easy credit during the 1990s and early 2000s Greenspan has termed the crisis a 'once-in-a-century phenomenon' (Greenspan, 31 July 2008). Defending Mr Cioffi, one of the Bear Sterns' financiers charged with the nine-count indictment with conspiracy, securities and wire fraud, his lawyer argued: 'the credit crisis took everyone by surprise, including the Fed and the Treasury.

Dozens of the largest financial institutions in the world have lost over $300 billion to date on the same investments' (Kelly, 2008: p. 15).

Baffled and incapacitated by the scope of the meltdown, regulators and policymakers also tend to emphasise the extraordinary character of the crisis and the fact that it had come as a shock to most people. In October 2008, Lord Turner, who had just taken over the FSA, noted: 'In April of this year everybody knew that something pretty big had happened to the world's financial system. What we had no idea, bluntly, was how extreme it was going to be' (Turner, 2008: p. 1). The Prime Minister, Gordon Brown, followed with the same line: 'We tend to think of the sweep of destiny as stretching across many months and years before culminating in decisive moments we call history. But sometimes the reality is that defining moments of history come suddenly and without warning.... An economic hurricane has swept the world, creating a crisis of credit and of confidence' (Brown, 4 March 2009).

Therefore, while Minsky's notion of destabilising stability is now informing most emergent theories of the credit crunch, it is disappointing that this uncontroversial statement has diverted the attention from the core of Minsky's political economy. Specifically, by building up a theory of the credit crunch as the end of the preceding credit boom, commentators and policymakers often chose to focus their analytical and policy responses on either fixing the isolated features of the recent bout of securitisation (for instance, suggesting to re-regulate certain financial products and practices), rather than confronting the actual source of financial fragility and crisis – the political regime of deregulated, privatised credit and the paradigm of welfare-enhancing, risk-optimising financial innovation. In Minsky's analysis, treating the crisis as an exogenous shock or a 'moment' simply does not make sense. Indeed, the risks unleashed and accentuated by the securitisation process, as well as the fragility of the US mortgage market and the economy as a whole had been noted repeatedly by many commentators long before the turmoil began in the summer of 2007. The trouble is that most whistleblowers were dismissed at the time, as in fact was the very message of Minsky and his followers.

5.5 The crisis of Ponzi finance

From its very start, the credit crunch has been described as the crisis of Ponzi finance. The increasingly popular use of the term, as well as the collapses of financial pyramids of Bernie Madoff and Allen Stanford, has put Minsky's model at the centre of crisis analytics. As noted above, for Minsky, 'Ponzi' is a method of financing old debt with new debt. In Minsky's original taxonomy, Ponzi finance is a phase in the transformation of the financial cycle; it corresponds to the expansion of the financial innovation spiral and the progressive underestimation of risk by financial agents, particularly during periods of economic optimism.

Essentially, therefore, a Ponzi collapse is a debt crisis: when there is too much debt accumulated by an economic agent, and there is no way to either get the resources to pay the debt (and interest), postpone the payments or shift the debt on to someone else, economic agents face insolvency: plain and simple. In a financial system relying on companies' ability to emit debt on the basis of internal risk strategies, however, the Ponzi mode has become the way for firms to manipulate, manage and trade a whole variety of financial risks. Structurally, the expansion of new markets for credit instruments, especially in Anglo-Saxon economies, has been underpinned by the policies of cheap credit, or the 'popularisation of finance', and has made the political regimes on both sides of the Atlantic dependent on the stability and growth of the financial and banking sectors (Montgomerie, 2007).

Institutionally, according to Kregel (2008), Ponzi finance is related to the way risk has been valued, assessed and modelled by banks and financial houses since the liberalisation reforms were introduced in the 1980s. In the post-Basle spiral of financial innovation, driven by the aggressive search for profits and desire to outperform your competitors, the 'old style' prudent banking was derided as boring and conservative, while the proactive risk-takers were considered sophisticated, innovative and shrewd. As long as this market atmosphere was supported by the belief in robust economic fundamentals, the under-valuation of risks, especially liquidity risk, the aggressive expansion of new borrowings and, in many cases, the use of quasi-legal investment techniques and outright swindling, flourished. In this element, Kregel notes, the ongoing financial crisis does differ from the context Minsky identified originally, yet the consequences will still be severe: it may still lead to a process of debt deflation and recession.

Debt crises are always destructive. But aside from the sheer scale of the collapse and uncertainty as to its long-term consequences, there is another crucial, yet so far overlooked, aspect of the current crisis. Ponzi finance, as the label suggests, implies a crucial role of intentional deceit: financing debts with new borrowings is the basic principle of a pure pyramid scheme. In the 1990s post-socialist Europe, for instance, many people repeated Carlo Ponzi's fate, and have been imprisoned for fraud through the construction of financial pyramids. The global credit crunch has also raised some uneasy political questions about the role of fraud, corruption and simple negligence in the recent expansion of the credit bubble and the securitisation industry.

Here, when analysing the workings of the Ponzi principle today, one should not forget that in essence Ponzi finance is a pyramid scheme, typically – as the allusion to the fraudster Carlo Ponzi implies – containing an element of deception or fraud. The charges against Bernie Madoff and Allen Stanford, as well as a series of money fraud investigations launched by the FBI in the wake of the subprime crisis, illustrates the degree to which financial innovation has helped disguise outright fraud and swindling. What is more worrying, however, is that the expansion of the subprime lending in the United States illustrates that Ponzi-type operations reached an industrial scale (Kirchgaessner and Weitzman, 2008). None of the policy debates or reform drafts that unfolded in the wake of the crisis actually addresses this troubling dimension of financial innovation.

Even in purely financial terms, the subprime industry was a giant Ponzi scheme. First, the practice of providing people with uncertain credit histories, no prospects of higher incomes and often no jobs, with 100 per cent (or sometimes higher) mortgages, was itself a deception on a very large scale. From the very start it was clear that many of those subprime borrowers would be unable to pay their mortgages if, or rather *when*, the interest rates on their loans rose. Any Ponzi scheme can thrive only as long as it attracts new participants. In the United States, subprime lending was justifiable only by the belief that the rising values of property would suffice to repay the loans, and like in any Ponzi scheme, this belief proved to be self-fulfilling. As Kregel (2008) argues, once the bottom layer of properties was inflated through the creation of massive demand, the entire US housing market entered into a bubble phase. Housing markets, however, are notoriously cyclical. It was this fact, along with the actual terms of the subprime loans, that the scores of financial advisers who sold the products forgot to mention to their clients.

Second, the terms of borrowing and the conditions for repayment appear, in retrospect, to be the key block in the Ponzi pyramid of subprime loans. Ponzi-type methods employed by lending institutions included large pre-payment penalties, low 'teaser' rates that reset at much higher rates, knowingly inducing a borrower to loan terms that she or he will not be able to meet (Wray, 2008).[2] What is more worrying is that the Ponzi mode seems to have spread far beyond the epicentre of the crisis – the US subprime industry. On the one hand, subprime lending mushroomed in the United States (and to a lesser extent in other Anglo-Saxon countries such as the United Kingdom, Australia and New Zealand) due to historically low interest rates in the 1990s and 2000s that presented ample opportunities for borrowers. On the other hand, low interest rates were available in many other regions – notably in continental Europe and Japan – which have avoided the spread of similar Ponzi schemes on the back of their own subprime sector. To me, this suggests that the Ponzi pyramid of subprime finance, and the related securitisation boom, had been shaped by the political climate in the Anglo-Saxon economies, and, correspondingly, by the benign and ill-informed view of financial and monetary authorities on the risks posed by the expanding bubble of artificial liquidity. Concealed by the plethora of innovative financial techniques and the illusion of liquidity, the process of securitisation has become a giant Ponzi scheme (Nesvetailova, 2010).

In this instance, the tale of Northern Rock is particularly revealing. The fall of the British bank does not only show how dangerously interconnected financial markets have become, although this seems to be the lesson most commentaries chose to draw from the Rock's collapse. Much more worryingly, the collapse of the bank revealed that the political regime of deregulated credit and the economic climate requiring companies to come up with evermore sophisticated ways to originate, value, manage and trade risk, actually helps disguise, if not encourage, fraudulent financial practices. Worse existing regulation of financial innovation helps 'clever' financiers make their frauds seem legitimate.

Two – very problematic – elements behind the Rock's story are relevant in this case. The first is what seems to be pure financial negligence and unaccountability: the management of the bank has failed to act on the rising riskiness of their financial strategy (Chick, 2008). The aggressive over-reliance on the wholesale capital markets for funds amidst the deteriorating credit markets and subprime crisis spreading in the United States raises a question: Why did Northern Rock continue with this mode of raising finance? One possible answer suggests simple negligence on the part of the bank's managers. That scenario implies that the crisis of Northern Rock is a one-off phenomenon and that it does not represent any systematic trends because banking crises, essentially, are the problem of the nineteenth century capitalism. In autumn 2007, this scenario seemed plausible: 'no other major lender is in quite the same situation but the banks and building societies that borrow most in the wholesale markets are the most vulnerable'.[3]

In the broader context of the credit meltdown that ensued, however, it appears that Nothern Rock was one of the many – and certainly not the biggest – examples of companies manipulating financial vehicles and investment techniques. Under the new 'originate and distribute' principle, banks seek to maximise their profits by moving lending to unrelated affiliates, and off their balance sheets (Kregel, 2007: p. 11; Wigan, 2009). That implies that seeds of a Minskyan Ponzi crisis stem not from individual undervaluation of risks by financial companies (as simple negligence by Rock's managers would imply), but from the very organisation of risk structures of the credit system as a whole.

While internally risk-managing models may work well for individual (or even a few) institutions, at a systemic level common risk strategies contribute to the build-up of fragility, rather than its dispersion. As Avinash Persaud explained back in 2002, 'the sophisticated internal risk models require a bank to reduce exposure to risk when the probability of losses increases as a result of falling or more volatile asset prices. If every bank uses these systems, and they have similar positions, and they try to sell assets at the same time, the system enters into a crisis' (Persaud, 2002: p. 1). This reading of the Rock's crisis, and the political economy of the credit crunch as a whole, would, just as Minsky argued back in 1986, be a much more radical, and comprehensive, political response. Individual bailouts, quantitative easing and even temporary nationalisation will not suffice to restore stability, at least not in the long run.

The second problem that has come into light after the Northern Rock crisis relates to deception more closely. Richard Murphy, an independent tax expert, investigated an artificial scheme employed by Northern Rock to disguise nearly £50 billion through the use of a private offshore trust (entitled Granite companies) and a charity based in the North-East of England, whose name was used, presumably, for financial gains and tax evasion purposes, and without its knowledge. The named charity seems to have been entirely unaware of the scheme, having received only one small donation from the Rock's staff in 2001.[4] (Similar schemes are reportedly common practice among all the major British banks.)

The precise ownership structure of Granite companies and the financial relationship with Northern Rock are murky. Because Granite is a Jersey-incorporated vehicle, and due to the secrecy laws of Jersey (generally considered an offshore financial centre), there is no way of knowing who precisely is the trustee or creditor of Granite. There is a consensus, however, that the Jersey-based offshore structure was used as a securitisation vehicle for mortgages issued by Northern Rock. It is suspected that Granite served as an equivalent of a price transfer channel for the Rock, a means through which the bank could transfer profits earned in the United Kingdom to a near-zero tax regime of Jersey.

As the British Treasury opted to nationalise Northern Rock, the exact relationship between the new owner – the UK government – and Granite never became clear. The UK government seems to believe that it owns Granite as well as Northern Rock. Others, however, are not sure.[5] An anonymous source close to Granite said that 'the obligations on Northern Rock as an originator of mortgages continue to exist.... It is a financial reality'. According to the source, in case Northern Rock stops supplying Granite with mortgages, it would have to pay back the £49 billion owed to its investors.[6] In the worst case scenario, therefore, the British taxpayer may end up paying twice for Northern Rock: first to nationalise it, then second to honour the Rock's obligations to Granite, which in turn may be owned by Northern Rock. Although some British MPs have raised questions about the precise links between Northern Rock and Granite, there have been no clear answers.

The scandal of Northern Rock has raised concerns about how many other companies might be benefiting from similar schemes through the use of structured finance and complex investment pyramids. According to the *Financial Times*, lead underwriters on the Granite programme were Lehman Brothers, Merrill Lynch and UBS; underwriters were Barclays Capital, Citigroup, JPMorgan and Morgan Stanley.[7]

The tale of another big casualty of the credit meltdown, Lehman Brothers, has reiterated the scale of the problem of obscure debt and financial manipulation. The post-crisis investigation of the fallen bank revealed that globally, at the time of collapse, Lehman is estimated to have held $1.2 million derivatives contracts with a total notional value of $6 trillion dollars. It held over $1.2 trillion of open positions spread between almost every market counterparty, all of whom were looking to minimise their exposure to Lehman. Just like in the case of Northern Rock, offshore facilities helped conceal the risks of the transactions. Lehman, and many other banks, accumulated MBAs in one country, securitised them, 'sliced and diced' them with other MBSs, then moved the resulting assets overseas, blurring the valuation basis of the original security (Thomson, 2009: pp. 9–11). This has not only triggered a liquidity crunch at Lehman, but also has made bankruptcy procedures very difficult.

Altogether, the secrecy and lack of transparency offered by offshore financial centres have facilitated the spread of outright fraudulent or quasi-legal Ponzi schemes, preventing public authorities from adjudicating in cases when private financial manipulation leads to systemic risks and public losses (Palan, 2004; Palan *et al.*, 2010). Unlike the 1920s America or 1990s Russia, however, the architects of today's Ponzi pyramids are much harder to identify (indeed, it was Madoff himself who came clean about the true scale of his Ponzi pyramid). Ponzi's successors today not only include financial gurus devising models in back offices across the City of London, Wall Street and the Cayman Islands; but governments and legislation that allowed the spiral of financial innovation to get out of control.

Therefore, while references to Ponzi schemes of isolated crooks like Madoff and Stanford have hit the headlines, Hyman Minsky again offers a deeper and more disturbing warning to crisis theories today. His message is actually not about these isolated pyramid schemes, but about the level of obscurity modern financial innovation has reached, facilitated by institutional changes in the financial institutions and, crucially, permitted by the new paradigm of credit risk management. The current crisis, therefore, is not the outcome of one malfunctioning institution, market segment or, contrary to what many believe, a financial model. Rather, it is an outcome of a political-economic and legal regime which has facilitated the privatisation of gains from financial risks, at a cost of socialising their losses. In other words, a regime that made the Ponzi principle a legitimate and prominent vehicle of financial innovation.

5.6 Conclusion: Minsky's political economy and the global credit crunch

Reviewing the emergent mainstream of post-crisis policy response, I conclude, therefore, that Minsky was partially rehabilitated. His insight into the cyclical nature of financialised capitalism, the endemic financial fragility and the role of leverage seem to have challenged, or at the very least compromised, the basic tenets of orthodox finance theory. Indeed, even Alan

Greenspan accepted that he had been wrong to assume that lending institutions would carry out proper surveillance of their counterparties, confessing that he

> made a mistake in presuming that the self-interest of organisations, specifically banks and others, was such that they were best capable of protecting their own shareholders.... I had been going for 40 years with considerable evidence that it was working very well.... The whole intellectual edifice, however, collapsed in the summer of last year.
>
> (cited in Beattie and Politi, 2008: p. 1)

Very few of these commentators, however, go deeper into the scholarly legacy of Minsky to challenge what I believe has been the essence of his political economy: namely, his profound and contentious observation that just as financial innovation marks any period of economic optimism and tranquillity, financial innovation inevitably drives the system towards the brink of a crisis. The mechanism that produces such tendency centres on the myth of liquidity-creating financial innovation. It is disappointing that amidst emerging critique of self-regulating finance and attempts to gain a better understanding of liquidity itself, this part of Minsky's message seems to have been ignored.

The G20 Plan for strengthening the global financial system, for instance, is disappointingly reminiscent of its rather impotent predecessor – the brief attempt to erect a New International Financial Architecture (NIFA) in the wake of the late 1990s crisis. As stressed in the G20 Communiqué: 'Regulators and supervisors must protect consumers and investors, support market discipline, avoid adverse impacts on other countries, reduce the scope for regulatory arbitrage, support competition and dynamism, and keep pace with innovation in the marketplace' (G20 2009: paragraph 14). The authors of the Geneva report are even more certain about the ultimately beneficial role of financial innovation: 'Our preference is for light-touch regulation (with one exception on housing loan-to-value ratios...). In general, restrictive control of financial intermediation stifles innovation and, especially if government starts to intervene with direct controls over bank lending, interferes with the appropriate allocation of capital' (Brunnermeier *et al.*, 2009: p. 10).

Thus, while noting the risk-valuing consequences of the general macroeconomic environment and investor expectations, most mainstream analysts of the crisis have opted to overlook the core of Minsky's framework. Especially once we consider the contentious issue of 'liquidity' in the crisis, it appears that only a fragmented and highly selective version of Minsky's theory of finance resonates in current readings of the meltdown. Very few of them, indeed, cast a critical eye on the very ability of financial intermediaries to stretch the frontier of private liquidity, ultimately accentuating financial fragility in the system and thus accelerating the scope for a structural financial collapse and economic crisis.

In this sense, with the global credit meltdown, the 'Minsky' moment has arrived indeed. Partly it is a moment of delight to his intellectual followers and students of political economy; partly it is a moment that accentuated the depth of his critique of financial capitalism. Indeed, amidst the euphoria about the resurrection of his work, let us not forget the message of the political economy of Minsky. It is not so much about Ponzi finance, and certainly not about a 'moment' in the financial development. It is rather his serious warning about the inherent conflict, embedded in a highly financialised economy, between the vagaries of financial innovation and economic stability generally. Despite the scale of the global meltdown – incidentally, foreseen by many Minskyans – this insight, it appears, remains far too controversial for the academic and policy orthodoxy in contemporary finance.

Notes

1. As we will see below, the ownership of the term 'Minsky Moment' is in fact claimed by Pimco's managing director, Paul McCulley.
2. Kregel notes that often borrowers were lured into taking a mortgage on their new home without being told that they would be unable to pre-pay it, to change the terms of the mortgage and that their interest repayments after the initial 'teaser' periods would be up to 6 per cent higher than the market average: in other words, they were simply trapped into the subprime net.
3. Among these names, commentators mentioned Paragon, the United Kingdom's biggest buy-to-let lender, Bradford & Bingley, Halifax owner HBOS and Alliance & Leicester (http://www.guardian.co.uk/business/2007/sep/14/money.northernrock1). Paragon has since crashed under the effects of the credit crunch.
4. Financial Times: Alphaville blog: 'The uncharitable tale of Northern Rock'.
5. http://www.guardian.co.uk/business/2008/feb/21/northernrock.banking
6. http://www.accountingweb.co.uk/cgi-bin/item.cgi?id=180124&d=1032&h=1024&f=1026
7. FT Alfphaville, blog archive.

References

Beattie, A. and J. Politi (2008) 'Greenspan admits to 'flaw' in ideology', *The Financial Times*, 24 October.

Bernanke, (2009) 'The crisis and the policy response', *Lecture at the LSE*, London, 13 January.

Brown, G. (2009) Speech to US congress, 4 March.

Brunnermeir, M. (2009) 'Deciphering the 2007–2008 Liquidity and credit crunch', *Journal of Economic Perspectives*, vol. 23, no. 1.

Brunnermeir, M., A. Crockett, C. Goodhart, A. Persaud and H. Shin (2009) 'The fundamental principles of financial regulation (The "Geneva Report"), Preliminary Conference Draft', *Geneva Reports on the World Economy*, vol. 11, CEPR: International Centre for Monetary and Banking Studies.

CGFS (Committee on the Global Financial System) (2001) Structural aspects of market liquidity from a financial stability perspective', vol. 2, CGFS *Discussion Paper, Base: BIS*, June.

Chick, V. (2008) 'Could the crisis at northern rock have been predicted? an evolutionary approach', *Contributions to Political Economy*, vol. 28, no. 1.

FSA 2009, "The Turner Review. A regulatory response to the global banking crisis", London: FSA, March.

G20 (2009) 'The global plan for recovery and reform', *Final Communique of the G20 Summit*, London, 2nd April.

Greenspan, A. (2008) Interview to CNBC, 31 July.

Guha, K. (2009) 'Paulson says crisis sown by imbalance', *The Financial Times*, 1 January.

IMF (2008), 'Asia: a perspective on the subprime crisis', *Finance and Development*, June.

Kelly, K. (2008) 'US Prosecutors to Focus on bear managers' email', *Wall Street Journal Europe*, 20–22 June.

Kirchgaessner, S. and H. Weitzman (2008) 'FBI eyes big business in mortgage fraud probe', *The Financial Times*, 19 June.

Knight, M. (2008) 'Some reflections on the future of the originate-to-distribute model in the context of the current financial turmoil' Speech at the Euro 50 Group Roundtable on *The future of the originate and distribute model*, London, 21 April.

Kregel, J. (2008) 'Minsky's cushions of safety. Systemic risk and the crisis in the U.S. subprime mortgage market', *Public Policy Brief No. 93, Levy Economic Institute.*

Magnus, G. (2007) 'What this Minsky moment means', *The Financial Times*, 22 August.

McCulley, P. (2009) 'The shadow banking system and Hyman Minsky's economic journey', *Global Central Bank Focus, PIMCO*, May.

Minsky, H.P. (1982) *Can 'It' Happen Again?* (New York: M.E. Sharpe).

Minsky, H.P. (1986, 2008) *Stabilising An Unstable Economy* (New York: McGraw Hill).

Montgomerie, J. (2007) 'Alchemy of Banks', in L. Assassi *et al.* (eds), *Global Finance in the New Century: After Deregulation* (London: Palgrave).

Morris, C. (2008) *The Trillion Dollar Meltdown* (New York: Public Affairs).

Nesvetailova, A. (2010) *Financial Alchemy in Crisis: the Great Liquidity Illusion* (London: Pluto).

Palan, R. (2004) *The Offshore World* (Ithaca: Cornell University Press).

Palan, R., C. Chavagneux and R. Murphy (2010) *Tax Havens: At the Heart of Globalisation* (Ithaca: Cornell University Press).

Persaud, A. (2002) 'Banks put themselves at risk in Basle', *Financial Times*, 17 October.

Soros, G. (2008) *The New Paradigm For Financial Markets* (New York: Public Affairs).

Strange, S. (1998) *Casino Capitalism* (Manchester, Manchester University Press).

Thomson, D. (2009) *'Unravelling Lehman', Business* (Turnaround) (London: Lyonsdown).

Trichet, J.C. (2008) Remarks on the recent turbulences in global financial markets, Keynote address at the Policy Discussion, 'Global Economic Policy Forum' (New York: New York University) 14 April.

Turner, L. (2008) 'Interview', *The Financial Times*, 17 October.

Wigan, D. (2009) 'Financialisation and derivatives', *Competition and Change*, vol. 13, no. 2.

Wray, L.R. (2008) 'Lessons from the subprime meltdown', *Challenge*, vol. 51, no. 2.

6
A Minsky Perspective on the Global Recession of 2009

Charles J. Whalen

6.1 Introduction

On 18 August 2007, a front-page story in *The Wall Street Journal* highlighted the ideas of economist Hyman Minsky. With the US economy in the midst of a worsening credit crunch, reporter Justin Lahart observed that although Minsky died in 1996, his views were 'reverberating from New York to Hong Kong as economists and traders are trying to understand what's happening in the markets' (Lahart, 2007: p. 1).

Since 2007, attention to Minsky's ideas has increased as global economic conditions have deteriorated (see, for example, Cassidy, 2008; Pollin, 2008). As an economist who has long appreciated Minsky's insights, I am happy to see this flurry of interest. Yet I fear that many observers have missed the full significance of his contributions.

Many of those now on the Minsky bandwagon treat his ideas as relevant to understanding a single economic event. Market analysts and traders even refer to that event as a 'Minsky moment', which arrives 'when over-indebted investors are forced to sell even their solid investments to make good on their loans' (Lahart, 2007: p. 1). If the trouble were to become so widespread that it threatened the banking system at the national or international level, then some would replace the word 'moment' with 'meltdown' (Magnus, 2008, see also Chapters 1 and 2). However, the focus is still on a single incident, not on the evolutionary path of economic activity.

Others exposed to Minsky's ideas acknowledge that his work was grounded in a dynamic conception of the economy. For most in this group, though, Minsky's place in economics rests on what he called the 'financial-instability hypothesis'. According to Minsky, capitalist financial systems tend to endogenous cycles – moving from a conservative state of affairs called 'hedge financing', to a more risky form called 'speculative financing', to an unsustainable form called 'Ponzi financing', and then back to 'hedge financing' for another round. This pattern of economic activity generates a series of booms and recessions, and the severity of the latter depends largely on the effectiveness of government regulation and stabilisation policies (Minsky, 1982, 1992a).

A full appreciation of Minsky's insights, however, must recognise that about the last dozen years of his life were devoted largely to synthesising the financial-instability hypothesis and an understanding of long-term capitalist development. Indeed, in an essay written for the hundredth anniversary of the birth of John Maynard Keynes and Joseph Schumpeter, Minsky wrote: 'The task confronting economics today may be characterised as a need to integrate Schumpeter's vision of a resilient inter-temporal capitalist process with Keynes's hard insights into the fragility introduced into the capitalist accumulation process by some inescapable properties of capitalist financial structures' (Minsky, 1986a: p. 121). A key conclusion of Minsky's pursuit of such a synthesis is that although the 'basic path' of real-world capitalism is cyclical (Minsky, 1975: p. 9), the 'money-manager capitalism' characteristic of recent decades differs substantially from the 'managerial capitalism' found in the United States immediately after Second World War (Minsky, 1990a, 1993a). A successful economic policy for the present era must be built upon recognition of the institutional features of this stage of capitalist development (Minsky and Whalen, 1996–1997).

This chapter offers a Minsky perspective on the global recession of 2009 by drawing on the insights Minsky gained from both Keynes and Schumpeter. While the Keynesian and Schumpeterian dimensions of Minsky's viewpoint are intertwined in the real world, the cyclical and structural aspects of the current crisis are highlighted separately in the analysis that follows. After examining the nature and causes of the global downturn from those two lenses, Minsky's policy proposals are compared with recent policy steps taken by the US government.

6.2 Cyclical dynamics

Minsky's financial-instability hypothesis can be seen as an alternative to the 'efficient-market hypothesis' of conventional economics (see also Chapter 5). According to that conventional view, investors, lenders and other financial-market participants are not, as a group, predisposed to overconfidence or other biases (Shefrin, 2000: p. 4). In contrast, the financial-instability hypothesis treats overconfidence and panic as regular features of the economic landscape.

Minsky traces this aspect of his perspective to Keynes, especially to the latter's 1937 article in *The Quarterly Journal of Economics*, 'The General Theory of Employment' (Keynes, 1937; Minsky, 1975: pp. 64–67). In that essay, Keynes describes his departure from the mainstream economics of his time, which he called 'classical economic theory', as the departure from a focus on long-period equilibrium (Keynes, 1937: pp. 213–214). Behind both the classical theory of Keynes' time and the efficient-market hypothesis of our own is an assumption that the future can be treated as a matter involving risk (reducible to the calculation of probabilities), not uncertainty. Keynes, however, dismisses this substitution of risk for uncertainty in the case of most economic analyses:

> The whole object of the accumulation of wealth is to produce results, or potential results, at a comparatively distant, and sometimes at an *indefinitely* distant, date. Thus the fact that our knowledge of the future is fluctuating, vague and uncertain renders wealth a peculiarly unsuitable subject for the methods of classical economic theory. This theory might work very well in a world in which economic goods were necessarily consumed within a short interval of their being produced. But it requires, I suggest, considerable amendment if it is to be applied to a world in which the accumulation of wealth for an indefinitely postponed future is an important factor; and the greater the proportionate part played by such wealth-accumulation the more essential does such amendment become.
>
> (Keynes, 1937: p. 213)

According to Minsky, the financial structure of our economy becomes more and more fragile over a period of prosperity. In the early stages of prosperity, enterprises in highly profitable segments of the economy are rewarded for taking on increasing amounts of debt. And their success encourages other firms to engage in similar behaviour.

This pattern was certainly evident in the high-tech sector during the late 1990s and in the housing sector during the early- and mid-2000s. In fact, construction companies and contractors were not the only ones taking on more debt in the 2000s. Homebuyers were also doing so as the housing market began heating up, in part because interest rates were low and the stock market had become less attractive in the wake of the dotcom boom and bust. While it had long been customary for US homebuyers to make a 20 per cent down payment on a home, 42 per cent of first-time home purchasers and 13 per cent of buyers who were not first-time purchasers put no money down to acquire homes in the mid-2000s (Irwin, 2005; Max, 2005; Baker, 2009a).[1]

In retrospect, it seems that enterprises and homebuyers should have resisted the impulse towards increasing indebtedness, but the incentives at the time were just too great. As Gary Dymski and Robert Pollin explain in a 1992 essay, nobody in a robust sector of the economy wants to be left behind due to underinvestment:

> Even if market participants did have full knowledge of the Minsky model, and were aware that financial crises will occur at some point, that would still not enable them to predict when the financial crisis will

> occur. In the meantime, aggressive firm managers and bank loan officers will be rewarded for pursuing profitable opportunities and gaining competitive advantages. Cautious managers, operating from the understanding that boom conditions will end at some uncertain point, will be penalised when their more aggressive competitors surpass their short-run performance.
>
> (Dymski and Pollin, 1992: p. 45)[2]

As the preceding quote indicates, lenders as well as borrowers fuel the tendency towards greater indebtedness in an expansion. The same climate of expectations that encourages borrowers to acquire more risky financial liability structures also eases lenders' worries that new loans might go unpaid (Minsky, 1975). Moreover, it is not just that borrowing and lending expand in the boom. There is also financial innovation. In fact, in a 1992 essay, Minsky wrote that bankers and other financial intermediaries are 'merchants of debt, who strive to innovate with regard to both the assets they acquire and the liabilities they market' (Minsky, 1992a: p. 6).

The boom cannot continue forever, however; we eventually arrive at what some have called the 'Minsky moment' (Lahart, 2007: p. 1). In other words, it eventually becomes clear that some borrowers have become overextended and need to sell assets (or secure a government bailout) to make their payments. In the current crisis, early high-profile cases involved the mortgage broker Countrywide, the British bank Northern Rock and two hedge funds run by Bear Stearns (Foley, 2007; Larsen and Giles, 2007; Reckard *et al.*, 2007; Stempel, 2007; Mildenberg, 2008).[3]

Then the problem spreads. Since bankers and investors hold subjective views about acceptable debt levels, once a shortfall of cash and a forced selling of assets materialise somewhere in the economy, it can lead to a widespread reassessment of how much debt or lending is appropriate. Moreover, the build-up can go on for years, but when anything goes wrong the revaluation can be sudden (Minsky, 1982: p. 67).

When banks decide to rein in their lending, we find ourselves in a credit crunch. It is easy to think of the present economic crisis as something that began with the world-wide stock-market downturn in the autumn of 2008. In fact, though, the difficulties of 2008 were preceded by a credit crunch that began in the summer of 2007, and signs of trouble – traceable in large part to the 'subprime' mortgage market – were evident as early as March 2007 (Foley, 2007; Magnus, 2007; Timeline, 2009).

Once a credit crunch emerges, financial difficulties are no longer confined to one sector. In fact, a crunch threatens not only business investment, but also household spending. This means that when a sectoral bubble bursts – in the high-tech sector nearly a decade ago or in the housing sector more recently – the collapse threatens to trigger an economy-wide recession.

And that sort of recession is what the United States and much of the world now experiences. Moreover, it is pretty clear the situation has gone beyond a 'Minsky moment' and is more akin to an economic 'meltdown', at least with respect to US housing, banking and stocks. The Dow Jones industrial average, for example, fell 37 per cent between 1 April 2007 and 1 April 2009 (Yahoo Finance, 2009). Meanwhile, the US unemployment rate rose from 4.4 per cent in March 2007 to 8.5 per cent in March 2009 (the latest monthly data available at the time of writing), and is widely expected to continue rising through 2009 (US Department of Labor, 2009; Obama's economic aide sees rising U.S. unemployment, 2009).

6.3 Structural evolution

In a pair of articles designed to integrate key contributions of Keynes and Schumpeter, Minsky mentions that Keynes and institutionalist Wesley C. Mitchell had a common perspective on business cycles (Minsky, 1993a, 1990a). Bringing Mitchell into the picture helps underscore the sort of synthesis towards which Minsky was aiming: Mitchell had long ago written that 'each new cycle presents idiosyncrasies. Business history repeats itself, but always with a difference' (Mitchell, 1941: p. ix). In the 1990s, Minsky still believed that the US economy moves along a cyclical path, but he also believed that the system had recently entered a new stage of capitalist development. The managerial era that matured in the immediate aftermath of Second World War had, during the 1980s, given way to a stage characterised by emergence of money managers as the nation's dominant economic decision-makers (Minsky, 1990a, 1993a, 1996; see also Whalen, 2001, 2002).

While Keynes offered insights into cyclical fluctuations, Schumpeter (Minsky's dissertation advisor at Harvard until the relationship was cut short by Schumpeter's untimely death) provided Minsky with insights into structural economic evolution over a series of cycles. In fact, Minsky underscored an aspect of Schumpeterian 'creative destruction' that few others recognised: 'Nowhere are evolution, change and Schumpeterian entrepreneurship more evident than in banking and finance and nowhere is the drive for profits more clearly the factor making for change' (Minsky, 1993a: p. 106). Thus, four institutional features of money-manager capitalism emerge to play a role in explaining the economic difficulties of the past few years. The origin of the current global crisis can be traced in large part to the following financial-sector innovations: unconventional mortgages, securitisation, the rise of hedge funds and the globalisation of finance.

At the heart of the current financial crisis are home mortgages that deviate from the traditional US home-loan arrangement, which involves a long-term loan on fixed-rate terms. Many of these unconventional – some have even called them 'exotic' – mortgages have adjustable interest rates and/or payments that balloon over time. Federal law allowed banks to issue adjustable-rate mortgages since 1982, but their use and complexity have exploded in the past decade. For example, industry experts estimate that a variant called the 'option adjustable rate mortgage' (option ARM), which offers a low 'teaser' rate and later resets so that minimum payments skyrocket, accounted for about 0.5 per cent of all US mortgages written in 2003, but close to 15 per cent (and up to 33 per cent in many US communities) in 2006. More precise figures are unavailable because banks have not been required to report how many option ARMs they originate (Der Hovanesian, 2006).

Many of these mortgages were created to target less-creditworthy customers, including those in what the banking industry calls the subprime market (Baker, 2009a). Others were marketed to people who wanted to speculate in the booming housing market, people who intended to buy and then quickly resell property. However, many unconventional loans were marketed to ordinary working families who could have handled conventional mortgages (Marks, 2008).

Unfortunately, it was clear from the outset that many of these exotic mortgages could never be repaid. (For an eye-opening look at the aggressive marketing of unconventional mortgages, see Morgenson (2007).) But why did this happen? Why did the mortgage market evolve in this dangerous direction?

This is where securitisation comes into the picture. Securitisation is simply the bundling of loans – which can include auto loans, student loans, accounts receivable and, of course, mortgages – and the subsequent selling of bundle shares to investors. In the mid-1980s, Minsky returned home from a conference sponsored by the Federal Reserve Bank of Chicago and wrote that securitisation was emerging as a key, new financial innovation. 'That which can be securitised, will be securitised', he wrote (Minsky, 1990a: p. 64). He was right, but way ahead of his time. Securitisation of mortgages exploded onto the scene in the past decade.

After the dotcom bubble burst in 2001, housing in the United States looked like a safer and more attractive investment than ever to many Americans, especially with low interest rates in place due to Federal Reserve policy. Still, returns on conventional mortgages were too mundane to satisfy the aims of most money managers. As a result, what Minsky and Schumpeter might have called the 'financial-innovation machine' turned its attention to housing and shifted in to high gear.

Securitisation of mortgages meant that home loan originators could be less concerned about the creditworthiness of borrowers than in the past. Thus, they had an incentive to steer customers towards the most profitable types of mortgages, even if they were the riskiest (which, of course, they were) (Der Hovanesian, 2006). The result was the explosive growth in option ARMs and in 'no money down' and 'no documentation (of income)' loans. Minsky warned of all this in 1992, when he observed that securitisation means mortgage originators are rewarded as long as they avoid 'obvious fraud' (Minsky, 1992b: p. 22–23).[4]

Securitisation worked like magic upon risky mortgages. Instead of 'garbage in, garbage out', risky loans went into the process, but out came bundles that received high credit ratings from agencies like Standard and Poors. According to Christopher Huhne, a member of the British Parliament and former rating-agency economist, part of the challenge of rating the bundles was 'that financial markets fall in love with new things, with innovations, and the [important] thing about new things is that it is very difficult to assess the real riskiness of them because you don't have a history by definition' (Huhne, 2007).

Another problem is that the rating agencies do not verify the information provided by mortgage issuers. Instead, they base their decisions on information received from intermediaries that, as Minsky put it, 'do not hazard any of their wealth on the long term viability of the underlying [loans]' (Minsky, 1992b: p. 23).

Moreover, there are so many middlemen in the mortgage securitisation game, including a number permitted to operate in a largely unregulated manner, that no one person or organisation can be easily assigned blame in the event of default. The chain between the borrower and the investor includes realtors, home appraisers, mortgage brokers, mortgage originators, investment banks that bundled the mortgages, agencies that rated the bundles and even companies (like American International Group) that insured many of the bundles (Whalen, 2008a: p. 235).[5]

Trillions of dollars worth of mortgage-backed securities were bundled and sold as shares to investors. In late 2008, Fannie Mae and Freddie Mac alone held $4.1 trillion (Lanman and Kopecki, 2008). Moreover, the private market in credit default swaps – used as a hedge against (mortgage-backed) securities losses, as a way to speculate that other companies will experience a loss, or as an arbitrage instrument – reached $45 trillion by late 2007 (O'Hara, 2009: p. 14).

Many of the mortgages underlying mortgage-backed securities are now in foreclosure or are headed there. In 2008, 2.3 million US homes went into foreclosure, up 81 per cent from 2007 and 225 per cent from 2006 (RealtyTrac, 2009a). There were another 803,489 filings in the first quarter of 2009 (the most recent period for which data are available at the time of writing), up 9 per cent from the previous quarter (RealtyTrac, 2009b).

Mortgage delinquencies are also up sharply. In February 2009, 7 per cent of US homeowners with mortgages were at least 30 days late on their loans, an increase of more than 50 per cent from a year earlier. Among subprime borrowers, that month's delinquency rate was 39.8 per cent (Chernikoff, 2009).[6] (Again, these are the latest available figures at the time of writing.)

There has been much public discussion over the past year or so in the United States about reckless homebuyers, but mortgage seekers could not and did not bring the economy to its knees on their own. Exotic home loans and mortgage securitisation are products of money-manager capitalism. As Minsky stressed at a pair of professional conferences in the late 1980s and early 1990s, there is a symbiotic relationship 'between the growth of securitisation and managed money.' Fund managers, he argued, 'have outgrown the orthodox high quality stock and bond portfolios of fiduciaries' (Minsky, 1990a: p. 71; 1992c: p. 32).

From a Minsky perspective, the economic participants most responsible for bringing down the economy are hedge funds and other investment funds, investment banks and other financial institutions. Looking at hedge funds offers a glimpse at what happened. Although the following discussion focuses on hedge funds because they are a relative newcomer to the scene and have become infamous for operating beyond the reach of much government regulation, the investment banks and other institutions played a similar role (and since 1999, US banking has operated without the Glass-Steagall firewall that separated commercial and investment banking for over a half century).

Some of the biggest purchasers of securitised mortgages have been hedge funds. The earliest of these funds were established in the first few decades after Second World War for the purpose of seeking absolute returns (rather than beating a benchmark stock-market index). They were indeed 'hedged' funds, which sought to protect principal from financial loss by hedging investments through short selling or other means. The number of hedge funds and the assets under their management expanded in the 1990s and grew even more rapidly in the 2000s. At the same time, these assets became increasingly concentrated at the top ten firms and funds became more diverse in terms of the strategies their managers employed. In mid-2008, the Alternative Investment Management Association estimated that the world's hedge funds (based primarily in the United States) were managing $2.5 trillion, though it acknowledged that other estimates were as high as $4 trillion (Ineichen and Silberstein, 2008: p. 16).

The total value of assets under hedge-fund management is uncertain because such funds are typically restricted to wealthy individuals and institutional investors, which exempts them from most financial-sector reporting requirements and regulation. Taking advantage of their largely unregulated status, managers of hedge funds used their mortgage-backed securities as collateral to take out highly leveraged loans. They then purchased an assortment of financial instruments, including still more mortgage bundles. As a result, the world's hedge funds used securitised mortgages to lay an inherently flimsy foundation for a financial 'house of cards' (Freeman, 2009; Holt, 2009).

The current crisis is unmistakably global. It is having economic and political ramifications on all continents (Timeline, 2009; Whalen, 2009). The trouble is even affecting unexpected places like rural China: factories in cities along that nation's coast are laying-off workers and sending them back to their villages (Lee, 2009).

The global nature of the current situation would not have surprised Minsky, who stressed early on that money-manager capitalism 'is international in both the funds and the assets in funds' (Minsky, 1990a: p. 71). Looking ahead to the current crisis, Minsky wrote: 'The problem of finance that will emerge is whether the... institutions of national governments can contain both the consequences of global financial fragility and an international debt deflation' (Minsky, 1995: p. 93). He worried that the United States would be unable to serve as 'the guardian angel for stability in the world economy' and stressed the need for 'an international division of responsibility for maintaining global aggregate gross profits' (Minsky, 1986b: p. 15; 1990a: p. 71).

In short, the global economy is now reeling from the consequences of a classic Minsky crisis. Its origins are in a housing boom fuelled by rising expectations, expanding debt and financial innovation. Then the bubble burst, creating first a credit crunch, then a broader banking and stock-market crisis and now a recession.

The consequences have been staggering. In the housing sector, an unprecedented one in nine US homes (14 million) sits vacant, while another 9.4 million are for sale (El Nasser, 2009). The US stock market lost an unprecedented $1.2 trillion of value in just a single day in late September 2008 (measured by the Wilshire, 5000), and for 2008 overall the Dow Jones industrial average had its worst year since 1931 (Blaine, 2008; Twin, 2008). Unemployment may soon hit double digits in the United States and has already reached double digits in some parts of Europe (Eurostat, 2009).

Since 2007, the global banking industry has seen an unprecedented shake-out (Timeline, 2009), but there is still uncertainty about how much more difficulty lies ahead. As the Bank for International Settlements indicated in a report released in June 2007:

> Assuming that the big banks have managed to distribute more widely the risks inherent in the loans they have made, who now holds these risks, and can they manage them adequately? The honest answer is that we do not know. Much of the risk is embodied in various forms of asset-backed securities of growing complexity and opacity. They have been purchased by a wide range of smaller banks, pension funds, insurance companies, hedge funds, other funds and even individuals, who have been encouraged to invest by the generally high ratings given to these instruments.
>
> (Bank for International Settlements, 2007: p. 145)

Warren Buffett made the point more vividly: 'You only learn who has been swimming naked when the tide goes out' (Buffett, 2008: p. 3). Although the risks are now being laid bare, it will still be some time before the world learns the full extent of the financial exposure.

6.4 Public policy

The current global economic situation requires a two-pronged economic-policy strategy: recovery and reform. Beyond stabilising the troubled financial sector and preventing the current downturn from becoming more severe, the overarching policy objective should be greater macroeconomic stability and broadly shared prosperity in the United States and abroad (Minsky, 1986c; Minsky and Whalen, 1996–1997). This section highlights some of the most important policy issues by comparing Minsky's recommendations with recent US government action.[7]

6.4.1 Recovery

A government strategy for recovery must have at least three components: fiscal policy, monetary policy and financial-market policy. Each is considered in turn.

The foundation of Minsky's strategy for avoiding another Great Depression is what he calls 'Big Government' (Minsky, 1986c: pp. 292–308). At the heart of Big Government is a federal budget that tends towards surpluses in inflationary periods and that produces deficits large enough to stabilise aggregate profits in recessionary periods. Minsky stressed that such countercyclical spending should be a 'built-in' feature of the budget structure, but he also recognised that discretionary action would be needed on occasion (Minsky, 1986c: pp. 132, 292).

Since the mid-1970s, however, policymakers have allowed the automatic stabilising features of the US federal budget to erode. As a colleague and I demonstrated in late 2002, income taxes, unemployment insurance, welfare expenditures and the minimum wage have all lost much of their ability to serve as countercyclical mechanisms. We concluded: 'It makes sense to shore up the economy's fiscal stabilisers. Better to fix the roof before the rain begins' (Whalen and Wenger, 2002: p. 91). By the time the storm finally hit, however, little had changed.

The erosion of automatic stabilisers has forced discretionary measures to do all the heavy lifting. In the current downturn, fiscal policy in the United States has moved in the right direction, but the initiatives have been too timid. The first stimulus attempt, passed in early 2008, included $100 billion in tax rebates and provided a modest boost to consumer spending (Broda and Parker, 2008), but the bill also included tens of billions in less stimulative business tax cuts. More recently, President Barack Obama signed into law a stimulus package totalling $787 billion over 2 years. However, Paul

Krugman was probably correct when he suggested the package should have been twice as big and even more tilted towards spending (as opposed to tax cuts), especially since recent data revisions show that fourth-quarter US gross domestic product fell by 6.3 per cent, not 4 per cent as reported originally (Earnshaw, 2009; Krugman, 2009a).[8]

Beyond giving a major role to the fiscal policy of Big Government, Minsky stressed that the central bank must intervene as lender-of-last-resort in response to the threat of a serious credit crisis and economic contraction. 'Central banks are the institutions responsible for containing and offsetting financial instability', he wrote in *Stabilising an Unstable Economy*, published in 1986 (Minsky, 1986c: p. 322). In that same year, Minsky also contributed an article emphasising the globalisation of finance and the need for international central-bank coordination to prepare for the next big financial crisis (Minsky, 1986b).

From a Minsky perspective, monetary policy has largely been on the right track since the credit crunch hit in mid-2007. In an effort to stabilise the financial sector and overall economy, the Federal Reserve has aggressively cut interest rates, allowed banks to borrow from it at nominal rates and given banks cash in exchange for risky assets (promising to take on the risk if those assets prove worthless).[9] The Fed has also engineered bank mergers and worked with other central banks to increase the supply of dollars world-wide. In a very short time, Fed chairman Ben Bernanke has moved a long way from the days when he was known as a champion of inflation targeting.[10]

In contrast, financial-market policy at the US Treasury Department has been woefully inadequate from a Minsky vantage point. The Troubled Asset Relief Program, more commonly known as the $700 billion Wall Street Bailout, seemed designed to clean up bank balance sheets by purchasing their bad assets. Instead, the Treasury was soon writing banks cheques and buying large quantities of bank stocks. The underlying problem of the 'toxic' assets remained unresolved, banks remained reluctant to lend and much of the added liquidity was transformed into bank stock dividends.

The Treasury's latest plan, a 'public–private partnership' that creates a market for troubled assets with government loans and guarantees, is not much better. The plan offers what Joseph E. Stiglitz calls a 'win-win-lose proposal: the banks win, investors win – and taxpayers lose.' He argues the plan encourages investors to bid high in that newly created market and socialises the losses that are likely to follow. In attempting to account for this proposal, Stiglitz writes: 'Perhaps it's the kind of Rube Goldberg device that Wall Street loves – clever, complex and nontransparent, allowing huge transfers of wealth to the financial markets' (Stiglitz, 2009: p. 1).

A different approach would likely have been endorsed by Minsky, who admired how the administration of President Franklin D. Roosevelt closed insolvent banks and assisted solvent ones during the Great Depression. Minsky would have almost certainly called for a more hands-on sorting-out of the current financial mess by means of bank restructuring.

Today, Krugman (2009b, 2009c), Dean Baker (2009b) and James K. Galbraith (2009) call for similar action. For example, Galbraith writes: 'If the subprime securities are truly trash, most of the big banks are troubled and some are insolvent. The FDIC should put them through receivership, get clean audits, install new management, and begin the necessary shrinkage of the banking system with the big guys, not the small ones' (Galbraith, 2009). The Obama administration recently ordered federal regulators to conduct 'stress tests' to gauge the condition of the nation's banks. As a next step, the receivership approach makes more sense than creation of a government-subsidised market for toxic assets.

Another aspect of financial-market policy that currently needs attention involves home mortgages. Throughout 2008, the United States largely avoided addressing the unaffordable mortgages that are at the heart of the current problem (Marks, 2008). The Obama administration has been encouraging the financial industry to voluntarily restructure those loans, but industry pressure has made many in the nation's capital reluctant to require it. For example, federal legislators have so far refused to let bankruptcy judges insist on home loan restructuring, despite the fact that judges can demand a restructuring of all loans except the mortgage on a homeowner's residence (legislation is stalled in the US Senate as of this writing). Although Minsky did not address this problem directly, his interest in social justice and a humane economy suggest he would have insisted that this problem be resolved by mortgage restructuring and would have been incensed that the problem has been unresolved for so long (Minsky, 1986c, 1993b).

6.4.2 Reform

Looking beyond the current downturn, a reform agenda must include stricter regulation and supervision of the financial system, a national commitment to the challenges facing America's working families and US participation in efforts that promote international economic stability and job creation.

Minsky believed that those responsible for government regulation and supervision of the financial system were in a 'never-ending struggle' with financial markets (Minsky, quoted in Phillips, 1997: p. 512). As he wrote in *Stabilising an Unstable Economy*, 'After an initial interval, the basic disequilibrating tendencies of capitalist finance will once again push the financial structure to the brink of fragility.' Still, he believed it was necessary for the Federal Reserve and regulators to continue the struggle: 'The evolution of financial practices must be guided to reduce the likelihood that fragile situations conducive to financial instability will develop' (Minsky, 1986c: pp. 322, 333).

Today, those adopting a Minsky perspective would hold the same view. Greater industry transparency, more rigorous bank examinations and broader regulatory oversight would be a good place to start. If policymakers had better information about the extent to which financial institutions were making use of option ARMs and other exotic instruments, perhaps at least a few would have more aggressively sought to address the mounting problem. It also seems appropriate to revive Minsky's notion of a cash-flow approach to bank examinations, which 'would use the examination process to generate information on not only the liquidity and solvency of particular institutions, but also on threats, if any, to the stability of financial markets' (Minsky, quoted in Phillips, 1997: p. 513). Similarly, mortgage brokers, hedge funds and other institutions that have gained increasing importance in the past decade deserve greater scrutiny from financial-system regulators.[11] In light of the current economic crisis, stricter oversight of securitisation and other recent financial innovations are clearly overdue, but the additional need is for regulators to be on the lookout for future innovations in an effort to head-off potential crises before they occur.

At the very least, the US government should not block state efforts designed to protect their citizens from gaps in federal law. Today, most Americans know about the 2008 Valentine's Day in Washington that cost former New York Governor Eliot Spitzer his job, but of greater national importance was his guest column that appeared in *The Washington Post* that day. It described how the federal government stopped states from cracking down on predatory lending practices. As Spitzer's essay documents, 'Not only did the Bush administration do nothing to protect consumers, it embarked on an aggressive and unprecedented campaign to prevent states from protecting their residents from the very problems to which the federal government was turning a blind eye.... The tale is still unfolding, but when the dust settles, [the Bush administration] will be judged as a willing accomplice to the lenders who went to any lengths in their quest for profits' (Spitzer, 2008).

In the age of managerial capitalism (approximately 1935–1982), it may have been sufficient to focus on full employment, low inflation and steady economic growth. In the age of money-manager capitalism (since 1982), these goals are still important, but the challenges facing America's working families require more direct attention as well. Americans, like citizens elsewhere around the world, want the opportunity to develop and utilise their talents and to increase their standard of living in the process. They also want the prospect of an even better life for their children.

Unfortunately, rising worker insecurity is the flipside of money-manager capitalism. Under pressure from money managers, corporate executives have largely put aside the employer–employee social contract of the New Deal and the early decades following Second World War. Employers have moved increasingly towards treating labour as just another 'spot market' commodity (Minsky, 1996; Minsky and Whalen, 1996–1997; Whalen, 1997; Zalewski, 2002; Whalen, 2008b).

Thus, the economic challenges facing the United States extend far beyond stabilising the financial system and preventing a long and deep recession, as Minsky and I discussed in an article written shortly before his death

(Minsky and Whalen, 1996–1997). The nation needs to spur the growth of domestic jobs that pay family-supporting wages and to ensure that Americans have access to the education and training such jobs require (Glover and King, 2010; Marshall, 2010). It needs to find a way to promote partnerships between workers and managers, so companies can compete on the basis of innovation, quality and customer service, rather than by outsourcing jobs or slashing wages and benefits. It needs to provide adjustment assistance to workers displaced by international trade (including service workers excluded from some existing benefits programs) and public-service employment to those unable to find private-sector work. And it needs health-care reform, retirement-system reform and labour-law reform to address medical insecurity, retirement insecurity and the insecurity of workers who seek to exercise their legal right to engage in union organising and collective bargaining (Whalen, 2008b, 2008c).[12]

To address the challenges facing America's working families, the Obama administration has created a Middle Class Task Force, headed by Vice President Joe Biden. Its goals suggest an awareness of the issues just mentioned (About the Task Force, 2009). Yet, only time will tell whether the administration devotes much attention and resources to these issues.

Finally, pursuit of greater economic stability and broadly shared prosperity cannot end at the borders of the United States. Indeed, as suggested above, Minsky recognised that money-manager capitalism is worldwide in scope and that stabilisation and development challenges must be addressed at a global level. From a Minsky perspective, Americans must help fashion international institutions that not only contain global financial instability, but also enhance labour rights and promote job growth (Minsky, 1995, 1993a, 1990b, 1986b; Palley, 1999: p. 55).

The world's key policymakers, however, have been reluctant to move in this direction.[13] Indeed, international economic policy has been dominated by a different outlook, as Stiglitz indicated after serving at the World Bank:

> During my three years as chief economist of the World Bank, labour market issues were looked at through the lens of neoclassical economics. 'Wage rigidities' – often the fruits of hard-fought bargaining – were thought part of the problem facing many countries. A standard message was to increase labour market flexibility. The not-so-subtle subtext was to lower wages and lay off unneeded workers.
>
> (Stiglitz, quoted in Komisar, 2000)

Stiglitz concluded, 'They had a strategy for job destruction. They had no strategy for job creation' (Stiglitz, quoted in Komisar, 2000). Economists who see the world from a Minsky perspective need to collaborate to develop that missing strategy.

6.5 Conclusion: standing on the shoulders of Minsky

Minsky used to say we should stand on the shoulders of giants to better understand the economy. Just as he stood on the shoulders of Keynes and Schumpeter, we can now stand on his shoulders to understand and address the current global recession. From a Minsky perspective, an explanation of this recession must include cyclical and structural dimensions, while a policy strategy requires attention to both recovery and reform.

The recent attention to Minsky's ideas, both outside and within the academy, is encouraging. Yet we do ourselves and his memory a disservice when Minsky's insights are reduced to an analysis of a single event or even of financial instability. Standing squarely on the shoulders of Minsky means understanding the latest business cycle within the context of money-manager capitalism, and it means seeking to guide the further development of the system in a more humane direction.

Notes

1. Homeowners were also able to fuel a consumption boom by taking on even more debt. That is because rising home prices encouraged banks to increase customers' credit-card limits and to heavily promote home-equity loans (Chu and Acohido, 2008; Story, 2008).
2. Dymski and Pollin add: 'When boom conditions do end, aggressive managers will already have been promoted, while cautious managers will have been demoted, if not dismissed. Moreover, during the slump, all aggressive managers will fail together, so no single individual will be singled out for blame. This is in contrast to the boom, where the miscalculating cautious will have been isolated' (Dymski and Pollin, 1992: p. 45).
3. Of course, Bear Stearns itself was to be a casualty of the crisis in early 2008.
4. Here are some figures that indicate the magnitude of US mortgage securitisation: in early 2007, about 65 per cent of mortgages were being turned into bonds via securitisation, up from 40 per cent in 1990; and, in the years 2004–2006, nearly $100 billion per year in option ARMs were sold to investors (Der Hovanesian, 2006; Pittman, 2007).
5. Mortgage brokers, who operate without much government regulation, accounted for 80 per cent of all US mortgage originations in 2006, double their share a decade earlier (Der Hovanesian, 2006).
6. According to the Federal Housing Finance Agency, mortgage delinquencies among the most creditworthy homeowners (prime borrowers) holding loans owned or guaranteed by Fannie Mae and Freddie Mac rose 50 per cent from December 2008 to January 2009 (from 497,131 to 743,686) 'as borrowers said drops in income or too much debt caused them to fall behind' (Kopecki, 2009).
7. The primary focus of this discussion is on the United States, not merely because this is where most of the recent economic trouble originated, but also because it is the main focus of Minsky's analyses.
8. Another reason for suggesting the 2009 stimulus was too timid is that the first-year tax-cut multipliers estimated by Christina Romer and Jared Bernstein were

considerably below 1.0 (Romer and Bernstein, 2009: p. 12). Thus, modifying the package in the direction of tax cuts (to ensure passage) seemed ill advised from a macroeconomic perspective.

9. It is interesting to observe the Federal Reserve's use of the discount window as a means of influencing the banking system during the current crisis. Minsky recommended that the Fed increase reliance on this mechanism throughout the business cycle, but he thought it was especially important to use this channel in a fragile financial environment (Minsky, 1986c: pp. 322–328).
10. For an unconventional look at Bernanke, including the suggestion of a surprising link between Minsky and Princeton University financial-market research convened by Bernanke, see Lahart (2008).
11. The use of leverage by hedge funds and the writing of no documentation home loans are among the practices in greatest need of regulatory attention. There is also a need to address the problem created by firms deemed 'too big to fail,' which is yet another issue Minsky (1986c) anticipated long ago.
12. Health-care reform was enacted as this chapter was being prepared for publication (March 2010).
13. The challenge of getting global leaders to cooperate for the purpose of establishing a foundation for greater stability and more widespread global economic well-being can be seen even in the current economic climate; see Zalewski and Whalen (2009: pp. 17–18).

References

'About the task force,' The White House Blog (30 January 2009), http://www.whitehouse.gov/blog_post/about_the_task_force_1/ (accessed 13 April 2009).

Baker, D. (2009a), 'The economic crisis: how we got here,' PowerPoint Presentation. Labor and Employment Relations Association Annual Meeting. 3 January. San Francisco, California.

Baker, D. (2009b), 'Geithner's plan will tax Main Street to make Wall Street richer,' *The Huffington Post* (30 March), http://www.huffingtonpost.com/dean-baker/geithners-plan-will-tax-m_b_181021.html (accessed 13 April 2009).

Bank for International Settlements (2007), 77th Annual Report. Basel, Switzerland: Bank for International Settlements Press and Communications.

Blaine, C. (2008), 'Wall Street says 'good riddance!' to 2008,' MSN Money (31 December), http://articles.moneycentral.msn.com/Investing/Dispatch/worst-year-since-1931-123108.aspx (accessed 13 April 2009).

Broda, C. and J. Parker (2008), 'The impact of the 2008 tax rebates on consumer spending: Preliminary evidence.' University of Chicago Graduate School of Business, 29 July, available at http://faculty.chicagobooth.edu/christian.broda/website/research/unrestricted/Research.htm (accessed 13 April 2009).

Buffett, W.E. (2008), Letter to shareholders, Berkshire Hathaway Inc., 2007 Annual Report.

Cassidy, J. (2008), 'The Minsky Moment?' *The New Yorker* (4 February), http://www.newyorker.com/talk/comment/2008/02/04/080204taco_talk_cassidy (accessed 28 April 2009).

Chernikoff, H. (2009), 'U.S. mortgage delinquencies up 50 percent,' Reuters UK, http://uk.reuters.com/article/economyNews/idUKTRE5374LT20090408 (accessed 13 April 2009).

Chu, K. and B. Acohido (2008), 'How rising home values, easy credit put your finances at risk,' USA Today (15 December), http://www.usatoday.com/money/perfi/credit/2008-06-17-credit-card-trap_N.htm (accessed 13 April 2009).

Der Hovanesian, M. (2006), 'Nightmare mortgages,' *BusinessWeek* (11 September), http://www.businessweek.com/magazine/content/06_37/b4000001.htm (accessed 13 April 2009).

Dymski, G. and R. Pollin (1992), 'Minsky as hedgehog: the power of the Wall Street paradigm,' in S. Fazzari and D.B. Papadimitriou (eds), *Financial Conditions and Macroeconomic Performance: Essays in Honor of Hyman P. Minsky* (Armonk, New York: M.E. Sharpe).

Earnshaw, A. (2009), 'Krugman: stimulus needs to be twice as big,' *Portland Business Journal* (2 February), http://www.bizjournals.com/portland/stories/2009/01/26/daily68.html (accessed 13 April 2009).

El Nasser, H. (2009), 'Open house anyone? 1 in 9 homes sit empty,' *USA Today*, http://www.usatoday.com/money/economy/housing/2009-04-09-vacanthomes_N.htm (accessed 13 April 2009).

Eurostat (2009), 'Euro area unemployment up to 8.5 percent,' News Release, Eurostat Euroindicators (1 April), downloaded from http:/ec.europa.eu/eurostat/euroindicators (accessed 13 April 2009).

Foley, S. (2007), Anatomy of a credit crunch,' *The Independent* (London, 27 July), http://findarticles.com/p/articles/mi_qn4158/is_20070727/ai_n19447440/?tag=content;col1 (accessed 13 April 2009).

Freeman, J. (2009), 'How the money vanished,' *The Wall Street Journal* (6 March), http://online.wsj.com/article/SB123630340388147387.html (accessed 13 April 2009).

Galbraith, J. K. (2009), 'The Geithner plan won't work,' *The Daily Beast* (24 March), http://www.thedailybeast.com/blogs-and-stories/2009-03-24/the-geithner-plan-wont-work/full/ (accessed 13 April 2009).

Glover, R.W. and C.T. King (2010), 'Sectoral approaches to workforce development: toward an effective U.S. labor market policy,' in C.J. Whalen (ed.), *Human Resource Economics and Public Policy: Essays in Honor of Vernon M. Briggs*, Jr. Kalamazoo, Michigan: W.E. Upjohn Institute for Employment Research, pp. 215–252.

Holt, C. (2009), 'A graphical look at hedge fund leverage,' Seeking Alpha (8 March), http://seekingalpha.com/article/124783-a-graphical-look-at-hedge-fund-leverage

Huhne, C. (2007) 'Comments on credit rating agencies and the U.S. credit crunch.' *World Business Review*, BBC World Service (1 September).

Ineichen, A. and K. Silberstein (2008), *AIMA's Roadman to Hedge Funds* (London: The Alternative Investment Management Association).

Irwin, G. (2005), 'No money down gains more buyers,' *Akron Beacon Journal* (31 July), http://www.policymattersohio.org/media/ABJ_No_money_down_gains_more_buyers_2005_0731.htm (accessed 13 April 2009).

Keynes, J.M. (1937), 'The general theory of employment,' *The Quarterly Journal of Economics*, vol. 51.

Komisar, L. (2000), 'Interview with Joseph Stiglitz,' *The Progressive* (June), http://www.progressive.org/0901/intv0600.html (accessed 13 April 2009).

Kopecki, D. (2009), 'Fannie, freddie defaults rise as borrowers cite lower income,' Bloomberg.com (21 April), http://www.bloomberg.com/apps/news?pid=20601087&sid=aw4.u4ryoAq0&refer=home (accessed 26 April 2009).

Krugman, P. (2009a), 'Stimulus arithmetic (wonkish but important),' *The New York Times* (6 January), http://krugman.blogs.nytimes.com/2009/01/06/stimulus-arithmetic-wonkish-but-important/ (accessed 13 April 2009).

Krugman, P. (2009b), 'Despair over financial policy,' *The New York Times* (21 March), http://krugman.blogs.nytimes.com/2009/03/21/despair-over-financial-policy/ (accessed 13 April 2009).

Krugman, P. (2009c), 'Geithner plan arithmetic,' *The New York Times* (23 March), http://krugman.blogs.nytimes.com/2009/03/23/geithner-plan-arithmetic/ (accessed 13 April 2009).

Lahart, J. (2007), 'In time of tumult, obscure economist gains currency,' *The Wall Street Journal* (8 August).

Lahart, J. (2008), 'Bernanke's bubble laboratory,' *The Wall Street Journal* (16 May), 1; http://online.wsj.com/public/article_print/SB121089412378097011.html (accessed 28 April 2009).

Lanman, S. and D. Kopecki (2008), 'Fed commits $800 billion more to unfreeze lending,' Bloomberg.com (25 November), http://www.bloomberg.com/apps/news?pid=20601103&refer=us&sid=a.IQxmdJnJMc (accessed 13 April 2009).

Larsen Thal, P. and C. Giles (2007), 'Bank of England to bail out Northern Rock,' *Financial Times* (14 September 2007), http://www.ft.com/cms/s/0/c6de12c8-6258-11dc-bdf6-0000779fd2ac.html (accessed 28 April 2009).

Lee, D. (2009), 'Migrant factory workers at a loss as China's economy slumps,' *Los Angeles Times* (23 January), http://articles.latimes.com/2009/jan/23/business/fi-chinamigrant23 (accessed 13 April 2009).

Magnus, G. (2007), 'The credit cycle and liquidity: have we arrived at a Minsky moment?' Economic insights – By George, *UBS Investment Research, London* (March).

Magnus, G. (2008), 'Is there time to avert a Minsky meltdown?' *The Financial Times* (14 October).

Marks, B. (2008), 'Bailout must address the foreclosure crisis,' *The Boston Globe* (24 September), http://www.boston.com/bostonglobe/editorial_opinion/oped/articles/2008/09/24/bailout_must_address_the_foreclosure_crisis/ (accessed 13 April 2009).

Marshall, R. (2010), 'Learning systems for a globalised economy: do Americans face tough choices or tough times?' in Charles J. Whalen (ed.), *Human Resource Economics and Public Policy: Essays in Honor of Vernon M. Briggs Jr.* (Kalamazoo, Michigan: W.E. Upjohn Institute for Employment Research), pp. 187–214.

Max, S. (2005), 'Risky real estate moves,' CNNMoney.com (4 April), http://money.cnn.com/2005/03/07/real_estate/financing/riskyloans/index.htm (accessed 13 April 2009).

Mildenberg, D. (2008), 'Bank of America to acquire Countrywide for $4 billion,' Bloomberg.com (11 January), http://www.bloomberg.com/apps/news?pid=20601087&refer=home&sid=aCbUSVliDIKQ (accessed 13 April 2009).

Minsky, H.P. (1975), *John Maynard Keynes* (New York: Columbia University Press).

Minsky, H.P. (1982), *Can 'It' Happen Again? Essays on Instability and Finance* (Armonk, New York: M.E. Sharpe).

Minsky, H.P. (1986a), 'Money and crisis in Schumpeter and Keynes,' in Hans-Jurgen Wagener and Jan W. Drukker (eds), *The Economic Law of Motion of Modern Society: A Marx-Keynes-Schumpeter Centennial* (Cambridge, UK: Cambridge University Press).

Minsky, H.P. (1986b), 'Global consequences of financial deregulation,' *The Marcus Wallenberg Papers on International Finance*, vol. 2, no. 1.

Minsky, H.P. (1986c), *Stabilising an Unstable Economy* (New Haven: Yale University Press).
Minsky, H.P. (1990a), 'Schumpeter: finance and evolution,' in Arnold Heertje and Mark Perlman (eds), *Evolving Market Technology and Market Structure: Studies in Schumpeterian Economics* (Ann Arbor: The University of Michigan Press).
Minsky, H.P. (1990b), 'Money manager capitalism, fiscal independence, and international monetary reconstruction,' in Miklos Szabo-Pelsoczi (ed.), *The Future of the Global Economic and Monetary System* (Budapest, Hungary: Institute for World Economics of the Hungarian Academy of Sciences).
Minsky, H.P. (1992a), 'The financial instability hypothesis,' *Working Paper Number 74, The Levy Economics Institute of Bard College.*
Minsky, H.P. (1992b), 'The capital development of the economy and the structure of financial institutions,' *Working Paper Number 72, The Levy Economics Institute of Bard College.*
Minsky, H.P. (1992c), 'Reconstituting the United States' financial structure: some fundamental issues,' *Working Paper Number 69, The Levy Economics Institute of Bard College.*
Minsky, H.P. (1993a), 'Schumpeter and finance,' in Salvatore Biasco, Alessandro Roncaglia, and Michele Salvati (eds), *Market and Institutions in Economic Development: Essays in Honour of Paulo Sylos Labini* (New York: St. Martin's Press).
Minsky, H.P. (1993b), 'Community development banks: an idea in search of substance,' *Challenge*, vol. 36, no. 2.
Minsky, H.P. (1995), 'Longer waves in financial relations: financial factors in the more severe depressions II,' *Journal of Economic Issues*, vol. 29, no. 1.
Minsky, H.P. (1996), 'Uncertainty and the institutional structure of capitalist economies,' *Journal of Economic Issues*, vol. 30, no. 2.
Minsky, H.P. and C.J. Whalen (1996–1997), 'Economic insecurity and the institutional prerequisites for successful capitalism,' *Journal of Post Keynesian Economics*, vol. 19, no. 2.
'Minsky's moment' (2009), Economist.com (2 April), http://www.economist.com/finance/displaystory.cfm?story_id=13415233 (accessed 28 April 2009).
Mitchell, W.C. (1941), *Business Cycles and Their Causes* (Berkeley, California: University of California Press).
Morgenson, G. (2007), 'Inside the countrywide lending spree,' *The New York Times* (26 August), http://www.nytimes.com/2007/08/26/business/yourmoney/26country.html?hp (accessed 13 April 2009).
'Obama's economic aide sees rising U.S. unemployment,' AFP [Agence France-Presse] (9 April 2009), http://www.google.com/hostednews/afp/article/ALeqM5g2urt_Wnm7T-ePnhznr5dLcBYY1w (accessed 13 April 2009).
O'Hara, P.A. (2009), 'The global securitised subprime market crisis,' paper prepared for the *Association for Institutional Thought Annual Meeting*, Albuquerque, New Mexico (17 April).
Palley, T.I. (1999), 'International finance and problems of capital account governance,' in Lynndee Kemmet, Karl Widerquist, and Ajit Zacharias (eds), *Conference Proceedings: Ninth Annual Hyman P. Minsky Conference on Financial Structure*, Annandale-on-Hudson, New York: The Jerome Levy Economics Institute of Bard College.
Phillips, R.J. (1997), 'Rethinking bank examinations: a Minsky approach,' *Journal of Economic Issues*, vol. 31, no. 2.
Pittman, M. (2007), 'Subprime bondholders may lose $75 billion from slump,' Bloomberg.com (24 April), http://www.bloomberg.com/apps/news?pid=20601087&sid=aq3flDbwBCbk&refer=home (accessed 13 April 2009).

Pollin, R. (2008), 'We're all Minskyites now,' *The Nation* (17 November).

RealtyTrac, S. (2009a), 'Foreclosure activity increases 81 percent in 2008,' RealtyTrac.com (15 January), http://www.realtytrac.com/ContentManagement/pressrelease.aspx?ChannelID=9&ItemID=5681 (accessed 13 April 2009).

RealtyTrac, S. (2009b), 'Foreclosure activity increases 9 percent in first quarter,' RealtyTrac.com (16 April), http://www.realtytrac.com//ContentManagement/PressRelease.aspx?channelid=9&ItemID=6180 (accessed 25 April 2009).

Reckard, E.S., E. Douglass and T. Petruno (2007), 'BofA invests $2 billion in Countrywide,' *Los Angeles Times* (23 August), C1, http://articles.latimes.com/2007/aug/23/business/fi-mortgage23 (accessed 13 April 2009).

Romer, C. and J. Bernstein (2009), *The Job Impact of the American Recovery and Reinvestment Plan*. (Washington, DC: Presidential Transition Team) 9 January.

Shefrin, H. (2000), *Beyond Greed and Fear: Understanding Behavioral Finance and the Psychology of Investing* (Boston: Harvard Business School Press).

Spitzer, E. (2008), 'Predatory lenders' partner in crime,' *The Washington Post*, http://www.washingtonpost.com/wp-dyn/content/article/2008/02/13/AR2008021302783.html (accessed 13 April 2009).

Stempel, J. (2007), 'Countrywide uses $11.5B credit line to pay for loans,' *USA Today* (16 August), http://www.usatoday.com/money/economy/housing/2007-08-15-countrywide-stock_N.htm (accessed 13 April 2009).

Stiglitz, J.E. (2009), 'Obama's ersatz capitalism,' *The New York Times* (31 March) http://www.nytimes.com/2009/04/01/opinion/01stiglitz.html (accessed 13 April 2009).

Story, L. (2008), 'Home equity frenzy was a bank ad come true,' *The New York Times* (15 August), http://www.nytimes.com/2008/08/15/business/15sell.html (accessed 13 April 2009).

'Timeline: credit crunch to downturn,' *BBC News* (3 April 2009), http://news.bbc.co.uk/2/hi/business/7521250.stm (accessed 13 April 2009).

Twin, A. (2008), 'Stocks crushed,' CNNMoney.com (29 September), http://money.cnn.com/2008/09/29/markets/markets_newyork/index.htm?cnn=yes (accessed 13 April 2009).

U.S. Department of Labor (2009), 'Employment situation summary.' Economic News Release, Bureau of Labor Statistics, http://www.bls.gov/news.release/empsit.nr0.htm (accessed 13 April 2009).

Whalen, C.J. (1997), 'Money manager capitalism and the end of shared prosperity,' *Journal of Economic Issues*, vol. 31, no. 2.

Whalen, C.J. (2001), 'Integrating Schumpeter and Keynes: Hyman Minsky's theory of capitalist development,' *Journal of Economic Issues*, vol. 35, no. 4.

Whalen, C.J. (2002), 'Money manager capitalism: still here, but not quite as expected,' *Journal of Economic Issues*, vol. 36, no. 2.

Whalen, C.J. (2008a), 'The credit crunch: A Minsky moment,' *Studi e Note Di Economia*, vol. 13, no. 1.

Whalen, C.J. (2008b), 'Post-Keynesian institutionalism and the anxious society,' in S.S. Batie and N. Mercuro (eds), *Alternative Economic Structures: Evolution and Impact* (London: Routledge).

Whalen, C.J. (2008c), 'A labor agenda filled with hope and change,' LERA Commons (18 December), http://lerablog.org/2009/03/18/a-labor-agenda-brimming-with-hope-and-change-by-charles-whalen/ (accessed 13 April 2009).

Whalen, C.J. (2009), 'The financial crisis: causes and consequences,' PowerPoint Presentation to the Finger Lakes Forum (19 January) Geneva, New York.

Whalen, C.J. and J. Wenger (2002), 'Destabilising an unstable economy,' *Challenge*, vol. 45, no. 6.

Yahoo Finance (2009), Dow Jones Industrial Average: Historical Prices, http://finance.yahoo.com (accessed 13 April 2009).

Zalewski, D.A. (2002), 'Retirement insecurity in the age of money-manager capitalism,' *Journal of Economic Issues*, vol. 36, no. 2.

Zalewski, D.A. and C.J. Whalen (2009), 'Financialisation and income inequality: a post Keynesian institutionalist analysis,' paper prepared for the *Association for Evolutionary Economics Annual Meeting* in San Francisco, California (revised 24 April).

7
Macroeconomic Imbalances in the United States and their Impact on the International Financial System

Julia S. Loe

7.1 Introduction

While most economies grow through investment or export which expands demand, the US economy has kept up its growth by increased consumption. Using its privileged position to borrow money, the United States has reached a historically unprecedented level of current account deficit, which has been followed by a debt crisis in 2007–2008. This chapter argues that the financial crisis of 2007–2008 is symptomatic of macroeconomic imbalances in the United States, because the imbalances eventually are resolved in financial markets, and passed on to the real economy. On the other hand, the international financial system is dependent on US trade deficits for feeding liquidity into financial and commodity markets.

The chapter breaks new ground in the analysis of the current financial instability in the United States by showing how it links up with macroeconomic imbalances and financial inflation in the US economy, and how, through the foreign trade deficit, those imbalances and that inflation are transmitting instability to the rest of the world. This approach is relevant because there is a dominant structural imbalance in the US economy, but little theory addressing the consequences of the US trade deficit for the international financial system. The academic debate, divided between monetarists and sceptics, has instead been centred on the question of whether the US trade deficit is sustainable or not, with emphasis on domestic factors. However, neither of these positions offer a sufficient explanation of the present situation since they do not account well enough for the global integration of capital markets. In this context, a more systematic view will be used to analyse the relationship between the US imbalances and the global financial markets. This will lead to the conclusion that the financial crisis in 2007–2008 is transmitted to the rest of the world through the US trade deficit; that there is a global financial dependence on the United States in addition to its political dominance; and that the US macroeconomic imbalances cannot be resolved without affecting the rest of the world whose financial systems are dependent on dollars supplied by the United States through its current account deficit.

Section 7.2 presents the main views currently put forward on the macroeconomic imbalances. Section 7.3 examines how the dominant US position in international finance is supported by the US balance of payments deficit. Section 7.4 examines the links between the US balance of payments and the current financial crisis. Section 7.5 discusses the effects of the US deficit on other countries. This is followed by a conclusion.

7.2 Theories

The United States has a higher level of current account deficits in the balance of payments than any other state has had before, because the value of imports to the United States is much higher than the value of their exports. This has happened simultaneously to the United States running a record high fiscal deficit, which is paid for by issuing new debt. The financing of the US national debt has been done primarily in Asia, and particularly in China, and has during the last 5 years included inflows of around 2 billion US dollars every day (Trichet, 2005: p. 6). The United States has in other words been the recipient of the world's savings, while emerging economies and developing countries have been the supplier. This has happened in combination with internationally low interest rates (Summers, 2006: p. 2).

The academic discussion about the US trade imbalances has been dominated by two opposite positions, the monetarists and the sceptics, that primarily disagree on whether the US current account deficit is sustainable or not. There has also been a debate on whether the United States is responsible for the global imbalances, or if emerging economies, like China, are to blame for saving too much without letting their currency appreciate.

7.2.1 The monetarist position

The theory of monetarism, developed by the economist Milton Friedman, has its main focus on the macroeconomic effect of the supply of money and central banking. Monetarism has been the dominating economic position in the United States and Europe since the 1980s. It is built on a basic assumption that markets tend towards equilibrium, and that deviations are random (Soros, 2008: p. 97). In contrast to the so-called sceptics, or heterodox economists, the monetarists have not seen the US current account deficit as an immediate threat to the US national economy, opposing the view that exports are always 'good', while imports are 'bad'. A central argument has been that the US dollar is different from all other currencies, so what happens in the case of the US economy cannot be compared to other countries with high trade deficits. As Serrano points out, the United States is in a unique position since the American dollar is the international means of payment, the Federal Reserve System (Fed) determines the basic interest rate of the dollar, and since public debt in the United States is the most liquid dollar financial asset (Serrano, 2003: p. 1). According to Griswold, the critique against the US trade deficit ignores the strength of the US economy during the past decades, and the positive correlation that imports have had to domestic production (Griswold, 2007: p. 1). He points out that, in light of developments before 2007, there is no evidence that an increasing current account deficit is related to slower growth (ibid.).

Since the market system tends towards equilibrium, the monetarists believe that the global trade imbalances will resolve themselves in the long run, so that there is no reason to worry too much about the US deficits. This position has been supported by the Bank for International Settlements (BIS). Although the BIS Annual report of 2005 pointed out that the deficit of the United States could result in long-time problems, leading to a decline of the dollar, financial turmoil and even recession (quoted in Glyn, 2005: p. 13) the monetarists have mainly rejected the notion that there is a high probability for an economic disaster due to the US deficit. They mostly believe that the only long-term effect of the dollar outflow will be inflation. Trade deficits are also defended because the dollar flow that is leaving the country is invested in the US financial markets, which is understood to make the deficits less harmful to the US economy. According to Griswold, economic growth has on average been twice as fast, during years when the US trade deficit increased much, compared to years when it was reduced (2007: p. 7). This is explained by the fact that foreign investment in US assets creates growth and helps to keep US interest rates low (ibid.). However, this line of argumentation was put forward before the outburst of the subprime mortgage crisis in 2007.

7.2.2 The sceptic position

In contrast to the monetarist position, a wide range of economists have claimed for years that the US current account deficit is unsustainable and might lead to disastrous consequences for the global economy. Their argument is that if the US external deficit is not drastically reduced, it might lead to a speculative attack against the dollar, and a serious crisis in the global economy. In a worst case scenario, the dollar might then lose the important role it has had in the global economy until today (Serrano, 2003: p. 1).

Paul Krugman is one of the scholars who have warned that the US current deficit might lead to a dollar crisis where the high level of foreign debt could lead to much higher capital losses to investors than expected, and great macroeconomic problems (Krugman, 2007: p. 438). Since the United States is running a current account deficit, it is building up debt to other countries, which is paid for by outflows in the financial account (Gosh and Ramakrishnan, 2006: p. 3). These liabilities have to be paid back in the future, so if the money is spent on consumption instead of investment that might create income in the future, there might come a day when it is no longer seen as a good investment to go for US dollars (ibid.). As Summers points out the willingness of investors to accept claims on the United States might not last forever (2006: p. 3) and he rejects the monetarist idea that the United States can continue to expand its level of foreign debt even if it is able to issue debt in its own currency (ibid.). The sceptics' solution to the US deficit has primarily been to force economic deflation on the United States, by spending less and increasing its level of exports. This would lead to unemployment and have other serious consequences to the real economy, but might be the only way to create a more stable international financial system in a long-term perspective. The warnings from Krugman and other heterodox economists have increased their credibility due to the financial crisis of 2007–2008. Some of the things they warned about seem to be happening right now.

7.2.3 It's China's fault

Finally it is worth noting that some economists, in particular the Chairman of the Federal Reserve in the United States, Ben Bernanke, have a different perspective of the current account deficit in the United States. He is pointing out that the focus on domestic factors in the United States in order to explain the deficit is one-sided and limits the understanding of the situation. Instead he hypothesises 'The Global Saving Glut' (Bernanke, 2007: p. 3) and underlines that increased savings and current account surplus in developing countries have to be counterbalanced with deficits somewhere else. This is because the total saving in the world must equal investment, and the sum of national current account balances must be zero.

Since a large part of the problem, according to Bernanke, is found in other parts of the world than the United States, it must consequently also be solved there (ibid.). One of the main examples he uses is the situation in China, where export growth has led to higher incomes, while the access to consumer credit has been low, and people still feel a need to save. Combined with the Chinese government's reluctance to appreciate their currency, this can help to explain the US deficit. Bernanke therefore rejects the idea that the decline in public and private saving in the United States is the main reason for the macroeconomic imbalances (2007: p. 2).

7.2.4 The argument in this chapter

The majority of the focus in the academic debate on the US economy is seen in domestic terms, ignoring the negative sides for other countries in the world of reducing the global trade imbalances. But, as an answer to the sceptics, using an opposite twist of Bernanke's argumentation, one cannot consider the consequences of a reduction in the US import-led growth without thinking through the consequences for the export-led growth of other countries (Summers, 2006: p. 3). If the United States goes into recession, something most economists agree is happening now, and reduces their level of imports; the rest of the world will suffer due to less demand for foreign export. Some countries might handle this better than others, but when it comes to the heavily indebted countries, they often export in order to be able to pay their foreign exchange debt, which is usually denominated in US dollars. If the export markets are reduced, this could lead to a severe debt-crisis in these countries. The global risk is very high since the US external deficit is creating an export stimulus demand close to 2 per cent of world GDP (ibid.). Many sceptics have worried about foreigners holding US assets, in the form of debts which then have to be repaid to them. However, the debt would still have to be repaid even if it were owned by Americans, and at the end of the day the central issue is the amount of the debt, and not who has lent the money.

7.3 The US dominant position in the world economy

7.3.1 The United States as supplier of global revenue

The United States has been a leading superpower since Second World War, partly because the dollar as the international reserve currency has given asymmetric power to the US economy.

As Figure 7.1 shows, the level of foreign exchange reserves held in dollars has declined slightly since 2001, mainly because the Euro is used more now. However, the US dollar is by far the most important reserve currency in the world. Most of the current account surpluses and foreign exchange reserves are held by Asian countries. According to Lim (2008: p. 9), 10 Asian countries hold $3.4 trillion or 59 per cent of the world's foreign reserves. China alone holds $1.3 trillion or 22 per cent of the world's reserves (ibid.). Much of the current account surplus has been built up in the aftermath of the East Asian financial crisis in 1997 and 1998 when some of these countries run out of reserves. Many of these countries have been building up their reserves precisely in order to avoid another crisis in the future.

When the US deficit has been lowered previously, it has led to a depreciation of local currencies against the dollar, and the price of borrowed US

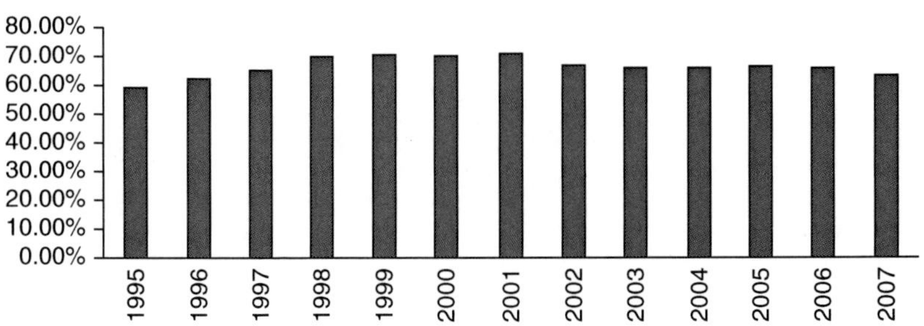

Figure 7.1 Percentage of global foreign exchange reserve in USD.
Source: IMF Statistics Department COFER database.

dollars has risen. This can be seen as part of the reason for the debt crisis in the 1980s and 1990s. It can therefore be argued that the US trade deficit is necessary to sustain the international financial system, since crisis has emerged when the United States has been closing the trade deficit. Galbraith has argued that a high dollar is beneficial since it gives the US cheap imports and capital inflows that can pay for domestic activity, while a declining dollar would reduce the value of reserves in developing countries (Galbraith, 2003: p. 4). In contrast to the focus in this chapter, his main concern is what is good for the US economy, regardless of the situation in the rest of the world. But in practice, the international monetary system has created a situation in which what is good for the United States is in many cases bad for the rest of the world, especially the dollar-indebted countries. A falling dollar makes dollar assets less attractive to foreigners, except central banks, but makes United States exports more competitive. In reality it might be in the interest of foreigners that are sufficiently indebted in dollars to have a weak dollar and a large current account deficit, which is a central point in this chapter. While the global growth previously depended upon the mining of gold, it is dependent on the creation of dollars today. If the United States reduces its deficit it might therefore have negative effects on the world and lead to an outflow slowdown.

7.3.2 The US balance of payment deficit

In 2007 the US balance of payment deficit amounted to $790 billion, which makes the United States the world's largest debtor state (Lim, 2008: p. 9). In this section, the main characteristics of the US current account deficit will be accounted for, including its relation to the public debt and its function to keep up domestic growth in the United States, despite the fact that the growth of industrial production in the United States has decreased while there has been significant GDP growth during the last 8 years.

The current account deficit related to personal over-consumption in the United States can be traced back to the 1980s, with the birth of consumer credit through the easy access to credit cards. Today every country trading with the United States runs a current account surplus with the United States (Shrik, 2007: p. 27). The level of the US trade deficit has varied through the years, but increased rapidly in the first part of this decade, hitting a record level in 2006 when it accounted for 6.2 per cent of GDP in the United States (Bernanke, 2007: p. 4).

As Figures 7.2 and 7.3 show, there was a temporary trade surplus in 1991, before a continued increase in the trade deficit started and rapidly changed the pattern of international trade balances in the world. In 2006 the aggregate current account surplus of emerging market countries rose to $643 billion, to a large degree because of China's growth (Bernanke, 2007: p. 4).

Bernanke claims that the deficit is related to a decline in United States saving since the second part of the 1990s, while investment rates have not been changed much, holding a level of about 19 per cent of US GDP (Bernanke,

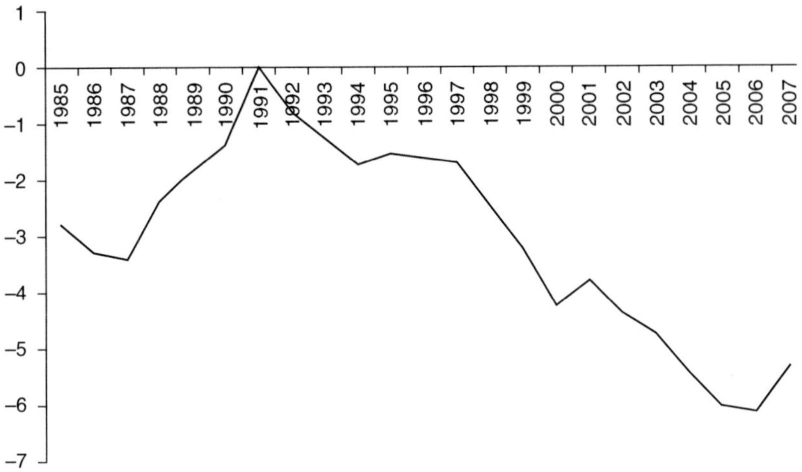

Figure 7.2 US current account balance as percentage of GDP.
See notes for GDP Current Prices (national Currency).

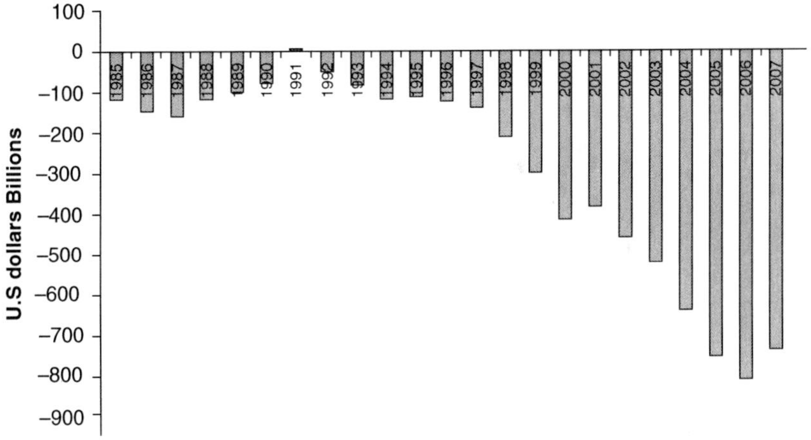

Figure 7.3 USA Current Account Balance. US billion dollar definition, balance on current transactions excluding exceptional financing.
Source: Haver Analytics.

2007: p. 1). But the decline in United States saving is not the cause of the deficit, as will be argued later. The cause of the deficit is rather that the rise in consumption has not been matched by a rise in industrial production or exports, because of under-investment in the industry.

With the large trade deficits in the United States, other countries have been using their saving to finance the American consumption. This is somehow ironic since according to neoclassical economics, the returns to capital are supposed to be lower in industrially developed countries than in developing countries where capital is supposed to be scarce. In reality the returns to capital are highest in emerging markets like China, who invest a lot in their industry, which are generating higher profits. At the same time there was a sustained decline in long-term real interest rates in many parts of the world. This phenomenon, which is closely related to the current financial crisis, is discussed more closely in Section 7.4.

Bernanke points out that 'deficit countries can raise funds in international capital markets only to the extent that other (surplus) countries provide those funds' (Bernanke, 2007). He therefore doesn't find it surprising that the increasing US current account deficit is related to the trade surplus in other countries (ibid.). It is obvious that the high level of imports to the United States is related to a low level of exports, since there is a great trade imbalance between the United States and the rest of the world. However, the global equilibrium view has never been borne out in practice and the international credit system exists to finance trade imbalances and trade in those credits determines exchange rates.

7.3.3 The fiscal deficit in relation to the foreign deficit

While the European Union has restrictions on the level of fiscal deficits, the United States has been running constant deficits on their budget. In September 2008 the level of national debt in the United States was $9,684 trillion, which means $32.000 for each inhabitant in the country, according to the so-called Debt Clock[1] based on statistics from the US Department of the Treasury. As Soros points out, the US budget deficit has been used to finance the current account deficit because the countries with trade surplus have invested their reserves in US bonds (Soros, 2008: pp. 97–98). This way, both the current account and the budget deficits of the US have led to a great expansion of credit (ibid.). China and Japan are today the major foreign holders of treasury securities; accounting for about 47 per cent of the US foreign owned debt.[2] In June 2008 each of these two countries held US treasury securities for over $500 billion (ibid.).

In the past, banks held large quantities of government bonds which they could easily convert into cash at the central bank, which would always stand ready to buy government bonds at a good price. But because of the buying of the US government bonds in the United States, where the Fed and other central banks have bought up some 60 per cent of US government bonds, the commercial banking systems in the United States and elsewhere do not have enough government bonds as secure assets in their portfolios. This is one reason for the current instability in the international financial markets. Another factor that has contributed to the increasing budget deficit is the rise in US military spending in recent years. According to Stiglitz, 'there is a very clear connection between the War in Iraq and the financial crisis we are experiencing now. The war has been fully financed through budget deficit' (quoted in Perelstein, 2008a: p. 1). He claims that the economic problems have not become visible before now because the US government have been stimulating the economy in the short run.

7.4 The US trade deficit and the financial crisis of 2007/2008

7.4.1 The deficit and the US financial markets

As Minsky pointed out back in 1986, success leads to the belief that failures cannot happen, and when a long time has passed since the last financial crisis, people within the financial system believe that it will not happen again, that things are different (quoted in Lim, 2008: p. 7). The US subprime mortgage crisis is an example of how fast a problem in one part of the internationally integrated financial system can be passed on to other parts and affect the real global economy.

The outflows of dollars from the United States, to a great extent reinvested in their country of origin, allowed all asset markets in the United States like the housing market, the stock market, NASDAQ as well as the commodity markets, to recover after the dotcom bubble collapse in 2000. But it also caused inflation in all dollar-denominated asset markets, for example in the housing market, as seen in the previous section. This section deals with a structural feature of the international financial market that allowed this bubble to grow.

The transmission of the US trade deficit to the financial markets goes through the payment mechanism for the US excess export which is paid for by crediting foreign exporters with dollar balances in US bank accounts. When, for example, a Chinese exporter of electronics receives these balances they need to sell their dollars for local currency in order to be able to spend the money at home, for example, to pay their workers, or make new investments. If the demand for local currency, in the case of China the Yuan, is too high, it can appreciate, which is not desirable since it will make Chinese exports more expensive to buy and lead to less demand, for example, from the United States. To prevent an appreciation, the local banking system and the central bank will usually buy the dollar inflow. The dollar credit balances would give low returns if they were put in a US bank account, so they are usually used to buy dollar securities that are issued by the US government, and give a better return. This is what inflates the US securities markets and has led to the buying of all sorts of securities whose risks are unknown, for example the collateralised debt obligations (CDOs) linked to subprime borrowing.

This cycle can be summarised as follows. The United States needs to pay for imports, since it buys more than it sells. US importers pay with dollar balances that are used to buy bonds issued by the US government to finance their budget deficit. This way the budget deficit is used to finance the US current account deficit, and brings an unbalanced economy into temporary equilibrium. The problem occurs when the bubble in the asset markets bursts, not only for the US economy, but also for all the countries that have been dependent on the dollar outflow.

7.4.2 Unbalanced US economic growth

In the case of the US Rogoff points out that 'Despite having one of the lowest savings rates in the industrialised world, the U.S. economy has enjoyed a remarkable period of sustained growth over the past eight years' (Rogoff, 1999: p. 22).

As Figure 7.4 shows, growth between 1996 and 2000 was following the same pattern as US industrial production, while the variables split in the beginning of the new millennium. The US growth in real GDP continued to increase, whereas the level of industrial production declined. One reason for this is that the rise of the US dollar has reduced US competitiveness (Glyn, 2005: p. 8). While the United States was previously a great exporter of industrial goods, it now depends heavily on imports, and growth has been achieved through increased consumption. If consumption declined, it would lead the economy into recession which would be very harmful for the whole economy. In order to keep the US economy out of recession after the dotcom bubble in 2000, interest rates were lowered, and reached a record level of 1 per cent in 2003 (Lim, 2008: p. 8).

The low interest rates were made possible by the access to cheap exports from China with lowered inflation and increasing asset prices in the United States, for example, in the real estate sector. In order to keep the system going, with increased consumption on the cost of the trade balance, combined with the high fiscal deficits of the United States, people had to keep spending money. In other words, the increasing dependence of US economic growth on inflation in asset markets was underpinning consumption, while the growth in insurance banking and financial consultancy was

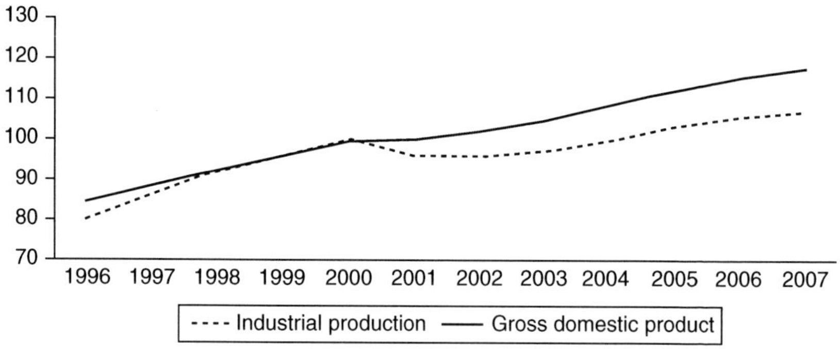

Figure 7.4 GDP and industrial production in USA index 2000 = 100.
Source: OECD Stat.

underpinning employment growth in the United States. As discussed in Section 7.4.1, foreign holders of dollar balances are looking for higher returns for their dollars; they invest in US securities to earn as much money as possible. Toporowski points out that when 'the demand for financial securities exceeds the amount of money that holders and issuers of those securities are prepared to take out of the market, prices rise' (Toporowski, 2009). And, when asset prices go up, the demand for those assets increases, due to a speculative demand from investors wanting to earn money from capital gains (ibid.). But the high demand for securities primarily leads to inflation of equities that do not have an exact agreed price of repayment. In fact, the price level of the CDOs in the subprime mortgage markets was highly unclear, and their presumed value was based on the rating done by US rating agencies. The asset inflation made it possible for people to keep borrowing money against rising housing prices, or selling them with profits (Lim, 2008: p. 9). Toporowski defines the process of inflating capital markets as *financialisation* or a 'major shift in the structure of economic activity towards turning over capital in financial markets' (Toporowski, 2009). It can similarly be argued that the boom in the US housing market is due to the high inflow of credit coming into that market, resulting in rising house prices. By the middle of this decade household consumption in the United States was the main engine of growth accounting for about 33 per cent of its GDP growth (Lim, 2008: p. 9). Much of the additional middle-class spending (ibid.) was financed by debt secured on real estate, and periodically written off when houses were sold at inflated prices. The security markets also recovered after the dotcom bubble burst because of the net credit inflow into the financial markets, which is a result of the US current account deficit financing the buying of US securities. This way, US real GDP growth has become dependent of growth in asset markets, and in this way it is linked to the US deficits in the balance of payments.

7.5 The effect of US deficit on other countries

7.5.1 The balance of payment deficit feeding inflation

When foreign exporters are credited with dollar balances due to the US current account deficit they are used to buy US national debt, financing its fiscal deficit, which has been a central topic in the previous chapters. Consequently, the dollar outflow from the United States has been flooding the international capital markets with American dollars, feeding asset or financial inflation to the rest of the world. Since the owners of the dollar debt are looking for a highest possible return, the situation has encouraged moral hazards, creating a bubble in the US housing market, and eventually an increase in the prices of oil, food and other commodities.

The reason that the dollar-balances are re-invested in the US capital markets is primarily that they have the most developed financial markets in the world, whereas most other countries are not able to invest the foreign capital safely in their own financial systems. It does not mean that there is no need for investment in emerging or developing economies, but rather that the United States has a comparative advantage in banking and finance, making it more profitable to invest there. The problem is that the systemic imbalances in the US economy create a phenomenon which is often referred to as *excess liquidity*. It means that there is more liquidity in the system than is needed, and since the money has to go somewhere they are invested in one asset market after another, inflating them in turn. When the bubble in the subprime mortgage market burst, it was followed by a jump in the prices of oil and food, mostly due to financial speculation via futures contracts. The excess liquidity of the United States can be seen as an example of how consumption in the United States directly affects millions of poor people in the world who suddenly had to deal with huge increases in the price of food and electricity, which they depend on to survive. On the other hand, the US macroeconomic imbalances are also a way of keeping the international economic system stable, as we will see in the following section.

7.5.2 Export-markets and dollar-debt in other countries

The US current account deficit has until now either been considered as unsustainable, like the sceptics argue, or as relatively sustainable and perhaps even beneficial to the growth of the United States, as the monetarists have claimed. However, there has been little focus on the consequences of the trade imbalances for countries in the rest of the world, which is the main focus of this section. If the demand for foreign imports to the US decreased the exporting countries in the rest of the world would suffer. Not only China, but all countries trading with the United States run a current account surplus with the US (Shrik, 2007: p. 27). There is also a continuous demand for the outflow of US dollars because many countries need them to service their dollar-debt.

It is possible to argue that a decline in the value of US dollars would make it easier to pay the debt, since it then will be less in terms of other currencies. But this argument ignores the fact that many countries export commodities priced in dollars in order to be able to pay their debt. According to Muchie, the IMF has demanded that 20–25 per cent of the export earnings, mostly from countries in Africa, should be used to service their debt (2001: p. 1). Boosting export earnings is a way for heavily indebted poor countries to raise money, which can be used to pay off old debt.[3] It is naturally relevant to discuss if it is right that some of the poorest countries in the world should be forced to export, for example, food that their own hungry population could have eaten. However, that is a question of development policies beyond the scope of this chapter.

If the US household sector starts saving more and buying fewer imports, the outflow of dollar will be reduced, and this would alter the per cent order in the world economy, due to the global integration of financial markets. As Bernanke points out, it became easier for many emerging-market countries to pay down their external liabilities and buy assets in developed countries when they became net lenders to the United States (Bernanke, 2007: p. 2). According to Summers the US current account deficit is equivalent to almost 2 per cent of GDP to global aggregate demand (Summers, 2006: p. 4). He points out that a reduction in the US trade deficit would lead to an impulse of contraction to the rest of the global economy, which would happen if goods produced in the United States replaced the export industry of other countries. He therefore argues that the reduction in the US current account deficit must equal the reductions in the surplus in other countries (ibid.). But people in the United States cannot increase their saving without leading the United States into recession, as if reduced expenditure would only affect expenditure on imports to the United States in relation to consumption, which is usually the most stable element of expenditure in the economy, since people normally adjust their savings to finance their current standard of living. One of the few ways in which household consumption can be squeezed is by increasing debt repayments. This is already happening in the United States as a result of the ongoing financial crisis, but there is a limit on how much more an already heavily indebted population is able to increase their payment. The countries that export to the United States will thus be in big trouble if the United States reduces its current account deficit – not primarily because of the danger for a depreciation of the US dollar, as Krugman has warned about, but quite simply because many countries have become dependent on the dollar outflow from the United States.

One can conclude that it is one thing to bring the US economy into equilibrium; but doing so with the world economy as a whole is another matter. There is not much literature on the problem as presented, but the findings in this chapter might be an indication that this field needs further investigation if the problems of the international financial system are to be resolved.

7.6 Conclusion

The United States, as the world's most powerful economy, has used its privileged position to borrow more money than any other country could gain access to, and now holds a historically unprecedented amount of foreign debt.

This chapter applies an original approach to the present situation of financial instability in the United States by showing how it is related to the macroeconomic imbalances and financial inflation in the US economy, and how this transmits instability to other countries.

The arguments presented assert first and foremost that the financial crisis of 2007–2008 is a consequence of the trade deficit in the United States. Due to the large balance of payment imbalances over the last 8 years, the United States has flooded the international capital markets with dollars which have been invested in US asset markets with high returns. A pertinent example is the case of the US housing market. Since demand for these securities was high, prices have inflated, creating a bubble. The growth of the US economy has been sustained by consumption made possible by easy access to credit. Secondly, this chapter has identified key structural features that determine the dynamics of an international financial system dependent on US trade deficits. These include the US dollar as the international reserve currency, the US trade deficit as a way of injecting reserves into the rest of the world financial system and the US provision of government bonds which are risk-free. This shows that the discussion on whether the US trade deficit is sustainable or not is too narrow, since both the monetarists and the sceptics focus little on the consequences of the deficit for the rest of the world. Clearly, the current financial crisis is not caused by frauds in the US financial markets, but results from trade imbalances being resolved in financial markets. But since the world has grown dependent on US deficits to keep up liquid markets and pay external liabilities in US dollars with incomes from exports, the US macroeconomic imbalances cannot be resolved without gravely affecting the rest of the world which now holds large amounts of dollar securities.

Notes

1. US National Debt Clock: http://www.brillig.com/debt_clock/
2. Department of the Treasury: http://www.treas.gov/tic/mfh.txt
3. Third World Network, http://www.twnside.org.sg/title/colo-cn.htm

Bibliography

Bank for International Settlements (BIS) Annual Report 2007, http://www.bis.org/publ/arpdf/ar2007e.pdf?noframes=1.

Bernanke, B. (2007) Speech: 'Global imbalances: recent developments and prospects' At the Bundesbank Lecture, Berlin, Germany. 11 September http://www.federalreserve.gov/newsevents/speech/bernanke20070911a.htm

Bjørklund, I., T. Erikstad, F. Frøyland and M. Ånestad (2008) 'Den grådige gaten' (The Greedy Street), in Dagens Næringsliv (Norwegian Business Daily) 5 April.

Dunn, R.M. and J.H. Mutti (2004) *International Economics* (London and New York: Routledge).

Galbraith, J. (2003) 'The larger international monetary problem' Adapted from a Levy Institute Policy note.

Gilpin, R. (2001) *Global Political Economy. Understanding the International Economic Order* (Princeton and Oxford: Princeton University Press).

Glyn, A. (2005) 'Imbalances of the global economy', *New Left Review*, vol. 34, July/August.

Gosh, A. and U. Ramakrishnan (2006) 'Do current account deficits matter', *Finance and Development*, vol. 43, no. 4.

Griswold, D. (2007) 'Are trade deficits a drag on US economic growth?' Free Trade Bulletin no. 27, 12 March. Published on Cato's Center for Trade Policy Studies, http://www.freetrade.org/node/598/print.

Harvey, D. (2006) *Spaces of Global Capitalism. Towards a Theory of Uneven Geographical Development* (London, New York: Verso).
International Monetary Fund (IMF) World Economic Outlook 2007.
Krugman, P. (2007) 'Will there be a dollar crisis?', *Economic Policy*, July.
Lim M. Mah-Hui (2008) 'Old wine in a new bottle: subprime mortgage crisis – causes and consequences', *Levy Institute of Bard College, Working Paper* No. 532.
Muchie, M. (2001) 'Wanted: a union government', *New African*, December.
Naughton, B. (2007) *The Chinese Economy. Transitions and Growth* (Cambridge, Massachusetts, London, England: The MIT Press).
Obstfeld, M. (1998) 'The global capital market: benefactor or menace', *The Journal of Economic Perspectives*, vol. 12, no. 4.
Perelstein, J. (2008a) 'Krigens økonomiske skygger' (The Economic Shadows of the War). Interview with Joseph Stiglitz on the occasion of the launch of his book The 3 Trillion Dollar War in London. Article in *Morgenbladet* (The Morning Magazine), 29 February–6 March, page 11.
Perelstein, J. (2008b) 'Derfor er finanskrisen poslitiv'(Positive Aspects of the Financial Crisis) Published 5th August, http://e24.no/utenriks/article2573426.ece
Perelstein, J. (2008c) 'Eksport-hopp i USA' (Export Increase in the US) Published 12 August, http://e24.no/utenriks/article2589065.ece
Perelstein, J. (2008d) 'Kina tar balletak på USA' (China Takes the US by the Balls) Published 9 July, http://e24.no/makro-og-politikk/article2525994.ece
Perelstein, J. (2008e) 'Kina vinner OL i finans' (China Win the Olympics in Finance) Published 4 August, http://e24.no/utenriks/article2573197.ece
Perelstein, J. (2008f) 'Oljeland finansierer USA' (Oil Countries Finance the US) Published 14 July, http://e24.no/olje/article2539442.ece
Rogoff, K. (1999) 'International institutions for reducing global financial instability', *The Journal of Economic Perspectives*, vol. 13, no. 4.
Serrano, F. (2003) 'The US Account Deficit under the Floating Dollar Standard' 14 October, http://www.networkideas.org/themes/finance/oct2003/fi14_US_Deficit_FDS.htm
Shirk, S. (2007) *China. Fragile Superpower. How China's Internal Politics Could Derail Its Peaceful Rise* (Oxford: Oxford University Press).
Soros, G. (2008) *The New Paradigm for Financial Markets. The Credit Crisis of 2008 and What it Means* (New York: Public Affairs).
Stark, J. (2006) 'Financial globalisation: Economic Policies in a new Era' Introductory remarks, *Conference on Financial Globalisation and Integration*. Frankfurt am Main, July, http://www.ecb.int/press/key/date/2006/html/sp060717_1.en.html
Stiglitz, J.E. and L. Bilmes (2008) *The 3 Trillion Dollar War* (London: Penguin).
Summers, L.H. (2006) 'Reflections on global account imbalances and emerging markets reserve accumulation' L.K. Jha *Memorial Lecture, Reserve Bank of India*, 24 March, http://www.president.harvard.edu/speeches/2006/0324_rbi.thml
Toporowski, J. (2009) 'The economics and culture of financial inflation', *Competition and Change*, vol. 13, no. 2.
Trichet, J. (2005) 'Reflections on the international financial system' Speech by Jean-Claude Trichet, President of the ECB. Bundesbank Lecture, Berlin 21 June, http://www.ecb.eu/press/key/date/2005/html/sp050621.en.html
Wade, R. (2008) 'The First-World debt crisis: How to Stop Globalisation from Eating Itself' Lecture at SOAS, 22 January.
Wolf, M. (2004) *Why Globalisation Works* (New Haven and London: Yale University Press).

Part II

Minsky and Development

8
Minsky, Financial Structure and Economic Development

Victoria Chick

8.1 Introduction

Hyman Minsky wrote very little on developing and emerging market economies. His theorising arose from his experience of the American economy from the 1950s until his death in 1996. A central question for us is how far his insights can be adapted to transitional and developing economies. We outline Minsky's theory of the role of finance in the functioning of the wider economy, against the background of the earlier theory of Keynes, his primary inspiration, and then address this central question.

All theories come to us from another place or time, or both, so the question of applicability is hardly new or peculiar to Minsky, though it is rarely addressed. Theories are usually put forward as universal, and the structural and behavioural assumptions on which they are based are rarely made explicit.

Minsky's inspirations were Marx, Keynes, Schumpeter and, perhaps surprisingly, Henry Simons. From Marx and Schumpeter he acquired an evolutionary view of the economic system which he so closely observed. From Keynes he understood the uncertainty surrounding decisions and the role of animal spirits in overcoming doubt, and the tendency of financial markets to depart from anything approaching 'real' returns: the 'casino capitalism' of Keynes's (1936) Chapter 12. From Simons he took the point that the banking system was inherently fragile. Simons's solution was to recommend 100 per cent reserve banking, while Minsky believed that the risks of instability were more than counterbalanced by the great flexibility of fractional reserve banking to lend in support of production and investment. In this, like Keynes, he assumed that banks were, from the point of view of the economy, 'functional' (Studart, 1995), that is, their loans supported productive activity. Although he saw the American economy evolve into 'money-manager capitalism', he did not live to see the banking system become a speculative engine which eventually went completely out of control. Since our purpose is to evaluate the applicability of Minsky's theory to other economies, in this essay we will ignore the evolution of banks in the 'first world' from the late 1990s, even though this decision gives the exposition an antiquated air.

The next section will sketch the main outline of Minsky's theory of finance and the economy. We concentrate on the structural relationships that Minsky posits rather than the dynamics, especially the theory of crises, which have been the subject of, for example, Nesvetailova (2007). It is useful to contrast Minsky's framework with Keynes's more familiar analysis. From there we go on to discuss the implications of his framework, first for transition economies and then for developing economies, and then conclude.

8.2 Asset markets and banking: Minsky's innovation

Before Minsky, the relation between banking and the 'real economy' was conceived mainly in terms of the flow of credit creation and its direction. For Keynes, asset markets played their role in determining the rate of interest at which the external financing of investment would be available. It was this external finance, specifically bank lending, which made investment an autonomous variable in his scheme (Chick, 1983: Chapter 9). 'The' rate of interest was determined by liquidity preference, the then very important Bank rate and open market operations. 'The' rate was the whole spectrum of rates, including the rates charged by banks to borrowers. A pure flow understanding of the relations between finance and other agents supposes an equilibrium in which the cash flow from sales is sufficient to pay current wages and other commitments; this is Keynes's 'revolving fund' (Keynes, 1937, p. 247). It is only when the economy is expanding that firms might borrow because their cash flow is insufficient. It is assumed that transactions and precautionary balances are sufficient to cope with stochastic variations in cash flow.

Minsky, by contrast, saw the problem of meeting variations in cash flow as a central problem in firms' management of their resources. This opened up options other than realising precautionary balances, namely, borrowing, either unsecured or against collateral, and issuing new liabilities. In other words, decisions about the whole structure of the balance sheet were involved.

Households also face cash flow problems, though it is more difficult to present these in balance-sheet terms, since households do not issue equity against themselves and their main asset, their human capital, is today, thankfully, totally illiquid.

Beyond this question of cash flow are the matters of financing the acquisition of new capital and adjusting the balance sheet when new plant and equipment are taken on: finance and funding. Minsky considered the balance-sheet implications of financing internally or externally (Minsky, [1975] 2008). For all sorts of reasons assumed away in Modigliani and Miller (1958), this choice matters. If nothing is done when the new capital comes onto the balance sheet, the value of equity will rise and its return will fall, which damages the attractiveness of that firm's equity. Firms must increase their liabilities to match additions to assets; typically they will increase debt, and thus they rely on active markets in such debt – a thriving capital market. This is usually called funding, but Minsky uses the language of the market to express this balance-sheet adjustment:

> The process of selling financial assets or [issuing] liabilities to fulfill cash-payment commitments is called 'position-making' the position being the unit's holdings of assets which, while they earn income, do not possess markets in which they can be readily sold. For corporations the 'position' which has to be financed is the capital assets necessary for production; for financial firms, the 'position' is defined by the assets with poor secondary markets.
>
> (Minsky, [1975] 2008, p. 122)

Poor secondary markets are the hallmark of assets called 'illiquid': such assets cannot be realised at all or only at a sharp reduction in price if they must be sold quickly, or their markets are very volatile, so that the price that can be realised is difficult to forecast. Keynes's definition of a liquid asset is one which is 'more certainly realisable at short notice without loss' (Keynes, 1930, v. 2, p. 67). Thus assets with a short time to maturity are more liquid than those with a longer time to run, and those traded on markets which are, in the old phrase, 'deep, broad and resilient', are more liquid than those whose markets are 'thin', that is, where participants are few and/or trading infrequent, because prices are more stable in broad markets.[1]

The considerations raised by Minsky for enterprises are familiar in the case of banks: traditional banking theory has always been framed in terms of balance sheets. The need for banks to balance earning power with liquidity had long been recognised, especially the need to keep as secondary reserves assets acceptable to the central bank as collateral ('eligible assets' in Britain), mostly government securities. And the need to fund the acquisition of illiquid assets, that is, loans, by means of deposits is a direct parallel to the firm's need to find long-term debt to match its holdings of real capital.[2]

Minsky makes clear that the capacity to borrow against liquid assets or to sell them is as important as income from productive activities in the meeting of cash flow commitments. This is central to the understanding of Minsky. Whereas neoclassical theory concentrates on the generation of income from production and claims on that income, Minsky recognised that the liquidity of balance sheets, rather than the generation of financial surplus, is the precondition of operating as an 'economic unit'. It is through balance-sheet adjustments that the activities of both financial institutions and the 'real economy' of production and consumption are articulated through financial markets. For this, well-functioning markets in financial assets, which make assets liquid, are essential. But stable financial markets cannot be guaranteed: confidence and optimism in these markets generate booms and facilitate productive investment. When confidence ebbs and pessimism takes hold, firms and households concentrate on repaying debt; demand and production fall and investment suffers.

Minsky proposed particular dynamic patterns. Economic booms result in accumulations of debt: 'During a boom the speculative demand for money decreases, and portfolios become more heavily weighted with debt-financed positions.... Households and firms substitute non-money financial assets for money as their liquid reserves' (Minsky, 1975, pp. 123–4).

Minsky then explained financial crisis as follows:

> When the speculative demand for money increases, owing to an increase in the danger seen as arising from liability structures, then firms, households, and financial institutions try to sell or reduce their assets to repay debts. This leads to a fall in the price of assets.... A major objective of business, bankers and financial intermediaries in this situation is to clean up their balance sheets.
>
> (Minsky, 1975, pp. 125–6)

Thus well-developed financial markets are both a blessing and a curse: they allow such situations to develop but also provide a mechanism for their eventual relief, albeit at a cost of increased market volatility and potential loss in the downturn. These mechanisms contribute cyclical instability to a fragility already inherent in the banking system. Minsky acknowledges that the existence of an activist central bank is important for maintaining the stability and liquidity of the system: the 'Big Bank' is needed, first to manage government debt to sustain moderately stable prices and secondly to act as lender of last resort when the banking system as a whole needs liquidity.

8.3 Minsky and economic development

8.3.1 Transition economies

Minsky wrote almost nothing about economies outside the United States. But he did write a short piece on transition economies shortly after the fall of communism (Minsky, 1991), when their financial systems appeared to be a *tabula rasa* with no clear indication of future direction, except towards a market economy. (In fact, the situation was rather more complicated, with a legacy of institutions and financial commitments that imposed certain constraints on the move towards a market economy. See, for example, Chick and Toporowski, 1995; Ruziev and Ghosh, 2009.) Minsky noted the variety of market and financial systems, but defined market economies as 'financial systems in which some personal incomes are derived from the profits made by industry and trade' (pp. 1–2). A common feature of transition economies is that '[b]ecause there is no significant private wealth in the economies emerging from socialism, markets for financial instruments, as well as the potential for market-based financing, are weak' (p. 18). In the light of this, he supposed that '[t]he initial choice of a financial structure is constrained to emphasizing universal banks or public holding companies', while 'special venture capital holding companies, and small, local and independent banks[,] should be part of the financial structure to facilitate the development of entrepreneurships' (ibid.).

In the 1991 paper (p. 11) Minsky sketched the historical evolution of balance sheets. His description of accounts in feudal times (which he calls early capitalism) as inventories of real property bears a striking resemblance to the accounts of enterprises dealing in material balances, though strangely he did not take this insight any further. In the early stage of American capitalism, enterprises, as sole proprietorships or partnerships, were financed by households, and banks lent to households and financed trade, rather than production or investment. It was only with the invention of the joint stock company that markets in equity and long-term corporate debt were developed.

During England's industrial revolution, enterprises and banks developed in a symbiotic way. As in the American experience, the development of joint stock ownership and limited liability were crucial to the emergence of capitalism as we know it today. There was, however, one important difference: that a secondary market for government securities had developed rapidly after the institution of a national debt, and the foundation of the Bank of England to manage it, in 1694. This pre-dated the main onset of industrialisation and provided the banks, both the London banks mainly financing commerce and the country banks financing industry, with a ready source of liquid assets. The markets in long-term corporate debt and equity, needed after the invention of joint stock ownership, thus had a model, and the habit of trading in secondary instruments was already established.

Banks already existed in planned economies,[3] but the job of the banks was to ensure that material balances were transferred to enterprises according to the plan and to provide a vehicle for the population's meagre savings. They performed few of the activities that characterised Western banks in the days of their functionality: the evaluation of potential borrowers and their projects, monitoring of payments, risk management and liquidity control. There was also little need for the balance sheets that we associate with the modern corporation and thus no need for the financial counterparts to capital that we call 'funding' and Minsky calls 'making position'. It is actually quite a long road from the institutional set-up inherited from planning to a full understanding of the role of financial institutions and markets in a market system. In Britain the evolution of the modern system took a good 200 years; in America the process was a few decades quicker. The transition economies have not the luxury of working out their system in an evolutionary way.

History suggests that it is more difficult to establish capital markets than banks. Thus Minsky looks to universal banks of the German type or to public holding companies as the solution to finding holders of corporate liabilities. (Universal banking was itself a response to the collapse of financial markets after the German hyperinflation of the 1920s.) He preferred the holding company option, in which a government-sponsored institution takes up the liabilities of firms, as this could be seen as a temporary arrangement which could be wound up as markets develop, but this has nowhere been taken up, possibly because the Western advisers had not experienced this possibility; it was last used as part of Roosevelt's New Deal.

The advisers, indeed, had little of Minsky's sophisticated knowledge of the importance of institutions: rather, they had a naive faith in 'markets' to solve problems automatically. But the markets did not exist. Nor did such institutions that did exist have much idea of their role in the new system: for example, in 1995, the balance sheets of Polish banks were dominated by interbank loans. Clearly they were not 'functional' (Chick and Toporowski, 1995). Later, Polish banking, and much of the banking systems in other East European transition economies, were largely taken over by international banks.

Monetary policy has not been particularly helpful to institution-building. Rather than fostering the smooth functioning of government securities markets to provide the banks with liquid assets, their attention has focused on implementing various stand-by agreements of the International Monetary Fund (see, for example, Gabor, 2009). These typically are concerned with inflation and macroeconomic stabilisation policies based on the Washington Consensus, rather than addressing the need to promote the development of appropriate institutions.

8.3.2 Developing countries

It is easy to exaggerate the differences between the developing and transition economies. Although developing economies have the possibility of a gradual adaptation of their institutions, the transition economies have been moving towards market economies for 20 years now, long enough to show individual characteristics, which various authors in this volume will deal with. But the history of economic development has concentrated on industrialisation, while the transition countries had plenty of industry, albeit inefficient and environmentally disastrous.

The chief perceived difficulties in most developing countries are, usually, finding a source of financing and funding industry and dealing with the instabilities of agricultural income. These have, in many cases, been catered for by specialist, state-sponsored development and agricultural banks. Development banks typically provide funding as well as financing of manufacturing, in the mode of universal banks. While these have supported industrialisation well, they can also cause havoc with the public sector budget, since these banks may have to sustain loans for an extensive period of time before repayments begin to appear. Their loans are not liquid, as there is no market for this type of debt in these countries. And the market for government securities is underdeveloped as well.

Private-sector banks too are faced with the absence of well-functioning markets for government debt, and in many countries they are, in addition, hampered in their development by an essentially cash economy. It is only when the majority of payments flow through the banking system that banks have the power to extend lending to a multiple of their cash reserves, and only then do they finance expenditure (particularly, investment) independently of prior saving (Chick, 1986).[4] Even if they could, loans to the productive sector in developing countries are seen as much more risky than similar loans in developed countries. Before banking has reached this stage of development, independence from saving does not hold, and a developing country is typically short of savings. Nor is saving channelled effectively: the lack of good second-hand markets for most securities means that saving is often diverted to unproductive uses (for example, gold). The banks tend to cater for the needs of only the most developed sectors of the economy and the richest households.[5] A variety of institutions has grown up to compensate for this, such as mutual societies, credit unions and micro-credit lenders. While these make a valuable contribution, they do not bulk large in the main scheme of development.

In recent years, in both the developing and the transitional economies, international banks have entered the field. These have the advantage of access to international capital markets. Their host countries no longer have to mobilise savings at home but can rely on the vast pool not only of savings but also of liquidity available in the developed world. This, however, is double-edged. Given the perceived riskiness of investment projects in these countries, it is as likely that international banks would siphon off funds from the developing countries for use in the 'first world'. At the very least, they are likely to approve loan applications which will give rise to products benefiting the first world – *dependencia* by financial means (Chick and Dow, 1988). And, depending on the way the loans are made and the vehicles these banks use for making position, the country may be exposed to foreign exchange risk.

8.4 Financial under-development

In the context of Minsky's analysis, developing and transitional economies are identified not so much by their lack of industrial infrastructure, but by the absence of well-functioning markets for financial assets and an underdeveloped banking system. The result of the former is that there are only limited markets for the financial-liability counterparts of productive capital. Those financial liabilities are assets for financial intermediaries and for households holding claims against those liabilities, claims such as bank deposits or insurance policies. This absence of financial liabilities/assets has two further consequences for the financial systems of emerging and transitional economies. In the first place, the possibilities for creating credit against the security of financial assets are correspondingly reduced if the range and value of those assets is restricted. This makes banking less efficient because credit has to be advanced more against prospective future income, rather than against collateral. Prospective future income from business activities is always going to be more uncertain than the value of collateral.

A second consequence of having a limited range and value of financial assets is that credit flows into the markets for financial assets have a restricted choice of assets, and those assets are correspondingly more prone to inflation of their values. This makes financial asset markets in emerging and transitional economies into better vehicles for speculation than for financing productive activities. If restrictions on inflows of foreign capital are removed, then these markets may become even more speculative.

A third consequence is that the promotion of privatisation may well result in the sale of state companies to foreign multinationals. This reinforces the financial backwardness of these economies by locating abroad the financial-liability counterparts of productive assets in those countries (Chick and Toporowski, 1995).

The structural limitations of banking, the limited scope for lending against collateral, the lack of breadth and depth of financial markets and their consequently very speculative character make the financial systems of emerging and transitional economies less 'functional' for development activities. As a matter of empirical observation, these features reproduce in emerging and transitional economies the instabilities that Keynes identified in the capital markets of the considerably more sophisticated financial systems of the United Kingdom and United States.

8.5 Conclusion

There is a whiff of complacency in Minsky's analysis: he thought that the financial system of the United States was something to aspire to. Perhaps his analysis also serves as a warning, especially considering what has happened to 'first world' finance since Minsky's death. The attempt to introduce financial complexity too soon can have unwelcome consequences: for example, opening an equity market in the context of a limited range of saving opportunities, where most people hold low-yielding bank deposits, can spark off a flurry of speculation, as it did in Brazil in the late 1980s. To encourage money-manager capitalism, as Minsky did in his 1991 paper, is to send transitional and developing economies down a road which Keynes warned would be even less stable than one characterised by private, individual speculation. And lurking around the corner, if the developed world is anything to go by, is the culture of takeover bids and the generation of paper wealth by financial manipulation. As for the transformation of banks into vehicles for originating and passing on loans, taking no responsibility for either the credit-worthiness of the borrower or his or her subsequent performance, we have seen that not all forms of financial development are healthy and beneficial.

While the concepts of Keynes's and Minsky's analyses have widespread application, the appearance in market economies of similar economic variables should not be taken to mean similar economic and financing structures. As banking and financial systems in emerging and transition economies evolve they may approach the degree of sophistication and what we now know to be the vulnerability of financial systems in the most financially 'advanced' economies. But until they reach that stage, the limited scope of banking and financial asset markets in developing and transition countries will always give a distinctive character to the problems of growth and development, and to the crises, experienced by those countries.

8.6 Acknowledgements

I wish to thank Jan Toporowski for his helpful contributions, without implicating him in the result.

Notes

1. It will be seen that we have resisted the current trend to speak of liquid markets, although it is properties of markets that make assets liquid.
2. The flow concept of banking does not see deposits this way, but rather as a source of money which the banks then lend. This is not at all what banks do: banks do not lend money; they guarantee the expenditures of those who make a borrowing agreement (in the United Kingdom, an overdraft agreement) with them. (In a loan system, they manufacture the deposit out of which the borrower spends.)
3. He commented that 'the so-called planned economies were not in any serious sense planned' (p. 1, n. 1), for they ignored the interdependence between production and consumption and acted to the detriment of labour and the environment.
4. Readers will recognise this ability as the foundation of Keynes's reversal of the classical causality between saving and investment.
5. This is most obvious in South Africa, where a 'first-world' economy coexists with a third-world economy. There is almost no contact between the two, certainly not through the banks, which are developed to a first-world standard but which would prefer to have no dealings whatever with the third world in their midst.

References

Chick, V. (1983) *Macroeconomics after Keynes: A Reconsideration of the General Theory* (Cambridge, Mass.: MIT Press).

Chick, V. (1986) 'The evolution of the banking system and the theory of saving, investment and interest', Economies et societes, Cahiers de l'ISMEA, Serie 'Monnaie et Production', no. 3: 111–126. Reprinted in M. Musella and C. Panico, Eds (1995) *The Money Supply in the Economic Process: A Post Keynesian Perspective* (Aldershot:

Edward Elgar) and in P. Arestis and S.C. Dow, Eds (1992) *On Money, Method and Keynes: Selected Essays by Victoria Chick* (London: Macmillan/New York: St Martin's Press).

Chick, V. and Dow, S.C. (1988) 'A post Keynesian perspective on the relation between banking and regional development', *Thames Papers in Political Economy*, Spring: 1–22. Reprinted in P. Arestis, Ed. (1988) *Post Keynesian Monetary Economics: New Approaches to Financial Modelling* (Aldershot: Edward Elgar), pp. 219–250.

Chick, V. and Toporowski, J. (1995) 'Evolution and sudden transition in banking: the Polish case considered', *Research Papers in International Business*, vol. 29 (London: South Bank University).

Gabor, D.V. (2009) Monetary Policy Processes in Post Communist Romania, PhD Thesis, University of Stirling. Forthcoming, as *Central Banking and Financialization: A Romanian Account of how Eastern Europe became Subprime* (London: Palgrave Macmillan).

Keynes, J.M. (1930) *A Treatise on Money*, 2 vols (London: Macmillan).

Keynes, J.M. (1936) *The General Theory of Employment Interest and Money* (London: Macmillan).

Keynes, J.M. (1937) 'Alternative theories of the rate of interest', *Economic Journal*, vol. 47.

Minsky, H.P. ([1975] 2008) *John Maynard Keynes* (New York: Columbia University Press). Republished, 2008, by McGraw-Hill Professional.

Minsky, H.P. (1991) 'The transition to market economy: financial options' Working Paper No. 66 (New York: The Levy Economics Institute of Bard College).

Modigliani, F. and Miller, M.H. (1958) 'The cost of capital, corporate finance and the theory of investment', *American Economic Review*, vol. 48.

Nesvetailova, A. (2007) *Fragile Finance: Debt, Speculation and Crisis in the Age of Global Credit* (London: Palgrave).

Ruziev, K. and Ghosh, D. (2009) 'Banking sector development in Uzbekistan: a case of mixed blessings', *Problems of Economic Transition*, vol. 52, no. 2.

Studart, R. (1995) *Investment Finance in Economic Development* (London: Routledge).

9

Minsky's Financial Instability Hypothesis in the New Financial Institutional Framework: What are the Lessons for Developing Countries?

Noemi Levy-Orlik

9.1 Introduction

The importance of financial instability and the revival of financial (and monetary) variables in the understanding of economic cycles are crucial elements of Hyman Minsky's theoretical legacy. The vehemence of Minsky discussions and the harsh critique to the Neoclassical Synthesis (Minsky, 1975) contributed to the revival of John Maynard Keynes' revolutionary and novel contributions, rescuing them from the partial attempt of John Hicks (1937) to corner 'The General Theory'. Minsky was among the founders of a new school of thought (post-Keynesian) that brought back the discussion of financial and economic instability, without indulging in apologetic defence of the capitalist system.

Following Irving Fisher (1933), who was a privileged (although unlucky) witness of the 1929 economic crisis, Minsky borrowed the concept of debt deflation and the changing behaviour of firms' financial structure through the economic cycle. Following the tradition of Joseph Schumpeter and Keynes, for whom money depends upon institutional arrangements, he rejected the neoclassical village fair image of capitalism, which relegates money to a mean of exchange that is exogenously determined and, more important, is neutral in terms of income, making credit demand supply determined.[1] Although Minsky did most of his theoretical thinking and writings in the capitalist golden age (the Financial Instability Hypothesis – FIH was put forward in the early 1970s) he was able to foresee that the capitalist system is a chain of economic stages that go from boom stages to economic stagnation. The latter took place first in developing countries (1980s and 1990s), shaking developed economies in 2008.[2] According to many observers, these cycles resembles Minsky's financial crisis analysis (see Kregel, 2008 and Davidson, 2008 for a critical assessment of this view).

This chapter revises critically the FIH concept taking into consideration the new financial institutions that modified economic units' financial relations as a result of the demise of the Bretton Woods system. The different stages of the business cycles are due to changes of investment expenditure resulted from modifications of income distributional variables (that is, interest rates) in which the Minsky FIH causation (from financial innovation, lower interest rates, higher investment spending and economic growth to higher leverage rates, higher interest rates and economic recessions) does not hold. Following Jan Toporowski's financial inflation theory (2000), this chapter argues that, in terms of the new financial settings, financial inflation is due to speculative activities, undermining investment spending and increasing consumption ratios, till the financial bubble bursts.

The main distinctiveness of developing countries financial inflation and deflation is their relation with external capital movements that, despite low investment expenditures, had relatively low impacts on consumption. Thereby the Latin American industrial recession of the 1980s was partially reversed by the globalisation of the capital markets that attracted external capital inflows, inflating stock index prices and overvaluing domestic currencies, generating mild economic recoveries; however, this was followed by deep external capital outflows that induced financial crises and deep economic stagnations (Tequila, Samba and the Argentinean crises). The new financial settings were fully imposed in the region around the year 2000, and were followed by a period of increased economic activity, strongly based on exports and capital inflows (foreign direct investment and foreign portfolio investment). This trend was stopped by the 2008 subprime crisis, which again reversed external capital inflows, inducing foreign exchange devaluations, reducing external demand.

The FIH is discussed in the first section of this chapter, highlighting its strengths and weaknesses; followed by an analysis of the Bretton Woods and the deregulated and globalised financial relation and economic activity in the second section. In the third section, developing economies growth is analysed in terms of the new financial settings. Finally, the main conclusions are put forward.

9.2 Minsky's financial instability hypothesis and the business cycle

Minsky maintained that 'the deeper cause of business cycles in an economy with the financial institutions of capitalism is the instability of portfolio and financial interrelations' (1975: p. 57). Right in the centre of the discussion 'the relations between investment and finance, and uncertainty, are the keys to understanding' (p. 60) the full significance of his contribution. He argued that 'each state whether [it] is the boom, crisis, debt, deflation, stagnation, or expansion, is transitory' (p. 61) since each carries 'the seeds of its own destruction' (ibid.). Consequently, Minsky showed that the capitalist system is structurally unstable due to changing enterprise financial structure that links past and present and determines future economic activity, making instability an endogenous phenomenon. Thus, uncertainty is linked to expected economic changes that, in turn, affect economic unit financial portfolios, which destabilise income. It should be highlighted that by not linking his analysis of uncertainty to speculative demand ('forecasting the psychology of the market', Keynes, 1936: p. 158) in terms of interest rates future variations, he dismissed Keynes' liquidity preference theory.[3]

Uncertainty modifies corporation balance sheet structures, since asset and liabilities 'set up cash receipts or expenditures over some fixed or variable future time period. In today's language... [they] set up a dated sequence of anticipated cash flows [which] differ in the nature of the cash... [that] may be dated, demand or contingent; they may be unconditional or may depend upon the functioning of the economy, they may be associated with owing or using an asset, or with the purchase or sale of an asset' (Minsky, 1975: p. 70).

In his analysis there are two prices (see also Chapter 5), which are the investment (or supply) and capital (or demand) prices, explained in terms of micro relations between investment, financial variables and business cycles. The supply price (P_I) initially considered to be determined by income flows from sales minus costs, therefore related to real variables (productive costs), with an upward slope curve, based in diminishing returns (Minsky, 1972, cited in Lavoie and Secarrecia, 2001); which afterwards was replaced by financial cost, reflecting the lenders' increasing risk (Minsky, 1975: pp. 106–113).[4] These costs are independent of the workings of the economy, determined by lenders (for example, banks) and are explicit in credit contracts, appearing only when corporations demand external finance. The underlying assumption is that corporations may not honour their debt commitments as a result of higher debt ratios.

In short, financial costs of P_I are explained in terms of: (a) banks' (lenders') evaluation of borrowers whose cost is depicted by an upward discontinuity curve of the P_I; (b) the lender risk shown by the upward increasing portion of the P_I curve rate, constructed on the assumption that interest rates vary according to the credit volume and (c) an additional marginal lender risk, assuming that contractual debt rises as interest rates increase, (ibid., 110), reflecting the changing financial structures that corporations face throughout the business cycle.

The demand price (P_K) reflects assets' future income flows. It changes according to market expectations (that is, they are conditional to the working of the economy), as the discount rate is an important element containing

Kalecki's borrowers' increasing cost. It is a subjective price, not written anywhere (only in the borrower's mind), highly dependent on the workings of the economy. Therefore, P_K can be modified by cash flows from asset sales (Minsky, 1975) and depends on asset price movements that in turn are affected by corporations leverage ratio, secondary market deepness and interest rate movements.

So far the relation between investment, financial variables and the business cycles is held at a micro level, with differing P_K and P_I among economic units that depend on the corporation sizes (Kalecki's increasing risk concept) as well as leverage rate and interest rate. However, Minsky applies these concepts at a macro level with the assumption that internal funds are given (or constant) and determined in previous periods. Lavoie and Secarrecia (2001) and Toporowski (2000) correctly assert that Minsky's analysis only holds in short periods, at micro levels, and cannot be transferred automatically to macro levels and long periods, since the analysis assumes that internal funds remain unchanged. But when investment spending rises so too do income and profits which, in turn, increase internal funds. It should be stressed that even though Minsky was aware that investment affects profits and internal returns (Minsky, 1975: pp. 113–116) he maintained the argument that higher investment spending leads to increasing leverage ratio, claiming that each state contains 'the seeds of its own destruction'.

A second important argument of Minsky's FIH is the corporations' financial structures. The starting point is that higher level of investment spending requires increasing credits, provided by commercial bank financial innovations at reduced interest rate. Over the course of the business cycle, banks' security margin diminishes, since borrowers are supposed to require extra-financing to cover the first year capital amortisation (speculative structure) and the first year interest payments (Ponzi structure). Thus, commercial banks raise the credit interest rates and diminish credit issuance. The main assumption of this argument is that commercial banks' liquidity is constrained and bank credit is interest rate elastic. Furthermore, central banks are supposed to act mainly as lenders of last resort and higher liquidity is related to inflation, neutralised by higher interest rates.

According to Minsky, non-financial corporations confront changing financial costs over the business cycles. Initially (at the boom stage) lenders risk is low, investment spending and, especially, credit go up, inducing higher leverage rates (internal funds are constant). Banks' uncertainty rises along with financing costs (since banks' liquidity is constrained) making it more difficult to cover previous debt commitments; corporations sell financial assets (to obtain liquidity and meet previous payment), asset prices fall, precipitating what Fisher (1933) labelled as asset price deflation, which set off corporate bankruptcies. The magnitude of the financial (and economic) crisis depends on the dominant corporation financial structure (see also Chapter 18).

From the above discussion two important issues emerge. The FIH is the result of increasing investment spending under conditions of unchanged internal funds; and the interest rate is endogenously determined.

9.3 Bretton Woods, deregulation, globalised periods and economic growth

In this section two arguments are considered. First, investment creates its own finance under conditions of limited capital mobility and, second, financial inflation reduces investment growth and prevents economic downturns through increasing consumption.

9.3.1 Kalecki's and Steindl's investment function

One of the main arguments of the post-Keynesian theory, including Kalecki's and Steindl's views (Toporowski, 2009), is that investment spending is financed through its profits, which constitute the firms' internal finance (or savings); hence higher investment spend is followed by higher income, profits and internal returns (due to the income multiplier). If banks accommodate the demand of increased liquidity for production purposes and interest rates remain constant there is no cause for financial instability to emerge.[5] Conversely, a reduction of investment sparks-off financial instability since profits and firms' internal funds are reduced, neutralised by increasing external finance to cancel out previous debt commitment and lowering effective demand. It should be noticed that Minsky's FIH causation is reversed since higher credits are caused by reduced investment spending that increases non-firm savings, reducing internal funds. The arguments can be formalised as follows:[6]

$$\text{Profits} = f(I) \tag{1}$$

Profits are constituted by non-distributed returns (NdR), which are also the firm's internal funds (IF), and distributed returns (dR). NdR can be divided among entrepreneurs' accumulation (EB) and depreciation D_P, while distributed returns represent the bulk of interest (II) assuming that firm external finance comes from bank lending, so that bonds and securities trade is negligible. Thereby the profits equation can be written as follow:

$$\text{Profits} = \text{NdR} + \text{dR} = \text{IF} + \text{II} = \text{EB} + \text{D}_\text{p} + \text{II} \tag{2}$$

If D_P is constant, internal funds are positively related to entrepreneurs' accumulation and negatively to interest rate

$$\text{IF} = f(\text{EB}, i) \tag{3}$$

Re-writing equation (2) in terms of IF determinants and considering equation (3), the rate of change of internal funds (if) can be expressed as follows:

$$\dot{\text{if}} = f(\underset{+}{\dot{\text{eb}}}, \underset{-}{i}) \tag{4}$$

eb is the rate of entrepreneur benefit, *i* is interest rate and the dot stands for the rate of growth.

Equation (4) shows that changes of internal funds are positively affected by the entrepreneurial benefit rate, which depends on past investment, and is related negatively to changes of interest rates, being no direct link between credits, investment and changes of interest rates. Consequently, Minsky's argument that the rate of interest is determined endogenously is also rejected, since investment is mostly financed by internal returns.

Thus, economic instability is derived from lower internal funds, caused by past lower investment spending and/or higher interest rates, creating a change in composition between non-distributed and distributed returns that reduces effective demand. Therefore, there is no reason why commercial banks should increase interest rates during boom periods since there are no grounds for debt increasing (leverage rates) when income rises. Additionally, if investment spending is above internal funds, profit are expected to rise in future periods, thereby debt repayments are guaranteed; finally, higher commercial bank credits issuance does not lead to balance sheet disequilibria because central banks provide all the necessary liquidity at constant interest rates.

9.3.2 Financial market inflation: The new conditions for economic growth

Toporowski (2009) argues that the economic growth engine in the *financialisation* era relies on consumption rather than investment spending, creating a paradoxical situation. On the basis of Kalecki's and Steindl's argument, Toporowski decomposes total savings into household – rentier and middle class distributed profits – and firms' saving (non-distributed profits). The former is defined as the residual income of households that is not consumed which is inelastic to changes in national income. Firms' savings are equal to investment spending minus household saving, and are income elastic.

Considering the above relation, Toporowski asserts that if investment falls below household savings, firms' savings shrink, reducing investment spending further. Firms become indebted (higher leverage rate) turning household saving into a threshold that investment spending must exceed if a financial deficit in the business sector is to be avoided. As a result, industrial recession emerges with no neutralising effects. Saving at all times equals investment. But the factor which equalises them in practice is not the rate of interest, as most text-books teach, but the net retained profits or financial deficit of the business sector. Hence, the increasing participation of financial gains (distributed profits or household savings) reduces effective demand and economic growth.

However, the new financial settings soften the downward stage of the business cycles through financial inflation (defined as excess demand for new securities). Security prices rise when demand for financial securities exceeds the amount of money that holders and issuers of those securities are prepared to take out of the market. A fall in household savings reduces the investment spending threshold. As a consequence of financial inflation, liquidity increases as well as financial gains, deterring investment spending, with a neutralising effect that comes from higher consumption, financed by households' credits and households' financial portfolio wealth effect.

Overcapitalisation of non-financial corporation is the main effect of financial market inflation. Enterprises with excess liquidity direct these resources to acquisitions and mergers instead of financing investment spending or productive activities. Consequently, corporations' excess capital is used to restructure the balance sheet (buying and selling financial assets; issuing new securities and repaying liabilities). Furthermore, non-financial sector corporations modify their internal organisation, making *financialisation* the most important source of their returns (even corporative managers are partially remunerated in securities). It needs to be highlighted that overcapitalisation is not used for ex-ante financing of investment (although corporation credit demand diminishes).[7]

Thus, corporations face larger financial market exposures since they hold more liquid assets. Additionally, as the issue of shares rises, although investment shrinks, corporations' treasury departments become the most important department in the internal corporate structure.

Moreover, industrial countries' financial inflation leads to increased capital movements (especially in the international financial market) promoting worldwide capital market development, extracting financial gains from developing financial markets. Throughout the world financial market (developed and developing markets), there has been a diversification of financial institutions (institutional investor, pension funds, investment banks and so on), increasing in number and adopting financial innovation methods, mainly derivatives and securitisation techniques. These new financial organisations demand more financial instruments, creating an ongoing financial inflation, which is the basis of further securitisation and derivative activities. Kregel (2008) argues that securitisation enables commercial banks to be made illiquid and transpose liquid assets distributing them throughout the financial system, with a limited effect on production, since most bank credits are unrelated to investment or productive activities. Bank credit is mainly used to finance consumption (that is, to realise production therefore increase profits) or finance speculation (buying and selling assets or securities such as derivatives).

These institutional changes modify corporations' balance sheet structures. On the asset side, bonds, derivatives and securities increase and bank credit diminishes replaced by holding of liquid asset; while on the liabilities side liquidity needs declined (see Kregel, 2008). Additionally, commercial bank credits for investment spending and production reduces, since most of their finance came from internal funds and eventually from bonds and share issuance. Banks increase household credits, which include finance for housing (mortgages) and, especially, for final goods (durable and non-durable) and for speculation.

In recent years, creditworthiness became less important and was replaced by probabilistic models of credit rating agencies that through algorithms determine the amount of finance that each borrower should be granted. In this context, commercial banks' financial returns became increasingly dependent on fees and commissions, displacing interest rate margins. In this process, undue payments seem to be unimportant since credit risk was passed on to other financial institutions (banks and non-banks) so long as financial prices rose and undue payments remained below certain margin. The commercial bank 'seeks to maximise its fees and commissions income from originating assets, managing those assets in off balance-sheet affiliate structures, underwriting the primary distribution of securities collateralised with those assets, and servicing them' (Kregel, 2008: p. 11). Therefore, the financial system became highly unstable since they issued credit to non-reliable agents; and once undue payment augmented, financial corporations (including commercial banks) went bankrupt. Guttman and Philon (2008) refer to new mortgage products, such as piggy-back loans, which covered down-payments requirement, Alt-A, which are loans that carried higher rates in return for relaxing income verification and other requirements for creditworthiness proofs and subprimes credits, channelled to low income borrowers (NINJA, no income, no jobs and assets). Thereby financial innovation induced higher debts. Once the financial bubble burst (September 2008) asset prices reversed, bringing on financial deflation and industrial recession.

Therefore, in the *financialisation* era household savings (of rentiers and middle classes) went down and even became negative, increasing household liabilities since they were able to borrow against the increasing capital values of their assets. As the result of this process, consumption and housing demand soared, facilitating the realisation of profits and stopping effective demand from falling. In this context Toporowski argues that 'Industrial crises no longer play an important part in bringing economic booms to an end. Such crises are largely eliminated by over-capitalisation, which increases the liquidity of large companies and thus makes it easier [for] them to maintain payments on their commitments'.

The main problem of this financial arrangement is that an ongoing process of financial inflation is required, entailing securities demand in excess.

The upper limit of this process is reached once the financial bubble bursts, unleashing a reduction of income through the wealth effect, which reduces house asset prices and effective demand; employment falls and borrowers are unable to pay debt commitments, house prices go down, non-bank financial institutions and banks bankrupt, finance is disrupted, resulting in an industrial recession.

9.4 Developing economies performance under the new financial settings

The most striking feature of the new financial settings is the behaviour of stock index prices. The representative price index of the US capital market is considered to be the Standard & Poor index price of the 500 most important corporations (US S&P-500) increased almost six times between 1987 (the last major world-wide stock exchange crisis) and 2006; while the Latin American and Caribbean (LA&C) Standard & Poor index price (in terms of the US dollar) rose almost 24 times, with an average value of 695, higher than the US S&P-500 that reached 490. The highest S&P index rises were Chile, Mexico and Argentina. This may be explained in terms of the financial globalisation (of the late 1980s).

In terms of financial inflation (change of corporation price indexes) the LA&C S&P index price doubled the US S&P-500. The leading markets were Brazil, Mexico and Argentina; while the Chilean market showed the lowest average price rise, explained by the tax imposed on external capital movement during the 1990s to deter capital outflows.

In terms of the market capitalisation (of the listed companies in relation to GDP) the US market is substantially larger and deeper than the LA&C market (110.1 per cent and 26.7 per cent, correspondingly), while Chile is biggest in the LA&C region, followed (with big gaps) by Mexico, Brazil and Argentina. The US capital market fortress is based on a high stock market turnover and a huge number of listed companies. The Chilean market capitalisation (the biggest in the region) has the highest stock price index, which is highly dependent of external capital movement inflows, with outflows deterrents till 1998; while Mexico (the second widest capital market) is distinguished by the highest turnover and Brazil (third in size) has the largest number of listed companies, as well high stock turnover movements.

From the above data it can be concluded that although LA&C S&P index prices increased above the US S&P-500, the operations of those markets have not achieved maturity, with financial speculation (especially from external capital inflow) a central element of the increased activity of this financial segment. The remaining bank-based system is the strongest financial structure of the region.

Minsky's argument that financial inflation is derived from higher investment expenditure (and higher economic growth) is not valid for the biggest

LA&C countries. This conclusion becomes stronger when the productive sector is analysed.

The average LA&C annual economic growth rate is lower than the previous period (characterised by industrialisation on the basis of import substitution, see Levy, 2008). In the 1987–2006 period, the LA&C big economies, with the exception of Chile, showed average economic growth values below 3 per cent (Chile showed an average value of 5.9 per cent).[8] The standard deviation of the LA&C region doubled US economic growth, which reflects the deep economic recessions of the region (for example, Tequila, 1994; Samba, 1998; Argentina, 2001). Mexico had a negative growth of 6.2 per cent in 1995; the Brazilian economy did not grow between 1988 and 1999 and Argentina had a negative growth rate between 1999 and 2001, reaching −10.9 in 2001). It is important to highlight that the causation movement went from external capital inflows, higher bank credits, high capital market index prices, higher stock turnover movements (Mexico and Brazil) and economic growth rates to external capital outflows, financial deflation and exchange rate devaluation and economic recession.

In addition, the economic structure modified. The US economy showed higher consumption ratio (in terms of GDP), with a minimum value of 83 per cent and a maximum of 87 per cent. The LA&C economies also experienced a rise in the consumption ratio (with the exception of Chile) which started from lower levels, reducing the gap in relation to the US economy. It is important to note that Brazil and Mexico during their crisis periods did not experience any drastic reduction in the ratio of consumption to GDP; while Argentina showed a drastic decline (from 84.5 per cent (2001) to 73 per cent in 2002, not followed by a reversal trend till 2007). Chile was the big exception, with a consumption ratio mean of 73 per cent and maximum and minimum value of 65.1 per cent and 76.8 per cent, correspondingly, albeit the capital market strengthening.

Gross fixed domestic capital formation as a ratio of GDP in the United States, Mexico, Argentina and Brazil taken together, oscillated between 18 per cent and 20 per cent, while Chile's average value was 22.5 per cent. The particular feature of the investment coefficient was that capital market booms (and stock index prices) did not induce noticeable rises, but the investment coefficient dropped immediately after financial crises (the Mexican investment coefficient between 1994 and 1995 went from 20 per cent to 18 per cent; the Brazilian dropped from 17 per cent to 15.6 per cent between 1988 and 1999; in Argentina it fell from 14.2 per cent to 12 per cent, between 2001 and 2002, and in Chile, between 1981 and 1982, it dropped from 19 per cent to 14 per cent). It should be stressed that this behaviour is linked to exchange rate devaluations due to external capital outflows (and financial crises) rather than stock index prices falls.

Finally, the most peculiar production structure adjustment took place in the external sector; soaring exports, reaching historic levels, above the USA economy. The Primary Export model (of the late nineteenth century and beginning of the twentieth century) reappeared, this time based on manufacture goods and services rather than on primary products, transferring the productive economic engine to the external market, with three major shortcomings. First, the domestic economic engine ceased to be in control of national policies; second and, most importantly, prices of export goods and services although from more technologically advanced sectors were determined by industrial economies or transnational corporations with overvalued domestic currencies (hence trade induced income losses, see ECLAC argument of terms of trade losses); and finally, the exports surge came along with commercial deficits (especially in the Mexican economy).

A final issue is the relation between the coefficients of investment and credit (investment/GDP and credits/GDP) and the stock index prices changes showing two different behavioural patterns. In the US economy, between 1987 and 2006, there is a strong correlation between the investment and bank-credit coefficients, completely independent of the US S&P-500 movement. It can be concluded that stock index prices are not strongly related to productive decisions. However, the relations of these three variables in the LA&C region (credit coefficients here are not directly available and the calculation here is the average credit ratio of the four biggest countries – Argentina, Brazil, Chile and Mexico) show important links between the stock index prices movement and the investment ratio, being relatively independent of the credit coefficient. This can be explained in terms of the strong links between stocks prices and exchange rate movements (both variables are highly influenced by external capital movements), and the independent relation between banks credits and investment.

The above observations provide evidence that Minsky's financial instability hypothesis causation does not hold in capitalist economies. In financially advanced countries there is no relation between stock prices and investment; and in developing countries the relation between investment and stock prices is explained in terms of a third variable, being completely independent of the credit coefficient.

9.5 Conclusion

Minsky's main contribution was to highlight capitalist financial instability which, according to him, was due to the relations between financial variables and investment expenditure. An important anchor of Minsky's argument was Kalecki's increasing risk concept, originally applied to microeconomic relation to understand the concentration process, a major concern of Kalecki's analysis. Therefore, Minsky's major shortcoming was shifting this concept to a macroeconomic framework, without acknowledging the dynamic relation between investment, profits and internal funds, and disregarding the rate of interest as a distributional variable. Thereby, under conditions of limited capital mobility, financial instability is related to falling investment spending resulting from the effect of that instability on the distribution of wealth and through interest rate changes.

Under conditions of *financialisation*, financial gains dominate and are a result of capital market speculative activities, independent of the financing needs of investment and production. Overcapitalisation is a consequence of trading financial instruments to obtain financial gains, modifying financial corporation balance sheet, regardless of investment finance requirements. The particular feature of the *financialisation* era is that despite investment spending reductions, economic downturns did not occur, since consumption increased. In this context, consumption spending rose and housing booms took place worldwide, especially in industrial countries.

Although developing countries underwent similar patterns in terms of capital market deepening, the impact in the productive sectors was different. The engine of growth moved from investment expenditure to exports and the share price index movements became related to the investment coefficient, not because of any association with the credit ratio, but because of external capital inflows, overvalued exchange rates, higher share index prices and boosting investment in the export sector, which nevertheless stayed relatively low due to industrial dependence.

Notes

1. Not all neoclassical economists regard money supply as exogenous reaching a wide consensus over long-term money neutrality (see Wicksell, 1907; Taylor, 1993; Blinder, 1998).
2. Before the 2008 financial crisis and industrial recession there were several important financial crises in developed countries that were short lived, such as the October 1987 world-wide crisis and the 2000–2001 Nasdaq crisis.
3. This argument was initially put forward by Jan Toporowski (2000).
4. Minsky's lender and borrower increasing risk concepts are borrowed from Kalecki's analysis, whose purpose was to highlight the effect of oligopoly markets on investment spending.
5. It is assumed that interest rates are determined by central banks and are independent of the workings of the capital market (neoclassical view) and of the monetary market (Keynes' liquidity preference theory). This argument is based on Keynes (1937) where liquidity preference was transferred to banks behaviour (see Kregel, 1984 for an ample explanation).
6. This section is based on a revised version of Levy (2001) Sections 2.4 and 3.3.
7. Toporowski (2000) argues that stock issuance equilibrates ex-post corporation balance sheet.
8. It should be recalled that in the early 1980s Chile underwent a deep financial crisis and economic stagnation, with a negative economic growth of –10.3 in 1982.

References

Blinder, A. (1998) *Central Banking in Theory and Practice* (Cambridge, Mass.: MIT Press).

Davidson, P. (2008) 'Is the current financial distress caused by the subprime mortgage crisis a Minsky moment? or is it a result of attempting to securitise illiquid noncommercial mortgage loans?', *Journal of Post Keynesian Economics*, vol. 30.

Fisher, I. (1933) 'The debt deflation theory of the great depression', *Econometrica*, vol. 1.

Guttmann, R. and D. Philon (2008) 'Consumer debt at the center of finance-led capitalism', *CEPN, Paris-Nord, working paper.*

Hicks, J. (1937) 'Mr. Keynes and the "Classics"; A suggested interpretation', *Econometrica*, vol. 5.

Keynes, J.M. (1936) *The General Theory of Employment, Interest and Money* (London: MacMillan Press, 1936).

Keynes, J.M. (1937) Alternative theories of the rate of interest, republished in Collected Writings of John Maynard Keynes, vol. 14, D. Moggridge (ed.) (London: Macmillan).

Kregel, J. (1984) 'Constrains on the expansion of output and employment: real or monetary?', *Journal of Pos Keynesian Economics*, vol. 7, no. 2.

Kregel, J. (2008) 'Minsky's cushions of safety Systemic Risk and the Crisis in the U.S. Subprime Mortgage Market', *Public Policy Brief No. 93. The Levy Economics Institute of Bard College.*

Lavoie, M. and M. Secarrecia (2001) 'Minsky's financial fragility hypothesis: a missing macroeconomic link? in *Financial Fragility and Investment in the Capitalist Economy. The economic legacy of Hyman Minsky*, Vol. II, in R. Bellofiore and P. Ferri (eds.) (Cheltenham UK: Edward Elgar).

Levy, N. (2001) 'Cambios institucionales del sector financiero y su efecto sobre el fondeo de la inversión'. México 1960–1994, DGAPA, UNAM.

Levy, N. (2010) 'Instituciones financieras para el desarrollo económico: Comparación del periodo de "sustitución de importaciones" y el "secundario exportador"' in M.G. Mántey and N. Levy (eds), *Cincuenta Años de Políticas Financieras para el Desarrollo en México, (1958–2008), Plaza y Valdez editores, UNAM,* pp. 149–178.

Minsky, H.P. (1975) *John Maynard Keynes* (New York: Columbia University Press).

Taylor, J. (1993), 'Discretion vs policy rules in practice', *Carnegie-Rochester Conference Series on Public Policy*, December, vol. 39.

Toporowski, J. (2000) *The End of Finance, Capital Market inflation, Financial Derivatives and Pension Fund Capitalism* (Routledge Frontiers of Political Economy).

Toporowski, J. (2009) 'The economics and culture of financial inflation', *Competition and Change*, vol. 13, no. 2.

Wicksell, K. (1907) 'The influence of the rate of interest on prices', *The Economic Journal*, vol. 17, no. 66.

10
Money Manager Capitalism in Primary Commodity-Dependent Developing Countries

Luigi Ventimiglia and Daniela Tavasci

10.1 Introduction

Capitalism comes in different forms. In the current form of capitalism, financial markets and arrangements are dominated by managers of funds. That is, we live in money manager capitalism. During the preceding form of paternalistic capitalism, countercyclical fiscal policy sustained profits when the economy faltered; the Federal Reserve kept interest rates low; government represented the main source of external financing. Money manager capitalism emerged out of this form not only because of increasingly speculative endeavours but also because of the emergence of plans that replaced and supplemented social security systems with private pensions (Minsky and Whalen, 1996).

This privatisation process released funds which were to be invested by money managers. These are institutions that manage large portfolios. A large proportion of the liabilities of corporations are today held by money managers who are guided by the maximisation of the value of investment; therefore, the real economy is, at present, sensitive to the valuation of money managers as reflected in financial markets. This chapter argues that within this context, money managers are also in a constant search for new asset classes, in order to 'make on the carry'.

The necessity to hedge large financial portfolios drives the money managers' search for new asset classes to invest in. The creation of a new asset class often involves the transformation of an existing market. One of the most recent asset classes corresponds to the derivatives on primary commodities. This market was initially formed to serve the need to hedge risk for primary commodity producers. Thanks to a number of characteristics, such as rising prices and lack of correlation to other asset classes, money managers chose this market to invest increasingly higher proportions of their assets. Commodity passive index funds have risen, in terms of assets allocated, from a value of $13 billion at the end of 2003 to $260 billion as of March 2008. Gradually, as both physical hedgers and money managers were exchanging in the derivatives market, this became one of the determinants of pricing in the real commodity market. That is, the real commodity market became 'financialised'.

How does the financialisation of one primary commodity market affect the producer country's economy? The Financial Instability Hypothesis (FIH), if appropriately adapted, may provide a framework to understand the sources of vulnerability of a small open economy, whose GDP is driven by the export of one or a few primary commodities. Export earnings drive the boom–bust cycle through its relation with the exchange rate and foreign borrowing, acting in a pro-cyclical way and interacting with the financial sector. The impressive result is that even a unit operating in the non-primary commodity sector is vulnerable to financial market dynamics outside the country.

Chile, a major copper exporter, is an example of a 'financialised' and 'liberalised' economy with a primary commodity-driven cycle. The country has attempted to stabilise the cycle by creating funds and by keeping the biggest mine under state ownership. However, in terms of development, these measures have been successful only up to a point, as the copper boom did not alleviate extreme poverty and inequality.

This chapter adapts Minsky in three ways. Firstly, Section 10.2 describes how, with respect to a long-term view of the evolution of a capitalist economy with developed financial institutions, the present phase of money manager capitalism has allowed the transformation of the commodity futures market and, consequently, at least to an extent, the evolution of the underlying real commodity market. This primary commodity market has become, then, broadly affected by changes in financial markets. Secondly, in Section 10.3 the concept of vulnerability put forth in the FIH (Minsky, 1992) is adapted to account for the increased vulnerability of a unit operating in a primary commodity-dependent developing country such as Chile. Here the export proceeds act pro-cyclically activating an internal mechanism.[1] This empirical component is described in Section 10.4. Finally, in the last section, a suggested policy prescription is introduced based on the idea of 'big government' acting counter-cyclically. Policy recommendations go beyond the scope of the present chapter and further research in this area is necessary.

10.2 Money managers and financialised commodity markets

From the end of the Great Depression until the post Second World War years, government represented the main source of external financing for the US economy. Minsky labelled this phase as 'paternalistic capitalism' (Minsky and Whalen, 1996). It was characterised by (a) the 'big government' which, with its spending at the level of 25 per cent of GDP, acted counter-cyclically to stabilise income, employment and profits (via the Kaleckian profit determination), and (b) the 'big bank', a central bank with the role of lender of last resort, kept low levels of interest rates.

However, from this a new form of capitalism emerged. Money manager capitalism evolved as result of increasingly speculative behaviour. For Minsky, this evolution took place for a number of reasons including the replacement of the system of social security with private pensions during the 1970s. However, the necessity of the financial sector to hedge against interest rate risk, especially after 1979–1982,[2] further stimulated financial innovations with securitisation of mortgages and other off-balance sheet operations and the creation (or new uses) of derivatives. Still today, this necessity to hedge drives the search for 'new asset classes', boosts the size of financial markets and involves, progressively, additional, 'fictitious', parallel markets. These may be created *ex novo*, or may be existing markets traditionally used for different purposes. The commodity futures market belongs to the second case. In these 'parallel' markets, 'asset classes' are simply paper claims on underlying 'real' assets, for example, real estate or, more recently, primary commodities. Eventually, once these 'parallel' markets have been 'financialised' and the money managers have turned these into an asset class, they may become determinants for the characteristics, i.e. price movements, of the corresponding 'real' market.

Clearly, money managers are the main actors of this transformation. They are institutions managing large portfolios and represent 'a new layer of intermediation in the financial structure' (Minsky and Whalen, 1996: p. 5). Table 10.1 describes the functions and actors in different markets: physical hedgers and speculators act in the commodity futures market and physical commodity producers, consumers and speculators act in the commodity market.

In order to bring some clarity to the 'financialisation' of commodity markets in general, and to the copper market in particular, it seems necessary to investigate, firstly, the behaviour of the actors involved, the

Table 10.1 Four distinct markets

Commodity markets	**Capital markets**
Crude Oil, Corn, Copper, etc. Physical commodity producers and consumers. Speculators	Stocks, Bonds, Real Estate, etc. Investors/Speculators
Commodities futures	**Financial futures**
Derive their value from physical commodities Physical hedgers ***AND*** Speculators	Derive their value from capital markets securities Investors/Speculators

Source: Adapted from Masters and White (2008: p. 3).

money managers; secondly, the creation of the new 'asset class', that is the transformation of the commodity futures market; and, finally, to what extent both these two elements (behaviour of money managers and the creation of the new asset class) have influenced the market of the underlying assets, the physical commodity market.

10.2.1 Money managers

Broadly, there are two groups of financial investors, active managers and passive index managers. The former type has been around for a while, surely before the last boom cycle. They mainly manage hedge funds and pension funds. Their style of trading varies depending on whether they use more a qualitative or quantitative technique, whether they are trend followers, momentum led, and so on. However, the second group is relatively new and has ballooned in size since the beginning of the new millennium. Commodity passive index funds have risen, in terms of assets allocated, from a value of $13 billion at the end of 2003 to $260 billion as of March 2008 (Masters and White, 2008).

Passive index funds have been created to attract larger number of investors such as pension funds and small retail funds as they are simple to manage and, consequently, require lower management fees. Passive managers investing in the commodity futures market use mainly two indexes,[3] each formed by a specific basket of future on commodities (Table 10.2). Size and depth of the market progressively increased as gradually more funds were invested, affecting all commodity futures prices according to benchmarks weights.

Passive index managers 'take position' in two ways. They can buy directly in the futures market through brokers as many futures-commodity-contracts

Table 10.2 Major primary commodity future index composition and relative future price increase

Index component weights as of 12 March 2008		**S&P GSCI (%)**	**DI-AIG (%)**	**Future price increase March 2003–March 2008 (%)**
Agricultural	Cocoa	0.2	0.0	34
	Coffe	0.6	2.9	166
	Corn	3.3	5.7	134
	Cotton	0.9	2.5	40
	Soybean Oil	0.0	2.9	198
	Soybeans	2.2	7.2	143
	Sugar	1.0	3.1	69
	Wheat	5.3	5.6	314
	Wheat KC	1.2	0.0	276
Livestock	Feed Cattle	0.3	0.0	34
	Lean Hogs	0.8	2.2	10
	Live Cattle	1.7	3.9	23

Table 10.2 (Continued)

Index component weights as of 12 March 2008		S&P GSCI (%)	DI-AIG (%)	Future price increase March 2003–March 2008 (%)
Energy	Brent Crude Oil	13.4	0.0	213
	WTI Crude Oil	38.3	12.9	191
	Gasoil	5.0	0.0	192
	Heating Oil	4.9	3.8	192
	Gasoline	4.2	3.6	145
	Natural Gas	6.8	13.1	71
Base metals	Aluminium	2.5	7.7	12
	Lead	0.5	0.0	563
	Nickel	0.9	2.7	282
	Zinc	0.6	2.7	225
	Copper	3.1	7.3	413
Precious metals	Gold	1.9	7.1	183
	Silver	0.3	3.0	331
Total		100.0	100.0	

Source: Standard & Poor's, Dow Jones, Bloomberg.

as the components of the index, according to the weights of the different commodities. These funds will be 'long only' and the futures positions get rolled generally every three months. Alternatively, they can buy, indirectly, one single contract representing the whole index. This would be a swap, a bilateral agreement with a broker who, in turn, does the dirty work of hedging every single component of the index through commodity futures on a commodity exchange.

10.2.2 A new asset class

Figure 10.1 shows the rapid expansion of dedicated primary commodity futures funds by just a sample of index managers. The number of futures and options contracts outstanding on commodity exchanges has increased about five fold and the notional amount of outstanding over-the-counter commodity related contracts increased about 20 times in the same period (UNCTAD, 2009: p. 41). This illustrates how commodity derivatives have become a new asset class, another category of investment for the managers of money.

The identification of a new asset class by financial investors depends, however, on a number of various factors related to (a) the way in which financial investors act and (b) the circumstances of specific markets. The fact that the interaction between these two sets of factors tends to change shows how markets do not exist in abstract but have a concrete evolution that needs to be investigated (Minsky, 1986).

In fact, the market for derivatives on commodities has traditionally shown a low correlation with bond and equity markets. An additional attractiveness

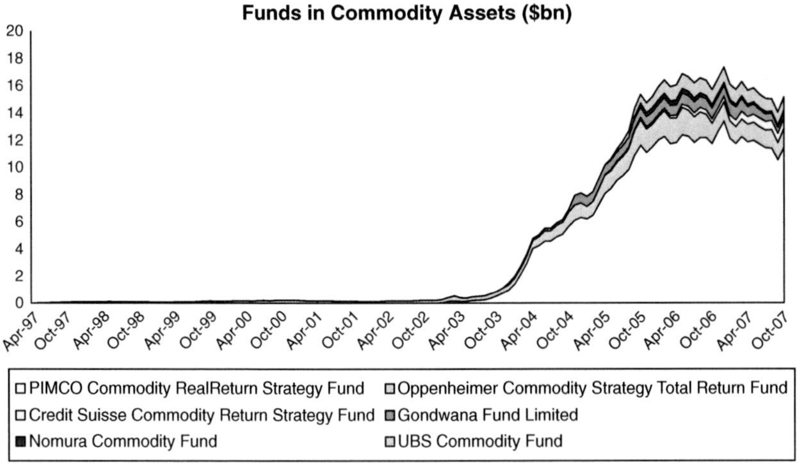

Figure 10.1 Sample of primary commodity-derivative dedicated funds during the primary commodity boom (1997–March 2008).
Source: Bloomberg.

of the derivatives on commodity markets was its natural hedge to inflation as energy and food prices have a strong component or secondary effects on consumer price indexes (core or non-core). However, low correlation with the other markets was partially given by the 'under-utilisation' of such market by financial investors. Indeed, historically, the notional size of the transactions on commodity futures has been marginal relative to bond and equities. But this lack of correlation has tended to fade with the expansion of the primary commodity derivative market, driving investors towards a new search for yet another unexploited asset class, in order to 'make on the carry' (Minsky, 1986: p. 211).

Furthermore, as real commodity prices were rising since the period 2002–2003, these were expected to support prices in the derivative market in which physical hedgers act. The fact that both exchange-traded commodities and non-exchange-traded commodities, or commodities not included in commodities indexes (UNCTAD, 2009, figure 3.1, p. 38), have seen a major increase in price underlines the idea that behind a boom there is always a 'fundamental' reason on which the financial market builds its euphoria. The proliferation of funds dedicated to the derivatives on commodity market, a financial 'mania' (Kindleberger, 1978), epitomises the fact that world liquidity has increased during the last boom given a progressive increase of leverage in the financial system.

10.2.3 The effects on the underlying market

The most apparent symptom of a dramatic change in the real commodity market is the increase in price, which has been extraordinary during the

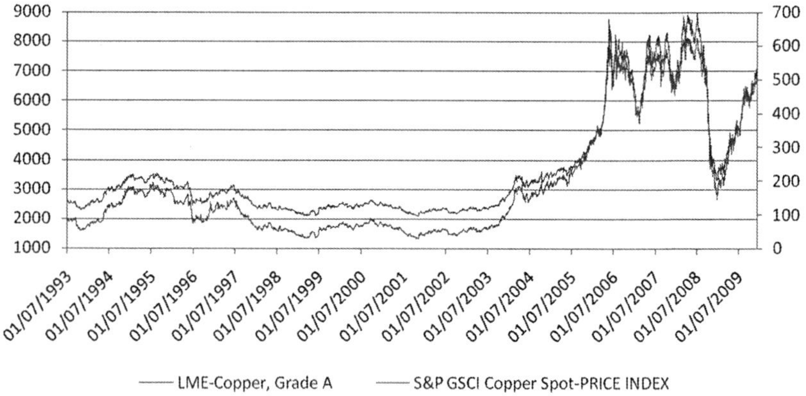

Figure 10.2 Copper futures price (three months buy) and 'real' copper price in US$ (1999–2009).
Source: Datastream.

period 2003–2008. However, it is difficult to say whether the price increase in both the real and the financial commodity markets has been driven by either the 'real' or by the derivatives on commodities (Figure 10.2). Generally, scholars and practitioners have identified three determinants of the price hike in the real commodity market.

The most popular explanation for the price increase of the real commodity market regards 'fundamentals' and refers also to 'China's fault' (see, for example, Chapter 7). In fact, the consistent high growth of China and, to a less extent, of India, created higher demand of primary commodities causing the surge of metal and energy prices (see, for example, Gros, 2008). China is the leading metal consumer and uses about 24 per cent of the world production. Geopolitical factors, such as the Middle East crisis, have contributed to the increase in energy prices too (Winters and Yusuf, 2007). Chinese demand is responsible for about 64 per cent of the total increase of world demand for copper during the period 2003–2008. Moreover, on the supply side, copper production has been disrupted for some time due to strikes in the Chilean mines.

A second explanation for the increase in copper price refers to speculation in the physical commodity market. This is not specific to any market in particular: for example, Wray (2008) mentions how British Petroleum monopolised 90 per cent of all TET propane supplies withholding some quantity from the market to drive prices up. Previously, Veneroso (2008) reported one million metric/tons (out of the 17–18 million produced every year) of copper missing, disappearing into un-recorded inventories in China. Some copper must have been held from the market for similar purposes.

A more recent account of the determinants of commodity prices, however, refers to the 'parallel' financial market, the commodity futures market.

In this, de-regulation policies and 'financial innovation' interacted in the Minskyan way (see, for example, Chapter 5). Regulation or, more accurately, the lack thereof, allowed the pervasiveness of financial markets to create a new asset class.

To explain this process, we should refer back to 1936 when the Congress passed the Commodity Exchange Act in order to limit speculators' domination in the commodity futures market. This had to serve exclusively the necessity to hedge for those acting in the underlying 'real' commodity market. During the 1990s, however, at the peak of money manager capitalism, the Commodity Futures Trading Commission (CFTC) granted Wall Street exemptions from speculative position limits, by which banks were allowed to hedge over-the-counter swap transactions. Until then, the associated index trades executed by index managers with a swap dealer were accumulated in dealers' portfolios of long futures position. This could reach its speculative position limit imposed by the CFTC rules. The removal of the limit 'actually happened in 1991 with a particular swap dealer that was hedging an OTC transaction with a pension fund, and the swap dealer came to us, and we said, "yeah, that qualifies for a hedge exemption", so we granted a hedge exemption to the swap dealer. And in the years since then, we've done the same for other swap dealers, as well' (CFTC, 2007: p. 66). This deregulation of the future commodity markets greatly contributed to the transformation of that market by allowing money managers to take positions. However, it was only in 2003, thanks to great levels of international liquidity, that the boom took place. Table 10.3 shows the increase in the demand for copper between 2002 and 2007 in metric tons. Index investors held 30 per cent of the total increase in the demand for copper.

A process of 'financialisation' of the commodity market, explainable through 'financial innovations' and the participation of money managers, then, has aligned this 'new' asset class to equities and bonds in such a way that it has incorporated those characteristics, including volatility and correlations, which are typically associated to booms and busts. By allowing the activity of money managers and their enormous amount of funds in this market, the correlation of commodity futures with other financial asset classes has radically increased.

Table 10.3 Increase in demand for copper (2002–2007)

	Metric tons
China	2,039,776
Index investors	1,160,192
Rest of the world	673,310

Source: Adapted from Masters and White (2008).

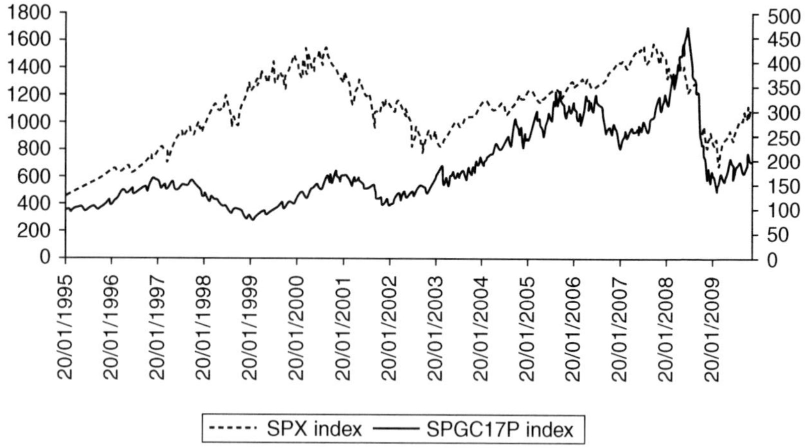

Figure 10.3 SPGC17P Goldman Sachs Future Commodity Index and S&P Equity Index.
Source: Bloomberg.

In order to verify this argument, we considered two time series, the Goldman Sachs commodity index (SPGC17P) and the S&P equity index, since the first day data for both series were available in January 1995 until November 2009. Figure 10.3 (the right hand side scale is for future commodity index) shows how the two indices were uncorrelated until 2003, when money managers started to invest in the commodity index.

Also, the correlation coefficient between the two series changes dramatically between the two periods. Until March 2003, the correlation coefficient is 0.07. During this first period, it is easy to see that while the S&P index increases the SPGC decreases. From March 2003 until November 2009, however, the correlation coefficient is 0.69.

As a result, given the close relation between the physical primary commodity market and the future commodity market, the dramatic change in the former discussed above, is related to the latter to a great extent. In the next section, we will discuss the relevance of this change with respect to those open economies which are particularly sensitive to fluctuations of primary commodity prices, such as the primary commodity-dependent developing countries. We argue that firms operating in these countries are exposed to an additional source of fragility.

10.3 Speculative units in primary commodity-dependent developing countries

The FIH was developed for a big closed economy, the United States. To what extent it can be used to analyse dynamics of smaller, emerging economies depends on a number of considerations. After the Asian crisis many have used Minsky in such contexts (see, for example, DJ Bezemer, 2001; Arestis and Glickman, 2002; Cruz *et al.*, 2006; Martinez, 2006; Arza and Español, 2008).

Amongst these, Arestis and Glickman (2002) have shown how an open economy, under certain conditions (that is, liberalisation), may show additional sources of vulnerability such as movements in the exchange rate which would impact the financial structure of units.[4]

According to the authors, Minsky offers two criteria for identifying a speculative unit, the need to roll over finance and the interest rate vulnerability. In the closed economy the two criteria are, for all intents and purposes, coterminous. Instead, Arestis and Glickman argue that, in an open economy, if a unit has to service its debt in foreign currency, it is vulnerable to changes in financial markets. Hence, taking Minsky's concept in its deepest sense, we must regard it as a 'speculative unit'. In other words, a unit may borrow short-term as well as in foreign currency. In that case, the firm is doubly vulnerable to financial market movements, hence it is 'super-speculative' (Arestis and Glickman, 2002: p. 242).

Nevertheless, for a smaller open economy, vulnerability comes in many different forms. For primary commodity-dependent developing countries, often only one (or very few) primary commodity is determinant for the economy. This is the case of Chile, for example, where the export of copper reaches about half of its exports and 16 per cent of its GDP. In Chile, one single primary commodity, copper, is so dominant that changes in its price affect the exchange rate. Hence, because the exchange rate moves with the commodity price and these exchange-rate movements in turn have an impact on firms, these can arguably be viewed as speculative units even when, on a literal interpretation of Minsky, they would be classified as hedged because they are entirely equity-financed.

Three different sets of mechanisms act pro-cyclically, from the price of the commodity to the financial posture of units. They operate in conjunction via a self-reinforcing dynamic, depending on the structure of the economy and its external sector. First, variations in prices and quantities demanded of the primary commodity directly affect the country's export earnings. Secondly, as their export earnings are re-valued in local currency, the real exchange rate is also affected, acting pro-cyclically by appreciating when prices and quantities of exports increase. The more a country depends on primary commodities, the higher the floating exchange rate is correlated to commodity prices. A currency that is highly correlated with the import earning of a primary commodity is known in the literature as 'commodity currency' (Cashin *et al.*, 2003). However, if the economy is financially 'liberalised' with no capital controls, then the exchange rate will be subject to financial account flows as well. Thirdly, foreign borrowing also acts pro-cyclically, interacting with export earnings, currency movements and the connection between them.

In this circumstance, 'the debt is incurred at the height of the boom when the international capital market, awash with seemingly unlimited surplus capital and liquid assets, rates the country as very creditworthy and puts a correspondingly high value on its currency' (Nissanke, 1993: p. 69). When commodity prices burst, not only does the country face lower export revenues, but its credit rating also tends to deteriorate, forcing more expensive re-financing.

In such a situation, the possibility of a crisis may have different origins. It can either start domestically and then spread to the external position of the country, or it can have an external origin and then impact the domestic economy. 'The latter one can be analysed on Minskyan terms on the basis that, once an economy is open to global financial markets, its state entity can be regarded as a financing unit in relation to the external value of its currency' (Arestis and Glickman, 2002: p. 243).

The third risk, however, from a perspective of a commodity dependent developing country, is the crisis triggered by a reduction in the price of the commodity. Even a Chilean firm that is entirely financed by domestic equity finance is intensely exposed to financial market movements: copper price affects the exchange rate, this can feed back on the firm through the impact in the real exchange rate and triggering international financial flows, which further impact on the exchange rate. So the firm becomes intensely vulnerable to financial market changes. Also as the copper price rises and, through it the real exchange rate goes up, profits of the copper-producers mount, ultimately inducing euphoria (Figure 10.4).

During a period of boom then, the increase of the price of commodity raises revenues, increasing liquidity in the domestic market. Local banks will experience an upsurge in deposits and will be able to expand their own

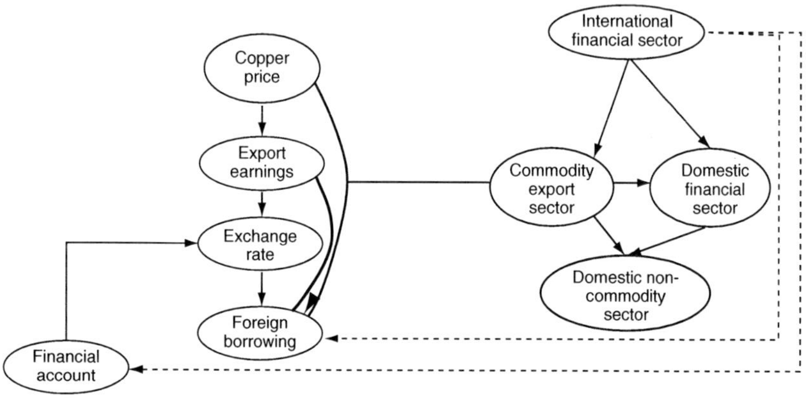

Figure 10.4 Transmission mechanisms of copper price movements.

international borrowing if the economy is financially 'liberalised'; prices of local stock market and securities of all kinds will also tend to rise. Thanks to the exchange rate appreciation, investors will buy domestic currency, either via derivatives or by acquiring local bonds and equities, in which the currency bet is implicit. This brings the collapse of the margins of safety and fuels domestic bubbles including real estate and consumer credit, for example.

In case of inflation, capital inflows will tend to offset the central bank's attempt to increase interest rates. With a floating exchange rate, there would be further appreciation improving the position of those indebted in foreign currency. Rising asset prices and profits, appreciation of the exchange rate and increasing export earnings validate foreign borrowing fuelling its expansion in an endogenous process.

10.4 Can 'it' happen in Chile?

Chile is a perfect example of a 'financialised' and 'liberalised' country. It is a primary commodity-dependent, open economy. It lifted capital controls in 1998 and adopted a floating exchange rate in 1999. In this section, we firstly discuss how the 2003–2008 boom and the consequent reduction of export earnings affected the exchange rate and foreign borrowing. Secondly, we illustrate how these movements hit the commodity export sector directly and then other sectors according to specific transmission mechanisms.

The price of copper started a sustained period of growth in 2003 from about US$1500/metric ton, reaching US$8714 in April 2008 and falling back to US$3105 in December 2008. This greatly affected Chilean export earnings.

The exchange rate is generally determined by movements of both trade and financial accounts. Firstly, from the definition of commodity currency described in the previous section, the higher the export of the primary commodity in relation to total exports, the stronger the correlation exchange-rate/primary commodity price. Furthermore, assuming the quantity of the primary commodity exported remains constant, the higher the increase of the primary commodity price the higher the correlation will be. Figure 10.5 highlights the copper price boom in the period 2003–2008 and the corresponding increase in the level of correlation with the exchange rate from 0.26 to 0.85 (horizontal lines). Similarly, Figure 10.6 shows the appreciation of the Chilean Peso since 2003 when the level of correlation between copper price and exchange rate is higher.

However, since the exchange rate is influenced by the financial account as well, the correlation between exchange rate and copper price breaks down when the former shows stability and the latter collapses as, for example, during the period June–December 2006 (Figures 10.5 and 10.6, 12-month rolling correlation). In fact, Chile had negative financial account flows during the

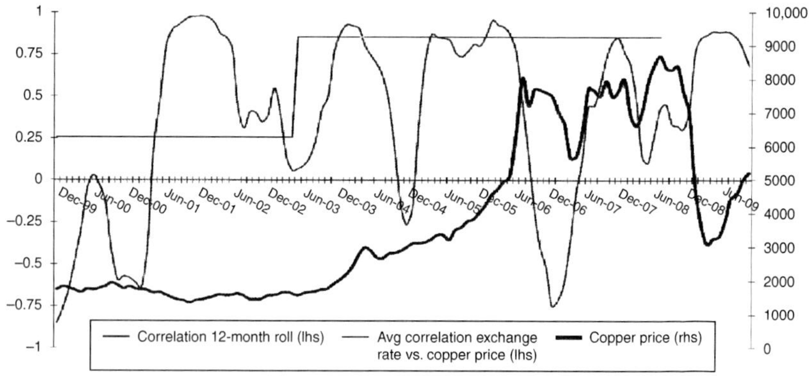

Figure 10.5 Copper price (right) rolling 12-month correlation and average correlation (left). (December 1999–July 2009).
Source: IMF.

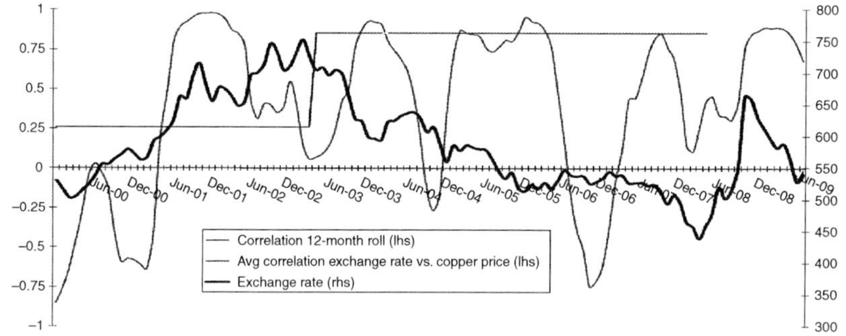

Figure 10.6 Exchange rate (right) and rolling 12-month correlation and average correlation (left). (December 1999–July 2009).
Source: IMF.

whole period until the break of the international crisis when portfolio flows were no longer invested abroad, in the second quarter of 2008 (Figure 10.7).

Despite positive investment flows for most of the period, the analysis of the financial account shows how, in reality, Chilean portfolios tended to invest abroad in search for higher yields. Indeed, during the commodity boom, from a financial investor's point of view, the healthy external position made Chile less interesting than other countries in the region, which could offer higher returns. Figure 10.8 shows how the Chilean spread over US Treasury has systematically been very stable and lower than the rest of the region since the beginning of the boom.

This observation leads us to reiterate that commodity-dependent developing countries face a 'complex issue of portfolio management' (Nissanke, 1993: p. 61) which departs from a simple inter-temporal optimisation

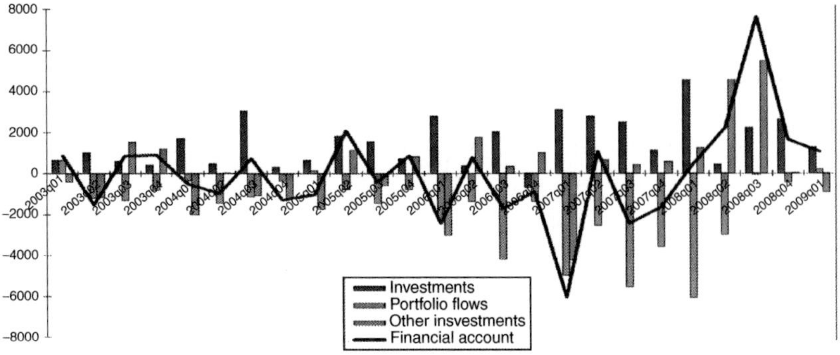

Figure 10.7 Financial account break-down since copper boom period (2003–2009).
Source: IMF.

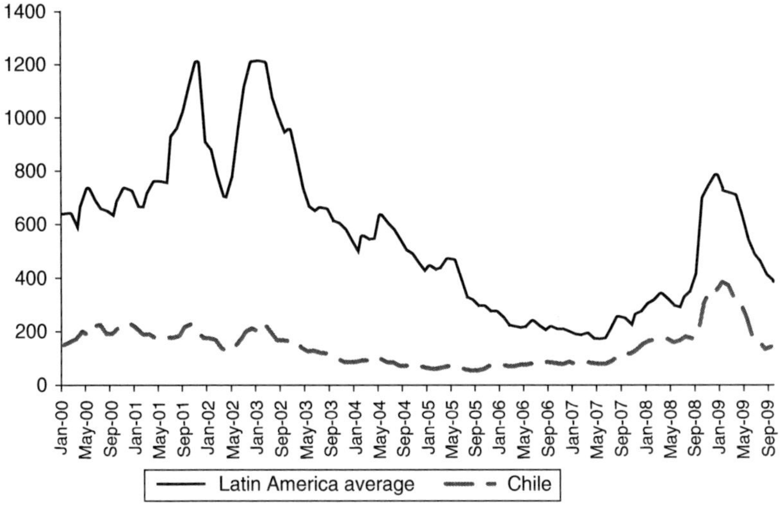

Figure 10.8 Chilean and Latin–American spreads (2000–2009).
Source: Central bank of Chile.

typical of closed economies (that is, allocation between current and future consumption). In fact, there are many dimensions involved such as the allocation of savings which needs to be distributed between domestic and net foreign investment, between real productive assets and financial assets, abroad or domestic, depending on the expected return on risk.

Finally, through the third link, rising prices and profits, increasing export earnings and exchange rate appreciation, validate foreign borrowing fuelling its expansion in an endogenous process.

However, the above dynamics affect the economy through different transmission mechanisms. The boom is passed on to the non-financial sector via the financial sector. During the upswing, the increased export earnings improve the financial posture of the commodity sector, favouring the spread of euphoria, driving up external debt (Figure 10.9) and liquidity in the domestic market which, in turn, directly affects the domestic credit market (Figure 10.10). Financial asset prices will also rise (Figure 10.11).

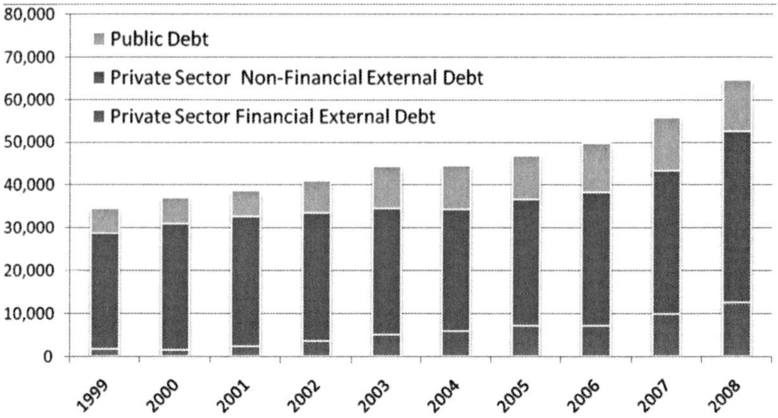

Figure 10.9 External debt and copper export earnings.
Source: Ministry of Finance.

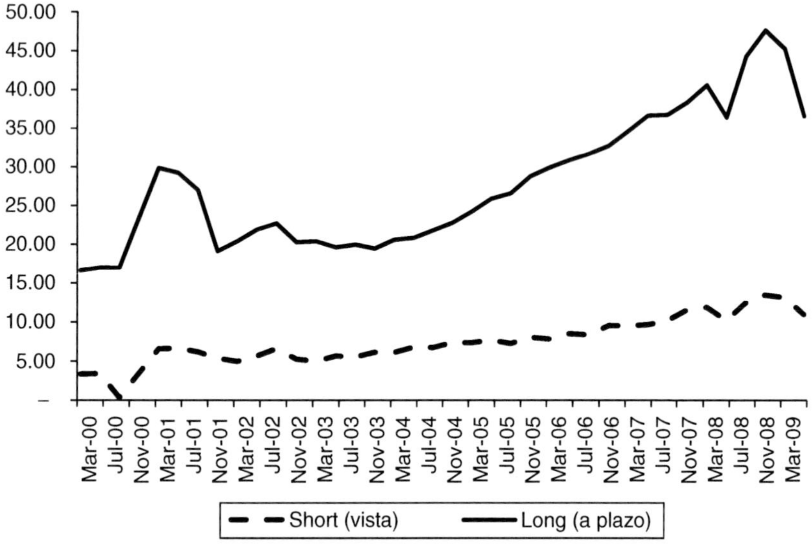

Figure 10.10 Increase in bank deposits.
Source: SBIF.

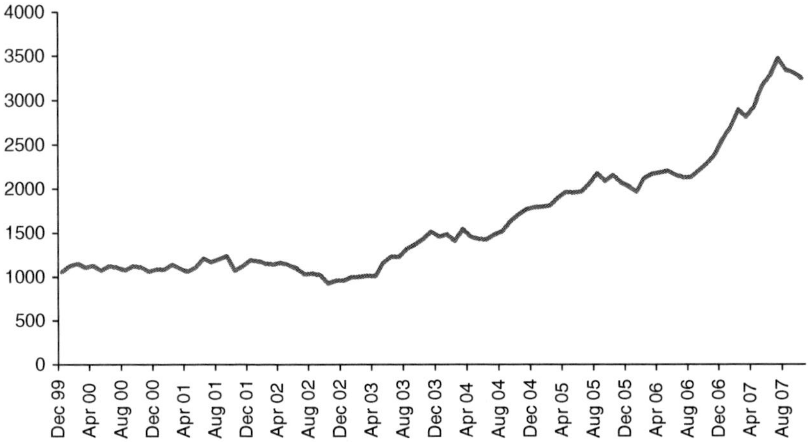

Figure 10.11 Ipsa Index.
Source: Bolsa Commercio de Santiago, Chile.

Figure 10.9 shows that between 1999 and 2008 public debt, private sector non-financial external debt and private sector financial external debt have increased respectively by 103 per cent, 48 per cent and 636 per cent.

Thanks to the exchange rate appreciation, investors bought domestic currency, either via derivatives or by acquiring local bonds and equities, in which, it is implicit the currency bet. This brought the collapse of the margins of safety and fuelled domestic bubbles including consumer credit (Figure 10.12).

Most importantly, the non-financial non-commodity sector also is affected as much as the mining sector. The transmission, then, does not materialise in terms of linkages between commodity and non-commodity sector as these are relatively small, but rather they concentrate in the north of the country where the mining sector is clustered and linked with business services, infrastructures and utilities (Aroca, 2001).

However, since the beginning of 2008, the price of copper has been declining so sharply that by the end of 2008 it had collapsed by 65 per cent. This newly difficult position of the commodity sector could have worsened the reduction of liquidity due to the effects of the global credit crunch in the domestic market with a decrease in deposits (Figure 10.10) and consumer credit (Figure 10.12).

Moreover, the cost of short-term external borrowing for resident banks that had always been only marginally above Libor until 2008, reached 170 basis points above in December 2008. Financial asset prices also collapsed: Ipsa went down from a high 3089 in April 2008 to 2500 in March 2009. It is likely that portfolio flows tended to stop investing abroad,

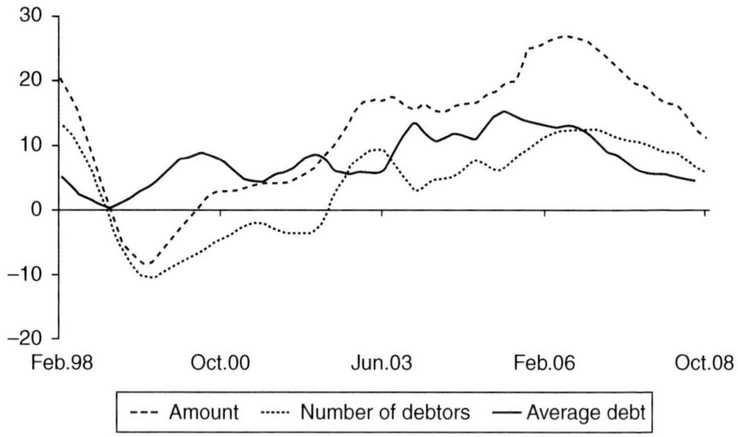

Figure 10.12 Consumers' bank debt (% annual change).
Source: SBIF and Central Bank.

counter-balancing the negative effects of the commodity price decline on the exchange rate.

The overall effect on the Chilean economy is still to be seen as the price of copper has recovered about 50 per cent of its recent decline. It is, nevertheless, difficult to disentangle the effect of the decline of the commodity price from the effects of the global crisis. However, it is important to establish that for a commodity-dependent developing country, the price of the commodity, especially in the presence of a 'financialised' market and with lack of capital controls, acts in a pro-cyclical way, making the country's vulnerability augmented by yet another dimension.

10.5 The role of the 'big government'

The necessity to hedge drives money market towards new asset classes. However, once an increasing quantity of funds are invested in the newly established asset class, this is no longer uncorrelated to other financial markets such as equities. Rather, as the case of copper shows, the price of the real commodity becomes influenced by the price of its derivative which, in turn, becomes correlated with financial markets.

The results are impressive for those countries which rely heavily on one of these commodities such as Chile. The export proceeds not only fuel euphoria in both financial and non-financial, primary commodity and non primary commodity, sectors. They also affect the exchange rate further stimulating external borrowing. The effects of a burst can only me mitigated with countercyclical policies. An effective and active monetary policy of 'big bank' and a countercyclical 'big government' are beyond the scope of this chapter. However, while the performances of Chile are commended, its results in terms of development indicators cannot be considered satisfactory.

Chile was the first country to experience the neoliberal turn. The military coup of 1973 and the Chicago boys were the symbol of a new era of free-market reforms. Today, the largest of the copper mines belongs to the government. Its website proudly indicates that 'all Chileans own it'. In 2007, the Chilean Government created the Economic and Social Stabilization Fund (ESSF). This fund replaced the original Copper Stabilization Fund. It receives fiscal surpluses which are above 1 per cent of GDP and came into existence with a one-off payment of approximately $5 billion (as a result of the closure of the original Copper Stabilization Fund). Through the ministry of finance of Chile, the financial committee proposed investment policy on the ESSF in March 2007. The investment strategy intends to diversify assets in the fund, putting 15 per cent of the portfolio into variable income assets, 20 per cent in corporate fixed income paper, gradually adjusting assets currently held, and especially liquid assets.

However, the stabilising function of the state-owned mining company, Codelco, has proven to be important also in terms of employment. The number of employees rose during the last 2 years even though the national unemployment rate remained slightly volatile and eventually increased in 2007.

These are important instruments that the Chilean state has been able to preserve. Other commodity-dependent developing countries have privatised their mines and have been unable to create stabilisation funds or to guarantee employment in times of crises and lack of demand. Nevertheless, for Minsky, not only is stabilisation destabilising (see Chapter 5), it does not necessarily mean development. Chile still faces a number of problems, including persistent income inequality and poverty with a Gini coefficient still above 52 and poverty headcount (people living below US$ 1.25) constant since 1996.

Chile needs to work towards a different model of development, including sources alternative to mining and especially towards the creation of those safety nets that should guarantee that 'it' won't happen again.

Notes

1. This trigger is external but the mechanism itself develops internally along the structure of the Chilean economy.
2. Volker played an important role within the US Treasury, in the suspension of the gold convertibility that led to the end of Bretton Woods system. At the Fed, he was credited for having ended stagflation by increasing federal funds rate and prime

rate to above 20 per cent in 1981, leading to the recession of the beginning of the 1980s.
3. The two benchmarks are the Standard & Poor's Goldman Sachs Commodity Index (S&P GSCI) and the Dow Jones-American International Group Commodity Index (DJ-AIGCI, recently changed into DJ-UBSCI).
4. It is now widely known that Minsky used to classify units according to their financial posture in hedge, speculative and Ponzi (see Chapter 2).

References

Arestis, P. and M. Glickman (2002) 'Financial crisis in Southeast Asia: dispelling illusion the Minskyan way', *Cambridge Journal of Economics*, vol. 26.
Aroca, P. (2001) 'Impacts and development in local economies based on mining: the case of the Chilean II region', *Resources Policy*, vol. 27: 2.
Arza, V. and P. Español (2008) 'Les Liaisons dangereuses: a Minskyan approach to the relation of credit and investment in Argentina during the 1990s', *Cambridge Journal of Economics*, vol. 32.
Banco Central de Chile, Financial Stability Report, various Years.
Banco Central de Chile, data and statistics.
Bezemer, D.J. (2001) 'Post-socialist financial fragility: the case of Albania', *Cambridge Journal of Economics*, vol. 25.
Cashin, P., L. Céspedes and R. Sahay (2003) 'Commodity currencies', *Finance and Development IMF Magazine*, vol. 40, no. 1.
Commodity Futures Trading Commission (2007) Remarks of Don Heitman, Division of Market Oversight, CFTC Agricultural Advisory Committee Meeting, Washington, D.C., 6th December, www.cftc.gov/stellent/groups/public/@aboutcftc/documents/file/aac_12062007.pdf.
Cruz M., E. Amann and B. Walters (2006) 'Expectations, the business cycle and the Mexican peso crisis', *Cambridge Journal of Economics*, vol. 30.
Gros, D. (2008) 'The China bubble fuelling record oil prices', *Financial Times*, July 9.
Kindleberger, C.P. (1978) *Manias, Panics, and Crashes: A History of Financial Crisis* (New York, Basic Books).
Martinez, G.X. (2006) 'The political economy of the Ecuadorian financial crisis', *Cambridge Journal of Economics*, vol. 30.
Masters, M.W. and A.K. White (2008) 'The accidental hunt brothers: how institutional investors are driving up food and energy prices', The Accidental Hunt Brothers Blog, special report posted July 31.
Minsky, H.P. (1986) *Stabilizing an Unstable Economy* (New Haven: Yale University Press).
Minsky, H.P. (1992) 'The financial instability hypothesis', *The Levy Economics Institute of Bard College Public Policy Working Paper No. 74.*
Minsky, H.P. and C.J. Whalen (1996) 'Economic insecurity and the institutional prerequisites for successful capitalism', *The Levy Economics Institute of Bard College Public Policy Working Paper No. 165.*
Nissanke, M. (1993) Economic Crisis in Developing Countries: New Perspectives on Commodities, Trade and Finance: Essay, Machiko Nissanke and Adrian Hewitt, Eds, (London and New York: Pinter Publisher).
UNCTAD (2009) 'The global economic crisis: Systemic failures and multilateral remedies'. Report by the UNCTAD Secretariat Task Force on Systemic Issues and Economic Cooperation New York, Geneva.

Veneroso, F. (2008) 'Financial crisis: on the prospect of a second wave of copper: A commodity calamity to come; Speculation to the point of manipulation in base metals', *Veneroso's View*, April 28.

Winters, L. and S. Yusuf (2007) *Dancing with Giants: China, India and the Global Economy* (Washington DC: The World Bank Institute of Policy Studies).

Wray, R.L. (2008) 'The commodities market bubble', *The Levy Economics Institute of Bard College Public Policy Brief*, no. 96.

11

Minsky au Vietnam: State Corporations, Financial Instability and Industrialisation

Scott Cheshier and Jonathan Pincus

11.1 Introduction

When considering application of Hyman Minsky's ideas to developing countries, an immediate issue is which Minsky?[1] Three different options present themselves.[2] Financial instability is an inherent and defining feature of capitalism in all three Minskys. The first variation is 'exogenous Minsky', used by Kindleberger and Aliber (2005) in one of the earliest attempts to apply Minsky to open economies.[3] In this view, a pool of global liquidity flows around the world seeking investment opportunities. As it enters a particular national market, it sets off asset inflation and an investment boom. Mania eventually becomes panic and global funds pull out and move on to the next opportunity, leaving the national authorities to cover the costs of the crisis.[4] The Minskyan movement from hedge to speculative to Ponzi finance is triggered by foreign inflows and the source of instability is therefore at least partly exogenous.

The second variation is 'endogenous Minsky' (see Chapter 1), incorporating the Kaleckian formulation of investment as the primary determinant of the level of profits (Minsky, 1992, 2008). Periods of tranquillity, in which hedge finance predominates and margins of safety are high, lead to an increased willingness by businesses and bankers to accept more debt-financing. 'Balance sheet adventuring' ensues, margins of safety are reduced and the shift to speculative finance begins. This leads to asset inflation and even more investment, improving 'employment, output, and business profits, which in turn proves to businessmen and bankers that experimenting with speculative finance was correct' (Minsky, 2008: p. 48). The movement from hedge to speculative to Ponzi finance is driven by profit-seeking units in the economy and instability is endogenous to the system.

The third option is 'institutionalist Minsky', emphasising structural evolution and change. Capitalism comes in as many varieties 'as Heinz has pickles' (Minsky, 1991), and these varieties have 'varying implications for stability, efficiency, and the distribution of market power' (Whalen, 2001: p. 807). Varieties of capitalism are defined in terms of institutional structures. Since production precedes exchange and finance precedes production, 'credit and finance are at the centre of capitalist development' (Whalen, 2001: p. 808). The financial structure is a key determinant of the behaviour of an economy. This institutional structure evolves over time due to profit-driven financial innovation and government regulatory responses (Minsky, 2008). Profit-seeking units innovate around and beyond existing regulations, setting off the 'endogenous Minsky' process. Eventually market mania becomes panic and the regulatory authorities intervene to prevent a crash or to reduce the likelihood of the sequence of events repeating itself. This regulation-innovation-regulation dynamic is at the core of institutional evolution in a capitalist economy. Regulatory responses and government imposed institutional change are needed to mitigate the financial instability that is inherent to the system and that takes the form of financial innovation, necessitating constant vigilance on the part of the authorities. The ability of the market players to innovate faster than regulators can respond ensures that there is no 'once and for all' solution to the problem of financial instability.

The institutional Minsky emphasis on the evolution of institutions, structures and financial practices provides a useful perspective on economic change in developing and transition countries. Minsky did not write much about countries other than the United States. He assumed that the government possesses the capacity to regulate financial markets and to discipline financial firms. This is not to say that Minsky's writing is apolitical or devoid of political economy considerations. His support for Big Government and opposition to the rise of giant financial firms are examples of his keen awareness of the political economy implications of his own work. Nevertheless, the interactions between politics and the evolution of financial institutions take different forms in developing and transition countries. Most crucially, we cannot assume that regulators have the knowledge, skills and political clout to control the behaviour of banks and other corporations, or to enforce regulations once promulgated. Minsky's assumption that technocrats possess the power to impose their will on the market is less than realistic in most developing and transition economies, including Vietnam.

While the re-emergence of Minsky's only article on developing countries is the occasion for this book, he did write one article on transition countries for the Levy Institute in 1991. The focus on technical solutions is prominent. The core element of his analysis is that reliable *pro formas* do not exist in transition settings. Since state enterprises have no relevant history of profits, there is no way to generate meaningful valuations of firms' assets. In the absence of acceptable *pro formas*, financing decisions depend on political considerations.

Minsky's main policy recommendation for transition countries is to create public holding companies that own shares in subsidiary enterprises.

Shares acquire value as these subsidiaries make profits, providing a guide to the valuation of firms' assets. Public holding companies would then sell their positions, transforming successful subsidiaries into private companies. Minsky views public holding companies as useful transitional institutions during the early stages of capitalist development in the specific situation in which information on financial flows is incomplete or unreliable and asset prices are not yet established. From a technical point of view, public holding companies could play this important role. However, their capacity to do so depends on the relative balance of power between bureaucrats and managers of state firms. The creation of holding companies does not occur in a political vacuum, but instead is shaped by and in turn influences the outcome of political conflict over access to capital, other assets and profits in the state sector. Consistent with the approach of institutional Minsky, unchecked innovation within state holding companies, including intra-group lending, underwriting and leasing, can contribute to system-wide financial instability.

Recent developments in Vietnam bring out the centrality of political conflict to the role and functioning of state holding companies in the process of capitalist development. In 2007 and early 2008, Vietnam experienced a relatively straightforward 'exogenous' Minsky boom. Foreign capital inflows surged into Vietnam throughout 2007 and early 2008. Banks boosted lending in response to the sudden rush of deposits, with the result that credit growth exceeded 60 per cent year on year by early 2008. Predictably, money supply, asset prices and goods price inflation soared. Stock market valuations increased several times before collapsing in late 2007. Property prices followed a similar although slightly delayed path, peaking in January 2008 (Harvard Vietnam Program, 2008b).

This chapter investigates the contribution of state corporations to financial instability in Vietnam. Although exogenous factors were largely responsible for Vietnam's recent boom and subsequent bust, the finance-related activities of the General Corporations both created the conditions for the boom and were themselves accelerated by the appreciation of asset prices. The period immediately prior to and during the boom saw a pronounced shift towards a new financial structure in Vietnam, in which state General Corporations have acquired the ability to self-finance. Our central contention is that institutional innovation by Vietnam's General Corporations has, in broadly institutionalist Minsky terms, increased the tendency towards financial instability in Vietnam and has at the same time undermined the capacity of policymakers to regain control over key macroeconomic variables.

We argue further that these changes in Vietnam have been heavily influenced by the institutional legacy of central planning. The behaviour of General Corporation managers reflects deeply ingrained habits of liquidity hunger, investment hunger and unrestrained diversification learned under the command economy. Left unchecked, the impulse to borrow, invest and diversify will lead to financial instability. However imperfect the capacity of bureaucrats was under central planning to control this behaviour, state corporations could not increase leverage without the consent of agencies and power holders external to themselves. Now that General Corporations have acquired the ability to self finance, bureaucrats are virtually powerless to control state companies' investment and diversification decisions. The result is a systemic tendency towards Ponzi finance and policymakers' progressive loss of control over the supply of money.

The rest of the chapter is organised as follows. The next section provides historical background with an emphasis on the importance of the planning period to the subsequent development of financial and corporate structures in Vietnam. Habits learned under central planning conditioned the behaviour of state company managers. Prominent among these habits is the drive to diversification, which was part and parcel of the functioning of the economy under central planning. We then present a short history of the General Corporations, followed by a discussion of key characteristics of their management, including liquidity and investment hunger, the drive to expansion, revenue shielding and hollowing out. These characteristics provide the historical context required for a fuller understanding of the recent moves of General Corporation into finance and real estate. These developments have important implications for Vietnam's ambitions to deploy state companies as the main vehicle through which the country achieves its ambitions for rapid industrialisation.

11.2 Historical elements

Diversification by state companies, including establishing banks, is not a new feature of Vietnamese business activity. Gainsborough (2003b) traces the rise and fall of Tan Binh Production Service Trading and Export Company (Tamexco) in the early 1990s prior to the creation of the General Corporations. The tendency for state companies to grow through horizontal diversification has a long history in Vietnam. Although these pressures are present in all centrally planned economies, they were perhaps even more pronounced in Vietnam because of the exceptional weakness of the planning bureaucracy. The war necessitated pragmatic decentralisation and compromise, as the need to supply the troops took precedence over the integrity of the planning system. Fforde points out that in the 1960s the government of the Democratic Republic of Vietnam failed to stamp out market transactions in rice conducted by collectivised northern farmers (Fforde, 1993: p. 297). State companies engaged in similar practices, with the result that markets were always more important to the northern economy than official documents of the period suggest.

Conditions were no more conducive to centralisation of control after reunification in 1976, as conflict with China and a reduction in Soviet aid derailed efforts to impose a traditional central planning model during peacetime. 'Fence-breaking', a euphemism for market and smuggling operations outside of the plan, proliferated as the system edged towards complete disintegration (Fforde, 1993; Dang Phong and Beresford, 1998).

Reforms introduced in 1981 increased formal decision making authority at lower levels for both state-owned enterprises and agricultural cooperatives. Although these reforms were intended to save the planning system, they accelerated its demise by legitimising the long established preference for market over plan transactions. The economy became increasingly commercialised and market oriented. In 1986 *đổi mới* (renovation) became official policy of the Communist Party and by 1989 formal central planning was abolished with the end of the two-price system (Fforde, 1993).

11.3 Diversification incentives in planned economies

While the planning system was particularly weak in Vietnam, it is important to remember that 'fence-breaking' was endemic to central planning wherever it was attempted. Gerschenkron's comment on 'the normalcy of Soviet mercantilism, concealed beneath a generous veneer of socialist phraseology' (1962: p. 295) applies equally well to Vietnam under central planning. Implementation of the plan gave rise to institutionalised disinformation and negotiation between bureaucrats and firm managers to overcome shortage and to serve the political interests of managers and bureaucrats. The authorities bemoaned this state of affairs in their official pronouncements while condoning it in practice. Evading the plan was required to fulfil it and market-oriented activity was a core feature of planning itself (Gerschenkron, 1962; Van Arkadie and Karlsson, 1992; Lavigne, 1999).

Toporowski (1998) identifies 'liquidity hunger' as a key aspect of socialist firms. Restrictions on the accumulation of financial wealth resulted in a lack of retained earnings, with most firms relying on borrowing to finance investment. Dependence on external financing increases the importance of cash flow to service liabilities.[5] Yet, revenues from deliveries under the plan are tightly circumscribed. Diversification is a means to secure cash flow outside of plan deliveries to meet debt obligations.

The concept of liquidity hunger derives from the idea of 'investment hunger' introduced by János Kornai in his classic analysis of central planning (1979) in which he explores the effects of soft budget constraints in resource constrained systems. When the state covers firms' losses profitability ceases to be a criterion for investment, which is instead driven by the desire of planners to achieve targets. The result is infinite demand. Every firm has an insatiable demand for inputs since the capacity to sell output is irrelevant. With infinite demand, the system becomes resource constrained as limits are imposed by the physical availability of inputs rather than prices. This produces chronic shortages as resource constraints – physical bottlenecks – are reached. It also produces uncertainty in input supply, resulting in hoarding, and more shortage.

The consequence of infinite demand is investment hunger. Investment is risk free because firms do not go bankrupt. Access to finance, which is controlled by planners, is the only limiting factor. Investment hunger is insatiable as each firm has infinite demand and a desire to secure as much of the finite resource pool as possible. Diversification is an outcome of the expansion drive created by investment hunger.

Investment hunger does not require the full apparatus of central planning. All that is required is a soft budget constraint, freedom from the threat of bankruptcy and political allocation of investment resources. Evidence of investment hunger in Vietnam during the reform period can be found both in public sector infrastructure investments and state companies. The failure of planners and politicians in Vietnam to impose discipline on local authorities and state firms has resulted in a sharp increase in the share of investment in national output accompanied by a secular decline in investment efficiency (Harvard Vietnam Program, 2008b). The next section will review the history of Vietnam's General Corporations, using expansion drive, investment hunger and liquidity hunger to understand their behaviour.

11.4 The General Corporations

The characteristics of planning systems described above were apparent in Vietnam during the centrally planned period. Porter (1993) describes the development of market relations among state companies to reduce imbalances, bargaining and concealment of production capacity to secure lower targets, and efforts to acquire larger quantities of inputs than needed in order to trade on parallel markets. Habits acquired during the period of central planning still condition the behaviour of General Corporations (GCs) more than two decades after the advent of reform. This in part reflects the fact that today's senior managers were trained under central planning and promoted largely on the basis of their loyalty to their superiors within the firm and party. But material conditions are also relevant. Today's GCs still enjoy soft budget constraints and easy access to state assets much like their predecessors under central planning.

This section provides a brief overview of the history of GCs and the role of liquidity hunger, investment hunger and the drive to expansion in the Vietnamese context. We also consider the implications of two additional factors, which we refer to as revenue shielding and hollowing out. These legacies of planning provide the historical context for recent GC moves into finance, real estate and other speculative ventures. The GC's acquisition of self-financing capabilities as part of the diversification drive is a key factor in Vietnam's tendency to financial instability in recent years.

11.4.1 Background

With the end of formal planning in 1989, the government progressively removed constraints on private sector activity. This did not mean, however, that the party had abandoned the idea that the state should remain as the leading sector (Van Arkadie and Mallon, 2003; Cheshier *et al.*, 2006). The creation of the GCs is appropriately viewed within the context of the government and party's search for a model to preserve state leadership of the economy despite the formal recognition of the private sector. Inspiration for the GCs came from the Korean *chaebol* and the creation of state business groups in China in the early 1990s. The legislation creating the GCs was promulgated in 1994, and over the next 2 years GCs were established in a variety of sectors. These corporations were predominately created from existing state firms and enterprise unions (Fforde, 1995; Marukawa, 1999; Cheshier and Penrose, 2007).[6]

The GCs were seen as the mechanism to achieve state-led industrialisation in a socialist-oriented market economy. The GCs were frequently established as near monopolies in their respective sectors and were provided with subsidised credit to implement sector development plans. Like other state companies they enjoyed preferential access to land and opportunities for foreign trade. Foreign investors were frequently directed to GCs and their members as suitable joint venture partners (Fforde, 1995; Van Arkadie and Mallon, 2003; Cheshier and Penrose, 2007). Even though the economy was changing rapidly as a result of ongoing reforms, the GCs remained a bastion of state intervention. The planning legacy was strong and expansion drive, investment hunger and liquidity hunger continued to influence GC decision making.

11.4.2 Liquidity hunger

General Corporations were responsible for sector development plans and were also directed to achieve social policy objectives. This latter role is a common feature of state firms in both planned and market economies. In addition to creating jobs and paying taxes, the GCs were required to operate in their core business sectors even if these activities were rendered unprofitable due to government-imposed price controls or other restrictions. For example, GCs were instructed to provide farmers with low cost fertilisers and to provide electricity to consumers at artificially low prices.[7] In a variation on liquidity hunger, diversification provides cash flow from profitable non-core activities to cover shortfalls from core businesses. The government could hardly restrict expansion into lucrative ventures like the development of industrial estates if at the same time it required state companies to make losses in their core businesses. Moreover, corporation targets are focused on profits and contributions to the state budget irrespective of how profits are generated. As a result, GCs pursued liquidity hunger driven diversification to meet their obligations to the state, presumably with the acquiescence of planners and politicians (Cheshier and Penrose, 2007).

11.4.3 Investment hunger and expansion drive

In other planned economies, the expansion drive, hoarding and systematic misrepresentation of real capacity generated a bizarre situation of general scarcity amidst excess capacity (Van Arkadie and Karlsson, 1992). However, socialist economies tended to create monopolies organised around particular ministries and their subordinate firms. This made expansion beyond the main areas of activity difficult since monopolies were vigorously defended. Firms were encouraged, though, to use excess capacity in related activities. Firms developed internal workshops and other productive units to meet their input needs, simultaneously utilising excess capacity and generating protection from shortages in goods and services (Lavigne, 1999).

This process also occurred in Vietnam, even after the end of formal central planning. Until recently, GC diversification to utilise excess capacity most often occurred in input supply and services required by the corporation. The Vietnam Coal and Mineral Industries Group (Vinacomin) moved into truck manufacturing to provide mining trucks to its member companies.[8] The Vietnam Paper Corporation (Vinapaco, formerly Vinapimex) moved into chemicals for paper production to supply its members (Cheshier and Penrose, 2007). Vietnam Chemical Corporation (Vinachem) member companies created workshops to supply spare parts. Unofficial activities were also prevalent. Both during and after planning, '[m]ost smuggling was either carried out or condoned by state organisations' (Fforde, 1993: p. 302, footnote 24; see also Porter, 1993; Beresford and Dang Phong, 2000).

The formal situation has also begun to change. As part of the reform process, several core monopolies were opened to 'bounded competition' primarily between GCs. The telecoms sector was dominated by the Vietnam Post and Telecommunications Group, but has seen the entry of the Army's Viettel, Electricity of Vietnam (EVN) through EVN Telecom and other providers. Vinachem's fertiliser base of operations has been penetrated by the Vietnam Oil and Gas Group (Petrovietnam). Both Petrovietnam and Vinacomin are moving into power generation, previously a monopoly of EVN (Cheshier and Penrose, 2007; Cheshier *et al.*, 2008). The situation is illustrated in Figure 11.1. Excess capacity is now being used to diversify beyond simple related within-group activities focused on input provision, and is now occurring in a range of upstream and downstream areas that were once off limits due to maintenance of monopoly positions.

GCs' ability to break out of their core activities and to invest in lucrative sectors outside of their mandate depends to a large extent on their access to cash. State corporations with access to larger revenue streams are in a better position to diversify. GCs operating in natural resource sectors like Petrovietnam and Vinacomin and military-linked companies (which control

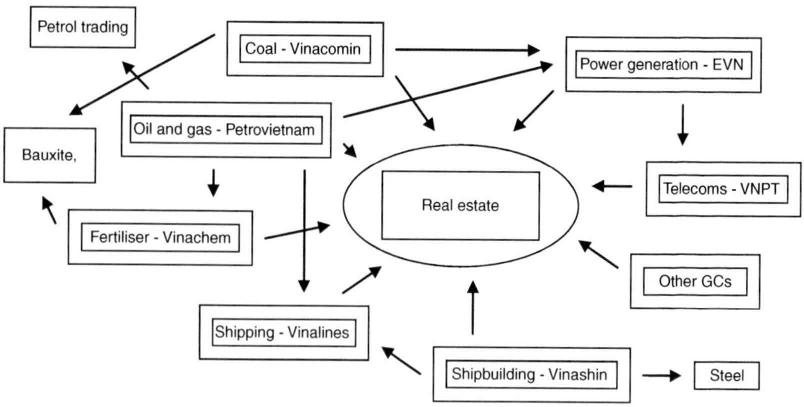

Figure 11.1 General corporation diversification.
Source: Adapted from Cheshier *et al.* (2008), p. 14.

large areas of forest land) are particularly well placed. As Kornai (1979) first pointed out, the presence of a soft budget constraint does not mean that financial resources are unlimited, and that investment hunger will enable all state companies to implement their plan and off-plan activities. Kornai's key insight is that the infinite investment demand of firms runs up against a finite pool of financial resources.

Investment hunger and the expansion drive are constant but constrained by the availability of finance. How these constraints are managed is a political issue, with results differing from place to place reflecting the balance of power among firms, planners and politicians.

In Vietnam, most state companies face a hard budget constraint (Beresford, 2008). However, the GCs are in a privileged position, and even among them important differences can be found. As noted above, companies operating in natural resource exploitation have easiest access to revenues. Vinachem must produce subsidised fertilisers and thus has less profit to invest in sideline activities. The garments base of the Vietnam Textile and Garment Group (Vinatex) provides thin margins due to intense competition with domestic private and foreign firms (Cheshier *et al.*, 2008).[9]

A spectacular example of expansion drive diversification resulting from a relaxation of financial constraints was the activities in 2008 of the Vietnam Shipbuilding Industry Group (Vinashin). At the end of 2005 the Vietnamese government issued its first sovereign bond managed by Credit Suisse First Boston, obtaining $750 million. This was on-lent to Vinashin in 2006 to facilitate upgrading and expansion of the shipbuilding industry. In 2007 Vinashin established 154 new member companies. Excluding weekends, there are 260 working days in the year. Vinashin therefore created a new subsidiary on average every 1.69 days (*Thời báo Kinh tế Sàigòn Online*,

2008). These include shipyards, investment and development companies, construction companies and import export firms.[10]

11.4.4 Shielding revenues and hollowing out

Differential core cash flow, access to limited finance, liquidity hunger and expansion drive have further consequences. The corporate governance structure of GCs gives them significant decision making authority over their member companies. The head office is the liaison between the government and corporation member companies. On paper, the head office is the representative of state capital invested in its subsidiaries, and as such is supposed to serve the interests of the state. Top corporate executives are appointed by senior levels of government, and for the largest GCs these appointments are approved by the Prime Minister (Cheshier *et al.*, 2006). However, within the corporation, the head office and corporate leadership wield ultimate control.[11] Under this arrangement, diversification becomes a useful method to shield revenues from the state. Creation of subsidiaries is a way to 'park' excess capital, keeping it under the control of corporate headquarters.[12] This has the added benefit of facilitating transfer pricing between member companies in order to meet targets and debt obligations.

An additional diversification incentive is private gain. The process is similar to revenue shielding but takes a different form. Rather than establish an official member company, a private (joint stock) firm is created with a relative or friend in charge.[13] The state firm directs profitable contracts to the private unofficial affiliate while keeping less profitable activities. State assets may be transferred to the new company at favourable prices. The result is large private profits and a weakened state enterprise. Diversification as 'hollowing out' becomes a means for diverting state resources for private gain (Fforde, 1993; Gainsborough, 2003a; Fforde, 2004).

11.4.5 Implications of GC diversification into finance and real estate

Liquidity hunger, investment hunger and expansion drive, revenue shielding and hollowing out form the backdrop for examining recent GC behaviour. GC entry into finance and real estate are part of a longer historical diversification process. However, diversification has moved beyond the traditional process of entry into related activities, upstream and downstream production, smuggling and asset accumulation. It now includes acquiring banks, establishing finance, insurance, leasing and securities companies, speculating in real estate and building golf courses, office buildings, five star hotels and tourist resorts. This represents a potentially permanent change in the political landscape, altering not only the relation between the state and GCs, but also the impact of the GCs on the financial stability of the economy.

Control over financial institutions is at the core of this change. Finance companies are non-bank credit institutions licensed and supervised by the

State Bank of Vietnam (SBV). In many respects similar to banks, they cannot provide payment settlement services. They are allowed to accept long-term deposits, borrow from domestic and foreign financial institutions, issue bonds and commercial paper, make loans and provide loan guarantees, buy shares, trade in foreign exchange and underwrite securities.[14]

The full details of GC involvement in finance are difficult to ascertain.[15] Nevertheless, a few facts and figures provides a picture of the scale of activity. Seventy-five per cent of existing financing companies are controlled by GCs (Vietnam Business Finance, 2008b). These include the largest corporate groups in Vietnam, such as EVN (electricity), Petrovietnam (oil and gas), Geruco (rubber), Vinacomin (mining), Vinashin (shipbuilding), Vinatex (garments) and Vietnam Post and Telecommunications Group.[16] Several other GCs have plans to create finance companies, including Vinachem (Vietnam Business Finance, 2008a).

GC holdings in banks are particularly difficult to identify.[17] Vietnam Petroleum Corporation (Petrolimex) has a 40 per cent stake in the Petroleum Group (PG) Bank. EVN has a 28 per cent stake in An Binh Bank (ABBank) (Vietnam Net, 2008a). Vinashin has a 7 per cent stake in Hanoi Building Bank (Habubank) and a finance leasing company under Vinashin Finance. Petrovietnam has a 9.5 per cent stake in Global Petrol Bank (GP Bank) (Vietnam Net, 2008b). VNPT has a 21 per cent stake in Maritime Bank (MSB) and has plans to turn its Vietnam Postal Savings Services Company (VPSC) into a bank (Vietnam Net, 2006, 2007b). Its member company, Vietnam Mobile Telecom Services Company (VMS, commonly known as Mobifone), is an investor in Tien Phong Bank. Vietnam Airlines is a major shareholder of Techcombank. Vietnam Airlines member company Southern Airport Services Company (Sasco) is an investor in Lien Viet Bank along with Saigon Trading Corporation (Satra) (Vietnam Stock Market News, 2008). Satra is also a strategic investor in Habubank (Vietnam Net, 2007a). Vinatex has an 11 per cent stake in Nam Viet Bank (Navibank) and holds equity in Maritime Bank (Morgan Stanley Gateway Securities, 2008). Both Vinacomin and Geruco have stakes in Saigon Hanoi Bank (SHB), which is a strategic partner of the Vietnam Machinery Erection Corporation (Lilama) (Vietnam News Agency, 2007).

Petrolimex also has an insurance company, Petrolimex Insurance (PJICO), as does Petrovietnam in Petrovietnam Insurance (PVI). Vietnam Airlines recently established an insurance company in which Vinacomin and Lilama are also investors (Thanh Nien News, 2008). Petrovietnam has real estate companies under Petrovietnam Finance Corporation (PVFC) and Petrovietnam Power Corporation (PV Power), and is involved in construction of office buildings, hotels, resorts and golf courses. Vinatex also has a real estate company and at least one of its member companies has invested in resort complexes (Cheshier and Penrose, 2007). Geruco is involved in construction of industrial zones, Vinacomin in commercial property development and Vinashin in industrial zone development and hotel construction. The finance–real estate nexus is illustrated by the Vinashin Hotel project in Nam Dinh. The hotel is being built by Vinashin member company Hoang Anh Shipbuilding using loans from Habubank, in which Vinashin holds a 7 per cent stake.[18] Several GCs are also involved in securities companies, but as with banks this is extremely difficult to trace. Control can be exercised through a GC invested bank which establishes a securities company, a GC independent investment in a securities firm or creation of a securities member company. Vinashin has a securities firm under Vinashin Finance. Saigon Hanoi Bank, in which Vinacomin and Geruco are investors, has its own securities company. Vinatex holds a stake in Empower Securities and EVN has member company Ha Thanh Securities.

For the GCs, finance companies create the capacity to self-finance. They also act as fungibility machines, with the finance company functioning as a black box for corporate funds and maturing debt obligations. Combine a finance company with a large stake in a bank, and the GC ability to self-finance increases exponentially. Combine these with a securities company, and the GC can underwrite, purchase, trade, manipulate and profit from the equitisation of its member companies – all within the same corporation. This is illustrated in Figure 11.2. The scope for intra-group lending, financial engineering, insider trading and speculative profiteering is enormous.

This process also extends the transmogrification of GCs into investment groups, turning interest away from sector development towards a focus on returns to investment.[19] It could be argued that this is a positive step as GCs increase the efficiency of capital by directing resources towards ventures yielding the highest returns. However, we should not fall into the trap of assuming that GCs confront equilibrium prices that reflect the economic value of the resources that they use and the products that they produce. Enjoying privileged access to cheap land and capital, and control over

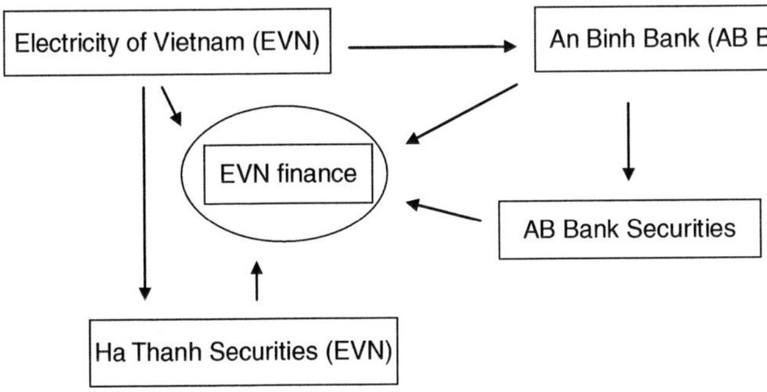

Figure 11.2 Interlocking investments – EVN finance.
Source: VCCI 2008.

natural resource and monopoly rents, the GCs respond to incentives that drive them towards land and capital intensive projects and into protected markets for goods and services. Moreover, an absence of transparency opens up profitable strategies that are based less on productivity and efficiency than creative bookkeeping.

The GCs, and state enterprise more generally, have a history of privileged access to land and most GCs and SOEs hold surplus land (World Bank, 2005). Diversification into real estate development is therefore not surprising. As equitisation of GC member companies proceeds, they will have an increasing interest in the stock market and the valuations of member firms. Combined with the capacity to self-finance, this will allow GCs to become self-contained speculators. Diversification into finance not only reduces the attractiveness of sector development, it also increases financial fragility.

The causes of the macroeconomic turbulence of 2007 and early 2008 were many and varied. The rush of foreign capital into Vietnam in the wake of the country's accession to the World Trade Organisation and excessive liquidity on international capital markets certainly played a major role. GCs participated in the boom and contributed to it by borrowing heavily from member company banks and other financial institutions to invest in real estate and shares and to diversify into a wide range of markets through the creation of child and grandchild companies. The penetration of GCs into banking and finance has resulted in intra-group lending, although even rough estimates of the extent of the problem are not publically available. Intra-group lending makes it difficult for the monetary authorities to monitor and control credit growth and the money supply, a problem that has contributed to financial crises in Chile, Korea and Indonesia (Pincus and Vu Thanh Tu Anh, 2008; see also Studwell, 2007; Harvard Vietnam Program, 2008b).[20]

One of the most pressing concerns of government is the limited progress made by GCs in increasing productivity and profitability in their respective core sectors. Production of textiles, steel, electricity, chemicals and other sectors have failed to keep pace with demand, leaving the country heavily dependent on imports and facing chronic trade deficits. In some sectors, production in terms of quality, complexity and efficiency is little changed from 20 years ago and equipment is often even older, in some cases dating from the 1960s (Cheshier and Penrose, 2007). While it is true that some GCs have done better than others, and most of them have at least a few dynamic and competitive member companies, the conglomerates as a whole continues to rely for profits on natural resource and monopoly rents.[21] Diversification has centred on lucrative ventures in residential and commercial properties, industrial estates, resorts, finance and distribution, and has for the most part studiously avoided export industries, which have largely been left to foreign and private domestic firms.

Liquidity hunger, investment hunger and expansion drive, all part of the legacy of central planning, combine to drive GCs towards diversification into sideline activities based on the groups' comparative advantage in terms of access to cheap land and capital and the corridors of power. Diversification helps the groups to finance their social policy obligations and unprofitable core business activities and to achieve profit and tax targets. Diversification also makes possible transfer pricing between member companies, which facilitates revenue shielding, the ability of groups to retain corporate control over excess capital and the diversion of state resources to private companies.

Thus the recent round of GC diversification into finance and real estate is appropriately viewed as part of a longer historical process. However, acquisition of self-financing capabilities represents a structural break with previous forms of diversification. The scope for risky intra-group lending and speculative investment increases with the presence of an intra-group bank and finance company. The attraction of investment in the group's core sector wanes as the GCs transform themselves into investment houses seeking out the highest returns available given their privileged access to land and capital. Financial fragility increases to the extent that GC financial firms engage in risky intra-group lending, leasing, insuring and underwriting, and the result impacts on asset prices and the balance sheet effects of GCs and related companies. An important dimension of the capacity of groups to self-finance is the decline in the relative bargaining power of bureaucrats and planners vis-à-vis GC managers. The increasing financial autonomy of GCs gives them the power to resist state pressure to invest in slow-gestating industrial and export projects that are unprofitable, at least in the short-term. A disjuncture has therefore emerged between the rhetoric of state-led industrialisation and the practice of the state sector's largest business groups.

11.5 Conclusion

Diversification is not new in Vietnam. The legacy of planning provides a context for understanding recent GC moves into finance, real estate and other activities outside of their core sectors. However, acquisition of self-financing capabilities represents a fundamental change in the structure of the Vietnamese financial and corporate system. From the perspective of institutional Minsky, the GCs have introduced financial innovations to increase their leverage, and they resisted the efforts of regulators to redirect their activities to state-approved investments in core sectors in pursuit of industrialisation and social objectives.

The government's commitment to state control over the 'commanding heights' of the economy through the vehicle of the GCs is a political decision, and one that is largely immaterial to the performance of the groups themselves (Harvard Vietnam Program, 2008b). Equitisation, or the conversion of public companies into joint stock companies with or without state majority control, is unlikely to improve the performance of the GCs. More relevant to the analysis presented in this chapter is the capacity of the government to impose discipline on the groups in the form of performance criteria in terms of exports, profitability or some other measure of productivity. The growing capacity of the groups to self finance has diminished the relative bargaining power of the state, making it less likely that bureaucrats and politicians will demand that the state's interests in industrialisation over the long period take precedence over the GCs' desire for profits in the short period.

Notes

1. This chapter is adapted from a United Nations Development Programme (UNDP) Vietnam Policy Dialogue Paper commissioned by the Country Economist Unit of UNDP, under the direction of Alex Warren-Rodriguez. Financial support from the Department for International Development (DFID) of the United Kingdom through the DFID-UNDP Strategic Partnership Initiative is gratefully acknowledged. The views expressed here are the authors' alone and do not necessarily reflect the views of the United Nations or the countries it represents. Special thanks are due to Sandhya Balasubrahmanyam, Do Le Thu Ngoc, Martin Gainsborough, Thaddeus Hostetler, Richard Jones, Jago Penrose, Jason Picard, Scott Robertson, Gerard Sasges, Daniela Tavasci, Markus Taussig, Jan Toporowski, Brian Van Arkadie and Alex Warren-Rodriguez. The authors are solely responsible for any errors of fact or omission.
2. This tripartite classification of Minsky is based on Toporowski (2005), which identifies the first two variations, and discussions with Daniela Tavasci, who identified the third.
3. The first edition of Kindleberger's classic appeared in 1978.
4. Palma (1998) uses this approach to explain the Asian Financial Crisis. Arestis and Glickman (2002) also apply Minsky's financial instability hypothesis to an open economy in their analysis of the Asian Financial Crisis. They remark on the existence of 'two' Minskys corresponding to the first two variations presented here. Arestis and Glickman add the concept of the 'super-speculative unit' borrowing in foreign currencies to Minsky's hedge-speculative-Ponzi trichotomy.
5. Although retained earnings are an important source of large firm financing in Vietnam (Cheshier and Penrose, 2007), high SOE debt–equity ratios indicate dependence on borrowing and hence liquidity hunger. See Harvard Vietnam Program (2008b), Figure 1, p. 4 for data on SOE finances. In addition, the degree of accumulation within Vietnamese state firms is complicated by the commercialisation process during planning and transition, manifested in the conflict over 'own capital'. See Fforde (1993) for details.
6. A full history of General Corporations and their ongoing reforms will not be provided here. Interested readers should refer to Fforde (1995); Marukawa (1999); Van Arkadie and Mallon (2003); Cheshier *et al.* (2006); Cheshier and Penrose (2007); Harvard Vietnam Program (2008a, 2008b); and Cheshier *et al.* (2008).
7. This is beginning to change as Vietnam moves towards market based prices in accordance with World Trade Organisation (WTO) commitments.
8. At the time it was the Vietnam Coal Corporation (Vinacoal). Economic Groups are a particular corporate structure that some General Corporations take as part of ongoing reforms. See Cheshier *et al.* (2006) and Cheshier and Penrose (2007) for details.

9. A key tool General Corporations use to reduce budget constraints and increase access to finance is loan guarantees. In a cascade of implicit coverage, the state guarantees the General Corporations and the corporations guarantee their member companies. Loan guarantees for member companies are a core function of the corporations (Cheshier and Penrose, 2007). The state itself typically only intervenes with state-owned commercial banks (SOCBs) to force lending for key strategic projects. These projects are invariably implemented by General Corporations and the SOCBs usually resist such lending due to exceptionally low profit expectations. However, political lending remains the norm (Malesky and Taussig, 2009), even without explicit state involvement. In addition, some General Corporations have begun accessing (until quite recently) enthusiastic international capital markets. Perceived state guarantees have been crucial in securing international loans. For example, in 2006 Vinashin secured a $1 billion Credit Suisse loan. More recently, Deutsche Bank provided a $2 billion to Vinashin and a $500 million loan to Vinatex following an official Prime Ministerial visit to Germany (Pincus and Vu Thanh Tu Anh, 2008).
10. See Vinashin website for details (www.vinashin.com.vn/members.aspx). In the English version only companies related to shipbuilding are listed, while in the Vietnamese version the scope of diversification becomes more apparent.
11. Not all corporate headquarters dominate their member companies, with some General Corporations quite weak in practice. The point is that the formal corporate governance structure of General Corporations provide head offices with jurisdiction over their members. The degree to which this is exercised, and the interest the head office takes in its members, varies by corporation (Cheshier and Penrose, 2007).
12. This strategy was conveyed to one author by several firms during interviews conducted under the project resulting in Cheshier and Penrose (2007). In the context of ongoing General Corporation reform and equitisation of member companies, this strategy also provides a way for senior corporate management to engineer significant personal income streams by appointing themselves to the management boards of new member companies. They would receive preferential access to shares should the member company be equitised. This is the authors' personal speculation, supported by Harvard Vietnam Program (2008a). Further research is needed.
13. Although this is illegal, it is quite frequent.
14. Decree 79/2002/ND-CP of 4 October on Organisation and Operation of Finance Companies.
15. Unless otherwise noted, the information presented here is drawn from the General Corporation website or bank website being discussed. Additional information is from interviews conducted for the project resulting in Cheshier and Penrose (2007).
16. See State Bank of Vietnam (SBV) website (www.sbv.gov.vn/en/home/htCtytchinh.jsp) for additional details. The SBV list is not current.
17. Some banks have received licenses but are not yet in operation. Others remain in the plan stage while some banks are still only ideas. For example, Vietnam Airlines had a 3 per cent stake in Hong Viet Bank and Hanoi Beer and Alcohol Corporation (Habeco) had a 5 per cent stake. Petrovietnam had a 20 per cent stake in the same bank but decided to pull out of the project. Investors' capital has been returned (Vietnam Net, 2008b). Lilama is involved in the proposed Kien Bac Bank and Vinachem is part of the Vietstar Bank project (Vietnam Net, 2008c).

Vinatex has plans for an Industrial Development Bank involving several other General Corporations (Morgan Stanley Gateway Securities, 2008). It is uncertain whether these projects will proceed.

18. http://www.habubank.com.vn/default.aspx?tabid=431&cateid=516&MainMenuID=1&MenuItemID=388.
19. This is increasingly the case for several General Corporations, for example, Geruco and many of its largest member companies (Cheshier and Penrose, 2007).
20. Vietnam does not publish reliable information on the sources of credit growth, and separating out the role of state versus private sector borrowing is impossible given the available data. The categories 'state' and 'non-state' are less informative than they appear at first glance because equitised joint stock companies, many of which still have minority state control, are listed as non-state.
21. For example, Mobifone and Vietnam Telecom Services Company (Vinaphone), both under VNPT, are significant players in the telecoms market. Nha Be Garments Company (Nhabeco), Viet Tien Garments Company (Vtec), and Garments Company No. 10 (Garco 10), all under Vinatex, are moving into higher quality garments products, expanding exports and developing brands.

References

Arestis, P. and M. Glickman (2002) 'Financial crisis in Southeast Asia: dispelling illusion the Minskyan way', *Cambridge Journal of Economics*, vol. 26.

Beresford, M. (2008) 'Doi Moi in review: The challenges of building market socialism in vietnam', *Journal of Contemporary Asia*, vol. 38: 2.

Beresford, M. and D. Phong (2000) *Economic Transition in Vietnam: Trade and Aid in the Demise of a Centrally Planned Economy* (Cheltenham: Edward Elgar).

Cheshier, S., J. Penrose and N. Thi Thanh Nga (2006) 'The state as investor: Equitisation, privatisation and the transformation of SOEs in Vietnam', *UNDP Vietnam Policy Dialogue Paper* 2006/3, Hanoi.

Cheshier, S. and J. Penrose (2007) 'The top 200: Industrial strategies of Vietnam's largest firms', *UNDP Vietnam Policy Dialogue Paper* 2007/4, Hanoi.

Cheshier, S., S. Robertson and B. Stoops (2008) 'SOE reform: The number-one challenge', *Vietnam Focus, Dragon Capital*, Ho Chi Minh City.

Dang, P. and M. Beresford (1998) *Authority Relations and Economic Decision Making in Vietnam: An Historical Perspective* (Copenhagen: Nordic Institute of Asian Studies, NIAS).

Fforde, A. (1993) 'The political economy of 'Reform' in Vietnam – some reflections', in Börje Ljunggren (ed.) *The Challenge of Reform in Indochina* (Cambridge: Harvard Institute for International Development).

Fforde, A. (1995) *Vietnam: Economic Commentary and Analysis, A Bi-annual Appraisal of the Vietnamese Economy* (Canberra: Aduki Pty Ltd.), Issue no. 7.

Fforde, A. (2004) 'Vietnamese state-owned enterprises: "Real Property" commercial performance and political economy', *Southeast Asian Research Center (SEARC) Working Paper Series no. 69*, August.

Gainsborough, M. (2003a) *Changing Political Economy in Vietnam: The Case of Ho Chi Minh City* (London: Routledge).

Gainsborough, M. (2003b) 'Corruption and the politics of economic decentralisation in Vietnam', *Journal of Contemporary Asia*, vol. 33, no. 1.

Gerschenkron, A. (1962) 'Industrial enterprise in Soviet Russia', *Economic Backwardness in Historical Perspective: A Book of Essays* (Cambridge: The Belknap Press of Harvard University Press).

Harvard Vietnam Program (2008a) 'Choosing Success: The Lessons of East and Southeast Asia and Vietnam's Future, A Policy Framework for Vietnam's Socioeconomic Development, 2011–2020', *Harvard Kennedy School Vietnam Program, Policy Discussion Paper* no. 1, Ho Chi Minh City, January.

Harvard Vietnam Program (2008b) 'The structural roots of macroeconomic instability', *Harvard Kennedy School Vietnam Program, Policy Discussion Paper* no. 3, Ho Chi Minh City, September.

Kindleberger, C. and R. Aliber (2005) *Manias, Panics and Crashes: A History of Financial Crises*, 5th Ed. (Hoboken: John Wiley and Sons).

Kornai, J. (1979) 'Resource-constrained versus demand-constrained systems', *Econometrica*, vol. 47, no. 4.

Lavigne, M. (1999) *The Economics of Transition: From Socialist Economy to Market Economy*, 2nd Ed. (Basingstoke: Macmillan Press).

Malesky, E. and M. Taussig (2009) 'Where is credit due? Legal institutions, connections, and the efficiency of bank lending in Vietnam', *Journal of Law, Economics and Organization*, vol. 25, no. 2.

Marukawa T., Tomoo (1999) 'Vietnam's General Corporations: Their Outline and a Comparison with Chinese Industrial Groups', in Ministry of Planning and Investment (MPI) and Japanese International Cooperation Agency (JICA) Follow-up Study for the Economic Development Policy in the *Transition toward a Market-oriented Economy in Vietnam*, Vol. 1: General Commentary/Industry and Trade.

Minsky, H.P (1991) 'The transition to a market economy: Financial options', *The Jerome Levy Economics Institute of Bard College Working Paper no. 66*, November.

Minsky, H.P. (1992) 'The financial instability hypothesis', *The Jerome Levy Economics Institute of Bard College Working Paper no.* 74, May.

Minsky, H.P. (2008 [1986]) *Stabilizing an Unstable Economy* (New York: McGraw Hill).

Morgan Stanley Gateway Securities (2008) 'Apparel-maker wants to set up bank', 22 November, http://www.gsi.vn/en/front-end/index.asp?website_id=39&menu_id=600&parent_menu_id=437&article_id=12832&fuseaction=DISPLAY_SINGLE_ARTICLE&hide_menu=0.

Palma, G. (1998) 'Three and a half cycles of "mania, panic, and [asymmetric] crash": East Asia and Latin America compared', *Cambridge Journal of Economics*, vol. 22.

Pincus, J. and A. Vu Thanh Tu (2008) 'Vietnam: A tiger in turmoil', *Far Eastern Economic Review*, vol. 5: 2.

Porter, G. (1993) *Vietnam: The Politics of Bureaucratic Socialism* (Ithaca: Cornell University Press).

Studwell, J. (2007) *Asian Godfathers: Money and Power in Hong Kong and Southeast Asia* (New York: Atlantic Monthly Press).

Thanh Nien News (2008) 'Vietnam Airlines to open insurance company', 3rd May, http://www.thanhniennews.com/business/?catid=2&newsid=38209.

Thời báo Kinh tế Sàigòn (Saigon Economic Times) Online (2008) 'Trật đường ray ngày mưa bão', 1 May, http://www.thesaigontimes.vn/Home/thoisu/sukien/5306.

Toporowski, J. (1998) 'Capital market inflation and privatisation in capitalist and post-communist economies', *Zagreb International Review of Economics and Business*, vol. 1, no. 2.

Toporowski, J. (2005) *Theories of Financial Disturbance: An Examination of Critical Theories of Finance from Adam Smith to the Present Day* (Cheltenham: Edward Elgar).

Van Arkadie, A. and M. Karlsson (1992) *Economic Survey of the Baltic States* (New York: New York University Press).

Van Arkadie, B. and R. Mallon (2003) *Vietnam: A Transition Tiger?* (Canberra: The Australian National University, Asia Pacific Press).

Vietnam Business Finance (2008a) 'Vinachem to establish finance arm', 11th July, http://www.vnbusinessnews.com/2008/07/vinachem-to-establish-finance-arm.html.

Vietnam Business Finance (2008b) 'New comers look to setting up financial companies', 7th August http://www.vnbusinessnews.com/2008/08/new-comers-look-to-setting-up-financial.html.

Vietnam Chamber of Commerce and Industry (VCCI) (2008) 'EVN Finance licensed', Ho Chi Minh City Branch, http://www.vcci-hcm.org/index.php?option=com_content&task=view&id=106795&Itemid=98&lang=en.

Vietnam Net (2006) 'VNPT to set up Post Bank', 12 December, http://english.vietnamnet.vn/biz/2006/12/643309.

Vietnam Net (2007a) 'When big corporations inject money into stocks', 9 March, http://english.vietnamnet.vn/biz/2007/03/671288.

Vietnam Net (2007b) 'VNPT và Maritime Bank nâng tầm hợp tác', October 29th, http://www.vietnamnet.vn/kinhte/2007/10/751829.

Vietnam Net (2008a) 'Malaysia's Maybank to buy 15 percent of ABBank', May 29th, http://english.vietnamnet.vn/biz/2008/05/785614.

Vietnam Net (2008b) 'Petrovietnam pulls out of Hong Viet Bank deal', July 28th, http://english.vietnamnet.vn/biz/2008/07/795878.

Vietnam Net (2008c) 'Setting up banks: investors now like cats on hot bricks', 5 August, http://english.vietnamnet.vn/biz/2008/08/797183.

Vietnam News Agency (2007) 'Sai Gon – Ha Noi Bank to issue shares', 11 October, http://www.vnagency.com.vn/Home/VNAStories/tabid/163/itemid/217699/Default.aspx.

Vietnam Stock Market News (2008) 'Lien Viet Bank: the new kid on the block', 11 April, http://www.vnstocknews.com/2008/04/lien-viet-bank-new-kid-on-block.html.

Whalen, C. (2001) 'Integrating Schumpeter and Keynes: Hyman Minsky's theory of capitalist development', *Journal of Economic Issues*, vol. 39, December.

World Bank (2005) 'Vietnam Development Report 2006: Business', Joint Donor Report to the Vietnam Consultative Group Meeting, Hanoi, December.

12
Financial Stability: The Significance and Distinctiveness of Islamic Banking in Malaysia

Ewa Karwowski

12.1 Introduction

Islamic banking is perceived to be at its 'tipping point' turning from a niche market phenomenon into a mainstream product (BBC, 2006; Credit Suisse, 2006). Although the total international assets of Islamic banks are still marginal, growth rates are phenomenal especially in the Middle East and Southeast Asia. Yet, Islamic banking seems incomprehensible to most Western economists. As discussed below due to the prohibition of interest and collateral Islamic banking is hardly reconcilable with Western economic theory dominated by the asymmetric information paradigm. Islamic scholars, however, claim that it is superior to conventional banking mainly due to the inherent stability of Islamic banking in reducing economic fluctuations and recurring crisis. The third section shows that these claims are questionable.

This chapter explores the significance of Islamic banking in Malaysia for stability of the economy as a whole. The fourth section shows that Malaysia's structural current account surplus causes the over-capitalisation of domestic firms. This results in the emergence of a financial (as opposed to an industrial), consumption-led (instead of investment-led) business cycle where banking favours destabilising asset price inflation. Islamic banks operating inter-dependently with conventional ones contribute to economic destabilisation channelling surplus funds from the corporate to the household sector, feeding asset price inflation.

The theory of financialisation and excess capitalisation – both originally developed for advanced economies – will be applied to an emerging economy. The chapter reveals the hitherto un-discussed dynamic interaction between the Islamic and the non-Islamic economy in Malaysia, showing how Islamic banking contributes to asset price inflation. Due to Malaysia's international integration, the country is a paradigm of the financial structures into which Islamic banking is emerging globally. In this way, the chapter contributes towards the understanding of Islamic banking as a financial phenomenon providing a systemic account – incorporating a macroeconomic and a microeconomic analysis – of its functioning and economic significance.

12.2 Islamic banking in conventional economic theory

In conventional economic theory banks are understood in a generic sense as financial intermediaries. Their main task is to provide indirect finance – in contrast to direct finance through financial markets. Households, businesses, the government and foreigners can in principle possess a surplus or a deficit in funds and supply or demand credit. However, households are identified as most important 'lender-savers' while businesses and the government are the major 'borrower-spenders' (Mishkin and Eakins, 2006: p. 18). Typically, economic analysis initially deals with a simplified setting of a closed economy without government and subsequently loosens these restrictions. Banks are understood to channel surplus funds from the household sector into the corporate sector facing a deficit, as the corporate sector invests more than internal or direct finance would allow. Hence, banks play a vital role in the economy enabling productive investment. So far Western and Islamic understandings of banking do not differ significantly (Siddiqi, 1981).

However, an asymmetric information understanding of banking must lead to the conclusion that Islamic banks are not viable. The distinguishing features of these banks are the prohibition of interest and collateral and, to a smaller extent, compulsory charitable spending (Khan and Mirakhor, 1992; Dhumale and Sapcanin, 2004). Profit has to be generated by primary and secondary modes of Islamic finance (Chapra, 2000). Primary modes include profit-sharing arrangements such as *mudharabah* (partnership) and *musyarakah* (equity participation).[1] Secondary financing modes are meant to take a subordinate position since they are essentially mark-up pricing or leasing arrangements, and not 'truly Islamic' because there is less emphasis on the productive element of investment (Sundararajan and Errico, 2002: p. 18).

It is the prohibition of interest combined with the common belief that banks channel funds towards productive investment that makes Islamic banking and Western economic theory inconsistent with each other. The supply price of credit disappears in a profit-and-loss sharing (PLS) framework because the profit is not known to the bank until the investment is realised. Therefore, asymmetric information models are difficult to apply to Islamic banking.

12.3 Islamic banking in Islamic economic theory

As far as Islamic scholars are concerned Islamic banks should engage primarily in PLS activities (Siddiqi, 1983; Chapra, 2000). They, and an increasing number of Western economists, regard Islamic banking to be superior to conventional banking because of the morality of the homo *Islamicus* (Khan, 1985; Chapra, 2000), the developmental character of the Islamic economic system (Lewis and Algaoud, 2001; Chapra, 2006) and its increased financial and economic stability.

Since economic stability is one of the main – if not the single main – preoccupations of Islamic economics, in the following, the most salient Islamic arguments for the increased stability of Islamic banking will be reviewed starting with microeconomic considerations and moving towards increasingly comprehensive macroeconomic theory.

Considering the demand side of financial funds, Islamic banks are arguably more run-proof than conventional ones. If the bank's value declines there is supposedly less incentive to withdraw funds invested on a PLS base (Lewis and Algaoud, 2001). Nonetheless, a substantial loss in funds would force the bank to withdraw already granted loans if it does not hold 100 per cent reserves. Given the favourable conditions granted to *mudharabah* clients enabling them to withdraw funds on short notice,[2] already an expected fall in profitability could cause a bank run since competing conventional banks might offer a higher (interest) return.

As to the macroeconomic perspective, W. M. Khan considers the work of Western economists to support his case against interest, most prominently Friedrich A. von Hayek and Milton Friedman (Khan, 1985). While Friedman advocated a 100 per cent-reserves system for commercial banks (Friedman, 1959) but was generally convinced that exogenous shocks – and not interest rate changes – altering the quantity of money in the economy caused economic disturbances, Hayek presented a more elaborated theory of the trade cycle. For the latter the idea that the disturbing influence of money only emerges with changes in the price level – as pronounced by Knut Wicksell – was naive (Hayek, 1929). PLS financing modes could eliminate disturbances in Wicksell's economic theory (Wicksell, 1907) since under PLS finance the equivalent of the money rate of interest would always adjust to the marginal return on capital. According to Hayek, the reason for the shortcomings in Wicksell's work lies in the marginalist methodology regarding the interest rate as the price equilibrating supply of savings and demand for credit – the loanable funds theory. In reality, growing economies can be observed to possess interest rates below those equilibrating demand and supply of funds since the former exceeds the latter (Hayek, 1929).

Shaikh Mahmud Ahmad, took up Keynes' concept of the marginal efficiency of capital to explain why interest rates destabilise the economy (Ahmad, 1952). According to Ahmad, Keynes failed to draw the decisive conclusion to eliminate economic crisis: the abolition of interest. Yet, Keynes understood interest as inherent to every commodity not only money. It is composed of the output an asset produces minus its carrying cost and plus its liquidity premium, which individuals are willing to pay for the convenience to possess the commodity. Money is unique since it is the only commodity for which the liquidity premium exceeds the carrying cost by definition. Therefore, the money rate of interest is the determinant rate of interest (Keynes, 1936). Replacing interest entirely by PLS would mean that return on money did not include the liquidity premium. This would under certain conditions – as in a liquidity trap – either deter agents from Islamic investment since they would lose liquidity or transfer the liquidity premium from demand deposit holders to the Islamic bank.

Ahmad's proposition is supported by Muhammad Akram Khan's and Sayyid Abdul A'la Mawdudi's ideas (Siddiqi, 1981). It is argued that recessions occur because interest payments introduce an imbalance between production and consumption. Wealth and purchasing power are transferred from the debtor to the creditor. By definition the former has a higher propensity to consume. While consumption demand decreases, since the debtor has to serve interest payments on the debt, supply increases as the creditor is assumed to invest the funds obtained into production. In the case of entrepreneurial credit, debt servicing causes prices to rise, which again transfers funds from those with a relatively high propensity to consume to those with a relatively low one (Khan, 1968). This analysis – explicitly referring to John A. Hobson (Ahmad, 1952) – stresses that large social income inequalities can be destabilising. However, while Hobson identified large inequality levels favourable to speculation and the emergence of a rentier class living from unearned profit (Hobson, 1938) as economically destabilising, according to Ahmad the sheer existence of interest is destabilising. Interest is seen to play a role in bringing about economic crisis (Ahmad, 1952). Yet, it is unclear what the systemic causalities behind booms and busts are.

Usually, none of the Islamic scholars 'really succeeded in establishing a causal link between interest, on the one hand, and employment and trade cycles, on the other' (Ariff, 1988: p. 50).

Generally, Islamic banking rarely exists in isolation and this co-existence is ignored. Islamic finance must be placed in the context of domestic and global economic and financial flows dominated by non-Islamic finance. Minsky's methodology (Minsky, 1986) and its development by Toporowski (2000) offer a systemic way to analyse financial sector dynamics examining the flow of funds. This makes it superior to New Keynesian approaches based on restrictive assumptions about markets subject to information, moral sentiments or data manipulation.

12.4 Islamic banking in Malaysia from a systemic perspective

In an open economy without government the saving identity takes the following shape (Steindl, 1989; Toporowski, 2009):

$$S \equiv S_H + S_F \equiv I + (X - M) \tag{1}$$

where, S = total saving; S_H = household saving; S_F = retained profits of firms; I = gross investment; $(X - M)$ = trade surplus.

Thus, retained profits are the sum of investment and the foreign balance minus household saving:

$$S_F = I + (X - M) - S_H \quad (2)$$

In an economy with a structurally positive foreign balance as in Malaysia the household saving leakage is less likely to induce 'enforced indebtedness' (Steindl, 1989) being off-set by a balance of payments surplus.[3] The case of emerging markets is interesting since many of them – particularly the East Asian ones – are accumulating vast balance of payments surpluses. But these surpluses are typically held in US dollars or US-treasury bonds. Hence, although emerging markets seem powerful in exporting commodities or (low-skill) manufactured goods, it is the developed world that dominates the international financial architecture. Thus, emerging markets face international financial institutions that are determined by the advanced economies. To a large extent emerging markets are forced to copy those institutions. Islamic banking explicitly tries to break with the Western financial dominance banning interest. The question is whether the autonomous development of this market segment is possible. The answer might differ for financially isolated countries such as Iran and internationally integrated ones such as Malaysia. This study reviews the latter case.

The role banks, and specifically Islamic banks, play depends on the purpose of their activity. The origin and direction of bank lending must be analysed to assess its overall impact on economic stability. Islamic banking in Malaysia exposes key economic and financial issues in Islamic banking. Malaysia possesses a comprehensive Islamic banking and financial system. Simultaneously, non-Islamic companies are allowed to offer Islamic products. Malaysia is an export- and foreign direct investment (FDI)-oriented country and therefore strives to ensure openness towards the international economic and financial system. Malaysia's domestic and international conditions make the country a paradigm of the effects that Islamic banking and international finance exert on each other. Hence, although this study focuses on the significance of Islamic banking for Malaysia, it is an indicator of the role Islamic banking will play in international finance once it leaves its niche (Table 12.1).

As equations (1) and (2) show a positive foreign balance can result in domestic firms' over-capitalisation. Nevertheless, households may be the main beneficiaries of the surplus instead of companies. To clarify whether Malaysian firms are over-capitalised, the balance sheets of a representative sample of large Malaysian companies will be examined. Since large non-financial companies typically undertake the bulk of fixed capital investment, the 25 companies holding the largest stocks at the Kuala Lumpur Stock

Table 12.1 Flows of funds (in RM billions)

Year		**1998**	**1999**	**2000**	**2001**	**2002**	**2003**
Sector	Transactions						
Public sector	Disposable income	72.5	80.5	92.7	96.4	113.5	129.5
	Consumption	–28.5	–33.5	–36.2	–42.9	–50	–54.9
	Investment	–32	–34.5	–43.6	–48.8	–53.7	–57.2
	Change in stocks	0.2	–0.2	–2.1			
	Balance	12.2	12.4	10.8	4.7	9.8	17.3
Private sector	Disposable income	186.8	192.4	211.8	204.4	211.5	232.9
	Consumption	–118.1	–124.8	–145.2	–150.6	–159.5	–172.4
	Investment	–44.3	–32	–43.5	–34.5	–30.1	–29.9
	Change in stocks	0.2	–0.2	–2	3.7	–1.3	2.8
	Balance	24.6	35.5	21.1	23	20.7	33.5
Non-financial balance		36.8	47.9	31.9	27.7	30.5	50.8
Rest of the world	Exports of goods and services	–325.3	–365.4	–427.5	–389.3	–415	–450.6
	Imports of goods and services	263.3	290.1	359.5	327.8	348.9	367.9
	Net factor payment abroad	15.3	20.9	28.6	25.6	25.1	22.5
	Net transfers	9.8	6.5	7.5	8.2	10.6	9.3
	Balance	–36.8	–47.9	–31.9	–27.7	–30.5	–50.8

Table 12.1 (Continued)

Year		2004	2005	2006	2007
Sector	Transactions				
Public sector	Disposable income	131.1	n/a	n/a	n/a
	Consumption	−59.3	n/a	n/a	n/a
	Investment	−53.4	n/a	n/a	n/a
	Change in stocks		n/a	n/a	n/a
	Balance	18.4	8.8	20.2	29.2
Private sector	Disposable Income	279.3	n/a	n/a	n/a
	Consumption	−192.8	n/a	n/a	n/a
	Investment	−38.4	n/a	n/a	n/a
	Change in stocks	−10	n/a	n/a	n/a
	Balance	38.2	67.2	70.8	63.8
Non-financial balance		56.5	76	91	93
Rest of the world	Exports of goods and services	−545	−611	−668	−726
	Imports of goods and services	449.3	495	540	595
	Net factor payment abroad	24.5	24	20	22
	Net transfers	14.6	17	17	16
	Balance	−56.5	−76	−91	−93

Exchange (KLSE) by market value are considered (Bloomberg, 2008). Excluding financial companies and only considering the group and not the specific subsidiaries in the case of conglomerates a sample of 13 representative companies remains, for which assets and liabilities are examined.

Excess capital is typically held in marketable securities and short-term investment but also as deposits, cash equivalents and bank and cash balances. Table 12.2 shows total assets (1.) and total liabilities (2.) – equal by definition – as well as banking and financial assets (3.) of these firms. The most interesting parameter is the percentage of banking and financial assets as share of total liabilities (4.). In marginalist theory companies hold liquid assets only to the extent that marginal revenue covers marginal cost of capital. This implies that banks mainly generate profit via the interest rate spread between the interest rate paid on deposits (borrowing) and that received from credit servicing by firms (lending). Liability management by companies (and banks) leading to speculative return on liquid assets is excluded (Toporowski, 2008). Hence, over-capitalisation should not occur.

On average, the sample of Malaysian companies holds an increasing share of liabilities in banking and financial assets. This trend is even more apparent if the first (1998) and the last observation (2008) are excluded. Since in both cases the average is based on one firm, Genting Group and PETRONAS, respectively, this exclusion is advisable. From 1999 to 2007 the average percentage of liabilities held as short-term investment and cash (equivalents) grew from 10.87 per cent to 28.95 per cent (Figure 12.1).[4]

If Malaysian companies are over-capitalised the question of what role banking – traditionally believed to supply under-capitalised firms with loanable funds – fulfils in the economic system arises. This chapter argues that the effect of financialisation is not merely a characteristic of certain developed economies (as argued in Toporowski, 2009) but equally arises in emerging markets. The large unmet demand of individuals for durable consumption goods and housing enables households to take on the role of the investing sector in the overall economy. Yet, this is only possible because the corporate sector shows signs of over-capitalisation and relinquishes this role to households. Excess capital puts firms in a position where they can acquire profit without undertaking industrial activity. While excess capital in the OECD world is often linked to monopolistic profits, a structural current account surplus can be the origin in emerging markets. Hence, bank credit especially if used by households to invest in real estate or purchases of securities destabilises the economic system.

Despite the claim to affect the economic system in a stabilising way, Islamic banks in Malaysia channel funds from corporates to households mainly financing durable goods and property purchases, which can be seen from their balance sheets.

There were 12 full-fledged Islamic banks active in Malaysia in 2008 (BNM, 2008). Two of them are excluded from the analysis since being subsidiaries

Table 12.2 Financial accumulation of the largest Malaysian quoted companies since 1998 (in RM'000)

Year	1998	1999	2000	2001	2002	2003	2004
Sime Darby Berhad							
1. Total liabilities	n/a	n/a	n/a	n/a	n/a	14,738,600	15,537,900
2. Total assets	n/a	n/a	n/a	n/a	n/a	14,738,600	15,537,900
of which							
3. Banking and financial assets[1]	n/a	n/a	n/a	n/a	n/a	2,676,000	2,862,900
4. Banking and financial assets as % of total liabilities	n/a	n/a	n/a	n/a	n/a	18.16%	18.43%
IOI Corporation Berhad							
1. Total liabilities	n/a	n/a	n/a	4,664,676	5,599,268	7,579,723	8,845,950
2. Total assets	n/a	n/a	n/a	4,664,676	5,599,268	7,579,723	8,845,950
of which							
3. Banking and financial assets[2]	n/a	n/a	n/a	431,559	505,688	501,896	697,907
4. Banking and financial assets as % of total liabilities	n/a	n/a	n/a	9.25%	9.03%	6.62%	7.89%
Tenaga Nasional Berhad							
1. Total liabilities	n/a	n/a	47,573,100	54,584,800	57,065,500	59,956,500	63,381,600
2. Total assets	n/a	n/a	47,573,100	54,584,800	57,065,500	59,956,500	63,381,600
of which							
3. Banking and financial assets[3]	n/a	n/a	827,800	918,000	1,164,700	2,301,800	4,220,300
4. Banking and financial assets as % of total liabilities	n/a	n/a	1.74%	1.68%	2.04%	4.67%	6.66%
MISC Berhad							
1. Total liabilities	n/a	n/a	n/a	n/a	n/a	14,726,303	22,355,514
2. Total assets	n/a	n/a	n/a	n/a	n/a	14,726,303	22,355,514
of which							
3. Banking and financial assets[4]	n/a	n/a	n/a	n/a	n/a	1,034,758	1,859,018
4. Banking and financial assets as % of total liabilities	n/a	n/a	n/a	n/a	n/a	7.03%	8.32%

[1] Cash hold under housing development accounts, bank balances, deposits and cash.
[2] Short-term funds, deposits with financial institutions, cash and bank balances.
[3] Short-term investment, marketable securities, deposits, bank and cash balances.
[4] Marketable securities, cash, bank deposits and bank balances.

Table 12.2 (Continued)

Year	2005	2006	2007	2008
Sime Darby Berhad				
1. Total liabilities	16,235,000	17,539,400	19,555,800	n/a
2. Total assets	16,235,000	17,539,400	19,555,800	n/a
of which				
3. Banking and financial assets	2,618,000	3,212,400	4,718,600	n/a
4. Banking and financial assets as % of total liabilities	16.13%	18.32%	24.13%	n/a
IOI Corporation Berhad				
1. Total liabilities	10,505,059	10,311,686	13,680,842	n/a
2. Total assets	10,505,059	10,311,686	13,680,842	n/a
of which				
3. Banking and financial assets	1,968,767	1,230,370	2,735,195	n/a
4. Banking and financial assets as % of total liabilities	18.74%	11.93%	19.99%	n/a
Tenaga Nasional Berhad				
1. Total liabilities	63,494,800	65,092,100	67,724,600	n/a
2. Total assets	63,494,800	65,092,100	67,724,600	n/a
of which				
3. Banking and financial assets	2,871,400	3,971,500	5,322,500	n/a
4. Banking and financial assets as % of total liabilities	4.52%	6.10%	7.86%	n/a
MISC Berhad				
1. Total liabilities	25,431,412	27,623,105	27,916,771	n/a
2. Total assets	25,431,412	27,623,105	27,916,771	n/a
of which				
3. Banking and financial assets	4,377,381	3,429,556	2,218,415	n/a
4. Banking and financial assets as % of total liabilities	17.21%	12.42%	7.95%	n/a

Table 12.2 (Continued)

Year	1998	1999	2000	2001	2002	2003	2004
Genting Group Berhad							
1. Total liabilities	8,340,100	9,438,800	9,300,800	10,221,100	11,445,800	14,207,400	16,596,500
2. Total assets	8,340,100	9,438,800	9,300,800	10,221,100	11,445,800	14,207,400	16,596,500
of which							
3. Banking and financial assets[5]	1,872,300	2,392,500	1,393,500	2,241,400	2,895,700	4,384,600	5,912,700
4. Banking and financial assets as % of total liabilities	22.45%	25.35%	14.98%	21.93%	25.30%	30.86%	35.63%
Petroliam Nasional Berhad (PETRONAS)							
1. Total liabilities	n/a	n/a	109,019,218	124,681,979	129,325,952	159,629,322	182,222,266
2. Total assets	n/a	n/a	109,019,218	124,681,979	129,325,952	159,629,322	182,222,266
of which							
3. Banking and financial assets[6]	n/a	n/a	45,604,970	53,734,478	51,335,830	64,586,315	67,584,624
4. Banking and financial assets as % of total liabilities	n/a	n/a	41.83%	43.10%	39.69%	40.46%	37.09%
DIGI Telecommunication Berhad							
1. Total liabilities	n/a	n/a	2,077,263	2,410,361	3,008,517	3,247,432	3,580,082
2. Total assets	n/a	n/a	2,077,263	2,410,361	3,008,517	3,247,432	3,580,082
of which							
3. Banking and financial assets[7]	n/a	n/a	211,473	157,663	245,672	338,516	634,719
4. Banking and financial assets as % of total liabilities	n/a	n/a	10.18%	6.54%	8.17%	10.42%	17.73%
Kuala Lumpur Kepong Berhad							
1. Total liabilities	n/a	n/a	n/a	3,738,122	4,071,108	4,524,442	4,896,361
2. Total assets	n/a	n/a	n/a	3,738,122	4,071,108	4,524,442	4,896,361
of which							
3. Banking and financial assets[7]	n/a	n/a	n/a	426,759	409,686	606,545	636,264
4. Banking and financial assets as % of total liabilities	n/a	n/a	n/a	11.42%	10.06%	13.41%	12.99%

5 Restricted cash, short-term investments, bank balances and deposits.
6 Cash, fund investment and other investment, other current assets.
7 Cash and cash equivalents.

Table 12.2 (Continued)

Year	2005	2006	2007	2008
Genting Group Berhad				
1. Total liabilities	18,553,700	28,224,700	30,178,900	n/a
2. Total assets	18,553,700	28,224,700	30,178,900	n/a
of which				
3. Banking and financial assets	6,079,100	8,078,300	9,745,300	n/a
4. Banking and financial assets as % of total liabilities	32.76%	28.62%	32.29%	n/a
Petroliam Nasional Berhad (PETRONAS)				
1. Total liabilities	214,389,358	252,481,519	290,348,806	361,292,900
2. Total assets	214,389,358	252,481,519	290,348,806	361,292,900
of which				
3. Banking and financial assets	92,450,151	111,438,309	127,509,930	161,257,949
4. Banking and financial assets as % of total liabilities	43.12%	44.14%	43.92%	44.63%
DIGI Telecommunication Berhad				
1. Total liabilities	4,232,319	4,123,031	3,877,491	n/a
2. Total assets	4,232,319	4,123,031	3,877,491	n/a
of which				
3. Banking and financial assets	1,182,962	869,549	577,144	n/a
4. Banking and financial assets as % of total liabilities	27.95%	21.09%	14.88%	n/a
Kuala Lumpur Kepong Berhad				
1. Total liabilities	3,556,813	5,692,760	7,003,292	n/a
2. Total assets	3,556,813	5,692,760	7,003,292	n/a
of which				
3. Banking and financial assets	644,754	460,471	495,634	n/a
4. Banking and financial assets as % of total liabilities	18.13%	8.09%	7.08%	n/a

Table 12.2 (Continued)

Year	1998	1999	2000	2001	2002	2003	2004
PLUS Expressway Berhad							
1. Total liabilities	n/a	n/a	n/a	16,796,338	9,980,384	10,478,293	10,782,763
2. Total assets	n/a	n/a	n/a	16,796,338	9,980,384	10,478,293	10,782,763
of which							
3. Banking and financial assets[8]	n/a	n/a	n/a	562,954	930,057	1,251,499	1,371,263
4. Banking and financial assets as % of total liabilities	n/a	n/a	n/a	3.35%	9.32%	11.94%	12.72%
PPB Group Berhad							
1. Total liabilities	n/a	n/a	4,958,795	5,211,283	5,338,335	5,805,156	6,133,912
2. Total assets	n/a	n/a	4,958,795	5,211,283	5,338,335	5,805,156	6,133,912
of which							
3. Banking and financial assets[9]	n/a	n/a	480,756	492,913	478,532	724,579	2,435,225
4. Banking and financial assets as % of total liabilities	n/a	n/a	9.70%	9.46%	8.96%	12.48%	39.70%
YTL Corporation Berhad							
1. Total liabilities	n/a	n/a	n/a	n/a	n/a	n/a	n/a
2. Total assets	n/a	n/a	n/a	n/a	n/a	n/a	n/a
of which							
3. Banking and financial assets[10]	n/a	n/a	n/a	n/a	n/a	n/a	n/a
4. Banking and financial assets as % of total liabilities	n/a	n/a	n/a	n/a	n/a	n/a	n/a
Telekom Malaysia Berhad							
1. Total liabilities	n/a	25,630,100	27,266,900	27,388,100	28,935,400	36,040,300	37,675,200
2. Total assets	n/a	25,630,100	27,266,900	27,388,100	28,935,400	36,040,300	37,675,200
of which							
3. Banking and Financial Assets[11]	n/a	1,206,700	2,381,900	2,742,600	2,032,500	3,609,500	8,951,800
4. Banking and Financial Assets as % of total liabilities	n/a	4.71%	8.74%	10.01%	7.02%	10.02%	23.76%

[8] Short-term investment, short-term deposits with licensed banks, cash and bank balances.
[9] Deposits, cash and bank balances.
[10] Short-term investments, food deposits, cash and bank balances.
[11] Short-term investments, cash and bank balances.

Table 12.2 (Continued)

Year	2005	2006	2007	2008
PLUS Expressway Berhad				
1. Total liabilities	12,007,791	12,588,363	15,893,005	n/a
2. Total assets	12,007,791	12,588,363	15,893,005	n/a
of which				
3. Banking and financial assets	2,555,419	2,634,764	2,480,944	n/a
4. Banking and financial assets as % of total liabilities	21.28%	20.93%	15.61%	n/a
PPB Group Berhad				
1. Total liabilities	6,369,313	7,288,922	11,984,045	n/a
2. Total assets	6,369,313	7,288,922	11,984,045	n/a
of which				
3. Banking and financial assets	752,839	762,712	700,658	n/a
4. Banking and financial assets as % of total liabilities	11.82%	10.46%	5.85%	n/a
YTL Corporation Berhad				
1. Total liabilities	28,213,103	30,370,822	33,912,520	n/a
2. Total assets	28,213,103	30,370,822	33,912,520	n/a
of which				
3. Banking and financial assets	5,787,093	5,578,020	9,033,066	n/a
4. Banking and financial assets as % of total liabilities	20.51%	18.37%	26.64%	n/a
Telekom Malaysia Berhad				
1. Total liabilities	41,184,300	41,843,500	44,221,300	n/a
2. Total assets	41,184,300	41,843,500	44,221,300	n/a
of which				
3. Banking and financial assets	6,690,300	5,000,500	4,549,900	n/a
4. Banking and financial assets as % of total liabilities	16.24%	11.95%	10.29%	n/a

Table 12.2 (Continued)

Year	1998	1999	2000	2001	2002	2003	2004
MMC Corporation Berhad							
1. Total liabilities	n/a	2,227,067	2,146,686	2,967,411	2,977,823	7,294,006	7,485,300
2. Total assets of which	n/a	2,227,067	2,146,686	2,967,411	2,977,823	7,294,006	7,485,300
3. Banking and financial assets[12]	n/a	455,667	628,510	806,292	364,394	251,530	551,307
4. Banking and financial assets as % of total liabilities	n/a	20.46%	29.28%	27.17%	12.24%	3.45%	7.37%
Average							
1. Total liabilities	**8,340,100**	**12,431,989**	**28,906,109**	**25,266,417**	**25,774,809**	**28,185,623**	**31,624,446**
2. Total assets of which	**8,340,100**	**37,295,967**	**28,906,109**	**25,266,417**	**25,774,809**	**28,185,623**	**31,624,446**
3. Banking and financial assets	**1,872,300**	**1,351,622**	**7361272,779**	**6,251,462**	**6,036,276**	**6,897,295**	**8,143,169**
4. Banking and financial assets as % of total liabilities	**22.45%**	**10.87%**	**25.47%**	**24.74%**	**23.42%**	**24.47%**	**25.75%**

[12] Marketable securities, deposits, bank and cash balances.

Table 12.2 (Continued)

Year	2005	2006	2007	2008
MMC Corporation Berhad				
1. Total liabilities	7,908,049	9,997,404	32,898,978	n/a
2. Total assets	7,908,049	9,997,404	32,898,978	n/a
of which				
3. Banking and financial assets	532,694	751,691	3,371,980	n/a
4. Banking and financial assets as % of total liabilities	6.74%	7.52%	10.25%	n/a
Average				
1. Total liabilities	34,775,463	39,475,178	46,092,027	361,292,900
2. Total assets	34,775,463	39,475,178	46,092,027	361,292,900
of which				
3. Banking and financial assets	9,885,451	11,339,857	13,343,020	161,257,949
4. Banking and financial assets as % of total liabilities	28.43%	28.73%	28.95%	44.63%

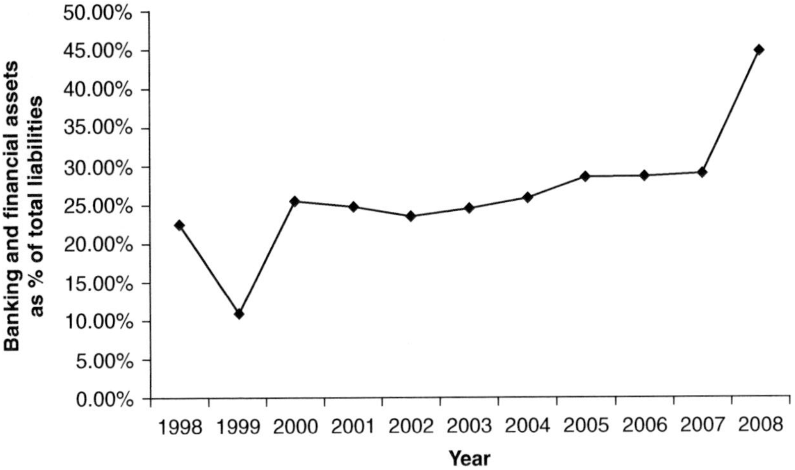

Figure 12.1 Average financial accumulation of the largest Malaysian firms listed at KLSE (as per cent of total liabilities held as financial assets, 1998–2008).
Source: Annual Reports of Sime Darby Berhad, IOI Corporation, Tenaga Nasional Berhad, MISC Berhad, Genting Group, PETRONAS, DiGi Telecommunication, Kuala Lumpur Kepong Berhad, PLUS Expressway Berhad, PPB Group Berhad, YTL Corporation Berhad, Telekom Malaysia, MMC Corporation Berhad, various years.

wholly owned by conventional banks – AmIslamic Bank Berhad and CIMB Islamic Bank – they do not possess separate balance sheets. Reviewing the liability side of the remaining 10 Islamic banks for 2007, deposits of non-financial companies constitute a higher share in total liabilities than deposits of individuals (Table 12.3). In 2007, the range of non-financial companies' deposits as share of total liabilities in the sample is huge starting with 11.20 per cent for Affin Islamic Bank and going up to 92.10 per cent for Al Rajhi Banking and Investment Corporation. Deposits of individuals as share of total liabilities for 2007 tend to be much smaller accounting for at least 0.26 per cent and at most 22.03 per cent of liabilities. Out of the 10 banks only two started operations before 2005, namely Bank Islam Malaysia (BIMB) in 1983 and Bank Muamalat Malaysia in 1999. They will be examined to identify trends in Malaysian Islamic banking.

For BIMB, available data about the composition of total liabilities goes back to 1993. Initially, the bank mainly drew on deposits of individuals to finance its lending. Household saving constituted 43.75 per cent of total liabilities in 1993 while non-financial companies contributed 16.68 per cent to the bank's liabilities (Figure 13.4). 'Others' – such as institutional investors[5] – deposited the residual. Until 1997 individual deposits constituted a share more than twice as big as company deposits. In 1998 and 1999 liabilities to households still exceeded those to companies. Yet, the non-financial

Table 12.3 Assets and liabilities of Malaysian Islamic banks (in '000RM)

Year	2004	2005	2006	2007	2008
1. Affin Islamic Bank Bhd					
Total liabilities			**3,706,190**	**6,031,419**	**5,906,852**
of which					
Deposits of non-financial companies			651,413	675,484	1,097,957
Deposits of non-financial companies as % of total liabilities			**17.58%**	**11.20%**	**18.59%**
Deposits of individuals			204,675	262,781	261,715
Deposits of individuals as % of total liabilities			**5.52%**	**4.36%**	**4.43%**
Total loans			**1,251,948**	**1,767,810**	**2,249,937**
of which					
Loans to companies			384,966	556,239	689691
(of which Loans to SME)			211,023	362,352	411,004
Loans to companies as % of total loans			**30.75%**	**31.46%**	**30.65%**
(of which loans to SME as % of total loans)			**16.86%**	**20.50%**	**18.27%**
Loans to households			756,622	1,093,088	1,315,779
Loans to households as % of total loans			**60.44%**	**61.83%**	**58.48%**
By purpose					
Purchase of vehicles			278,087	496,390	614,750
Purchase of vehicles as % of total loans			**22.21%**	**28.08%**	**27.32%**
Purchase of landed property			517,747	693,368	803,342
Purchase of landed property as % of total loans			**41.36%**	**39.22%**	**35.71%**
of which					
Purchase of residential property			470,279	636,864	714,957
Purchase of residential property as % of total loans			**37.56%**	**36.03%**	**31.78%**
Purchase of non-residential property			47,468	56,504	88,385
Purchase of non-residential property as % of total loans			**3.79%**	**3.20%**	**3.93%**
Purchase of securities			0	5,405	26,041
Purchase of securities as % of total loans			**0.00%**	**0.31%**	**1.16%**

Table 12.3 (Continued)

Year	2004	2005	2006	2007	2008
2. Al Rajhi Banking & Investment Corporation (Malaysia) Bhd					
Total liabilities			**66,489**	**2,112,913**	**2,436,876**
of which					
Deposits of non-financial companies			29,0'8	1,945,941	2,236,436
Deposits of non-financial companies as % of total liabilities			**43.64%**	**92.10%**	**91.77%**
Deposits of individuals			12,3'5	113,399	132,595
Deposits of individuals as % of total liabilities			**18.52%**	**5.37%**	**5.44%**
Total loans			**2,444**	**1,896,916**	**2,013,790**
of which					
Loans to companies			0	209,624	254,346
Loans to companies as % of total loans			**0.00%**	**9.92%**	**10.44%**
Loans to households			2,4'6	159,788	226,137
Loans to households as % of total loans			**3.63%**	**7.56%**	**9.28%**
By purpose					
Purchase of vehicles			0	1,427	2,234
Purchase of vehicles as % total loans			**0.00%**	**0.08%**	**0.11%**
Purchase of landed property			0	10,457	15,387
Purchase of landed property as % of total loans			**0.00%**	**0.55%**	**0.76%**
of which					
Purchase of residential property			0	10,457	n/a
Purchase of residential property as % of total loans			**0.00%**	**0.55%**	n/a
Purchase of non-residential property			0	0	n/a
Purchase of non-residential property as % of total loans			**0.00%**	**0.00%**	n/a
Purchase of securities			0	1,509,118	1,524,420
Purchase of securities as % of total loans			**0.00%**	**79.56%**	**75.70%**

Table 12.3 (Continued)

Year	2004	2005	2006	2007	2008
3. Asian Finance Bank Bhd					
Total liabilities			**361,899,146**	**906,319,456**	**991,139,703**
of which					
Deposits of non-financial companies			0	822,490,358	707,603,638
Deposits of non-financial companies as % of total liabilities			0.00%	**90.75%**	**71.39%**
Deposits of individuals			0	6,209,213	10,589,860
Deposits of individuals as % of total liabilities			0.00%	**0.69%**	**1.07%**
Total loans			**0**	**93,304,970**	**133,899,402**
of which					
Loans to companies			0	93,096,595	111,218,141
Loans to companies as % of total loans			0.00%	**99.78%**	**83.06%**
Loans to households			0	208,375	261,331
Loans to households as % of total loans			0.00%	**0.22%**	**0.20%**
By purpose					
Purchase of vehicles			0	99,650	22,515,152
Purchase of vehicles as % of total loans			0.00%	**0.11%**	**16.81%**
Purchase of landed property			0	65,968,830	66,720,807
Purchase of landed property as % of total loans of which			0.00%	**70.70%**	**49.83%**
Purchase of residential property			0	65,968,830	66,613,568
Purchase of residential property as % of total loans			0.00%	**70.70%**	**49.75%**
Purchase of non-residential property			0	0	107,239
Purchase of non-residential property as % of total loans			0.00%	0.00%	0.08%
Purchase of securities			0	0	0
Purchase of securities as % of total loans			0.00%	0.00%	0.00%

Table 12.3 (Continued)

Year	1993	1994	1995	1996	1997	1998
4. Bank Islam Malaysia Bhd						
Total liabilities	**1,694,301**	**2,736,508**	**3,015,111**	**3,352,349**	**4,231,032**	**3,976,501**
of which						
Deposits of non-financial companies	282,535	377,157	454,513	573,225	827,748	1,163,727
Deposits of non-financial companies as % of total liabilities	**16.68%**	**13.78%**	**15.07%**	**17.10%**	**19.56%**	**29.27%**
Deposits of individuals	741,286	1,050,446	1,151,490	1,574,696	1,844,284	1,780,376
Deposits of individuals as % of total liabilities	**43.75%**	**38.39%**	**38.19%**	**46.97%**	**43.59%**	**44.77%**
Total loans of which						
Loans to companies						
(of which SME)						
Loans to companies as % of total loans (of which loans to SME as % of total loans)						
Loans to households						
Loans to households as % of total loans						
By purpose						
Purchase of vehicles						
Purchase of vehicles as % of total loans						
Purchase of landed property						
Purchase of landed property as % of total loans						
of which						
Residential						
Residential as % of total loans						
Non-residential						
Non-residential as % of total loans						
Purchase of securities						
Purchase of securities as % of total loans						

Table 12.3 (Continued)

Year	1999	2000	2001	2002	2003
4. Bank Islam Malaysia Bhd					
Total liabilities	**5,797,698**	**7,513,853**	**9,338,008**	**11,384,235**	**12,604,029**
of which					
Deposits of non-financial companies	1,480,091	2,190,427	3,079,043	3,398,141	3,813,361
Deposits of non-financial companies as % of total liabilities	**25.53%**	**29.15%**	**32.97%**	**29.85%**	**30.26%**
Deposits of individuals	2,606,659	1,188,837	1,355,097	1638431	1,780,557
Deposits of individuals as % of total liabilities	**44.96%**	**15.82%**	**14.51%**	**14.39%**	**14.13%**
Total loans			**5,452,885**	**6,144,323**	**7,194,386**
of which					
Loans to companies				3,407,146	3,569,119
(of which SME)				223,119	312,136
Loans to companies as % of total loans				**55.45%**	**49.61%**
(of which loans to SME as % of total loans)				**3.63%**	**4.34%**
Loans to households				2,299,382	3,394,269
Loans to households as % of total loans				**37.42%**	**47.18%**
By purpose					
Purchase of vehicles				298,641	533,068
Purchase of vehicles as % of total loans				**4.86%**	**7.41%**
Purchase of landed property				2,000,347	2,619,987
Purchase of landed property as % of total loans				**32.56%**	**36.42%**
of which					
Residential				1,386,971	1,957,964
Residential as % of total loans				**22.57%**	**27.22%**
Non-residential				613,376	662,023
Non-residential as % of total loans				**9.98%**	**9.20%**
Purchase of securities				163,493	158,627
Purchase of securities as % of total loans				**2.66%**	**2.20%**

Table 12.3 (Continued)

Year	2004	2005	2006	2007	2008
4. Bank Islam Malaysia Bhd					
Total liabilities	**11,795,326**	**15,118,725**	**14,886,724**	**18,076,963**	**19,988,773**
of which					
Deposits of non-financial companies	3,790,872	4,832,010	5,433,895	6,097,683	5,629,120
Deposits of non-financial companies as % of total liabilities	**32.14%**	**31.96%**	**36.50%**	**33.73%**	**28.16%**
Deposits of individuals	1,951,383	2,144,688	2,292,431	2,549,629	4,551,916
Deposits of individuals as % of total liabilities	**16.54%**	**14.19%**	**15.40%**	**14.10%**	**22.77%**
Total loans	**7,985,959**	**10,041,562**	**10,311,593**	**9,888,297**	**10,303,913**
of which					
Loans to companies	3,386,093	3,102,573	2,761,928	2,515,603	2841419
(of which SME)	1,268,243	1,346,481	1,189,561	1,051,169	909,282
Loans to companies as % of total loans	**42.40%**	**30.90%**	**26.78%**	**25.44%**	**27.58%**
(of which loans to SME as % of total loans)	**15.88%**	**13.41%**	**11.54%**	**10.63%**	**8.82%**
Loans to households	4,380,151	5,419,025	6,507,234	6,471,960	6,620,477
Loans to households as % of total loans	**54.85%**	**53.97%**	**63.11%**	**65.45%**	**64.25%**
By purpose					
Purchase of vehicles	919,526	1,309,112	1,965,984	1,772,269	1,545,061
Purchase of vehicles as % of total loans	**11.51%**	**13.04%**	**19.07%**	**17.92%**	**14.99%**
Purchase of landed property	3,172,102	3,300,910	3,281,292	3,371,965	3239644
Purchase of landed property as % of total loans	**39.72%**	**32.87%**	**31.82%**	**34.10%**	**31.44%**
of which					
Residential	2,503,093	2,674,078	2,743,033	2,891,457	2,838,237
Residential as % of total loans	**31.34%**	**26.63%**	**26.60%**	**29.24%**	**27.55%**
Non-residential	669,009	626,832	538,259	480,508	401,407
Non-residential as % of total loans	**8.38%**	**6.24%**	**5.22%**	**4.86%**	**3.90%**
Purchase of securities	182,495	572,266	487,421	221,905	172,763
Purchase of securities as % of total loans	**2.29%**	**5.70%**	**4.73%**	**2.24%**	**1.68%**

Table 12.3 (Continued)

Year	2003	2004	2005	2006	2007	2008
5. Bank Muamalat Malaysia Bhd						
Total liabilities	**6,962,922**	**7,563,267**	**9,745,964**	**12,750,283**	**13,814,692**	**12,472,880**
of which						
Deposits of non-financial companies	2,506,642	3,020,004	5,133,138	5,749,625	5,747,947	5,310,917
Deposits of non-financial companies as % of total liabilities	**36.00%**	**39.93%**	**52.67%**	**45.09%**	**41.61%**	**42.58%**
Deposits of individuals	666,331	753,292	822,511	957,164	886,771	915,058
Deposits of individuals as % of total liabilities	**9.57%**	**9.96%**	**8.44%**	**7.51%**	**6.42%**	**7.34%**
Total loans	**2,272,526**	**2,887,415**	**4,154,021**	**5,373,343**	**5,870,585**	**6,336,185**
of which						
Loans to companies	1,187,969	1,362,125	1,665,552	2,062,288	2631406	3254184
(of which SME)	554,763	557,929	748,468	594,538	923,564	1147331
Loans to companies as % of total loans	**52.28%**	**47.17%**	**40.09%**	**38.38%**	**44.82%**	**51.36%**
(of which loans to SME as % of total loans)	**24.41%**	**19.32%**	**18.02%**	**11.06%**	**15.73%**	**18.11%**
Loans to households	1,004,703	1,380,911	2,353,284	3,155,184	3,053,412	2,826,378
Loans to households as % of total loans	**44.21%**	**47.83%**	**56.65%**	**58.72%**	**52.01%**	**44.61%**

Table 12.3 (Continued)

Year	2003	2004	2005	2006	2007	2008
By purpose						
Purchase of vehicles	63,497	128,261	706,155	1,239,719	1,399,305	1,407,281
Purchase of vehicles as % of total loans	**2.79%**	**4.44%**	**17.00%**	**23.07%**	**23.84%**	**22.21%**
Purchase of landed property	956,710	1,131,287	1,486,493	1,841,364	1,635,945	1,700,703
Purchase of landed property as % of total loans	**42.10%**	**39.18%**	**35.78%**	**34.27%**	**27.87%**	**26.84%**
of which						
Purchase of residential property	772,994	938,126	1,279,587	1,574,975	1,346,710	1,396,726
Purchase of residential property as % of total loans	**34.01%**	**32.49%**	**30.80%**	**29.31%**	**22.94%**	**22.04%**
Purchase of non-residential property	183,716	193,161	206,906	266,389	289,235	303,977
Purchase of non-residential property as % of total loans	**8.08%**	**6.69%**	**4.98%**	**4.96%**	**4.93%**	**4.80%**
Purchase of securities	37,961	39,496	32,332	25,678	4,714	1,796
Purchase of securities as % of total loans	**1.67%**	**1.37%**	**0.78%**	**0.48%**	**0.08%**	**0.03%**

Table 12.3 (Continued)

Year	2004	2005	2006	2007	2008
6. EONCAP Islamic Bank Bhd					
Total liabilities			**4,724,271**	**5,678,114**	**6089452**
of which					
Deposits of non-financial companies			2,099,168	2,096,528	1926115
Deposits of non-financial companies as % of total liabilities			**44.43%**	**36.92%**	**31.63%**
Deposits of individuals			483,452	512,222	546460
Deposits of individuals as % of total liabilities			**10.23%**	**9.02%**	**8.97%**
Total loans			**4,198,999**	**4,688,774**	**4741873**
of which					
Loans to companies			1,049,985	1,145,406	1040646
(of which loans to SMEs)			367,700	454,132	461402
Loans to companies as % of total loans			**25.01%**	**24.43%**	**21.95%**
(of which loans to SMEs as % of total loans)			**8.76%**	**9.69%**	**9.73%**
Loans to households			3,134,973	3,427,078	3438014
Loans to households as % of total loans			**74.66%**	**73.09%**	**72.50%**
By purpose					
Purchase of vehicles			1,664,208	1,558,425	1537781
Purchase of vehicles as % of total loans			**39.63%**	**33.24%**	**32.43%**
Purchase of landed property			1,177,013	1,413,664	1460581
Purchase of landed property as % of total loans			**28.03%**	**30.15%**	**30.80%**
of which					
Purchase of residential property			1,096,736	1,324,042	1371464
Purchase of residential property as % of total loans			**26.12%**	**28.24%**	**28.92%**
Purchase of non-residential property			80,277	89,622	89117
Purchase of non-residential property as % of total loans			**1.91%**	**1.91%**	**1.88%**
Purchase of securities			7,854	4,740	3683
Purchase of securities as % of total loans			**0.19%**	**0.10%**	**0.08%**

Table 12.3 (Continued)

Year	2004	2005	2006	2007	2008
7. Hong Leong Islamic Bank Bhd					
Total liabilities			**5,892,378**	**5,624,155**	**6722743**
of which					
Deposits of non-financial companies			3,572,117	3,060,132	3,939,899
Deposits of non-financial companies as % of total liabilities			**60.62%**	**54.41%**	**58.61%**
Deposits of individuals			925,347	1,239,059	1,286,107
Deposits of individuals as % of total liabilities			**15.70%**	**22.03%**	**19.13%**
Total loans			**4,031,824**	**3,758,749**	**4,329,988**
of which					
Loans to companies			980,475	911,250	972,805
(of which loans to SMEs)			304,939	290,564	303,876
Loans to companies as % of total loans			24.32%	24.24%	22.47%
(of which loans to SMEs as % of total loans)			7.56%	7.73%	7.02%
Loans to households			2,985,206	2,768,069	3,249,786
Loans to households as % of total loans			**74.04%**	**73.64%**	**75.05%**
By purpose					
Purchase of vehicles			2,568,499	2,144,169	2,448,681
Purchase of vehicles as % of total loans			**63.71%**	**57.04%**	**56.55%**
Purchase of landed property			585026	793745	1,079,461
Purchase of landed property as % of total loans			**14.51%**	**21.12%**	**24.93%**
of which					
Purchase of residential property			483,381	654,425	899,547
Purchase of residential property as % of total loans			**11.99%**	**17.41%**	**20.77%**
Purchase of non-residential property			101,645	139,320	179,914
Purchase of non-residential property as % of total loans			**2.52%**	**3.71%**	**4.16%**
Purchase of securities			3,575	1,123	1,053
Purchase of securities as % of total loans			**0.09%**	**0.03%**	**0.02%**

Table 12.3 (Continued)

Year	2004	2005	2006	2007	2008
8. Kuwait Finance House (Malaysia) Bhd					
Total liabilities		**134,781**	**2,630,883**	**5,555,934**	**6,720,237**
of which					
Deposits of non-financial companies		100,106	861,964	2,016,878	2,264,211
Deposits of non-financial companies as % of total liabilities		**74.27%**	**32.76%**	**36.30%**	**33.69%**
Deposits of individuals		1627	13,637	14,503	22,934
Deposits of individuals as % of total liabilities		**1.21%**	**0.52%**	**0.26%**	**0.34%**
Total loans		0	**817,986**	**3,219,726**	**3,874,457**
of which					
Loans to companies		0	752,159	2,558,550	2,899,467
(of which loans to SMEs)		0	238,308	1,063,253	1,375,060
Loans to companies as % of total loans		0.00%	**91.95%**	**79.46%**	**74.84%**
(of which loans to SMEs as % of total loans)		0.00%	**29.13%**	**33.02%**	**35.49%**
Loans to households		0	9,453	66,021	70,234
Loans to households as % of total loans		0.00%	**1.16%**	**2.05%**	**1.81%**
By purpose					
Purchase of vehicles		0	1,510	2,674	2,648
Purchase of vehicles as % of total loans		0.00%	**0.18%**	**0.08%**	**0.07%**
Purchase of landed property		0	430	14,031	20,629
Purchase of landed property as % of total loans		0.00%	**0.05%**	**0.44%**	**0.53%**
of which					
Purchase of residential property		0	430	14,031	20,629
Purchase of residential property as % of total loans		0.00%	**0.05%**	**0.44%**	**0.53%**
Purchase of non-residential property		0	0	0	0
Purchase of non-residential property as % of total loans		0.00%	**0.00%**	**0.00%**	**0.00%**
Purchase of securities		0	16,871	94,928	93,273
Purchase of securities as % of total loans		0.00%	**2.06%**	**2.95%**	**2.41%**

Table 12.3 (Continued)

Year	2004	2005	2006	2007	2008
9. Maybank Islamic Bhd					
Total liabilities					**23,349,620**
of which					
Deposits of non-financial companies					4,230,270
Deposits of non-financial companies as % of total liabilities					**18.12%**
Deposits of individuals					5,411,265
Deposits of individuals as % of total liabilities					**23.17%**
Total loans					**20,802,549**
of which					
Loans to companies					7,138,969
(of which SME)					4,207,354
Loans to companies as % of total loans					**34.32%**
(of which loans to SMEs as % of total loans)					**20.23%**
Loans to households					11,969,255
Loans to households as % of total loans					**57.54%**
By purpose					
Purchase of vehicles					6,934,651
Purchase of vehicles as % of total loans					**33.34%**
Purchase of landed property					6,170,717
Purchase of landed property as % of total loans					**29.66%**
of which					
Purchase of residential property					5,560,850
Purchase of residential property as % of total loans					**26.73%**
Purchase of non-residential property					609,867
Purchase of non-residential property as % of total loans					**2.93%**
Purchase of securities					81,627
Purchase of securities as % of total loans					**0.39%**

Table 12.3 (Continued)

Year	2004	2005	2006	2007	2008
10. RHB ISLAMIC Bank Bhd					
Total liabilities		**7,058,512**	**7,440,591**	**7,665,002**	**7,507,781**
of which					
Deposits of non-financial companies		3,864,254	4,149,826	4,222,990	3,529,206
Deposits of non-financial companies as % of total liabilities		**54.75%**	**55.77%**	**55.09%**	**47.01%**
Deposits of individuals		702,101	723,189	770,047	817,983
Deposits of individuals as % of total liabilities		**9.95%**	**9.72%**	**10.05%**	**10.90%**
Total loans		**3,524,373**	**4,273,454**	**4,691,096**	**4,842,376**
of which					
Loans to companies		2,221,072	2,496,765	2,596,281	2,472,383
(of which loans to SMEs)		208,876	548,509	557,394	643,183
Loans to companies as % of total loans		**63.02%**	**58.42%**	**55.34%**	**51.06%**
(of which loans to SMEs as % of total loans)		**5.93%**	**12.84%**	**11.88%**	**13.28%**
Loans to households		1,251,623	1,623,648	1,942,677	2,080,667
Loans to households as % of total loans		**35.51%**	**37.99%**	**41.41%**	**42.97%**
By purpose					
Purchase of vehicles		23,225	140,519	359,898	515,660
Purchase of vehicles as % of total loans		**0.66%**	**3.29%**	**7.67%**	**10.65%**
Purchase of landed property		1,241,303	1,543,217	1,732,443	1,739,784
Purchase of landed property as % of total loans		**35.22%**	**36.11%**	**36.93%**	**35.93%**
of which					
Purchase of residential property		1,199,980	1,461,866	1,610,779	1,613,650
Purchase of residential property as % of total loans		**34.05%**	**34.21%**	**34.34%**	**33.32%**
Purchase of non-residential property		41,323	81,351	121,664	126,134
Purchase of non-residential property as % of total loans		**1.17%**	**1.90%**	**2.59%**	**2.60%**
Purchase of securities		343,173	366,627	185,180	399
Purchase of securities as % of total loans		**9.74%**	**8.58%**	**3.95%**	**0.01%**

Source: Annual Reports of Affin Islamic Bank Bhd, Al Rajhi Banking & Investment Corporation (Malaysia) Bhd, Asian Finance Bank Bhd, Bank Islam Malaysia Bhd, Bank Muamalat Malaysia Bhd, EONCAP Islamic Bank Bhd, Hong Leong Islamic Bank Bhd, Kuwait Finance House (Malaysia) Bhd, Maybank Islamic Bhd, RHB ISLAMIC Bank Bhd, various issues.

corporate sector increased their deposits substantially from RM828 billion (19.56 per cent) to RM1164 billion (29.27 per cent) between 1997 and 1998. This surge in banking assets held by companies might have been a precaution taken during the Asian financial crisis of 1997/1998, as the following pages show.

Interestingly, firms did not withdraw their money from BIMB in subsequent years. On the contrary, corporate deposits kept growing overtaking individual deposits as share in bank liabilities by 2000. From 2001 to 2007, non-financial enterprises contributed more than twice as much as households to BIMB's liabilities. Data for 2008 suggest that contributions by the two groups converge towards a share somewhere around 25 per cent. Yet these data are derived from the March quarterly report and are due to their preliminary character less reliable. Financial statements available for Muamalat Bank Malaysia, covering 2003–2008, support the evidence that on the liability side non-financial companies are the major depositors of Islamic banks in Malaysia. While individuals contribute less than 10 per cent and a decreasing share of bank liabilities, companies' deposits amount to 36 per cent of liabilities in 2003 increasing to 42.58 per cent in the first quarter of 2008. These results are representative for most of the Islamic banks in Malaysia. With the exception of Maybank Islamic and BIMB before 2000, non-financial enterprises contribute significantly more to bank liabilities than households. For the period 2000–2008, firms' percentage share is typically 30 per cent or more with the exception of Affin Islamic Bank.

On the assets side, only Asian Finance Bank and Kuwait Finance House focus their lending activity completely on non-financial companies.[6] Both banks lend more than 70 per cent of their asset value to corporates and less than 3 per cent to individuals. Al Rajhi Banking, RHB Islamic Bank and Mualamat Bank Malaysia provide approximately the same share of their assets as credit to households as to companies. The remaining five Islamic banks provide a significantly larger share of total loans to individuals than to non-financial companies. Hence, there is convincing evidence that funds flow from companies to households and not the other way around (Table 12.3). Since there is little data available for the years before the Asian financial crisis firms' over-capitalisation could be a cyclical phenomenon arising as precautionary measure after periods of economic distress. The effect on the housing market – or other markets where the surplus funds are channelled to – remains the same. If anything over-capitalisation as cyclical phenomenon can only increase economic instability since a slowdown in the flow of funds into an inflated market stops prices rising and triggers a downward price spiral.

Analysing the purpose of credit, purchases of transport vehicles and residential property figure most prominently for all Islamic banks apart from Asian Finance Bank, Kuwait Finance House and Al Rajhi Banking. This observation is in accordance with data collected by the Malaysian Central

Table 12.4 Direction of Islamic lending in Malaysia as per cent of total lending, 2000–2005

Year	**2000**	**2001**	**2002**	**2003**	**2004**	**2005**
Sector						
Real estate	1.70%	2.00%	1.82%	1.67%	1.57%	1.44%
Construction	7.50%	6.00%	6.20%	6.03%	6.10%	4.95%
Purchase of residential property	19.00%	24.30%	29.31%	29.51%	26.66%	23.71%
Purchase of non-residential property	7.60%	5.90%	5.52%	4.92%	4.46%	3.93%
Consumption credit	19.40%	24.20%	25.29%	30.59%	30.76%	36.19%
of which						
Purchase of consumer durables	0.20%	0.20%	0.17%	0.11%	0.08%	0.06%
Purchase of transport vehicles	17.50%	21.50%	22.07%	26.79%	25.91%	29.89%
Total credit to private sector (in RM million)	20,891	28,201	36,718	48,615	57,883	67,365

Source: Annual Reports, BNM, various issues.

Bank, Bank Negara Malaysia (BNM), on the direction of Islamic lending. Since 1996, the sum of Islamic credit for purchases of residential property and consumption rose from 24.3 to 59.9 per cent in 2005. Consumption credit increased steadily while loans for property purchases experienced a less steady upward trend. Since 2000, BNM disaggregates consumption credit demonstrating that the major part is used for the purchase of transport vehicles confirming the results found analysing bank balance sheets (Table 12.4 and Figure 12.2).

The evidence suggests that Islamic banks in Malaysia channel funds from the over-capitalised non-financial corporate sector towards households investing into housing and durable consumer goods. However, if this is the case Islamic banks – just as conventional ones – are far from exercising a stabilising effect on the economic system because housing markets inflate similarly to capital markets.

Price changes – if positive – tend to attract further funds with investors hoping for continued price appreciation. If the household sector is unwilling to increase its borrowing for house purchases, prices stop rising. New investors stay away while current ones try to exit destabilising the housing market through price deflation (Table 12.5).

A secondary result of this study is that the dominance of Western financial and economic patterns is paramount. A niche phenomenon such as Islamic

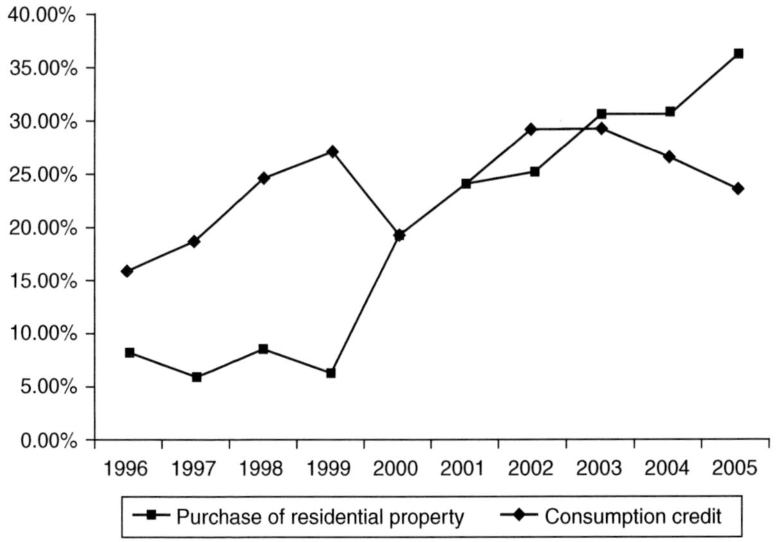

Figure 12.2 Islamic lending for residential property and consumption as per cent of total credit to the private sector, 1996–2005.
Source: Annual Reports, BNM, various issues.

Table 12.5 Direction of credit to major sectors by the financial system (% of Total Credit)

Year	**1996**	**1997**	**1998**	**1999**	**2000**	**2001**	**2002**
Construction and real estate	12.20%	15.30%	15.60%	14.40%	12.98%	12.07%	9.96%
housing	10.10%	10.50%	11.10%	11.90%	13.12%	15.94%	17.09%
Consumption credit	8.70%	9.00%	8.50%	8.50%	8.81%	9.80%	11.26%
Investment in corporate securities	26.70%	23.30%	24.00%	26.30%	28.12%	28.09%	30.05%
Credit to private sector (in RM billion)	462.2	594.5	590.1	595,7	633,4	696,8	766,7
Year	**2003**	**2004**	**2005**				
Construction and real estate	9.84%	9.07%	8.68%				
housing	17.98%	19.26%	19.31%				
Consumption credit	11.73%	12.66%	13.72%				
Investment in corporate securities	31.50%	30.33%	29.72%				
Credit private sector (in RM billion)	822,1	878,3	972,5				

Source: Bank Negara Malaysia, Annual Reports, 1996–2005.

banking willing to isolate itself from debt-based banking and its destabilising impact should be able to shield itself from Western post-modern, financialised institutions. Yet, this is not the case because of interdependence between Islamic and non-Islamic economic agents.

12.5 Conclusion

A flow of funds analysis reveals that (at least) since 1998 a current account surplus has been steadily channelled into the Malaysian economy resulting in the over-capitalisation of domestic firms and the emergence of a financial business cycle. Contrary to the claims of Islamic scholars Islamic banks channelling funds from companies to households play a destabilising role in the economy as a whole. Credit granted to the household sector is used for housing purchases and therefore inflates asset markets increasing the system's economic fragility and encouraging speculation. These trends are reflected by the Islamic banks' balance sheets.

Through financial inflation and over-capitalisation, banking in emerging markets in general and Malaysian Islamic banking in particular are reproducing those features that give rise to Minskyan instability.

Notes

1. The partners in an Islamic finance contract are: the depositor, the bank and the borrower. Concerning supply of savings and capital, the depositors entering either into a non-remunerated safeguarding agreement or a remunerated partnership agreement with the bank. While the bank is not obliged to share profits with holders of current or savings deposits it must encash these deposits on demand. Investment accounts are entitled to a share in profit but typically demand a long-term commitment and also a share in losses. Concerning the demand for finance, the entrepreneur receiving credit is only liable with his time and effort. The profit is shared at a predetermined ratio between the bank and the entrepreneur. While in the case of *mudharabah* projects the bank does not possess any direct influence on the investment, a *musyarakah* arrangement entitles it to rights of the type a joint venture partner possesses (Chapra, 2000, Dhumale and Sapcanin, 2004).
2. Often a notice of 1 month suffices.
3. If (X–M) is positive, retained profits (S_F) increase. In corporations listed on the stock exchange this means that a firm's assets and liabilities to the shareholders grow. Since shareholders are mainly interested in selling shares on at a higher price, they focus on the firm's balance sheet, commonly regarded as profitability indicator. Increased liabilities bring the firm under pressure to improve its balance sheet. As productive investment only generates income in the long-run, financial operations are more suitable to meet expectations of increased profitability. Therefore, a structural balance of payments surplus might favour the accumulation of excess capital.
4. The data presented – as all data – are prone to error. In big conglomerates incorrect data are even more likely to occur since mistakes are added up while putting

together the group's financial statement. On the balance sheet assets and liabilities have to match by definition. Deviations are often arbitrarily eliminated with a potentially adverse effect on the data.

5. The employees' pension fund managing the retirement savings of the majority of the population became an important investor as the requirement to hold funds in government securities was gradually relaxed since the mid-1980s (Suto, 2001).
6. Both banks are owned by Middle Eastern investors and are likely to concentrate on Middle Eastern companies operating in Malaysia.

References

Documentary sources

Affin Islamic Bank Berhad, (2006, 2007) Annual Reports, Kuala Lumpur.

Affin Islamic Bank Berhad, (2008) Quarterly Report, Kuala Lumpur, March.

Al Rajhi Banking & Investment Corporation (Malaysia) Berhad, (2006, 2007) Annual Reports, Kuala Lumpur.

Al Rajhi Banking & Investment Corporation (Malaysia) Berhad, (2008) Quarterly Report, Kuala Lumpur, March.

Asian Finance Bank Berhad, (2007) Annual Report, Kuala Lumpur.

Asian Finance Bank Berhad, (2008) Quarterly Report, Kuala Lumpur, March.

Bank Islam Malaysia Berhad, (1994–2007) Annual Reports, Kuala Lumpur.

Bank Islam Malaysia Berhad, (2008) Quarterly Report, Kuala Lumpur, March.

Bank Muamalat Malaysia Berhad, (2004–2007) Annual Reports, Kuala Lumpur.

Bank Muamalat Malaysia Berhad, (2008) Quaterly Report, Kuala Lumpur, March.

BNM, (1996–2006) Annual Reports, Kuala Lumpur.

DiGi Telecommunication Berhad, (2001–2007) Annual Reports, Sham Alam.

EONCAP Islamic Bank Berhad, (2006, 2007) Annual Reports, Kuala Lumpur.

EONCAP Islamic Bank Berhad, (2008) Quarterly Report, Kuala Lumpur, March.

Genting Group Berhad, (1999–2007) Annual Reports, Kuala Lumpur.

Hong Leong Islamic Bank Berhad, (2006, 2007) Annual Reports, Kuala Lumpur.

Hong Leong Islamic Bank Berhad, (2008) Quarterly Report, Kuala Lumpur, March.

IOI Corporation Berhad, (2002–2007) Annual Reports, Putrajaya.

Kuala Lumpur Kepong Berhad, (2002–2007) Annual Reports, Ipoh.

Kuwait Finance House (Malaysia) Berhad, (2006, 2007) Annual Reports, Kuala Lumpur.

Kuwait Finance House (Malaysia) Berhad, (2008) Quarterly Report, Kuala Lumpur, March.

Maybank Islamic Berhad, (2008) Quarterly Report, Kuala Lumpur, March.

MISC Berhad, (2004–2007) Annual Reports, Kuala Lumpur.

MMC Corporation Berhad, (2000–2007) Annual Reports, Kuala Lumpur.

Petroliam Nasional Berhad (PETRONAS), (2001–2008) Annual Reports, Kuala Lumpur.

PLUS Expressway Berhad, (2002–2007) Annual Reports, Kuala Lumpur.

PPB Group Berhad, Kuala Lumpur, (2001–2007) Annual Reports.

Sime Darby Berhad, (2004–2007) Annual Reports, Kuala Lumpur.

RHB ISLAMIC Bank Berhad, (2006, 2007) Annual Reports, Kuala Lumpur.

RHB ISLAMIC Bank Berhad, (2008) Quarterly Report, Kuala Lumpur, March.

Telekom Malaysia Berhad, (2000–2007) Annual Reports, Kuala Lumpur.

Tenaga Nasional Berhad, (2001–2007) Annual Reports, Kuala Lumpur.
YTL Corporation Berhad, (2006, 2007) Annual Reports, Kuala Lumpur.

Books and articles

Ahmad, S.M. (1952) *Economics of Islam* (Lahore: Ashraf Press).

Ariff M., Mohamed (1988) 'Islamic banking', *Asian-Pacific Economic Literature*, vol. 2, no. 2.

BBC News (2006) Banks Move into Islamic Finance, 9 June.

Chapra, M.U. (2000) *The Future of Economics, An Islamic Perspective United Kingdom* (Leicester: The Islamic Foundation).

Chapra, M.U. (2006) 'Why has Islam prohibited interest? Rationale behind the prohibition of interest', in A. Thomas (ed.), *Interest in Islamic Economics* (London: Routledge).

Credit Suisse (2006) Islamic Banking, Der Profit des Propheten, 13 June.

Dhumale, R. and A. Sapcanin (2004) 'An application of Islamic banking principles to microfinance', Technical Note, Washington: Study by the Regional Bureau for Arab States, United Nations Development Programme in Cooperation with the World Bank.

Friedman, M. (1959) *A Program for Monetary Stability* (New York: Fordham University Press).

Hayek, F.A. (1929) *Geldtheorie und Konjunkturtheorie* (Wien: Hölder-Pichler-Tempsky A.G.).

Hobson, J.A. (1938) *Imperialism: A Study* (London: George Allen and Unwin).

Keynes, J.M. (1936) *The General Theory of Employment, Interest and Money* (London: MacMillan Press, 1936).

Khan, M.A. (1968) 'The theory of employment in Islam', *Islamic Literature*, vol. 14, no. 4.

Khan, W.M. (1985) *Towards an Interest-Free Islamic Economic System, A Theoretical Analysis of Prohibiting Debt Finance* (United Kingdom: The Islamic Foundation, Islamabad: The International Association for Islamic Economics).

Khan, M.S. and A. Mirakhor (1992) 'Islamic banking', in P. Newman, M. Milgate and J. Eatwell (eds), *The New Palgrave Dictionary of Money and Finance* (London: MacMillan Press).

Lewis, M.K. and L.M. Algaoud (2001) *Islamic Banking* (Cheltenham: Edward Elgar).

Minsky, H.P. (1986) *Stabilizing an Unstable Economy* (Haven: Yale University Press).

Mishkin, F.S. and S.G. Eakins (2006) *Financial Markets and Institutions* (Boston: Pearson Addisson Wesley).

Siddiqi, M.N. (1981) 'Muslim economic thinking, a survey of contemporary literature' Jeddah: International Centre for Research in *Islamic Economics*, King Abdul Aziz University, United Kingdom: The Islamic Foundation.

Siddiqi, M.N. (1983) *Banking Without Interest* (Leicester: The Islamic Foundation).

Steindl, J. (1989) 'Saving and debt', in A. Barrere (ed.), *Money, Credit and Prices in Keynesian Perspective* (London: MacMillan Press).

Sundararajan, V. and L. Errico (2002) 'Islamic financial institutions and products in the global financial system: key issues in risk management and challenges ahead', IMF Working Paper, Washington: International Monetary Funds.

Suto, M. (2001) 'Capital structure and investment behaviour of Malaysian firms in the 1990s – a study of corporate governance before the crisis', *CEI Working Paper Series*, No. 2001-9, Tokyo: Center for Economic Institutions.

Toporowski, J. (2000) *The End of Finance, The Theory of Capital Market Inflation, Financial Derivatives and Pension Capitalism* (London: Routledge).
Toporowski, J. (2008) Notes on Excess Capital and Liquidity Management Working Paper no. 549, *The Jerome Levy Institute.*
Toporowski, J. (2009) 'The economics and culture of financial inflation', *Competition and Change*, vol. 13, no. 2.
Wicksell, K. (1907) 'The influence of the rate of interest on prices', *The Economic Journal*, vol. 17, no. 66.

Websites

BNM, Kuala Lumpur (http://www.bnm.gov.my/). July 2008.
Bloomberg, London (www.bloomberg.com). January 2008.

13

Ponzi from the Start: The Human Cost of Financial Instability in Latvia

Jeffrey Sommers, Dirk Bezemer and Michael Hudson

13.1 Introduction

Most models of financial markets, trade and business cycles start from an assumed state of equilibrium and then describe how the economy becomes increasingly unbalanced and stressed. Prices rise as full employment and full capacity are approached. The trade balance falls into deficit as raw materials and import prices rise. Interest rates also rise as business upswings heat up. Higher interest rates attract foreign loan inflows to stabilise the balance of payments, but this builds up foreign indebtedness, whose carrying charges are met by yet new borrowing.

Hyman Minsky's (1978, 1980) model of the financial cycle focuses on domestic debt relationships. Economies start in balance. Loans can be paid off out of earnings (the 'hedge' stage). The self-amortising 30-year home mortgages common in the United States until the 1980s typify this stage. But real estate and industrial investment becomes increasingly debt-leveraged, to the point where – in the 'speculative' stage of the financial cycle – only interest can be paid, not any amortisation. And in the third and culminating 'Ponzi' stage, interest is simply added onto the debt balance, so that debts grow exponentially – beyond the ability of the 'real' economy to produce a large enough surplus to keep pace. Defaults and bankruptcies occur, property is forfeited to foreclosing creditors and asset prices decline until balance is restored by bringing debts back in line with the ability to pay.

Over the past decade a fourth stage to this cycle emerged to delay the financial crash: loosening credit standards to enable debt pyramiding to reach utterly fictitious (that is, un-payable) proportions. The central bank and commercial banking system flood economies with enough credit to inflate asset prices, enabling debtors to keep paying interest by refinancing their loans against more and more inflated prices for property pledged as collateral, far beyond the ability of actual earnings to justify. Regulatory standards are relaxed to the point where substantial fraud and misrepresentation occur. This may be thought of as 'Ponzi phase #2'.

In the United States, Federal Reserve Chairman Alan Greenspan convinced the public that debt-leveraged gains in asset prices were 'wealth creation', not just debt creation. His successor, Chairman Ben Bernanke (2004), euphemised the great 1979–2004 credit boom as 'the Great Moderation'. He was not being sarcastic, merely tunnel-visioned. His financial blind spot was an essential precondition for the Ponzi phase #2. Like the neoliberal advisors who shaped Latvian and other Baltic and post-Soviet economic policies, Mr Bernanke defined 'moderation' as relatively stable prices for goods and services (while real estate, stock and bond prices soared) and a steady growth in output and employment, despite the increasing economic focus on the finance, insurance and real estate (FIRE) sector. The build-up of un-payable debt was ignored, giving predatory finance free rein to load down property and income streams with debts that had no foundation in the 'real economy'. In this chapter we trace Latvia's Ponzi experience from a political economy perspective.

13.2 Latvia: 'Ponzi from the start'

Reckless lending without regard for the 'real' economy marks the Ponzi phase #2 into which the Baltic countries and most other post-Soviet economies passed almost directly in the 1990s. They were in a state of disequilibrium from the time the Soviet Union's far-flung production interconnections were unplugged when the USSR broke up in 1991. Left without fully integrated industrial sectors, each economy (including Russia itself) was obliged to import the great bulk of its consumer and capital goods. The result was a structural trade deficit that has now persisted for nearly 19 years.

This deficit was financed by foreign borrowing and investment inflows, not to rebuild the former USSR's industrial export capacity and create domestic banking systems, but to buy property already in place (creating a stock market boom starting from the near-zero price at which public resources and enterprises were privatised) and to lend foreign-currency mortgage credit against it. Property was given away almost freely to political insiders, turning them into oligarchs. This was essentially the neoliberal plan, promoted by the Washington Consensus organised via the World Bank, IMF and US Agency for International Development (A.I.D.) and administered by the 'Harvard Boys' in Russia and their counterparts in other countries (Wedel, 1998; Klein, 2008; Hudson and Sommers, 2009). As expected, the early kleptocrats in due course sold large shares of these enterprises to Western investors, and borrowed heavily against the real estate and other property they took.

George Bernard Shaw quipped that America was a country that went from barbarism to decadence without the intervening stage of civilisation. In a similar fashion the post-Soviet economies since 1991, above all the Baltics, went directly from debt-free economies to the Ponzi stage with only the faintest intervening stage of productive industrial credit. Not only did the Baltic States live by 'borrowing the interest' from the outset, but most of this credit was borrowed in foreign currency.

The result can be summarised as 'Ponzi from the outset'. Trade deficits were financed by inflows of foreign-currency mortgage credit and direct investment in real estate and privatised infrastructure, and to a much lesser extent in building up a few industries, such as Volkswagen's investments in Hungary and Slovakia, and substantial European investment in the Czech Republic and Poland. The largest direct investment inflows were for construction of buildings and renovation of industry that only belatedly began to generate income on the eve of the post-2007 crash. On balance, few capital inflows found their counterpart in earnings able to pay down the debt or even to carry its interest charges. Most were secured by the collateral put in place for more than a half-century and inherited from the Soviet Union debt-free. Rising property 'bubble' valuations thus formed the basis for foreign-currency inflows, not current earnings. For the Baltics and other post-Soviet economies, neoliberal policies caused enormous social and personal devastation that no Western democracy could have sustained: declining birth rates, deteriorating public health, rising worker injury rates, accelerating emigration and in Russia itself, shortening life spans. In addition to these demographic effects, neoliberal extremism put in place the world's most oligarchic tax structure: in Latvia a total social tax of over 50 per cent and a marginal tax on labour of 57 per cent but virtually no tax on real estate or financial property.

The collapse of the post-Soviet economies is hurting the Western European economies as well, and IMF and EU 'stabilisation' loans aim almost exclusively at helping EU creditor institutions recover losses on their bad loans, not the indebted economies, which so far have received almost no relief. Swedish and Austrian bank branches in the Baltics and Hungary imagined that they were protecting themselves by denominating loans in their own currency. Left out of the equation was the debtors' ability to pay, not only by individuals (headed by kleptocrats who gained possession of the prime real estate and public enterprises) out of current income, but also of economies to service the foreign-currency debts being run up. Like Iceland, the Baltics, Hungary and other post-Soviet economies violated the Prime Directive of sound national financial policy: Do not borrow in a hard currency against assets whose revenue stream is in a soft currency. These currencies are now plunging as we write, rendering un-payable the real estate debts and other obligations denominated in foreign currencies. Latvia's economy post 1990 was literally 'Ponzi from the start'. In the next sections we delve into the details of *how* Ponzi structures were forged.

13.3 The political economy of financialisation in Latvia

Latvia became a money-laundering centre for flight capital by Soviet party bureaucrats and army officers already in the late 1980s. This activity was pioneered by figures such as Grigori Loutchansky. Removed from his post for corruption as vice-rector of the University of Latvia in 1982, he went on to engineer the sale of Soviet oil and raw materials to global markets through offshore instruments (Tocs, 2008). This was done in cooperation with Americans such as Marc Rich, seeking to share in the windfall profits.[1] Loutchansky, a founding member of Nordex, bought Russian aluminium and other commodities at give-away prices. This process marked the beginnings of Latvia's offshore economy in the 1980s. It continues to shape its economy today.

Other fortunes were made in arbitrage on the Ruble between Riga and Moscow in the late 1980s. This was caused by the slight price differential between the value of the Ruble in Moscow and Riga as the USSR was slowly disintegrating. Banks involved in this eventually grew into financial offshore operations handling vast sums of Russian money seeking outlets to the West in order to avoid taxation in Russia.[2]

As in other Baltic post-Soviet economies and Hungary, Latvia's growth model favoured financialisation over tangible investment to increase output and exports sufficiently to cover the trade deficit. The EU and IMF encouraged this disastrous policy by providing economic advice that neglected real-sector investment. They pushed for domestic giveaways to political insiders, financed by foreign banks taking over the domestic market rather than developing public financing. It is as if Europe viewed the post-Soviet economies as competitors rather than helping them to build sustainable economic systems and real democracies.

Domestic policy elites also must bear part of the blame for un-taxing finance and real estate so that their surplus cash flow and capital gains could be capitalised into interest payments. This policy left governments to rely on a hopelessly high flat tax on industry and, especially, labour. The flat tax falling on labour amounts to 58 per cent, composed of an income tax of 25 per cent, plus a social benefits tax that falls on employers (24 per cent) and workers (9 per cent). Deregulation (or more accurately, non-regulation from the start) removed most sensible barriers to explosive credit growth. The combination of this advice with reliance almost entirely on foreign bank credit broke the prime directive of avoiding debts denominated in foreign currency to be paid out of revenue earned domestically.

It is important to stress that this development was not the outcome of democratic deliberation. What Latvia got after exit from the USSR was a far cry from the transition to social democracy that most people in the former Soviet Union were promised (Kotz and Weir, 1997). Instead of being openly discussed and democratically decided upon, economic policy was captured by a group of neoliberals known as the Georgetown Gang, following the patterns of 'Shock Doctrine' reforms that had been repeated from Chile in the 1970s to Iraq post-2003 (Klein, 2008). Led by Latvian-American economist George (Juris) Viksnins, this cadre of neoliberal activists crafted a policy that de-industrialised Latvia and reordered its economy along financialised lines. Their ranks included students recruited and mentored by Viksnins and placed in powerful positions as heads of the central bank, finance ministry and indeed as prime ministers. They held key policy positions throughout much of Latvia's 19 years of independence.

The US government played a key role in bringing together these young neoliberals, joined by former mid-level Soviet-era figures whose vision of Latvia was as an appendage of Western finance. USAID and the usual complement of US organisations guided Latvian policy along neoliberal lines (Morica, 2008), as exemplified by the 'Latvia 2000' report. Viksnins there describes the strategy of maintaining dialogue with the public regarding the new policy, but seeing that 'the reform has to continue despite changes in government' (Viksnins, 2008: p. 111). The Washington Consensus was to be applied regardless of the people's will as reflected in changes of government. Again, this is entirely in line with the anti-democratic neoliberal reforms pushed by Milton Friedman in Chile and later by his disciples in Bolivia, the US, the UK, Poland, Russia, South Africa, the Tiger economies during the Asian crisis, Argentina and Iraq (Klein, 2008). Policy was planned by elites (in an eerie resemblance to the Soviet period) and presented to the public as the only way forward – or in Mrs Thatcher's celebrated phrase, as if 'There Is No Alternative'. These policies led to the social fragmentation seen in Latvia today.

Einars Repse, the current finance minister, and Ilmars Rimsevics, presently head of the Central Bank, stand out as the most prominent of these policymakers active over the entire length of Latvia's independence. Rotating through the positions of finance minister and prime minister, their policy was based on a stable exchange rate linked to the euro, and low inflation based on curtailed government spending. Most critics of this 'Great Moderation' were dismissed as Russian revanchists or ignorant populists.

The consequence was that Latvia, a country of only 2.3 million people, mostly poor, had some 100 banks in the early 1990s, and still has 23 today. Some of these banks, such as VEF, have over 80 per cent of their deposits held by foreigners, and routinely deal with foreign shell companies. Latvia has hosted several conferences for 'Shorex', the main organisation for the offshore industry. Figures such as Lucy Edwards, a vice president at the Bank of New York, gave a presentation in 1999 for the Shorex meeting in Riga on 'Money Laundering's Latest Developments and Regulations'. This was done in cooperation with Parex (Block and Weaver, 2004: p. 167). Edwards later pled guilty for her part in the Bank of New York's handling of 160,000 transfers from Russia, with suggestions that some of this money represented

IMF credits (Moyer, 2007). Later, as some banks became more established, they 'off-shored' this specialised activity via corporately distinct businesses they created to stay clear of regulation[3].

The example of Parex bank illustrates the kind of financialisation that was at work. Started by two young ethnic Russians living in Latvia, Valery Kargin, a journalist, and Victor Krasovitsky, a computer specialist, it became Latvia's largest domestic bank, and the second largest bank operating in Latvia. Seizing an opening provided by *perestroika*, the two men opened Latvia's first travel agency in the late 1980s. In 1990 they obtained a for-ex license legitimising the currency trading in which they previously had engaged illegally. In just a few months they made millions on black market arbitrage on the Ruble between Riga and Moscow. They used this money to launch Parex in 1992. It became huge, with billions of dollars in assets and offices throughout West Europe and Asia. Parex was heavily involved in offshore banking, with connections to the infamous correspondent trade mentioned above, run by the Bank of New York that ended in indictments.

Parex was nationalised in the fall of 2008. The tipping point occurred when the Swedish banks announced their government would guarantee deposits. Latvians took this to suggest that deposits in non-Swedish banks were in danger and a run ensued on Parex. In December 2008 the Latvian government gave Parex a €285 million loan and took a 51 per cent control of the bank. Karagin and Krasovitsky retained 34 per cent. It has been speculated that significant sums of Latvian state money have been poured into Parex since, with much of the money coming from IMF and EU loans, for which the public will be burdened. In August 2009 the European Commission launched an investigation into the viability of Parex and Latvia's bailout plan for the bank, while Latvians are disputing the legitimacy of bailing out Karagin and Krasovitsky, whose fortunes are estimated to run into hundreds of millions of dollars each.

Similar stories could be cited to illustrate the extent to which Latvia's economy has been intermeshed with offshore activities and the domestic kleptocracy. The dominating idea on the country's development at the time of independence was that it could be another Switzerland. Creating the policies necessary for building agriculture and industry was not considered a priority. This idea ignored the reality that Switzerland was also an industrial power, with high-value added production in metals, pharmaceuticals and other industries. And its role as a safe financial haven for criminals and kleptocrats is being phased out in response to the global clampdown on facilitators of tax evasion, embezzlement and other crime.

13.4 Latvia's experience in wider perspective

There are three reasons why Latvia took the financialisation route and let international banks and the EU take over the economy and load it down with debt without building its real economy. As in a detective novel, there were means, motive and opportunity. Means were provided by the globalisation of banking in the 1980s and the development of financial instruments (and dismantling or blocking of public regulation) to vastly increase leverage. The motive for financial liberalisation was the large gains that financialisation offered these global creditors in the form of a short-term hit-and-run asset-price and debt boom. And opportunity was provided by the shock therapy imposed on Latvia immediately upon independence. Neoliberal economist John Williamson suggested (in the 1993 book that coined the phrase 'Washington Consensus') that policy makers should 'think of deliberately provoking a crisis so as to remove the political logjam to reform.' Naomi Klein's 2008 *Shock Doctrine – the Rise of Disaster Capitalism* describes this as typical neoliberal policy to dismantle public authority over property and finance. It is the policy that was applied in Chile as a dress rehearsal after that country's 1974 military coup, and then in Bolivia, the United States, the United Kingdom, Poland, Russia, South Africa, the Tiger economies during the Asian crisis, Argentina and Iraq. It is a prime reason why so many developing countries ended up in a Ponzi profile (Kregel, 2004) where real capital cannot be built so that the continuous attraction of financial capital remains as the only option to finance imports.

Latvia fits into this sorry sequence in tandem with the other post-Soviet economies after 1991. Opportunities to privatise and 'liberalise' (that is, steal) were unrestrained. But perhaps the most important element of opportunity was the fact that the post-Soviet economies emerged practically debt-free, offering ample opportunity to take on loans against income 'free' to be pledged as a carrying charge.

Financialisation came to Latvia and most other post-Soviet republics in two phases. The first was the proliferation of private Ponzi schemes posing as mutual funds, benefiting from the kleptocratic privatisations arranged by Western advisors. Most notorious was the Russian MMM scheme operated by Sergei Mavrodi from 1989 to 1994. As one of us has documented (Bezemer, 2001), this wave of pyramid schemes was a form of financial fragility accompanied by all the elements typical in the Minskian sequence: misinformation about what 'the markets' were, gullibility on the part of investors, exponential indebtedness of funds at the cost of real-sector development (by diverting savings to 'make money from money' rather than by direct investment in actual means of production) and co-opting the media and government. Yet only in Albania during 1996–1997 did such schemes take over an entire economy. On the economy-wide level they were essentially microeconomic phenomena.

The more macroeconomic form of financialisation developed as the Ponzi schemes enjoyed their heyday. Official policy backed borrowing abroad rather than developing industry, agriculture and other 'real economy' sectors. Exchange-rate, interest-rate and flat-tax policies aimed at financialising the post-Soviet economies to support this route. Neoliberal 'development' policy took on its own Ponzi features, encouraging large debt overhead (and capital flight), often with maturity and currency mismatches that lay the groundwork for the debt deflations of 2007–2009.

This Iceland-style scenario has now become familiar. Instead of providing productive credit to put in place the means of paying off the debt and its interest charges, finance was predatory. It aimed to extract interest simply by 'capitalising' existing property, loading down assets with debt up to the point where interest charges would absorb all the cash flow over and above bare outlays. Little productive service was supplied, not even reasonable economic analysis of the capacity to pay. Bank officers were given bonuses simply in proportion to the volume of loans they advanced, with no more concern for loan quality than US mortgage bankers showed.

Hardly by surprise, the disastrous effects were similar – defaults, foreclosures and vast personal displacement of debtors. In the absence of real-sector development, the expansion of predatory finance involves enormous human costs. The population shrinks, along with the 'real' economy. Latvia, for example, has experienced plummeting birth rates and large-scale emigration of the most productive part of its labour force, while Russian demographers have pointed out that their nation has lost more population as a result of Western neoliberal policy than it lost militarily during all of Second World War. In both cases the brunt of demographic loss was borne by men between the ages of 20 and 35 years old – the prime working age as well as the typical military draft age.

To the World Bank, the social and labour policies that drove workers to emigrate and held down living standards and workplace democracy qualified Latvia and its Baltic neighbours as being among the world's leading 'business friendly' economies. Its 'Doing Business Indicator' ranks the three Baltic countries plus Georgia as the top four of 25 post-Soviet countries (World Bank, 2009). It is as if the Great Moderation really was working, not polarising economies and leaving bankruptcy in its wake – and for the Baltics, with their property owned largely by foreigners or pledged to foreign creditors.

Economic polarisation, foreign dependency and rising indebtedness was inevitable from the start, being implicit in the neoliberal dismantling of the private sector, of government banking and privatisation of the public domain to local kleptocrats dependent on foreign bank credit. Central planning was dismantled, not to make place for private initiative but in favour of another type of planning. The blueprint produced jointly by the IMF, IBRD, OECD and the European Bank for Reconstruction and Development (EBRD) dated 19 December 1990, entitled *The Economy of the USSR: A study undertaken to a request by the Houston Summit. Summary and Recommendations*, shows that the dismantling of Russia's economy has not been merely an accidental result of bad administration. 'There is no example of a successful modern centrally planned economy', the report asserted. Discussion of ways 'to enhance performance under the old system' was foreclosed by the bald assertion that government planning had 'proved to be counterproductive'. The system was not to be fixed but replaced by an equally one-sided privatised economy, called 'the market system', as if markets could not exist in mixed economies such as the Western social democracies.

Accordingly, Latvia's economy was privatised in stages. Small enterprises were done first in the early 1990s. Large enterprises followed in the mid 1990s with delays reflecting concerns about possible corruption, but also intra-oligarchic jockeying for position. Latvia imposed high labour and social taxes (in effect, both are labour taxes), without any capital gains tax at all. This provided special tax subsidy for privileged insiders making supergains (what John Stuart Mill called the 'unearned increment') by selling off or borrowing against formerly public assets, while encouraging foreign companies to incorporate and invest in Latvia.

Anticipating what the American advisor Jeffrey Sachs would call 'shock therapy', the Houston Summit report claimed not to know of any 'path of gradual reform ... which would minimise economic disturbance and lead to an early harvesting of the fruits of economic efficiency.' Existing savings throughout the Soviet Union – that is, purchasing power in the hands of consumers in excess of goods on which to spend this money – were dismissed callously as 'the overhang problem'. This left the only funding available to purchase public property or modernise the economy to be foreign creditors. From the start, the terms of financing were that business cash flow be paid to foreign banks as interest, denominated in foreign currency.

The initially proposed way to deal with the 'overhang problem' was to let the population use its savings to buy shares in the industries that were being sold by the government. However, the report warned, 'workers' ownership in enterprises ... would run counter to the desired objectives of enterprise reform.' There were to be no worker constraints on management. An almost unparalleled corruption in looting enterprises was tolerated on the premise that the most important need was to create a capitalist class, and that workers were to be without a voice. Once given property, according to the theory, these newly enriched managers would run their factories and other businesses along economically rational lines. But the way this was done was a travesty of providing 'free choice'. Natural monopolies in the public domain were the crown jewels to be privatised and their shares sold off to foreigners, with the proceeds kept abroad by the emerging financial oligarchy.

As in the other post-Soviet republics, Latvia issued vouchers to privatise state property, giving out one voucher for each year of life. Additionally, citizens were given 15 extra vouchers if their families had roots in Latvia predating the 1940 Soviet occupation. Latvians who left during Second World War even as children were given these extra vouchers, but not those who settled in Latvia after 1940, not even their children born in the country. This discrimination was designed to provide an advantage for ethnic Latvians and exclude Soviet era migrants, adding to social tensions among Latvian ethnic groups. However, little consequence resulted from this voucher inequality.

As in Russia, they proved to be of little worth individually, and a cash market rapidly developed by individuals to pool them and take over valuable state property.

Identical voucher plans occurred in nearly each post-Soviet republic. Latvia's plan was a clone of the Russian version, and equally effective in concentrating control in the hands of red directors and voucher buy-up companies who turned around and sold them to domestic and foreign buyers. The effect was to funnel wealth upward, providing a symbolic cover for local kleptocracies throughout the post-Soviet economies.

13.5 Summary, reflections and conclusions

Woody Allen quipped that economics is about money and why it is good. From this perspective – an economic logic benefiting financial interests – Latvia did well, just what the neoliberals advised. The common story in the financial and business press, as in many academic studies and official assessment by IMF and EU, is that Latvia was a star student in the class of reforming economies under IMF tutelage. In this view, Latvia reaped benefits from privatisation, market liberalisation and free movement of goods and labour within the EU. From the start of its 1991 resurrection as an independent state, it embraced the Washington Consensus lock, stock and barrel, and persisted through the 1990s and 2000s even as that Consensus lost credibility. Latvia's 2008–2009 collapse was dismissed as an aberration in an otherwise coherent mainstream story commonly attributed to the global financial turmoil.

The evidence that we find bears out the analysis of Minsky rather than John Williamson (he of the Washington Consensus). Starting from miniscule levels of national indebtedness and widespread asset ownership, Latvia's politicians acted in concert with the EU and the IMF to favour the financial sector, which consisted overwhelmingly of European and other Western institutions. The result was to load down Latvian real estate and other assets and income streams with debt, extracting an exponentially rising outflow of interest while transferring asset ownership abroad. When the economy hit the inevitable debt wall, EU and IMF credit was extended only to support the currency's exchange rate long enough for assets to be pulled out and portfolios to be transferred with minimum loss of value. The foreign financial sector was bailed out, with little attempt to promote domestic recovery. Indeed, falling employment and profits were exacerbated by EU and IMF demands that the government run budget surpluses to squeeze out income to pay back these foreign creditors rather than counter-cyclical deficits to prevent unemployment and dismantling of basic public services from education to medical care.

For Latvia, this neoliberal policy dismantled its public sector and much of its productive capacity. It failed to capitalise on the nation's potential for international competitiveness, and caused widening income inequality, social polarisation and declining health and education standards (not discussed here). In contrast to glowing recommendation by the investment rating agencies, many Latvians voted with their feet and out-migrated in large number.

The inference is that, what results when economic planning is shifted out of the hands of government to private financial institutions is an economy run an oligarchy – not a 'free market'. The problem with this is that oligarchies tend to be lawless. 'Free enterprise' austerity planning, IMF and EU style, aims at shifting the tax burden off finance and its major clients – real estate, monopolies and other property – onto labour. This prevents growth of the domestic market, and also the rise in living standards, education, medical care and public infrastructure investment that tends to be a precondition for rising labour productivity to keep production costs down. The effect tends to be a deteriorating spiral of asset stripping, emigration, capital flight and declining population.

This is not what post-Soviet populations were promised, and the consequences are serious. Breaking the promises made in the early 1990s has now prepared the ground for a re-examination of the benefits and costs of pro-Western alignment and even membership in the EU. Outside Latvia and the Baltics, Iceland provides another example of a population traumatised by predatory credit practices promoted by neoliberal planners.

If this policy continues, one might quip that the final stage of the dynamics set in motion by Soviet Communism is debt peonage. It also means that the new 'final' stage of the financial cycle tends to be kleptocracy, bankruptcy and government bailouts – funded in the last instance by the IMF and EU, to be paid to Western European bankers out of taxes on labour set at levels so high as to render debtor economies uncompetitive in world markets.

Rather than being an aberration, these developments followed the same logic that prevailed in the Anglo-Saxon economies, much of the Third World and many post-Soviet economies during the long credit boom since the mid 1990s. Gina Antczak of Lymington, Hampshire (UK) noted the striking parallels in a recent letter written to *The Economist*:

> SIR – You say that Latvia has enjoyed a colossal boom 'fuelled by reckless bank lending, particularly in construction and consumer loans'. You then state that 'conventional wisdom would have suggested applying the brakes hard, by tightening the budget and curbing borrowing. But the country's rulers, a lightweight lot with close ties to business, rejected that'. Hang on a minute. That sounds remarkably like the ten years leading up to the recession in Britain. I'm no expert on Latvian economic history but it seems rather harsh to blame Latvia's rulers, who were probably doing no more, in their new-found freedom, than emulating what they doubtless perceived as the conventional wisdom of Western capitalist policies.

Notes

1. Rich, whose spouse was a major donor to President Clinton, was pardoned on the last day of Clinton's administration for his former indictments on tax evasion and trafficking in Iranian oil (Willi Semmler, 2002).
2. This practice was pioneered by Parex, Latvia's largest bank until it imploded under the weight of its speculative deals in fall 2008 and was nationalised.
3. Sommers interviewed some of the actors involved in this activity.

References

Bernanke, B. (2004) Remarks by Governor Ben S. Bernanke To the Conference on Reflections on Monetary Policy 25 Years after October 1979, Federal Reserve Bank of St. Louis, St. Louis, Missouri, 8 October 2004: Panel discussion: 'What have we learned since October 1979?', and 'The great moderation', remarks before the Eastern Economic Association, Washington, DC, 20 February 2004.

Bezemer, D.J. (2001) 'Post-socialist financial fragility: the case of Albania', *Cambridge Journal of Economics*, 25(1): 1–23.

Block, A. and Weaver, C. (2004) *All Is Clouded by Desire: Global Banking, Money Laundering, and International Organised Crime* (New York: Praeger).

Hudson, M. and Sommers, J. (2009) 'How neoliberals bankrupted the New Europe', in Martijn Koenigs, 2009 *Verso*.

Kregel, J. (2004) 'Can we create a stable international financial environment that ensures net resource transfers to developing countries?' *Journal of Post Keynesian Economics*, 26(4).

Klein, N. (2008) *The Shock Doctrine. The Rise Of Disaster Capitalism* (London: Penguin Books).

Kotz, D. and Weir, F. (1997) *Revolution from Above* (London: Routledge Press).

Minsky, H. (1978) *The Financial Instability Hypothesis: A Restatement, Thames Papers in Political Economy* (London: Thames Polytechnic).

Minsky, H. (1980) 'Capitalist financial processes and the instability ff capitalism', *Journal of Economic Issues*, 14(2).

Morica, I. (2008) 'The Latvian-American partnership in building civil society in Latvia', in Auers, D. (ed.) *Latvia and the USA: From Captive Nation to Strategic Partner*, (Riga: University of Latvia Press).

Moyer, L. (2007) 'Bank of New York's bad Russian suit,' Forbes.com, 17 May, http://www.forbes.com/2007/05/17/bony-russia-lawsuit-biz-services-cx_lm_0517suit.html

Tocs, S. (2008) 'Louchantsky: beating the times.' Interview with Loutchansky. The Baltic Course. http://www.baltic-course.com/archive/eng/fall_2001/profile.htm.

Viksnins, G. (2008) 'The Georgetown university syndrome and Latvian economic reforms,' in Auers, D. (ed.) *Latvia and the USA: From Captive Nation to Strategic Partner* (Riga: University of Latvia Press).

Wedel, J.R. (1998) *Collision and Collusion: The Strange Case of Western Aid to Eastern Europe 1989–1998* (New York: St. Martin's Press).

World Bank (2009) Latvia. Europe and Central Asia Transport. http://web.worldbank.org/WBSITE/EXTERNAL/COUNTRIES/ECAEXT/EXTECAREGTOPTRANSPORT/0,,contentMDK:20647605~pagePK:34004173~piPK:34003707~theSitePK:571121,00.html.

Part III

Minsky and Crises in the Emerging Markets

14

Financial Crises in an Asian Transitional Economy: The Case of Mongolia

Richard Marshall and Bernard Walters

14.1 Introduction

Minsky's analysis of the endogenous evolution of a financial system from stability through euphoria to fragility has, as its often-explicit example, the United States and presupposes a highly developed financial system. By contrast, the Central Asian transition economies of the former Soviet Union (FSU), and its client states such as Mongolia, had no experience of capitalist development and, at the time transition began, lacked even the most basic capitalist financial institutions, such as commercial banks. Nevertheless, a Minskyan perspective is both possible and useful. In the first decade of transition, for both internal reasons and due to external pressure, Mongolia very quickly became an enthusiastic implementer of the shock therapy transition strategy. This was predicated on the supposed efficiency and welfare implications of unfettered markets. Even the strongest adherents to this approach now consider that, at best, the immediate application of these ideas to financial markets in transition economies was inappropriate and destabilising (see Williamson and Mahar, 1998). Mongolia's first decade of transition provides a striking example of why this change in viewpoint was necessary.

The second decade provides an equally interesting commentary on current notions of the appropriate degree of financial control and regulation for a small developing economy. During this period, Mongolia succeeded in stabilising the banking system, instituted reforms based on Western best practice, and believed it had left its crisis prone history behind. The financial system, largely still dominated by the banks, grew rapidly, and expanded its deposit and asset base during a long period of boom conditions created by high commodity prices. However, it also developed a degree of fragility that has been dramatically exposed by the 2009 global recession.

In this chapter, a first section provides a brief discussion of the way in which Minsky's approach is relevant for a central Asian transition economy.

This is followed by a discussion of banking and financial privatisation and liberalisation in the early period, in which severe domestic banking crises were a prominent feature. The developments since the early 2000s follow with a discussion of the extent to which this evolution and the subsequent crisis can be placed within a Minskyan framework.

14.2 Transition economies and Minsky

A central implication of Minsky's ideas is that a fully deregulated and liberalised financial system will not behave as a stable and automatic mechanism transferring savings to the highest return investments. The reason for this is that the financial system does not operate as a simple conduit channelling savings to investment but is itself a sector searching for profitable opportunities, which will gradually transform the asset and liability structure of financial organisations, including banks, from a stable state, judged in terms of their ability to withstand shocks, to a fragile state in which they are vulnerable to such shocks. A number of mechanisms support this transformation. First, expectations are judged to evolve endogenously with agents' perceptions of current profitable opportunities; they are not rational in the sense of the rational expectations hypothesis and thus, immediately, a Minskyan framework dismisses the efficient market hypothesis. Second, as agents' perceptions of profitable opportunities become embedded, due to the experience of a period of profitable expansion, there is an increasing likelihood of greater mismatch between the time structure of asset repayments and liability demands as agents sense that short term liabilities can be easily re-paid through accessing other sources of funds. These changes in the behaviour of agents are captured by characterising the evolving financial structure of firms (including financial organisations) in terms of three categories: hedge, speculative and Ponzi units. Hedge units have balance sheets which allow the full repayment of all commitments in the face of shocks. However, after a period of robust growth many organisations judge that such conservative financing means that profitable opportunities are being missed. An increasing number of firms engage in more adventurous financing in which mismatches in their asset and liability structures mean that they must roll over their debts on a regular basis. Speculative units are vulnerable to adverse shocks as financial conditions now determine the terms on which they can access further finance. Finally, Ponzi units must continuously seek new finance in order to remain able to discharge their current obligations, expanding debt in order to pay debt. Once the proportion of speculative and Ponzi units grows an economy becomes fragile.

Although it is evident that Minsky primarily had the advanced Anglo-Saxon financial system in mind when he was developing his framework, there are a number of ways in which his insights are important to the case of a small transition economy such as Mongolia. First, on a basic level, his analysis would reject the argument that a deregulated, liberalised financial system would automatically deliver the benefits claimed by the McKinnon-Shaw hypothesis (McKinnon, 1973; Shaw, 1973) and the more elaborated claims of the efficient market hypothesis (Fama, 1991). In Minsky's view financial markets are even less likely to have the claimed efficiency and welfare characteristics than other markets. Mongolia provides a striking example of this insight.

In addition, however, Minsky's analysis has considerable purchase over a financial system, like Mongolia's (and most less developed countries), dominated by banks. For Minsky, banks are the characteristic speculative financial unit (Minsky, 1986; see also Chapter 18). Following a Minskyan approach it would be expected that a period of boom conditions would lead to an endogenous movement towards a more fragile state, with an increasing proportion of financial organisations developing speculative features – broadly, increasingly dangerous mismatches between the time-profile of their asset repayments and the claims represented by liabilities. The early part of the present century was a boom for Mongolia as its economy grew robustly on the back of rising commodity prices. The balance sheets of the commercial banks grew dramatically during this period and their fragility to interest rate and exchange rate shocks correspondingly rose.

The extension of Minsky's approach to an open economy setting is particularly relevant for a small open economy such as Mongolia. Arestis and Glickman (2002) develop the notions of hedge, speculative and Ponzi units in an open economy context. An organisation which deals in both domestic and foreign currency liabilities has another important dimension of fragility. A depreciation of the domestic currency means that the local currency debt corresponding to foreign exchange liabilities rises. This means that a financial organisation, which may be hedged from the perspective of its domestic financial structure, may be speculative from the perspective of its foreign exchange exposure. They characterise an organisation which borrows short-term in foreign currency to finance domestic long-term assets as a super-speculative-financing unit (Arestis and Glickman, 2002: p. 242). The existence of super-speculative financial units also opens up the possibility that the economy as a whole may come to resemble a speculative financing unit. If super-speculative units attempt to re-finance their foreign exchange positions by selling domestic currency to the central bank this may lead to pressure on the reserves of the central bank. If the short-term foreign exchange liabilities of the banking system are large relative to the size of reserves then the economy as a whole may resemble a Ponzi unit, needing to continuously re-finance its position. It is argued that, in fact, this is what has happened in Mongolia.

14.3 The evolution of the financial system in Mongolia during the early years of transition

Mongolia's transition to the market began in the spring of 1990, with large-scale, peaceful demonstrations in the capital Ulaanbaatar, which were quickly followed by the establishment of multi-party elections in early summer and by the embrace of a Western, liberal capitalist model of development. The transition strategy that was adopted was one of shock therapy and there was an immediate and enduring commitment to a staunchly neoliberal approach to economic restructuring predicated on the efficiency characteristics of markets. Harsh stabilisation of the macro economy, interpreted exclusively in terms of price stability, was implemented and a simultaneous and extensive liberalisation and privatisation in all areas of economic life followed quickly (see Nixson *et al.*, 2000 for a detailed examination of this period).

The privatisation of the banks proceeded rapidly and this was accompanied by a general deregulation of financial activities. Two-tier banking was introduced in 1991 when the communist era monobank was split into a division taking on central bank responsibilities, christened the Mongolbank or Bank of Mongolia, and five privatised banks, which inherited elements of the monobank's balance sheet. Ownership was privatised by distributing shares rather than by sale, often to enterprises and co-operatives, which later re-sold (Baumann and Dash-Ulzil, 2003). This meant that there was no injection of fresh capital to protect against insolvency risk. Meanwhile the number of banks expanded very quickly; the privatised banks were joined by eleven new private banks of different sizes during the period 1991–1996 (IMF, 2002: p. 33). Equally quickly, financial innovation in pursuit of profit through financial dealing rather than more traditional banking intermediation became a noticeable feature of the emerging financial system. The result was that, as in many developing countries, Mongolia became surprisingly 'over-banked', with the capital city dominated by large numbers of banking organisations, with a large proportion being fully or partially owned by international firms. The population of the whole of Mongolia, approximately 2.6 million, was, therefore, in the early period of transition, nominally served by up to 16 private banks. In fact, however, most of these banks had no branch network and so did not really provide banking services to the population at large. The majority of Mongolia's population were and are nomadic pastoralists who had little contact or knowledge of the new banking structures. Their experience of banking was limited to the dispersed branches of the former state bank, which distributed pensions and other basic services, such as money transfer. This part of the monobank was inherited by the new Agricultural bank, which had a network of 358 branches across the country's different *aimags* (provinces) concentrated in the *soum* (district) centres. The only other bank with a substantial network was the Investment and

Technological Innovation (ITI) bank with 74 branches. The other 14 banks had practically no branch networks and operated out of offices in Ulaanbaatar. In short, the banking reforms did not lead to an extension of banking services across the whole economy.

A number of further features are also worth highlighting. First, there was no attempt made to establish a development bank. As with other developing and transition economies it was presumed that liberalising and privatising the financial system would encourage savings and the direction of resources to high returns investment projects, without any state guidance, following the basic precepts of the neoliberal template. Second, although the banking system was privatised in 1991, a deposit insurance system for retail deposits was not introduced. The dominance of traditional views about the ubiquity of moral hazard, alongside the confidence in the power of competition to discipline banking practice, meant that little attention was paid to this aspect of banking in the early period. Third, the banking liberalisation proceeded with no attention to retraining staff or introducing systems for credit risk evaluation. Fourth, full currency convertibility was established quickly, effectively from July 1991, and full convertibility with a freely floating exchange rate was established in 1993 and maintained throughout the period. Finally, although a law of banking was passed in 1991, financial supervision and regulation developed slowly and noticeably lagged behind even the prudential standards prevalent in more mature transition economies. There was little development of supervisory structures and the new central bank lacked even the basic expertise to oversee the system (IMF, 1999: p.30). It is important to note that this was not just an oversight in a chaotic period of transition. Instead it reflected the drive to weaken and minimise the state's role in the economy; there was a deliberate, although often not fully articulated, attempt to remove functions from the state.

The blithe confidence of the early reformers in the automaticity and immediacy of welfare and efficiency improving outcomes was quickly undermined. Mongolia's experience of finance in the first decade of transition was dismal and Mongolians were noticeably unenthusiastic. The period was punctuated by frequent and often major crises.

The first major banking crisis occurred in 1994. The proximate cause was lack of liquidity but this, in turn, reflected the effective insolvency of several banks. The Co-operative Bank, spun off from the original state monobank, was effectively insolvent due to a combination of inherited bad debts, bad lending practice and inadequate capitalisation (IMF, 2002). Much of the inherited loan book, which constituted the asset base of the bank, was non-performing and it was compulsorily merged with the Ardyn or People's Bank. However, the problems within the banking sector were not confined to the progeny of the former state bank. A newly established private bank, the Selenge, was also forcibly merged with a larger rival, the ITI. More generally, all of the banks, privatised or newly established, operated without any attention to changing lending practices or employing any form of risk management (IMF, 2002). There appeared to be little connection between bank licensing and evidence of banking experience or expertise, as shown by the large number of extremely small banks established without branch networks to collect deposits and support their operations. In addition, to a considerable extent, the banks spun off from the former monobank continued (and were encouraged to continue, see IMF, 2002: p. 36) to behave as arms of the state, a state however, which now reflected the interests of the newly emerging political elite. Lending to political figures was commonplace and rolling over credit to bankrupt state firms, many of which were in the process of real or spontaneous/wild privatisation was routine; there was clearly little intention of these loans ever being paid back. The banking system in the early years was an adjunct to the process of dismembering state assets.

A further crisis erupted in 1996. In the early part of the year, rumours of banking problems circulated. In the summer, two small banks failed and the central bank was forced to inject large amounts of liquidity as the public withdrew large amounts of currency and attempted to diversify into foreign currency holdings at banks which retained their reputations, for example, the Trade and Development Bank, which specialised in foreign currency dealing (IMF, 2002: pp. 37–38). Finally, in December two relatively large banks (the People's Bank and the Insurance Bank), which had been spun off the original monobank, became bankrupt, weighed down by non-performing loans and disastrous lending practices. At this stage, the authorities were forced to institute reforms, as the entire banking system was now in danger of collapse (IMF, 2002: p. 40).

A Central Bank Law and a new Banking Law were enacted, which attempted to introduce more stringent liquidity and solvency rules, while expanding the power of the central bank to intervene in the commercial banking sector (IMF, 2002). A number of new institutions were created: a Savings bank, with a brief to absorb the retail deposits of the failed banks; a Reconstruction bank, which was to retain all the performing loans of the failed banks; and, finally, a 'bad' bank, the Mongolian Asset Recovery Agency (MARA) in which the non-performing loans were vested and which attempted to pursue and recover unpaid loans (for details, see IMF, 2002: Section IV). The losses in this episode alone were estimated at 7.1 per cent of GDP (IMF, 2002: Table 9, p. 45).

In order to attempt to forestall further crises and amend banking behaviour, Mongol Bank also signed memoranda of understanding with owners and management of the Agricultural Bank and the ITI Bank. However, these measures were insufficient (IMF, 1999: p. 32) and 1998–1999 was punctuated by a further major series of crises. During that year, six banks had their licenses revoked and/or were liquidated (although three new banks were established). The Agricultural Bank and the ITI bank were, successively, taken into conservatorship and, subsequently, the Agricultural bank was placed in receivership, while the ITI and Reconstruction Bank (only established after the 1996 crisis) were liquidated (BoM, Annual Report 2000). The narrative of successive banking crises is reflected in the behaviour of a number of key ratios and statistics, which are shown in Table 14.1.

A traditional claim of the proponents of liberalisation and deregulation is that such reforms will lead quickly to a greater degree of monetisation of the economy, with the implicit claim that this will raise efficiency and garner increased monetary savings. A typical measure is the ratio of broad money, M2, to GDP. Row 1 in Table 14.1 shows this ratio. It is evident that the ratio falls rather than rises and is lower at the end of the decade than at the beginning. Of course, this is partly due to the very high inflation experienced in the early period, shown in the sixth row. This rises precipitously in the early period, peaking at over 325 per cent. However, this fails to explain why the ratio fails to rise later in the decade; inflation had fallen to only 6 per cent by 1998. A similar story is evident in the clear preference of the public to hold legal tender currency outside the banking system and the extent to which it attempts to substitute into safer assets, such as foreign currency.

Table 14.1 Indicators of banking health

	1991	1992	1993	1994	1995	1996	1997	1998	1999	2000
M2/GDP		24.3	14.3	18.5	16.3	17.1	17.4	20.6	20.9	20.4
Proportion of currency outside banks	84.6	63.5	81.1	86.1	86	90.5	87.6	91.4	95.3	94
Currency outside banks/M1	23.3	24.1	47.2	57.1	60	64.9	65.4	68.4	76	77.2
Currency outside banks/M2	17.1	14.1	20.5	24.4	25.1	32.5	29.3	33.7	39.6	39
Ratio of total foreign to total bank deposits	7.4	8.8	41.5	25.8	27.3	33.4	41	35.9	45.4	43.7
Inflation rate (CPI)	52.7	325.5	183	66.3	53.1	44.6	20.5	6	10	8.1
Maximum time deposit rate			100	63.8	42.6	34.5	34.5	19.6	13.2	13.2
Minimum time deposit rate			24	10	12	12	3.6	3.6	3	1.2
Maximum current account rate			2	2	2	2	2	6	6	6
Average lending rate less average deposit rate			19.8	163.5	59.8	43.2	45.7	19.3	15.9	15.9
Ratio of NPL to total loans						38.4	19.7	31	50.5	21.9

Sources: Mongolian Monthly Statistical Bulletin (May) 2009; World Development Indicators (June) 2009; authors' calculations.

Domestic currency as a proportion of M1 and M2 rises over this period and is at a higher level in 2000 than at any previous point. At the same time, foreign currency, chiefly dollar, deposits rise throughout the period. Once again, this continues long after the incentives generated by high inflation have subsided; the impact of inflation on this ratio is evident in the sharp spike in holdings in 1993, but the ratio subsequently rises to even higher levels later in the decade.

Although it is often conceded that newly liberalised banking systems inevitably face problems adjusting to a newly competitive banking, a strong claim of this approach to transition was that privatised, competitive banking would deliver better rates of interest to savers and provide a more transparent and straightforward allocation of resources to investment projects. In other words, following the McKinnon-Shaw hypothesis (McKinnon, 1973; Shaw, 1973), a privatised and liberalised banking system would encourage both saving and investment. A good index of the competitiveness of a banking system can be gleaned from the spreads between deposit and loan rates of interest. A competitive banking system should, *ceteris paribus*, reduce these spreads. Table 14.1 shows a number of different interest rate spreads and their evolution over this period. It is clear that there was no competition among the banks to secure instant access current account deposits during this period. The maximum rate is, during the entire period, below and often far below the rate of inflation. The typical rate for most banks remains zero throughout the period. Rates on time deposits of various maturities are higher but even the maximal rate is rarely above the inflation rate and the minimum rate far below. There was clearly little incentive for agents to deposit their savings in the banking system. At the same time, the spread of lending rates over deposit rates are large and although they fall towards the end of the decade, are still ruinous for long-term productive investment. By contrast, it is worth noting that the rates on offer for dollar deposits are strikingly higher than those available during this period in Western banks. It is evident that the Mongolian banks, especially those with international ownership, were actively seeking such deposits.

By the end of 1999 public confidence in the banking system reached a new low, with the ratio of M2 to GDP falling to 21 per cent. Similarly, total assets to GDP fell to 22 per cent while, correspondingly, the ratio of currency outside banks to M2 rose to 40 per cent. The ratio of non-performing loans was over 50 per cent. Even after excluding the figures from the liquidated banks, this ratio was 37.3 per cent. This figure calls into question the technical solvency even of those banks that escaped the crises. The overall balance sheet shows that the banking system as a whole made a substantial, albeit declining loss vis-à-vis 1998 of 2.8 billion Togrog. However, this apparent improvement is mostly explained by the exclusion of the liquidated banks (BoM, 1999: pp. 40–41).

At the end of the decade, the experiment with fully deregulated, liberalised banks had produced a banking system that was undercapitalised, unprofitable, prone to crisis and lacking any form of public confidence in its core functions.

14.4 The evolution of the financial system in Mongolia during the second decade of transition

The multiple banking crises of 1996–1999 threatened the whole financial structure and generated, at last, a firm response from the Mongolian authorities. However, this response was still constrained by the evolving conventional wisdom that, while poorly sequenced in practice relative to other reforms, financial liberalisation remained a necessary condition for improved economic performance. The corollary was that the appropriate policy response was an improvement in banking supervision and regulation, but with no retreat from the liberalisation framework. To this end, the Mongol Bank made a much more determined attempt to police and enforce capital adequacy and liquidity ratios (although the full implementation of Basel II was not completed). At the same time, further attempts were made to introduce modern banking practices, both in terms of risk management and an attack on the corrupt influences on bank lending. The early part of this period was largely free of crises and major bank failures but witnessed a string of changes to banking regulation and supervision in the wake of the almost continuous problems of 1999. According to BoM it had begun to inculcate international banking standards (BoM, 2000).

The apparent success of these changes was illustrated through the reform of the Agricultural Bank, which, having earlier been taken into receivership, instead of being liquidated was placed under foreign management control in July 2000, with a brief to improve its efficiency with a view to its later sale as a solvent commercial bank. By 2003 the renamed Khan Bank was the most profitable bank in Mongolia and was sold to H.S securities of Japan, with the World Bank's International Finance Corporation arm and the management team of Development Alternative Incorporated buying a stake in 2004 (Baumann and Dash-Ulzil, 2003; Khan Bank, 2004).

In addition, standard indicators showed a return of faith in the banking system. Table 14.2 illustrates these changes. The ratio of M2 to GDP rose strongly throughout the period, from 20.4 per cent in 2000 to 42.4 per cent in 2007. Money held outside banks dropped sharply, especially as a proportion of M2, from 39 per cent in 2000 to only 14.2 per cent in 2008. Both the deposit to GDP and loans to GDP ratios also rose strongly. In addition, the proportion of non-performing loans fell and became comparable for the first time with those in more mature economies, although there is a noticeable jump in 2008.

Table 14.2 Banking after 2000

	2000	2001	2002	2003	2004	2005	2006	2007	2008
M2/GDP	20.4	23	28.3	35.3	36	36.1	36.1	42.4	
Proportion of currency outside banks	94	91.6	89.7	86	85.2	79.5	75.5	77.8	80.7
Currency outside banks/M1	77.2	69.9	64.3	61.8	64.8	56.6	55.8	48	49.8
Currency outside banks/M2	39	33	25.7	18.7	16.9	13.4	12	11.8	14.2
Deposits/GDP	13.5	17.3	24.7	34.4	32.7	35.5	36.4	46.0	
Loans/GDP	5.7	10.5	16.4	26.6	28.2	30.9	32.9	44.7	
NPL/Total loans	21.9	6.7	5.1	4.8	6.4	5.8	4.9	3.3	7.2

Source: Mongolian Monthly Digest of Statistics, May 2009, World Development Indicators (accessed June 2009) and authors' calculations.

At the same time the Bank of Mongolia gained experience and instituted and policed capital adequacy and liquidity rules. Capital and liquidity ratios rose, and became comparable with many developed countries. By 2005, capital adequacy, measured in terms of the Tier 1 capital ratio was 15.8, while total regulatory capital to risk weighted assets was a respectable 18.2 and the liquid asset ratio was 36 per cent (IMF, 2009). The early experience of the present century suggested bank failures were a thing of the past and there appeared reason to suppose that the problems described in Section 14.3 had been successfully addressed.

The improvement in the apparent health of the banking sector reflected the strong economic growth which occurred on the back of rising mineral prices, especially copper but also gold. The growth rate of GDP rose strongly from 0.5 per cent in 2000 to 10.6 per cent 2004, falling back slightly in 2005 before rising to 10.2 per cent in 2007. Although inflationary pressures also rose, the inflation rate was, until 2008, not a major problem. The nominal exchange rate was relatively stable against the dollar and, in fact, slightly strengthened between 2004 and the end of 2008. Given the level of inflation, the real exchange rate clearly strengthened during this period.

However, despite this widely trumpeted success (see, for example, BoM, 2008), the seeds of the subsequent crisis are clear. The growth of overall deposits is extremely high during this period. This undoubtedly reflects the expansion of gold purchases by the Bank of Mongolia. Until 2002 the Bank of Mongolia was the monopoly purchaser of gold from the rapidly expanding gold mining sector. After that date, some commercial banks also purchased gold from the mines, but subsequently sold it to the central bank. The Bank of Mongolia has, therefore, effectively injected large amounts of reserve money, which, judging from the behaviour of the issue of central bank bills, has been largely unsterilised (IMF, 2007: Section C, p. 33). As shown in Table 14.3, the nominal value of deposits rose explosively, rising by 63.7 per cent in 2003 alone and by 56.7 per cent in 2007 before contracting in 2008. The overall growth over the period 2000–2007 was 1241 per cent, a 12-fold rise. Foreign currency deposits also rose by over 1000 per cent between 2000 and 2007, with an annual rate of 85 per cent in 2003. As row 6 indicates, they remained an extremely high proportion of overall deposits, rising to 46 per cent in 2004, before declining to 36 per cent in 2008. In fact, in the early months of 2009 this ratio continued to rise, reaching 41.5 per cent of total deposits in February (BoM, 2009). Row 7 shows that a very large proportion of these foreign currency deposits were in instant access accounts; this ratio was over 50 per cent at the start of the period and was still 39 per cent in December 2008. It is worth

Table 14.3 Economic and credit indicators 2000–2008

	2000	**2001**	**2002**	**2003**	**2004**	**2005**	**2006**	**2007**	**2008**
Real GDP growth rate	0.5	3.0	4.7	7.0	10.6	7.3	8.6	10.2	
Inflation rate (CPI)	8.1	8	1.6	4.7	11	9.5	6	15.1	23.2
Exchange rate index against $ (December 1999=100)	97.8	97.3	95.3	91.8	88.7	87.8	92.0	91.7	91.6*
Growth rate of total bank deposits	18.8	40.5	57.4	63.7	23.0	40.4	36.8	56.7	−6.0
Growth rate of foreign currency deposits	14.6	26.4	54.8	85.1	29.8	37.0	15.1	36.1	3.9
Total foreign deposits/total bank deposits	43.7	39.3	38.7	43.8	46.2	45	37.9	32.9	36.4
Instant access/total foreign currency deposits	51.2	46.2	47.4	50.7	33.3	44.8	40.8	46.1	39.2
Growth rate of net domestic credit	−27.3	52.4	54.7	157.3	25.8	18.8	−3.1	78.4	59.1
Growth rate of credit to the private sector	44.8	152.1	77.5	79.3	0.0	38.3	34.8	77.0	34.7

*November 2008.
Source: Mongolian Monthly Digest of Statistics, May 2009 and authors' calculations.

noting that the foreign exchange market in Mongolia is relatively undeveloped, with almost no operational forward market. The practical upshot of this weakness is that the commercial banks' foreign currency exposure was (and is) effectively unhedged (IMF, 2007: p. 41). Meanwhile, credit growth to the private sector expanded even more quickly, rising by over 3000 per cent between December 2000 and December 2008, much of this to support construction, especially in central Ulaanbaatar. Correspondingly, the loan to deposit rate rose to 132 per cent by the end of 2008.

In summary, although the banks were now technically solvent and held a reasonable proportion of liquid assets, it is clear that the balance sheet disguised considerable risk in terms of exchange rate shocks. The Bank of Mongolia had effectively been following a *de facto* peg for several years during which foreign exchange liabilities had been growing enormously. The Togrog had by the early part of 2008 become an important determinant of the liquidity position of the banking system as a whole; any fall in its value would raise the foreign currency cost of discharging the very large liabilities held by the banking system as a whole, compromising its solvency, which in more traditional terms was well backed. The Bank of Mongolia was in a situation where it felt forced to defend the currency while, at the same time, the very high proportion of instant access accounts made the possibility of a crisis run on the banks a realistic risk. The scale of these liabilities was, by the end of the period, a significant proportion of the reserves (for practical purposes, the same as the net foreign assets (NFA)) held by the central bank. The comparative figures are given in Table 14.4. This exposure therefore compromised the solvency of the Mongolian state.

In the second half of 2008, as the global financial crisis gained momentum, large amounts of foreign currency deposits started to be withdrawn. For some months the central bank preserved the exchange rate and the reserves tumbled, by over 330 billion Togrogs between December 2007 and December 2008. The commercial banks were now extremely exposed. In addition to liquidity risk, the banks started to suffer from insolvency risk. The coverage of their liabilities in terms of foreign assets started falling precipitously, well before the crisis erupted. Net foreign assets, while initially adequate, become negative in 2008; the size of the turnaround corresponds precisely to the central bank's reserve loss; Mongolia's international solvency was being directly compromised by the rapid withdrawal of foreign exchange deposits.

Two events or shocks finally precipitated the crisis of 2009, exposing the fragility of the overall banking system. The Anod bank was declared insolvent in January 2009, after having been taken into conservatorship in December 2008. The bank was discovered to have extended credit to its own shareholders which had not been paid back, to have transferred large amounts of money abroad and to have engaged in a variety of improper accounting and operating procedures. Almost simultaneously, the Bank of

Table 14.4 Foreign assets and liabilities (billions Togrogs)

	2000	2001	2002	2003	2004	2005	2006	2007	2008
NFA BoM	154.4	176.7	254.3	150.7	198.9	368.5	797.6	1137.5	804.9
Foreign currency liabilities of the non-official financial organisations	5.9	8.8	16.5	51.4	53.7	54.8	76.0	209.0	422.2
NFA of non-official financial organisations	47.3	43.5	54.2	105.6	112.1	201.7	334.2	214.5	−127.8

Sources: Mongolian Monthly Digest of Statistics, May 2009 and authors' calculations.

Mongolia acceded to market pressure and allowed the Togrog to depreciate by 25 per cent, as shown in Table 14.5. The banking system was now under severe pressure. Key indicators in Table 14.5 show the speed and size of the deterioration in their liquidity and solvency position and they approached the Bank of Mongolia for liquidity injections. In August 2008, the commercial banks' coverage of their short-term liabilities (demand deposits in domestic and foreign currency) was only just over 36 per cent. The balance sheet of the Bank of Mongolia reveals the extent of its operations, with its claims on the commercial banks rising in just seven months from 64 billion Togrogs to over 250 billion; the liquidity position of the banks improved but it is clear that they remain severely exposed. At the same time, there is a rapid deterioration in the solvency position, with the proportion of non-performing loans rising very sharply.

Despite the degree of support being provided it was clear by March that the Bank of Mongolia did not have the foreign exchange resources to survive a further intensification of the crisis and an approach to the IMF was made. A letter of intent and a memorandum of understanding were signed on 17 March which requested a Stand-By Arrangement with the Fund for 18 months for 153.3 SDR or $224 million. In order to re-build its reserves, the Mongolian authorities committed themselves to a tight monetary policy without, however, any change in the basic policy stance, except an Article VIII restriction, in the case of rationing foreign exchange to critical (food) imports. The weaknesses in the banking system are to be addressed though strengthening supervision and up-dating the legal framework (IMF, 2009). Simultaneously, the Mongolian Government made strong commitments to stabilising the budget deficit.

Table 14.5 Banking during the crisis

	August 08	September 08	October 08	November 08	December 08	January 09	February 09	March 09	April 09
Ex rate T:$ (August 08=100)	100.0	100.4	100.6	98.3	90.8	83.3	78.3	75.5	80.8
Liquid assets/ short-term liabilities	36.6	40.1	41.3	52.4	68.9	63.7	71.0	72.1	72.8
NPL/total loans	2.8	2.8	3.1	3.3	7.2	7.3	7.4	9.9	10.6
BoM claims on commercial banks (bn togrog)	64.2	53.5	92.3	185.1	234.1	244.4	250.4	234.1	208.1

Sources: Mongolian Monthly Digest of Statistics, May 2009 and authors' calculations.

Although Mongolia, with its dependence on copper and gold mining, was inevitably caught up in the global downturn, with an on-going risk that its exchange rate would be determined by the international prices of copper and gold, it is difficult to avoid the conclusion that the degree of foreign exchange exposure which the banks were allowed to develop, in a fully deregulated framework, seriously exacerbated the risks and the costs of the downturn.

14.5 Conclusions

This chapter has provided a review of banking and financial liberalisation in a small open transition economy: Mongolia. The first decade of transition provided a number of straightforward lessons: privatisation prior to setting up supervisory and regulatory structures is likely to generate crises; supervisory and regulatory structures take time to evolve and, evidently, cannot be directly imported; rapid liberalisation does not lead to greater monetisation; banks do not automatically compete for domestic retail deposits, when alternative routes to profitability are available. The licensing of large numbers of small banks is a mistake; Mongolia is overbanked. In terms of development, the substitution of foreign loans (purchase of assets) instead of directing loans to the domestic economy is clearly deleterious. However, the more important general conclusion is that the optimistic assumptions about the efficiency and welfare impact of rapid liberalisation are evidently contradicted by the evidence.

The second decade since transition began tells a more nuanced, but no less important, story. The banking system was stabilised and, in terms of the standard measures of liquidity and capital adequacy, performed creditably. However, as the commodity boom proceeded, the balance sheets of the commercial banks soon indicated an extremely large rise in deposits, with a high proportion of these being in foreign currency and instant access. At the same time, loans in foreign currency expanded and were largely unhedged. This meant that the liquidity position of the banking system, and by extension the Mongolian state, became a function of the exchange rate; the system had endogenously developed a more fragile state. While the exchange rate was bolstered by high commodity prices for Mongolia's staples, copper and gold, this situation was sustainable. However, the global downturn put downward pressure on the exchange rate and exposed the liquidity and solvency fragility of Mongolia's banks. Their attempts to discharge their short-term liabilities drained foreign exchange out of the central bank and left the central bank itself in a dangerously exposed position. Its approach to the IMF was, at this juncture, probably inevitable. However, the policy packages that it is now implementing seem likely to exacerbate some of these problems in the short-run, through increased interest rates and general retrenchment of government finances, and seem unlikely to address the true causes of these banking crises; namely the ability of the banks to raise their foreign currency exposure to systemically dangerous levels. Allowing banks the unrestricted right to deal in foreign currencies and, in particular, allowing their exposure to foreign currency liabilities to grow unchecked raises the risk of crisis substantially.

References

Arestis, P. and Glickman, M. (2002), 'Financial crisis in Southeast Asia: dispelling illusion the Minskyan way', *Cambridge Journal of Economics*, vol. 26, 237–260.

Baumann, H. and Dash-Ulzil, B. (2003), *The Ag Bank's Turnaround: From Insolvency to Profits, Report prepared to USAID* by Development Alternatives Inc.

Bank of Mongolia (2009), Monthly Bulletin of Statistics (May, 2009), Bank of Mongolia, Ulaanbaatar.

Bank of Mongolia (2008), Annual Report 2007, Mongolia, Ulaanbaatar.

Bank of Mongolia (2001), Annual Report 2000, Mongolia, Ulaanbaatar.

Bank of Mongolia (2000), Annual Report 1999, Mongolia, Ulaanbaatar.

Fama, E.F. (1991), 'Efficient Markets II', *Journal of Finance*, vol. 46, no. 5.

International Monetary Fund (2009), IMF Country Report No. 09/130, IMF, Washington, DC.

International Monetary Fund (2007), IMF Country Report No. 07/39, IMF, Washington, DC.

International Monetary Fund (2002), Banking Crises and Bank Resolution: Experiences in Some Transition Economies, IMF Working Paper WP/02/56, IMF, Washington, DC.

International Monetary Fund (1999), IMF Country Report No. 99/4, IMF, Washington, DC.

Khan Bank (2004), Annual Report 2004, available as pdf file at www.khanbank.com.

McKinnon, R.I. (1973), *Money and Capital in Economic Development* (Washington, DC: Brookings Institute).

Minsky, H. (1986), *Stabilizing and Unstable Economy* (New Haven: Yale University Press).

Shaw, E.S. (1973), *Financial Deepening in Economic Development* (Oxford and New York: Oxford University Press).

Nixson, F.I., Suvd, B., Luvsandorj, P. and Walters, B. (eds) (2000), *The Mongolian Economy: A Manual of Applied Economics for a Country in Transition* (Cheltenham, UK: Edward Elgar).

Williamson, J. and Mahar, M. (1998), A Survey of Financial Liberalisation, *Princeton Essays in International Finance*, no. 211, Printon, NJ, Princeton University, International Finance Section.

World Development Indicators (June 2009), World Bank accessed via ESDS at http://www.esds.ac.uk/international/access/dataset_overview.asp.

15

Speculative Financial Behaviour and Financial Fragility in Developing Countries: The Case of Argentina 1992–2001

Valeria Arza and Paula Español

15.1 Introduction

Financial market liberalisation used to be the most controversial policy among those included in the agenda of the Structural Adjustment Plans developed in the late 1980s for Latin American countries. Some claimed that financial liberalisation promoted domestic financial development, enhancing, therefore, efficiency in credit allocation: credit would be better allocated to the most productive activities, which in turn would contribute to long-term growth. Others suggested that financial liberalisation would mostly motivate speculative behaviour, boosting, therefore, financial fragility and thus increasing the risk of economic crises.

This chapter contributes to this debate by providing evidence of financial behaviour in Argentina before the financial and currency crisis of 2001. The evidence supports the latter of those views. As in developed countries, in developing countries speculation is to be facilitated by financial markets and is also to be endogenous to the normal functioning of their markets. Our contention is that with less quality controls after liberalisation, financial markets promoted undervaluation of risks in Argentina, and, as in Minsky's presumptions, actors disconnected their borrowing strategies from their repayment capacity. In this case, however, we claim that the disconnection was related to currency and maturity. Firstly, actors borrowed in foreign currency but their real market operations continued to be predominantly in domestic currency. Secondly, regardless of the maturity of their investment plans, actors borrowed mostly short-term. Thus, speculative behaviour in Argentina took the form of neglecting the mismatch between financial behaviour and real market operation in terms of currency and maturity.

Based on a Minskyan approach we analyse the case of Argentina in the aftermath of the financial liberalisation of 1992, undertaken in the context of the Convertibility regime. Our arguments will be empirically illustrated using descriptive macro and micro data from Argentina during the period 1992–2001. In particular, we discuss the extent to which a Minskyan cycle of optimistic expectations during the upward phase of the business cycle triggered speculative behaviour which contributed to macroeconomic financial fragility.

The chapter is organised in three further sections. Section 15.2 discusses our conceptual framework. Section 15.3 presents and discusses the empirical evidence for Argentina. Finally, Section 15.4 concludes.

15.2 Conceptual framework

Our conceptual framework relies on Minsky (1982, 1986) who suggested that the normal dynamics of a capitalist economy create the forces for its own destruction with financial markets playing a key role in this process. On the one hand, during booms, in a pervasive context of optimistic expectations, there is a widespread undervaluation of risks by firms asking for loans. On the other hand, in the aftermath of a recession, firms recompose their balance sheets and enjoy an increased ratio of cash flow to debt. This abundance of firms' liquidity appeals to banks, which are then particularly willing to provide firms with fresh funds, since banks 'are in business to maximise profits' and 'their profits result from charging for funds they make available' (Minsky, 1986: pp. 229–230).

In other words, the Minskyan hypothesis states that every capitalist economy goes through a situation of over-borrowing and over-lending which typically occurs in the upsurge of the business cycle. This is triggered by undervaluation of risks due to optimistic expectations and abundant liquidity, which has characterised the aftermath of recessions.[1] As a consequence, the economy goes through a rapid indebtedness process, which is rarely subject to quality control, propitiating financial fragility. Not only is there an increasing in the debt-net worth ratio but also actors need to roll over their debt commitments constantly, becoming very attuned to interest rates. This latter financial behaviour is called *speculative* behaviour by Minsky.

This framework was originally developed for closed-economies, particularly for central economies with unregulated and well developed financial markets. This is not normally the case in developing countries, which, more often than not, operate with financial constraints in underdeveloped financial markets. However, our analysis refers to the aftermath of financial liberalisation in a developing country, defined both in terms of international capital mobility and domestic financial deregulation. In most countries, financial liberalisation was deliberately intended to develop financial markets; therefore, we believe, it creates an ideal context to explore the validity of Minskyan arguments in a developing country, such as Argentina.

Some studies started to reformulate the Minskyan framework to be applied to open developing economies, notably, to analyse financial crisis episodes in the aftermath of the Southeast-Asian crisis.[2] Some of these studies point out that speculative behaviour is exacerbated in a liberalised context.

Firstly, without capital controls, portfolio investors – who are naturally seeking for investment opportunities around the world – will be keen on investing in emerging economies which usually offer higher rates of returns. This increases foreign indebtedness and implies that actors in the local economy add a *new source of financial vulnerability*: movements in the *exchange rates* would also affect their repayment capacity. However, this risk is to be commonly disregarded by investors in these countries since market sentiments tend to be positive in a context of financial liberalisation. Not only has such policy the blessing of conventional think-tanks in economics including those in the international community (notably, the International Financial Institutions – IFIs), but capital inflows triggered by liberalisation also reconfirm optimistic expectations about the well-being of these economies.

Secondly, with the liberalisation of financial market, financial opportunities mushroom since previous constraints are swept away. As a consequence, there are new opportunities for speculative finance. Let us bring, for example, the case of up-to-then hedge-financed local firms, which had been constrained to finance their normal operations either with internal funds or with the few – usually expensive – sources of funds available under a situation of underdeveloped financial systems. Say these firms notice there are much cheaper sources of finance, although these are *short-term* and denominated in foreign currency. If these firms had optimistic expectations about the well-being of the local economy and therefore they foresaw no change either in the interest rates or in the exchange rate, they would have no reason for not accepting such a better deal. As a consequence, previously hedge-financed firms are to be pulled by newly available opportunities to become speculative units. They would more likely need to roll over this newly acquired foreign short-term debt (because it was taken to cover normal operations or to substitute other more expensive alternatives) which make them vulnerable to both interest rates and exchange rates.

In sum, as Arestis and Glickman (2002) put it, financial liberalisation acts as a 'key-euphoria-inducing factor'. The authors define a new category of 'super-speculative financing unit' adding the exchange rate risk to classical Minskyan risk of default, since a large part of firms' debt becomes denominated in foreign currency (Arestis and Glickman, 2002: 242).

Frenkel (1983, 2003) largely studied the financial cycles driven by financial liberalisation in Latin America during the *Southern Cone liberalisation experiment*, as he called financial liberalisation pursued principally in Argentina and Chile in the late 1970s. During the initial phase of the cycle, capital inflows were attracted by the spread between domestic and international interest rates. Those capital inflows together with fixed or semi-fixed exchange rate regimes enhanced real currency appreciation which prompted trade deficit. As a result, there was an increase in foreign currency requirements. Since capital inflows weighted heavily in underdeveloped domestic financial markets, abundant liquidity soon became evident in these markets. This in turn pushed financial activity and raised asset prices. Given the fixed or semi-fixed exchange rate, the massive entrance of capital continued to enjoy high profitability – especially when compared with prospective profitability elsewhere in developed economies – and consequently expanded rapidly. However, foreign funds eventually became insufficient to cover the ever increasing deficit in the current account, and, as a consequence, Central Bank reserves declined. When reaching this point, actors began to distrust the sustainability of the exchange rate regime and therefore higher interest rates became necessary to keep on attracting capital inflows, which is somehow a signal of increasing currency risk and default risk. Moreover, higher interest rates negatively affected investment and GDP stalled. This made even more unsustainable the indebtedness dynamics, which usually ended up in financial and currency crises. In fact, the financial crisis triggered by these experiments in Argentina soon brought back pre-liberalisation policies in the early 1980s, which implied higher financial and trade barriers.

During the 1990s, liberalisation policies return vigorously in Latin America, and, as in the 1970s, they were accompanied by an excess of liquidity in international financial markets. International over-liquidity, in a context of financial deregulation, created the opportunities for actors to borrow internationally cheaper than at home, allowed by low spreads (the so-called country risk) even at the eve of financial crises.[3]

In fact, financial fragility is not just a macroeconomic phenomenon. Taylor (1998), who revisited Frenkel's thesis to describe Asian crises, pointed out that the other side of the coin of the macro indebtedness process described above was the intensification of foreign debt in private balance-sheet positions. This process not only affected firms' financial vulnerability but in due time contributed to the systemic risks for the whole financial system. In the same vein, Arestis and Glickman (2002) argued that the new opportunities opened up by financial liberalisation pushed many firms into speculative finance in Southeast Asian countries during the period that preceded the financial crisis in 1997 and Palma (1998) also claimed this was the process that characterised the pre-crisis periods both in Asia and Latin America.

Similarly to these authors, we claim that speculation in developing countries is not necessarily associated with over-borrowing but wrong-borrowing. In Latin America, even after financial liberalisation, financial markets were never deep. During the period under analysis, deposits or credits as a proportion of GDP were much lower for developing countries in Latin America than they were in developed countries.[4] In fact, García Herrero *et al.*

(2002) compared the financial development of Latin America against other European and Asian countries and found that all Latin American countries except Chile conformed a fifth cluster (out of five) in terms of financial depth.[5] The group of Latin American countries had on average in 1996 a financial depth equal to 43 per cent of GDP, while the first cluster (consisting of the United States and Japan) had a financial depth of 346 per cent and the second cluster (Western Europe and some Asian countries) showed a financial depth of 229 per cent.

However, the importance of foreign capital in their economies, especially short-term capital, was usually larger and more volatile than in developed countries. Figure 15.1 represents movements in capital flows – excluding Foreign Direct Investment (FDI) – as proportion of GDP. Columns illustrate these flows for a selection of Latin American countries, while lines do so for a selection of developed countries. The first clear pattern that emerges from the figure is that the underdeveloped financial markets of Latin America receive similar, if not larger, proportions of their GDP of no-FDI capital flows as developed financial systems in advanced economies. Three periods can be identified. Until the Mexican crises (December 1994), capital flows to Latin American were on average proportionally much larger than in the selection of developed countries. From the Mexican crisis until the Asian

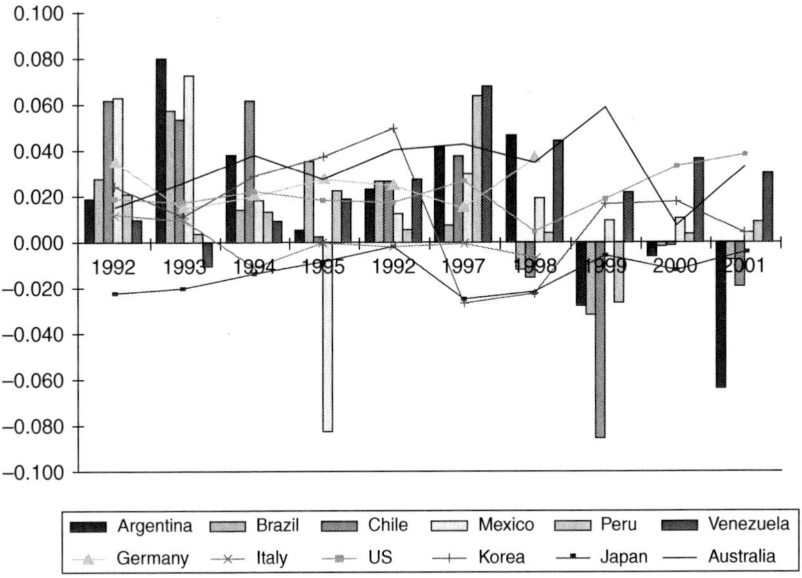

Figure 15.1 Capital flows – excluding FDI – as proportion of GDP in developing and developed countries, 1992–2001.
Source: IFIs – IMF.

crisis (1995–1997), no-FDI capital flows continued to flood these markets, although less intensively. From 1998 onwards, reversals began and outflows represented intense proportions of GDP as inflows used to do.

Therefore, our claim is that speculative behaviour in developing countries is not necessarily associated with the level of financial indebtedness in relation to real market operations but with the *type* of the indebtedness process: mostly *short-term* and in *foreign currency*. Thus, in the context of financial liberalisation and international over-liquidity seeking for investment opportunities, more domestic firms managed to obtain credit in foreign markets, and this regardless of whether their business provided them with foreign currency or whether they could produce the corresponding collateral. This propitiated *maturity* and *currency mismatch* at micro level. This claim would be supported by other scholars studying financial crises in developing countries.[6]

As most of the literature that follows the Minskyan framework would argue, our main explanation for speculative behaviour is related to the normal functioning of international financial markets, which operate fully in the context of financial liberalisation that took place in the 1990s in Latin American. As in the 1970s, the 1990s brought excess of liquidity in international markets. However, most capital flows were footloose and driven by the immediate profitable opportunities that emerging economies offer. Typically, as soon as signals from emerging economies did not appeal to investors, capital flows would reverse. In sum, financial liberalisation in developing countries increased both currency and capital flight risk at macro level. Both of those risks are at the very heart of the typical balance of payment crises of developing countries as described by Grabel (2003) contributing to the intrinsic macroeconomic volatility that characterise these economies. Moreover, contagion effects imply that capital reversals generally affect more than one country creating financial crises in a whole region, sometimes even with a certain level of independence from national policies.

This chapter is largely inspired by the literature that applied the Minskyan approach to explain the escalation towards financial crises in developing countries, particularly recent research that has provided empirical evidence to illustrate the Minskyan dynamics described above.[7]

15.3 A Minskyan cycle illustrated with data for Argentina

This study covers the period 1992–2001, which was fairly successful in terms of economic growth of recent Argentinean economic history. The limits were chosen so as to include the whole Convertibility era, over which GDP grew at an annual cumulative rate of 2.8 per cent in constant PPP (between 1991–2001). During the decade, there were two clearly defined *growth* periods: 1991–1995, interrupted by the Mexican Crisis in December 2004, and 1996–1998. Although the Argentinean economy resisted the first shocks of the Asian crisis, the Russian and finally the Brazilian crises – combined with domestic macro and micro inconsistencies – triggered a long lasting recession that culminated in probably the most intense financial and currency crisis of the country in 2001.

At the beginning of the 1990s, a package of structural reforms was fully carried out by the Argentinean government. Those reforms were part of Structural Adjustment Programmes (SAP) implemented with slight variations in most Latin American countries. These programmes respected the spirit of what was known as the Washington Consensus (WC), whose stated aim was to overcome regional stagnation and to boost growth by means of implementing the so-called market-friendly policies.

Although the currency board regime – that kept the exchange rate fixed by law – was the most prominent feature, the government was committed to every 'must' included in the WC. Most public companies (all public utilities) were privatised, Basel agreements on financial liberalisation were carried out fully, there were no restrictions on capital movement, FDI was given equal treatment, trade liberalisation (which started earlier) was speeded up, most industrial promotion regimes were eliminated and flexibility in the labour market was initiated in the public sector and rapidly adopted by the private sector as well.

The Convertibility Plan finally succeeded in controlling inflation and in stabilising a national currency. These policy reforms were celebrated by the economic establishment, nationally and also internationally. For example, Lora (2001) – from the Inter-American Development Bank – constructed an index that measured the magnitude and efficacy of policy reforms in 19 Latin American countries in five areas, all of which were firmly associated with SAPs recommended by IFIs: (i) trade policy, (ii) financial policy, (iii) tax policy, (iv) privatisation and (v) labour legislation. Figures 15.2A and 15.2B show that Argentina ranked highest among all Latin American countries from 1991 onwards, both for the compound index and in particular for the one referring to financial liberalisation reform. The index seeks to measure neutrality in policymaking in these areas (Lora, 2001: 20), or, in other words, it measures the extent to which policy reforms were carried out as recommended by IFIs.

The rapid implementation of financial liberalisation, which placed Argentina at the top of Latin American countries as early as 1992 – when Basel Capital Requirements started to be adopted – is striking.[8]

As a result, the country soon received important doses of capital inflows (see Figure 15.3). From 1991 onwards, they were large enough to finance trade deficit, interest payments and to roll over existing debt. Besides, a positive balance of the capital account was indispensable to sustain the currency board regime without restricting monetary supply.

Without external constraints – because capital inflows were sufficient to finance current account deficits – the economy grew persistently until the

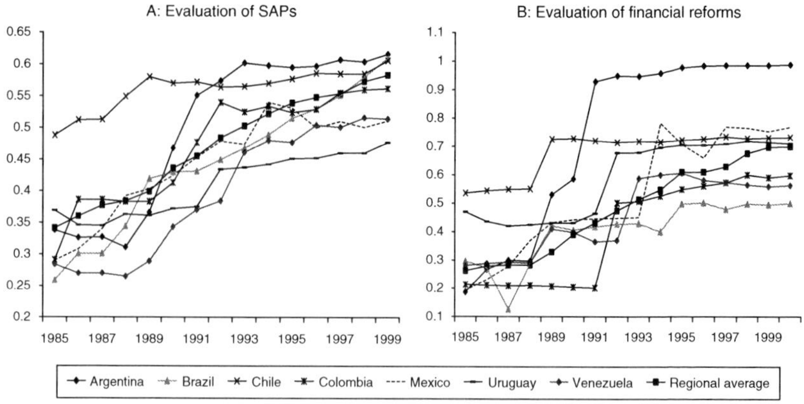

Figure 15.2 Lora (2001)'s indices of efficacy of policy reforms associated to SAP (1985–1999).
Source: Lora (2001).

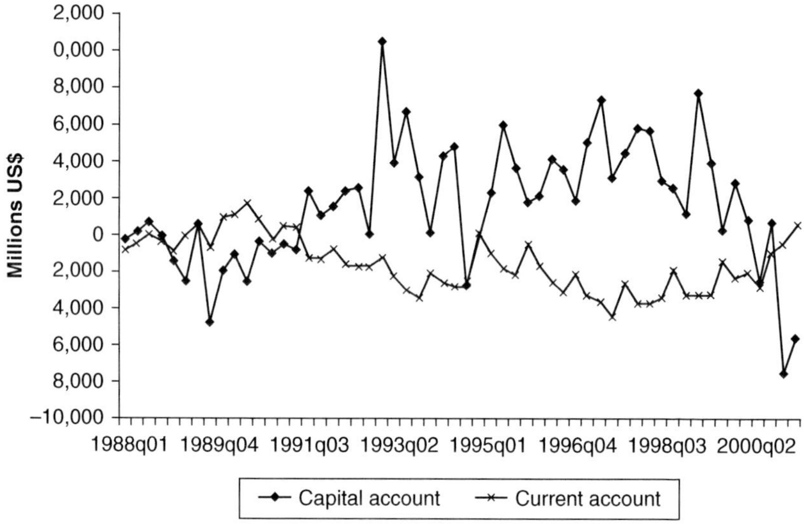

Figure 15.3 Current and capital account balance (1989–2001).
Source: IFS – IMF.

Mexican crisis in December 1994. In fact, GDP in constant PPP grew at 7.2 per cent annual cumulative rate during the period 1991–1994. After a short recession originated by contagion, a rapid agreement with IMF stopped capital flight. In 1996 GDP growth rate was positive again (GDP in constant PPP grew 6 per cent annually between 1995 and 1998). Moreover, Argentinean GDP per capita also grew in most of the analysed period (1992–2001) and during the first half of the decade Argentina GDP per capita was of a similar size and grew at comparable rates as Korean GDP per capita.[9]

This fast growth under the blessing of the IFIs[10] rapidly triggered optimistic expectations as can be seen in Figures 15.4 and 15.5. The former draws an index that anticipates the business cycle[11] and the latter are the expectations of devaluation measured as differences in interest rates between similar types of deposits in national currency and in US dollars, which in a the context of currency board regimes provides evidence on the regime general trustworthiness.

Both figures can be read in the same lines and represent the euphoria of the upward phase of a typical Minskyan business cycle. In the onset of a

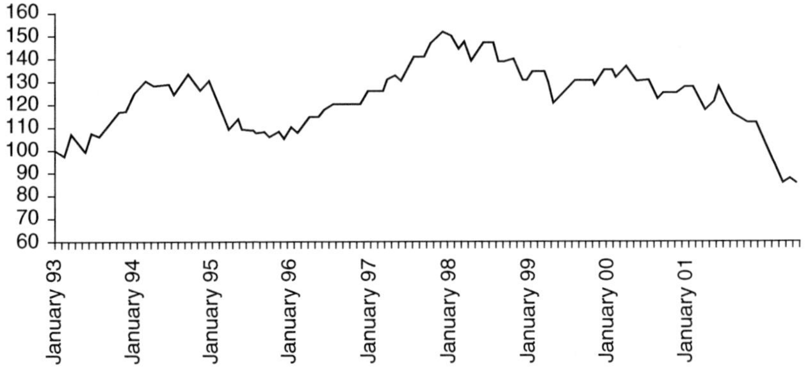

Figure 15.4 Leader Index, expectations on the business cycle (1993–2001).
Source: *Universidad Torcuato Di Tella* (UTDT).

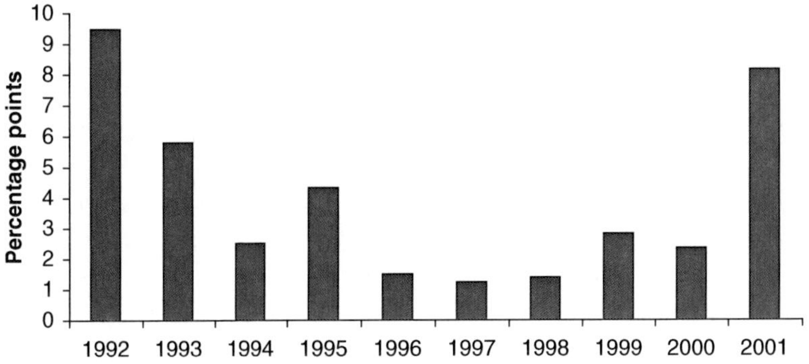

Figure 15.5 Expectations of devaluation: differences in interest rates of 60 days deposits denominated in pesos and denominated in US dollars (1992–2001).
Source: BCRA (Argentine Central Bank).

change in a macroeconomic regime, which proved to stabilise main macroeconomic indicators and counted with the blessing of the international community, expectation raised systematically accompanying the phase of high-economic growth. Expectations rose continuously between 1992 and 1998, except for a short period of unsettlement provoked by the Mexican crisis at the end of 1994. They only reversed clearly during the last year of the regime (2001), but by then the country was already at the prelude of its major financial and currency crisis. Why did it happen?

We believe that a Minskyan framework will be useful to explain the process. As will be seen, we suggest that a Minskyan dynamic of speculative behaviour in a context of abundant liquidity and undervaluation of risks – triggered by optimistic expectations during the high-growth phase of the business cycle – provides interesting insights to the explanation.

After financial liberalisation and under a Convertibility Regime, liquidity clearly increased in Argentina. This is reflected by the surplus in the balance of payment due to the abundant entrance of capital flows showed in Figure 15.3; and by the increase in total deposits and credit presented in Figure 15.6. While in 1991 deposits represented 5 per cent and credit 20 per cent of GDP at the beginning of 2001 they were both around 35 per cent.

However, this increase in liquidity was highly unstable since it was nurtured by short-term capital inflows, as can be seen in Figure 15.7. This Figure shows that there was a large increase in capital inflows but they were clearly dominated by no-FDI short-term capital flows (which are mainly portfolio operations). This situation increases the risk of capital flight: different to FDI

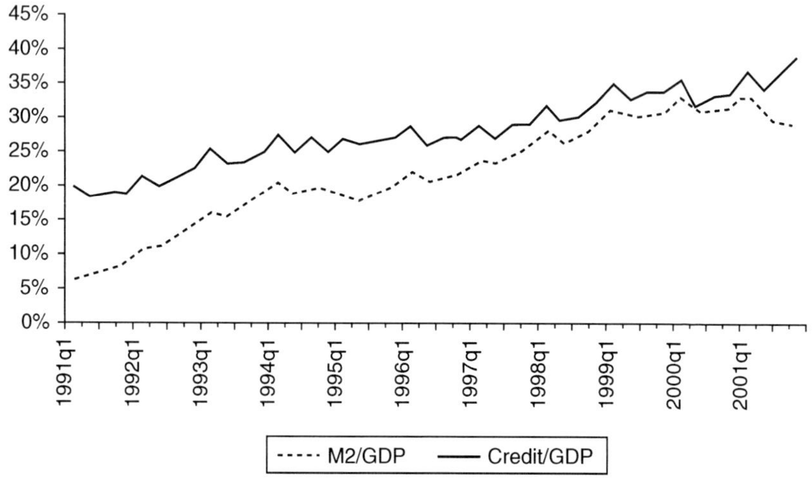

Figure 15.6 Liquidity, deposits and credit as percentage of GDP (1991–2001).
Source: IFS – IMF.

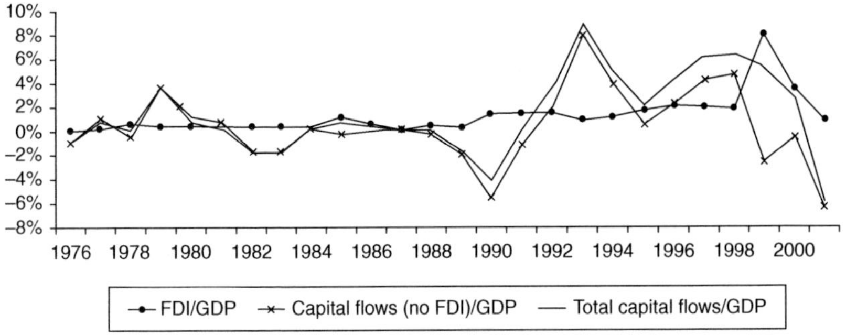

Figure 15.7 Capital flows over GDP (1976–2001).
Source: IFS – IMF.

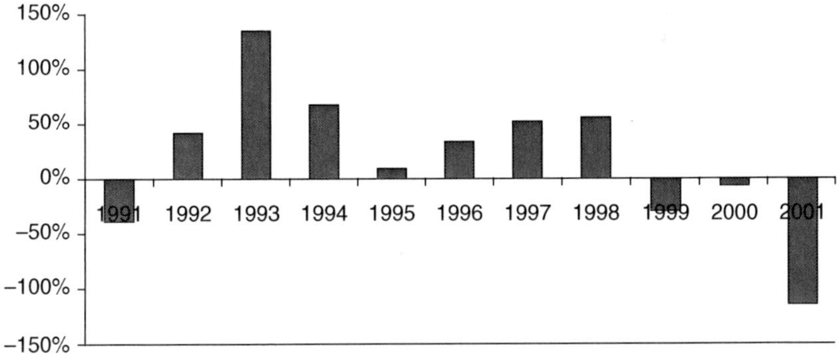

Figure 15.8 Capial flows excluding FDI as a percentage of reserves (1991–2001).
Source: IFS – IMF.

flows, short-term flows are highly volatile and can be easily reversed. Moreover, these flows represented around 50 per cent of total reserves between 1992 and 1998 (Figure 15.8); in a fixed exchange regime such situation may have been highly destabilising since it implied that not only was there a risk of capital flight but also of devaluation (that is, currency risk).

This massive entrance of international capital in combination with the currency board pushed the dollarisation of the local financial system further. The proportion of deposits in foreign currency over total deposits in the domestic financial market grew from around 50 per cent in 1991 to almost 75 per cent in 2001 (Figure 15.9). Credit in foreign currency over total credit also grew, and to a large extent it was absorbed by the private sector, which highly increased participation in total credit at the beginning of the decade.[12]

Moreover, Figure 15.10 shows that although the public sector absorbed a higher share of total foreign debt, the private sector led the increase in

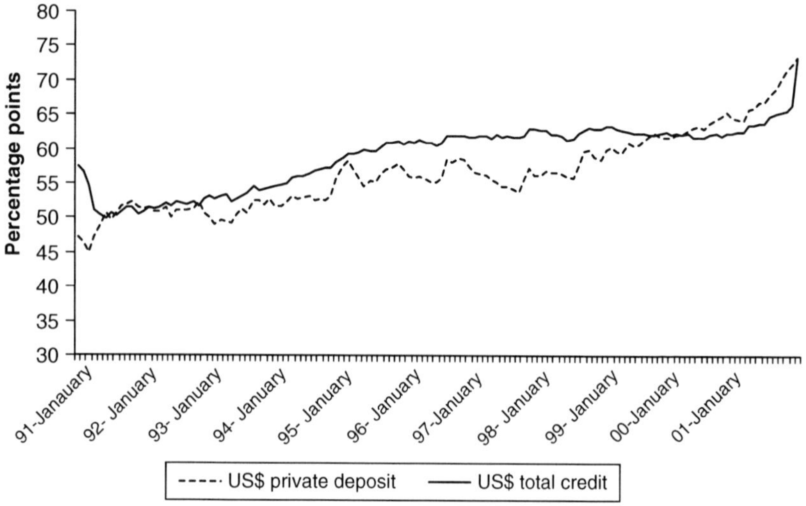

Figure 15.9 US Dollar denominated credit and deposit as proportion of total credits and deposits (1991–2001).
Source: BCRA (Argentine Central Bank).

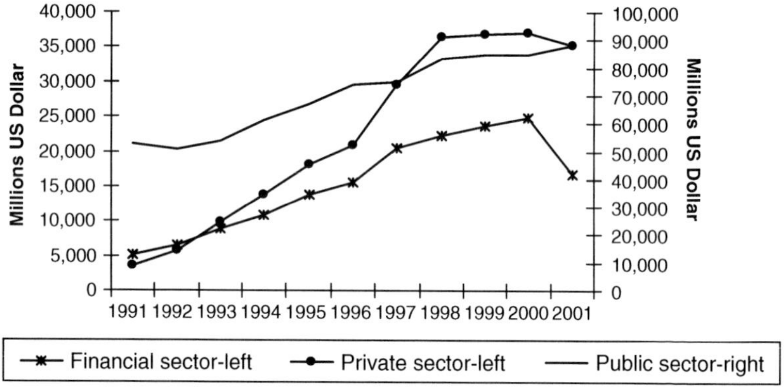

Figure 15.10 Foreign debt by sector (1991–2001).
Source: National Direction of International Accounts – National Institute of Statistics and Censuses Argentina.

external indebtedness throughout the decade. Firstly, the non-financial sector (private firms) constantly increased their adoption of foreign debt after financial liberalisation and until 1998. This process may have pushed many up-to-then hedge-financed firms into (super) speculative finance in the sense of Arestis and Glickman (2002). Secondly, the domestic financial system also intensively increased its foreign indebtedness, which was use to supply credit in domestic markets. Therefore, foreign currency liabilities (heavily fed by short-term capital flows) were used to finance domestic credit (very often, long-term credit, for instance for real estate).

In fact, as occurred in other countries during the upsurge of the cycle in a context of optimistic expectations, there was an increase in credit for real estate operations, especially in foreign currency. While in 1991 real estate credit represent 15 per cent of total credit, by 2001 it had more than doubled to 35 per cent, 80 per cent of which was in foreign currency.[13] This suggests that until the crisis actors did not seem to have suffered currency risk, since they continued to take debt in foreign currency. This is especially worrisome if one admits that most of such external debt was fed by short-term funds. In fact, by 2001 there was a clear accumulation of short-term debt. It represented almost 200 per cent of total reserves;[14] a ratio larger than the corresponding one for Indonesia, Thailand, Philippines and Malaysia at the peak of the Asian crisis in 1997 (see Arestis and Glickman, 2002: p. 249).

Besides this macro picture of an increasing financial fragility due to the intensification of capital flight risk and currency risk, undervaluation of risks may also be found at micro level. As we said in the conceptual section, in the presence of liquidity from international source in the context of financial liberalisation, in Latin America and in Argentina in particular, firms' undervaluation of risks took the form of currency and maturity mismatch. This was to be expected given that, as we showed above, the increasing liquidity took a very precise form: a widespread dollarisation of the domestic financial system fed predominantly by short-term flows.

Thus, investors in Argentina took debt that was short-term and in foreign currency regardless of their repayment capacity. Figure 15.11 shows the relation between the median of gross capital formation and the median

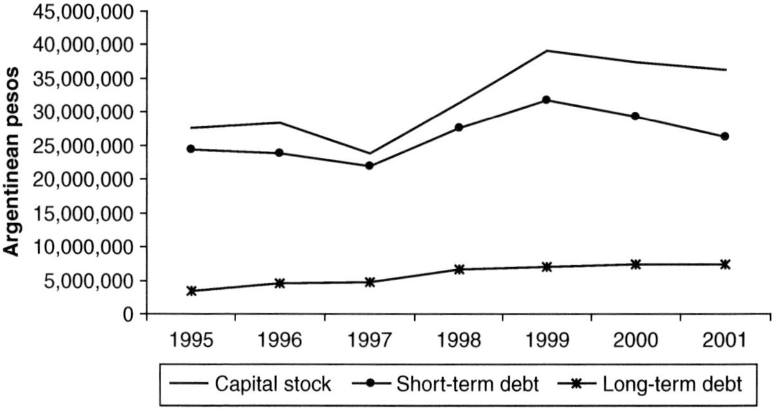

Figure 15.11 Maturity mismatch for the 500 biggest enterprises in Argentina, median values (1995–2001).

Source: ENGE (Survey of big enterprises) – INDEC – Argentina.

of short-term domestic indebtedness for the 500 biggest enterprises of Argentina (data available only since 1995). As Cruz *et al.* (2006) found for the Mexican case, in Argentina for a typical (median) firm an important proportion of gross capital formation during the period under analysis was financed with short-term debt.

Interestingly, firms that obtained the highest proportion of foreign debt belong to the non-tradable sector, as can be seen in Figure 15.12. These firms could not produce foreign currency through their normal operations, because they were, by definition, non-exporters. This mismatch in currencies pushed some of these firms to establish tariffs for their services in foreign currency – notably most privatised utilities – which constitute further proof of unsustainable behaviour in a context of optimistic expectations.

Finally, not only firms that could not produce foreign currency were particularly indebted in foreign currency, this indebtedness process occurred regardless of their possession of collateral in foreign currency. Figure 15.13 illustrates median values for a micro database that gathers all firms listed in the Buenos Aires stock exchange (74 firms). As can be seen, a typical firm increased their foreign debt as a proportion of total debt and did so regardless of their collateral in foreign currency. Actually, until 1998, the median ratio of foreign liabilities to foreign assets increased over time until 1998.

In sum, this section has showed that, after financial liberalisation, Argentina was characterised by an increasing risk of capital flight and currency devaluation at macro level, and by speculative behaviour in the form of currency and maturity mismatch at micro level.

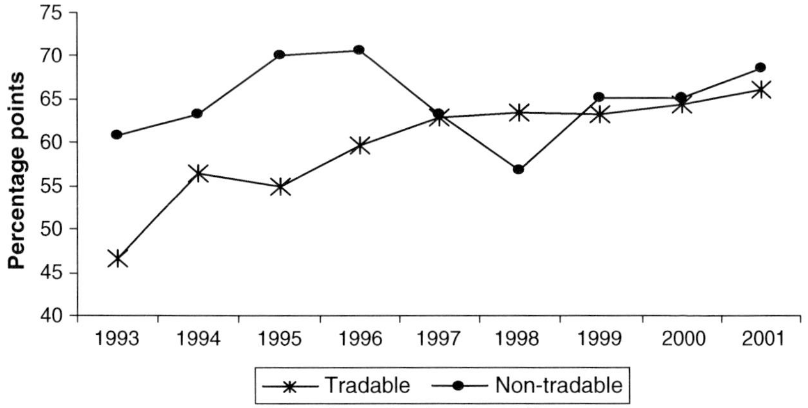

Figure 15.12 Currency mismatch: proportion for foreign currency debt over total debt, median values (1993–2001).

Source: Database built on Economatica, Buenos Aires SE, Regulatory Agencies, Nosis External Trade and IADB calculations. It contains between 130 and 180 firms per year. For more details, see Kamil (2004).

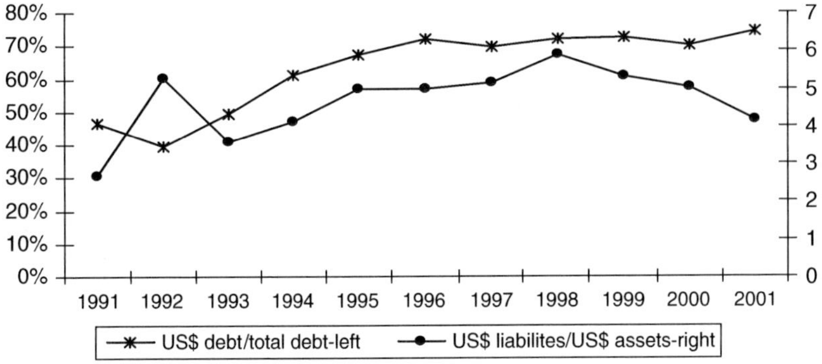

Figure 15.13 Currency mismatch: foreign debt for firms listed in Buenos Aires Stock Exchange, median values (1991–2001).
Source: Buenos Aires Stock Exchange.

15.4 Conclusions

This chapter applies a Minskyan framework to explain financial behaviour that drove Argentina to one of its major financial and currency crises.

Minsky believed that every capitalist economy goes, at some point, through a situation of undervaluation of risks and abundant liquidity both of which would propagate speculative behaviour, disconnecting borrowing from repayment capacity. Therefore, boosted by optimistic expectations, the economy systematically increases its indebtedness, which accentuates financial fragility because outflows due to debt commitments become larger than inflows due to real operations.

According to Minsky, speculative behaviour occurs when actors constantly need to roll over their debt commitments and consequently their financial sustainability becomes very wise to movements of the interest rates. However, the original Minskyan approach referred to advanced and close economies and therefore it needs to be adapted to take into consideration the particularities of open economies in a development context. This chapter has adopted many lines of argumentation that have addressed such a task. In particular, it draws heavily on Arestis and Glickman (2002) and other authors who have applied the Minskyan approach to understand financial crises in developing countries.

We use macro and micro data to analyse the case of Argentina after financial liberalisation in 1992 and before the financial and currency crisis of 2001. We claim that, after financial liberalisation, Latin American countries in general and Argentina in particular received high doses of capital flows.

We show that capital flows were enough to cover current account deficits, which to some extent contributed to sustaining optimistic expectations. However, most of those funds were short-term. Similarly, foreign debt was primarily short-term, and this was used increasingly to fund normal operations of domestic firms – usually non-tradable firms – and to feed the domestic financial system. Domestic credit increased largely, but usually denominated in foreign currency even if it was to finance intrinsically domestic operations such as real estate businesses.

These dynamics propitiate, on the one hand, currency risk and capital flight risk, at macro level; and on the other hand, maturity and currency mismatch, at micro level. In other words, financial liberalisation lifted the barriers for international capital to nurture domestic unities with short-term and foreign fresh funds, risking their financial sustainability and accentuating financial fragility of the whole system.

At macro level, the country was subject to the risk of reversal (capital flights) because most flows were short-term. Since foreign currency was needed to finance current account deficits in a context of real appreciation of the exchange rates, reversals also imply currency risks.

At micro level, domestic units adopted speculative behaviour, disconnecting their borrowing strategies from their normal operation. As in Minskyan dynamics, firms' financial sustainability depended on their capacity to roll over their debt because their long-term investment plans were financed by short-term debt.

Using micro datasets, we show that a typical firm borrowed short-term to finance their gross capital formation, which clearly represents a long-term investment. However, they depended not only on the behaviour of the interest rates but, as Arestis and Glickman (2002) claimed, also on the behaviour of the exchange rate, since their indebtedness was largely in foreign currency. We also show that a typical non-tradable firm, non-exporter by definition, was much more indebted in foreign currency than a tradable firm. Moreover, for the typical firm, the foreign liabilities to foreign assets ratio was ever increasing, indicating that not only did firms disconnect their borrowing strategy from their normal operation but they also disconnected borrowing from the broadly defined repayment capacity given by their collateral.

In sum, we believe that *speculation in developing countries in general and in Argentina in particular was expressed in terms of maturity and currency mismatch.* The outcome of this specific type of speculative behaviour was typically Minskyan: it increased financial fragility of the whole system and a financial (and currency) crisis closed the Minskyan cycle in 2001.

Notes

1. Keynes also proposes the connection between expectations along the business cycle and financial risks. In his words, 'during the boom the popular estimation of the magnitude of these risks, both borrower's risk and lender's risk, is apt to become unusually and imprudently low' (Keynes, 1997: 147).

2. See, for example, Arestis and Glickman (2002), Foley (2003), Kregel (1998a, 1998b), Palma (2000) and much of the academic research from *The Levy Economics Institute*.
3. See Arestis and Glickman (2002), Palma (1998) and Taylor (1998).
4. For example, in 1996 deposits over GDP in Argentina and in Mexico were 23 per cent and 20 per cent, respectively, while in the United Kingdom and in Japan they were 73 per cent and 175 per cent, respectively. In turn, credits over GDP in the former countries were 30 per cent and 53 per cent, while they were 122 per cent and 222 per cent in the latter (source: International Financial Statistics (IFS), from the International Monetary Fund (IMF)).
5. Financial depth is measured as bank liquid liabilities (M2), stock market capitalization and public private bonds outstanding over GDP. García Herrero *et al.* (2002).
6. For example, Arestis and Glickman (2002), Palma (1998) and Taylor (1998).
7. See, for example, Abeles (2005), Arestis and Glickman (2002), Arza and Espanol (2008), Cruz (2005), Cruz *et al.* (2006), Frenkel and Rapetti (2009), Martinez (2006), Schroeder (2002), among others.
8. See Calomiris and Powell (2000) for a review of main regulatory changes on finance carried out in Argentina during the 1990s.
9. However, the effect of the recession from 1998 onwards is outstanding: while during 1992–1994 Argentina GDP per capita was just 5 per cent lower than that of Korean, in 2001 it was 31 per cent lower.
10. Seven years after the set up of the Convertibility Plan, Argentina was still being presented by the IFIs as an example for the world. Michel Camdessus, Managing Director of IMF said in a press conference at the end of 1998: 'It is true that in many respects the experience of Argentina in recent years has been exemplary, including in particular the adoption of the proper strategy at the beginning of the 1990s and the very courageous adaptation of it when the tequila crisis put the overall subcontinent at risk of major turmoil. It is noteworthy that Argentina was probably the first in reacting by immediately strengthening its policy stance and, in particular, pushing ahead with banking sector reform, which of course turned out afterward to be one of the main elements of trouble in other parts of the world. *Notable, too, are the efforts of Argentina since that time to continue its excellent compliance with the performance criteria under our arrangements and much progress in implementation of the structural reforms'* (...). 'So, clearly, *Argentina has a story to tell the world: a story which is about the importance of fiscal discipline, of structural change, and of monetary policy rigorously maintained.* Of course, in the case of Argentina, in the framework of its convertibility plan, the basic principle that you cannot solve problems by relaxation of monetary discipline has demonstrated its virtues' Camdessus, 1 October (1998). The emphasis is ours.
11. This index is called 'the leader index' and it is built with a mix of expectations variables (such as the domestic stock market index and a consumer confident index) and actual economic variables (sectorial performance, use of spare capacity, bankruptcies and money supply, among others). For more details of the index's methodology, see http://www.utdt.edu/ver_contenido.php?id_contenido=3159&id_item_menu=6221.
12. Private credit reached a peak of 80 per cent of total credit at the end of 1994, then it stalled around 75 per cent until the recession of 1998/99, when there was a clear increase in the needs of financial sources from the public sector (Source: BCRA, Argentine Central Bank).

13. Source: Argentina Central Bank.
14. Source: IFS – IMF.

References

Abeles, M. (2005). 'A Minksyan analysis of argentina's convertibility an assessment through corporate finance', *Eastern Economic Association Annual Conference*, New York.

Arestis, P and M. Glickman (2002). 'Financial crisis in Southeast Asia: dispelling illusion the Minskyan way', *Cambridge Journal of Economics*, Vol. 26, No. 2, pp. 237–260.

Arza, V and P. Espanol (2008). 'Les Liaisons dangereuses: a Minskyan approach to the relation of credit and investment in Argentina during the 1990s', *Cambridge Journal of Economics*, Vol. 32, No. 5, pp. 739–759.

Calomiris, C and A. Powell (2000). 'Can emerging market bank regulators establish credible discipline? The case of Argentina, 1992–1999', *National Bureau of Economic Research Working Paper*, Vol. No. 7715, pp. 1–45.

Camdessus, M (1998). 'Press conference of Michel Camdessus, Managing Director International Monetary Fund', IMF Meeting Hall. IMF Headquarters. Washington, D.C.: http://www.imf.org/external/np/tr/1998/tr981001.htm.

Cruz, M. (2005). 'A three-regime business cycle model for an emerging economy', *Applied Economics Letters*, Vol. 12, No. 7, pp. 399–402.

Cruz, M., E. Amann, and B. Walters (2006). 'Expectations, the business cycle and the Mexican peso crisis', *Cambridge Journal of Economics*, Vol. 30, No. 5, pp. 701–722.

Foley, D.K. (2003). 'Financial fragility in developing economies', in A.K. Dutt and J. Ros (eds) *Development Economics and Structuralist Macroeconomics: Essays in Honor of Lance Taylor* (Cheltenham: Edward Elgar).

Frenkel, R. (1983). 'Mercado financiero, expectativas cambiarias y movimientos de capital', *El Trimestre Económico*, Vol. 200, No. October–December, pp. 2041–2076.

Frenkel, R. (2003). 'Globalization and financial crisis in Latin America', *ECLAC Review*, No. 80.

Frenkel, R and M. Rapetti (2009). 'A developing country view of the current global crisis: what should not be forgotten and what should be done', *Cambridge Journal of Economics*, Vol. 33, No. 4, pp. 685–702.

García Herrero, A, J. Santillán, S. Gallego, L. Cuadro, and C. Egea (2002). 'Latin American financial development in perspective', *Madrid Seminar of the Eurosystem and Latin American Central Banks* (Madrid: Banco de España).

Grabel, I. (2003). 'Averting crisis? Assessing measures to manage financial integration in emerging economies', *Cambridge Journal of Economics*, Vol. 27, No. 3, pp. 317–336.

Kamil, H. (2004). 'A database on currency composition of firm liabilities in Latin America', *IADB*, Vol. RES F12.

Keynes, J.M. (1997). *The General Theory of Employment, Interest, and Money* (Amherst, New York: Prometheus Books).

Kregel, J. (1998a). 'East Asia is not Mexico: the difference between balance of payment crises and deft deflations', *Working paper The Jerome Levy Economics Institute*, Vol. 235.

Kregel, J. (1998b). 'Yes, "It" did happen again': a Minsky crisis happened in Asia', *Working Paper The Jerome Levy Economics Institute*, Vol. 234.

Lora, E. (2001). 'Structural reforms in Latin America what has been reformed and how to measure it', *IADB Working Paper*, Vol. 466, pp. 1–135.

Martinez, G.X. (2006). 'The political economy of the Ecuadorian financial crisis', *Cambridge Journal of Economics*, Vol. 30, No. 4, pp. 567–585.

Minsky, H. (1982). 'The financial-instability hypothesis: capitalist processes and the behaviour of the economy', in C. Kindleberger and J.-P. Labargue (eds) *Financial Crises. Theory, History and Policy* (London, New York, New Rochelle, Melbourne, Sydney: Cambridge University Press).

Minsky, H. (1986). *Stabilizing an Unstable Economy (A Twentieth Century Fun Report)* (New York: Yale University Press).

Palma, G. (1998). 'Three and a half cycles of 'Mania, panic, and [asymmetric] crash': East Asia and Latin America compared', *Cambridge Journal of Economics*, Vol. 22, No. 6, pp. 789–808.

Palma, G. (2000). 'The magical realism of Brazilian economics: how to create a financial crisis by trying to avoid one', *Center for Economic Policy Analysis-CEPA. Working Paper*, Vol. III, No. 17, pp. 1–51.

Schroeder, S.K. (2002). 'A Minskian analysis of financial crisis in developing countries', *Working Papers, Center for Economic Policy Analysis (CEPA), New School University*.

Taylor, L. (1998). 'Capital market crises: liberalisation, fixed exchange rates and market-driven destabilisation', *Cambridge Journal of Economics*, Vol. 22, No. 6, pp. 663–676.

16
Dealing with Financial Crises the Latin American Way: The Argentinean, Brazilian and Mexican Experiences

Moritz Cruz and Bernard Walters

16.1 Introduction

According to Minsky (1982, 1986), a crisis can be mitigated if, during the economy's evolution from robustness to fragility, the central bank and fiscal authorities apply counteractive economic policies. These consist of acting as lender of last resort and running a large government deficit, thereby blunting the fall in profits. In other words, the seminal financial instability hypothesis (FIH) framework suggests an activist government may be able to block the endogenous evolution of expectations progressing to instability (see Part I and, with respect to Argentina, previous chapter). However, it is striking that during the recent financial crises in Latin America,[1] such policies were, in most cases, not adopted.

The reason for this is that, in a financially deregulated context, the options open to a government to pre-empt a crisis are limited and precarious. They amount to a reliance on maintaining portfolio inflows at the expense of other internal objectives. The active economic policies to block the endogenous process leading to a crisis, discussed in the seminal FIH, are simply not feasible after the implementation of a financial liberalisation strategy.

This chapter explores this issue by examining the way the three major affected Latin American economies, Argentina, Brazil and Mexico, responded to their immediate crises, and the policies which they adopted to insure against any potential recurrence. The chapter argues that financial liberalisation and consequent 'compromised policy autonomy' (Grabel, 1996: p. 1763) disallowed the application of Minsky's policy recommendations, forcing the countries to fashion alternative responses. It is suggested that these responses, both to the immediate financial crisis and to guard against future financial instability can, to a considerable degree, explain their subsequent economic performance.

The chapter is set out as follows. The next section explains why Minsky's policy recommendations to avert a financial crisis vanish in a financially deregulated context. The different crisis responses and emerging policy frameworks that Argentina, Brazil and Mexico adopted are then outlined and discussed. Finally, Section 16.4 presents the concluding remarks.

16.2 Why recent financial crises could not be avoided in a Minskyan way

Minsky (1982, 1986) developed his FIH in the context of the US economy, which, at that time, was relatively insulated from the problems generated by surges or reversals in capital inflows or a massive run on the currency. It is not surprising that his policy recommendations to avert financial crises concentrated on influencing firms' expectations regarding their future cash flows. Since the economy is an interlinked system – a network of intertemporal, uncertain cash flows – non-payment of debts by one firm to another (especially banks) generates further, multiple defaults. This succession of defaults may, in certain circumstances, provoke the overall collapse of the economy (Bellofiore and Ferri, 2001: p. 13).

For these reasons, on the cusp of a period of financial instability with an imminent prospect of crisis, Minsky (1986) prescribed a policy of stabilising business cash flows (profits). This is to be achieved partly by expanding fiscal policy; government spending has effects both on final demand and on sectoral and business balance sheets. '[T]he income and the employment effect, which operates through government demand for goods, services and labour; the budget effect, which operates through generating sectoral surpluses and deficits; and the portfolio effect, which exists because the financial instruments put out to finance a deficit must appear in some portfolio' (Minsky, 1986: p. 21).

At the same time, Minsky recommended that the central bank, in cooperation with other government agencies and private financial institutions, act as lender of last resort. The actions of the central bank will tend to stabilise asset prices and financial markets. In this sense, the 'institutions that perform a lender-of-last-resort function guarantee that the terms of some contracts will be fulfilled, regardless of market conditions or the business situation of the particular debtor. Thus a lender of last resort diminishes the risk of default...' (Minsky, 1986: p. 41).

In sum, 'both sets of stabilising efforts are necessary to contain and reverse an income decline associated with financial trauma' (Minsky, 1986: p. 38). As a result, 'the combined behaviour of the government and of the central bank, in the face of financial disarray and declining income, not only prevents deep depressions but also sets the stage for a serious and accelerating inflation to follow' (Minsky, 1986: p. 15).

This account generates an immediate question. If these policies are the correct responses to incipient financial instability, why were they not applied to avoid the recent 'boom' of financial crises in developing economies, particularly in Latin America? The answer is that the policy choices that these economies applied prior to their crises undermined their ability to respond in a Minskyan fashion and, in fact, accelerated and deepened the endogenous processes leading to the subsequent collapses. In particular, all the economies that suffered financial crises applied the so-called neoliberal financial liberalisation strategy (see Grabel, 2003). Indeed, the common feature that distinguishes recent financial crises all over the developing world is that they were *all* preceded by rapid domestic and external financial liberalisation. Latin America, of course, was no exception, with the three major economies, Argentina, Brazil and Mexico, undergoing significant financial liberalisation and deregulation.

The adoption of the financial liberalisation strategy not only introduces a set of negative reinforcing risks (see Grabel, 2003), which translate into explosive financial instability, but also constrains policy *ex-ante* and *ex-post*. In other words, in a financially liberalised context, especially a developing one, Minsky's fiscal and monetary policy recommendations cannot be effectively implemented: faced with an imminent crisis, the fiscal and monetary authorities lack the policy space to prevent it. Instead, they are forced into a reliance on attracting portfolio inflows, which introduces, according to Grabel (1996: p. 1763), the problem of 'compromised policy autonomy'.

Compromised policy autonomy emerges when a country's government (especially a developing one) seeks to attract and maintain external investment inflows (direct but particularly portfolio) as a strategy to boost growth. For a government to create an adequate climate to attract capital, it is necessary to adopt a set of policies aimed at securing investors' confidence and reward. These policies include restrictive monetary and fiscal policies aimed exclusively at price stabilisation, maintaining interest and exchange rates higher than otherwise would be preferred and sound public finances. Thus, policies to expand aggregate demand and/or promote industrialisation and growth are discounted *ex ante*. In addition, in the event of a run of capital that triggers a financial crisis, the government is compelled to adopt reinforcing measures aimed at rapidly reversing the outflow and attracting new inflows. These measures involve an intensification of the policies initially adopted. Thus, policy autonomy will be *ex-post* constrained, a situation which can be aggravated if or when the country receives financial support from multilateral agencies (Grabel, 1996).

Hence, policymakers, once they have implemented the neoliberal financial liberalisation strategy, have little room to 'thwart' the endogenous process leading to a crisis. Thus, the government's ability to avoid a crisis, assumed in the seminal FIH, effectively disappears in a financially liberalised context. Their options are either to reinforce the liberalisation policies hoping in this way they can reverse the speculative outflow or, more radically, to rethink the whole approach, reverse the liberalisation strategy and implement a more coherent policy in terms of control and stability.

The next section illustrates the policy choices that the major crisis-affected economies in Latin America followed in the midst of their crises in their search for financial stability and the measures they subsequently took to maintain it.

16.3 Achieving financial stability in Latin America

There has been relatively little concern in the literature for the precise way in which the authorities in Argentina, Brazil and Mexico sought to achieve financial stability in the midst of the financial turmoil and, subsequently, to ensure future financial stability. Shedding light on these issues is important because a significant part of the post-crisis economic performance can be ascribed precisely to the policies adopted to address the crisis and achieve financial stability.

Table 16.1 shows the post-crisis economic performance of Argentina, Brazil and Mexico. As can be seen, Argentina has experienced outstanding economic growth among these crisis-affected economies. On the other hand, Brazil and Mexico, perhaps not coincidentally, exhibit similar economic records. Although one could argue that these economies have grown relatively well after their respective crises, their rates of growth have been both unstable and below those necessary to recover the output loses sustained.[2]

In the next subsections, we describe the policies that Brazil and Mexico followed to address the immediate crisis, that is, to stop the outflow of capital and to attract new capital, and so regain financial stability. We argue that their choices largely explain their lack-lustre economic post-crisis performance: these policies consisted in essentially reinforcing the neo-liberal agenda. By contrast, we argue that the economic success of Argentina relied on her capacity to adopt alternative measures to achieve financial stability.

16.3.1 Brazil and Mexico: reinforcing the neoliberal agenda

In order to stop the outflow of capital and try to attract new capital back during their respective crises, the Brazilian and Mexican authorities intensified

Table 16.1 Argentina's, Brazil's and Mexico's post-crisis economic evolution (GDP rates of growth)

	1996	1997	1998	1999	2000	2001	2002	2003	2004	2005	2006	2007	2008	Average
Argentina								8.8	9.0	9.2	8.3	8.7	7.0	8.5
Brazil					4.3	1.3	2.7	1.1	5.7	3.2	4.0	5.7	5.1	3.7
Mexico	5.2	6.8	5.0	3.8	6.6	0.0	0.8	1.4	4.0	3.2	4.8	3.3	1.3	3.5

Source: ECLAC on-line (available at www.eclac.cl).

the neoliberal strategy of financial liberalisation. Their aim was to stabilise the fundamentals (mainly the exchange rate and the interest rate, but also to reduce the rate of inflation and keep under control the fiscal and external balances) and thus regain (international) investors' confidence. It is important to stress that the sort of policy measures adopted, illustrates clearly that their policy autonomy was indeed constrained in the *ex-post* sense.

In the case of Mexico, for example, during the first months of 1995, three measures were announced in order to halt the capital outflow. First, the government promised to reinforce the economic policies recommended by the neoliberal liberalisation view, that is, to continue the process of financial and trade deregulation as well as the adoption of a tighter monetary policy, and the reinforcement of fiscal retrenchment. Second, the government guaranteed to honour outstanding debts. This was done thanks to the massive financial bailout (around $50 billion) provided by the US government. Finally, a federal insurance savings fund was created (this instrument was known as the FOBAPROA). This measure was taken essentially to rescue from bankruptcy several banks that were unable to discharge their foreign currency denominated debts.

These measures were successful in halting the capital outflow, though it took until the last quarter of 1995 to restore investors' confidence, that is until new capital inflows were attracted. From the last quarter of 1994 until the third quarter of 1995, Mexico's economy registered large, although declining, portfolio capital outflows. However, once the exchange rate stabilised, the rate of interest, though still very high, had started to decline, and the external disequilibrium was corrected, capital flows arrived once again (around $1.7 billion in the last quarter of 1995).

The set of policy measures applied in Brazil to halt the outflow of capital and attract capital back, was essentially no different from those applied in Mexico. First, during the first quarter of 1999, the Brazilian government promised that it would honour its outstanding debts. Second, it received a gigantic bailout (or assistance package as it was called) from the IMF of $41.5 billion 'in support of its program of adjustment, considered being a program of a "preventive nature"' (De Paula and Alves, 2000: p. 610). In the adjustment programme, announced during the last quarter of 1998, the authorities promised to set a clear monetary framework, including an inflation target scheme, and promised further fiscal tightening worth about 1 per cent of GDP (there was also a commitment to achieve a fiscal surplus). Moreover, there were announcements proposing the intensification of the privatisation programme and further trade and financial liberalisation.

Unlike the Mexican experience, the effects of the policy measures taken by the Brazilian authorities in restoring invertors' confidence are more difficult to identify because of contagion effects. While Brazil was experiencing its crisis, several other crisis episodes elsewhere were finishing (Asian and Russian) or unfolding (Argentinean); portfolio inflows accordingly were disrupted across the world, including in Brazil. However, an examination of the evolution of portfolio inflows suggests that the restoration of investors' confidence can be traced, more or less clearly, to the second quarter of 1999. At this time, after the stabilisation of the exchange rate and the rate of interest, portfolio inflows reached $5.4 billion and from then onwards, they followed a more stable though declining trend. Prior to this, from the last quarter of 1997 (that is at the onset of the crisis after a significant speculative attack in October) to the first quarter of 1999, portfolio inflows exhibited sharp variability, going, for example, from $−5. 4 billion in the last quarter of 1997 to $12.4 billion the next quarter, to fall sharply again to $−6 billion in the third quarter of that year. During this period, as expected, both the exchange rate and the rate of interest were very unstable.

It is worth noting that the reinforcement of the neoliberal agenda also explains the recent economic policy response that Brazil and Mexico have applied as their *alternative* strategy to avoid future financial crises. They have simply been increasing liquidity through the accumulation of international reserves. However, stockpiling reserves does not provide full insurance. With full capital account liberalisation, no matter how high the level of international reserves rise, the economy remains highly exposed to the punishing vicissitudes of hot money.

In summary, Mexico and Brazil followed an identical strategy to address their immediate crises and re-establish financial stability. This consisted of strengthening the neoliberal liberalisation agenda. By directing their economic policy exclusively to establish, maintain and then re-establish investors' confidence and reward, their policy room to maintain business' profits, and avoid a crisis, as well as to implement successful policies to promote growth and industrialisation disappeared. There seems little doubt that this explains the unsatisfactory and unstable post-crisis economic performance of both economies.

16.3.2 Breaking the mould in the search of financial stability: the Argentinean experience

Among Latin America crisis-affected economies, Argentina stands apart in the policy measures that it took both to address its crisis and to establish the mechanisms to avoid future episodes. The approach that Argentina took was to abandon the neoliberal agenda, implementing instead a set of radical alternatives.

The first break with the neoliberal agenda was to announce, in December 2001, that the government would default on its public debt (both to private and multilateral creditors), which amounted to $141 billion. Through this announcement, the government signalled that international investors were not its major concern. Moreover, by defaulting on its sovereign debt, the government explicitly broke its relationship with the IMF, demonstrating its independence in terms of economic policymaking.

The second major decision was taken during the first days of 2002 with the end of the so-called convertibility system (which pegged the peso to the dollar under a currency board), signalled by partially freezing the ability to withdraw deposits. This measure allowed the authorities to decide on an exchange rate regime more appropriate to their growth objectives, and to recover control of monetary policy.

The alternative strategy was sealed during early 2003, when the government imposed *controls* on short-term capital inflows, enforcing a minimum stay of 1 year. This measure was further strengthened in early January 2005 when the government obligated investors bringing capital into the country to lock away 30 per cent of the total amount for 12 months.

The benefits that could be achieved by imposing controls on capital inflows are diverse. In the first place, the probability of a sudden exit of investors is reduced by allocating investment towards longer-term activities. Second, the effects of large inflows on the exchange rate and exports are mitigated and, at the same time, the economy is protected from the instability associated with speculative excess and the sudden withdrawal of external finance (see Grabel, 2003).

Finally, it is important to stress that, unlike Brazil and Mexico, Argentina has not needed to hoard foreign exchange to the same degree and, therefore, has not been diverting resources from other developmental objectives.

In summary, the set of alternative policies that Argentina took to address its crisis gave their authorities the policy space to implement pro-growth measures. In this sense, the strong economic growth that Argentina has been registering since the end of their financial crisis has been the result of the set of radical measures implemented. At the same time, Argentina has effectively recovered the space to prevent future financial crises in a Minskyan way.

16.4 Concluding remarks

In this chapter, the crisis and post-crisis policy choices of Latin America's three most important economies, Brazil, Mexico and Argentina, have been discussed using the device of a counter-factual question. Why were Minsky's prescribed policy responses to a financial crisis not adopted in these cases? The chapter argues that the neoliberal financial liberalisation strategy precluded such a response.

This is because the justification for a neoliberal policy of full capital account convertibility is to attract capital inflows. Such inflows require not just formal openness but also a policy framework which maintains the confidence of international investors. This requirement excludes activist policies directed at other objectives *ex ante*. In the midst of a crisis, of course, this bias intensifies, as the overriding objective becomes the restoration of capital inflows; policy is constrained *ex post*.

The chapter argues that the choices made by Mexico, Brazil and Argentina were shaped by this dilemma of compromised policy autonomy. In the case of both Brazil and Mexico, it was demonstrated that the policy choices taken represented an intensification of the neoliberal strategy, which eventually restored investor confidence reflected in the return of capital inflows. However, it was argued that these countries' relatively anaemic subsequent performance represented the effective results of this response.

By contrast, Argentina's response was to reject the liberalisation strategy, substitute domestic goals for international investor sentiment as the key objective of policy and fashion a set of policies to support growth and development. It was suggested that Argentina's subsequent growth performance, in no small measure, reflected this radical choice.

The corollary of this brief analysis of the different experiences of Latin America's major economies is that the restoration of policy space to implement effective measures to pre-empt a crisis and devote resources to industrialisation and development requires the rejection of the neoliberal financial liberalisation strategy.

Notes

1. The Latin American region has been severely affected by financial crises in recent times. Mexico's 'peso crisis' of 1994–1995 was followed by Brazil in 1998–1999, Ecuador in 1999, Argentina in 2001 and finally the Dominican Republic in 2003.
2. According to Cerra and Saxena (2008) the loss of output due to a currency crisis varies between 1 and 5 per cent, and output loss persists even at a 10-year horizon. In the case of a banking crisis, the output impact is, on average, 7.5 per cent and is as persistent as for a currency crisis. Finally, in the case of a twin crisis, the authors find that the output loss is deeper than either of the individual crises and that by the third year after the crisis output loss reaches and remains at 10 per cent.

References

Bellofiore, R. and Ferri, P. (eds) (2001). *Financial fragility and the investment in the capitalist economy. The legacy of Hyman Minsky*, Vol. I (Aldershot, UK: Edward Elgar).

Cerra, V. and Saxena, S. C. (2008). Growth dynamics: the myth of economic recovery *American Economic Review*, 98(1).

De Paula, L. and Alves, A. (2000). 'External financial fragility and the 1998–1999 Brazilian currency crisis', *Journal of Post Keynesian Economics*, 22(4), 589–617.

Grabel, I. (1996). 'Marketing the third world: the contradictions of portfolio investment in the global economy', *World Development*, 24(11).

Grabel, I. (2003). 'Averting crisis? Assessing measures to manage financial integration in emerging economies', *Cambridge Journal of Economics*, 27.

Minsky, H. P. (1982). *Inflation, Recession and Economy Policy* (Great Britain: Wheatsheaf Books).

Minsky, H. P. (1986). *Stabilizing an unstable economy* (New York: Columbia University Press).

17

The Role of Banks in the Korean Financial Crisis of 1997: An Interpretation Based on the Financial Instability Hypothesis

Juan Pablo Painceira

17.1 Introduction

This chapter shows the fundamental role of Korean banks in the explosion of South Korea's financial crisis in 1997 using an adapted Financial Instability Hypothesis (FIH) as an analytical tool to explain it unfolding.[1]

At the core of Hyman Minsky's FIH lies the process of investment and the way ownership and operational control of capital assets are financed by companies. Financial instability emerges from the evolution of the companies' financial structure in undertaking their investment plans during the business cycle. These become more and more fragile during the business cycle as investment is increasingly financed through funds borrowed from banks. As such, this process can be grasped through the performance of banks, analysing banks' balance sheet dynamics during the business cycle. Banks' relations with the corporate sector are represented mainly through banks' assets side: securities and loans. Minsky's framework considers the solvency of the corporate sector as a condition for the solvency of the banking system.

The 2007–2009 global crisis has, once more, revealed how important financial conditions are for the process of capital accumulation. The abrupt interruption of credit flows in September 2008 caused one of the largest drops ever in industrial production around the global economy during the last quarter of 2008. Korea is no exception. So today, more than ever, it is crucial to understand how financial conditions shape the business cycle. Minsky's analysis on banking relations and business cycle can offer some insight into the current situation in which the relationship between finance and capital accumulation has become more complex as global banks focus their business on trading activities and housing lending and large companies increasingly raise their funding through open markets.

Section 17.1 analyses the role of banks and the concept of banks' liquidity preference as being the main economic unit in the determination of the business cycle in Minsky's writings. Section 17.2 addresses critically two hypotheses underlying Minsky's original model: First, the role of the equality between 'two' prices – the demand price of investment goods and the price of capital assets – for the determination of the investment level. Second, the model's assumption of a closed economy, given the new characteristics of financial markets. Section 17.3 discusses the causes of the 1997 Korean financial crisis based on the FIH. It is shown that the main cause of Korea's financial and currency crisis can be found in the performance of Korean financial institutions during the business cycle of the 1990s. Section 17.4 concludes.

17.2 Banks' liquidity preference and the FIH

> Banking is a dynamic and innovative profit-making business. Bank entrepreneurs actively seek to build their fortunes by adjusting their assets and liabilities, that is, their lines of business, to take advantage of perceived profit opportunities. This banker's activism affects not just the volume and the distribution of finance but also the cyclical behaviour of prices, incomes, and employment.
>
> (Minsky, 1986: pp. 225–226)

Banks influence liquidity and should be understood in terms of their dual role as financial intermediaries (origin of investment banks) and as issuers of means of payment (origin of commercial banks). The role of banks in the creation of means of payments is crucial and it is done through customers' deposits. Deposits can be created by acquiring assets and/or through lending operations.

However, the nature of banks should be understood not only by their functions as intermediaries and issuers of means of payments, creating credit risk, but also by their capacity to transform maturities of assets and liabilities, known as assets and liabilities management, creating price (interest rate) and liquidity risk (Kregel, 1998). Banks try to adjust maturities by considering different liquidity *premiums* on their assets and by paying different interest rates on their liabilities.

In post-Keynesian theory, banks adjust their portfolio decisions according to their liquidity preference (Carvalho, 1999). On the asset side, the most important factor on the aggregate level is not the absolute levels of banking investment operations or of reserves, but the proportion in which banks allocate their resources among possible asset positions. In decreasing order of liquidity, different investment forms are: (1) short-term loans in the money market; (2) securities in general; (3) loans in general. Normally, the returns on these asset classes are inverse functions of their liquidity.

On the liabilities side, the main accounts are: banking deposits (cash and time); borrowing operations through money markets and debt securities, and other liabilities (banking capital included). The investment positions and the financing of those positions in capital assets rely on the banks level of confidence in their return expectations (assets) and sources of funding (liabilities). The introduction of the liabilities structure in the analysis of liquidity can show the level of risk taken by the economic units in their portfolio decisions; shaping the Minskyan financial postures, hedge, speculative and *Ponzi* (see Chapter 1).

Banks cannot be hedge units because these units do not raise their level of debt beyond their expected revenue flow in a period of time. Given their reliance on short-term finance to 'take position' in capital assets of longer maturity, banks are essentially speculative units. Banks have always to refinance their liabilities in order to acquire assets with maturities longer than their liabilities. For Minsky, the greater the proportion of speculative and Ponzi units in the economic system, the higher is the degree of financial fragility. The perception of the level of financial fragility is a decreasing function of the safety margins which is given by assets held for their liquidity *premiums* and not by their expected income. These assets are hold as liquidity cushion against possible events of wealth loss (Chapter 5) financial fragility is not the level of indebtedness, but it is the 'coherence' between assets and liabilities of an economic unit. Banks which incur liquidity risk – from maturity transformation – can finance themselves by selling assets, decreasing their reserves or by issuing new debt. In the first case, banks will be incurring only liquidity risk. By issuing debt, banks will also incur interest rate risk due to the possibility of higher interest rates on future debt issuances. The drawdown in reserves is important in terms of liquidity as it can cause an unexpected need to sell assets which could also damage the issuance of debt. The drop in banking reserves may be severe in crisis time. Thus, banks' liquidity preference will be mirrored in their portfolio management.

Over the last decades there have been fundamental changes in the financial system related to the end of Bretton Woods and to the process of financial liberalisation.[2] Financial institutions had to re-adapt themselves. 'The main banks' objective is not the investment income neither the banknotes issuance, but the risk management' (Kregel, 1998a: p. 78) operated via assets and liabilities management.

Due to the institutional changes in financial markets it has become possible to split liquidity and interest rate risks (Fed-NY, 1990) through a periodic re-arrangement of financial contracts. Thus, the maturity mismatch can be drastically reduced through adequate contractual intervals. In this case, however, it is only possible to eliminate the interest rate risk, while the liquidity risk remains. Nevertheless, liquidity risk can be drastically reduced if financial institutions have access to liquidity-shortage credit lines.

Derivatives and secondary markets were believed to allow banks to have smaller exposure to risk through hedging operations and greater flexibility.

Derivative markets increase the liquidity through increased flexibility of positions and reduce costs, but can also raise financial instability through higher volatility in assets prices. In this view, derivative markets are a double-edged sword: they reduce individual risks but introduce difficulties in supervising and regulating the financial operations raising the instability through the increase of the financial fragility of financial institutions.[3] The relationship between banks' liquidity preference and the business cycle is fundamental to explain the inherent instability of the capitalist system as an endogenous market process. During the cycle, there is a rise in the level of investment. Units decrease their liquidity preference, favour more risky capital assets with higher return and are more likely to hold less liquid capital assets and to incur short-term debt with higher interest rates.

> Once euphoria sets in, they accept liability structures – their own and those of borrowers – that, in a more sober expectational climate, they would have rejected. (...) The shift to euphoria increases the willingness of financial institutions to acquire assets by engaging in liquidity-decreasing portfolio transformations.
>
> (Minsky, 1982: pp. 122–3)

Favourable financing conditions are fundamental to the process of investment and to sustain growth. An analysis of how banks expand credit is crucial. Table 17.1 shows a bank's balance-sheet model during the boom phase of the business cycle: when banks' balance sheets expand, there is a shift towards less liquid assets such as long-term securities (corporate bonds) and mainly long-term loans in general. On the liabilities side, it is possible to identify a drop in net worth and a higher importance of liabilities management with a rise of time deposits and interbank borrowing and a drop in the net worth (in relation to total liabilities) due to the fall in the reserves of capital and profits.

The contraction phase of the business cycle is characterised by a rise in uncertainty, causing an increase in their liquidity preference. In this phase

Table 17.1 Banks' balance sheet during the expansionary phase of business cycle

Assets	**Liabilities**
Banking reserves (–)	Demand deposits
Liquid assets (public securities and CP) (–)	Time deposits
Long-term securities (+)	Interbank borrowing
Lending operations (+)	Net worth (–)
Short-term (–)	
Long-term (+)	

Table 17.2 Banks' balance sheet during the contraction phase of business cycle

Assets	Liabilities
Banking reserves (+)	Demand deposits
Liquid Assets (public securities and CP) (+)	Time deposits
Long-term securities (−)	Interbank borrowing
Lending operations (−)	Net worth (+)
Short-term (+)	
Long-term (−)	

one can observe a rise in safety margins through an increase of liquid assets holdings in banks' portfolios (Table 17.2).

In moving towards liquid assets, that is, public debt securities and banking reserves, banks decrease their credit supply with a fall in long-term securities and loans, and through a rise in short-term assets and reserves. The reduction of credit supply damages the sustainability of capital assets positions, mainly for non-financial units. On the liabilities side, proportionally one can observe a rise in net worth and a decrease in the importance of liabilities management due to a rise in deposits in relation to the other sources of funding. The crisis is reflected in banks' performance towards assets with lower return, but higher liquidity.

During the boom, banks' liquidity preference decreases as capital asset markets become more dynamic and a rise in confidence among economic units raises anticipated capital gains (see, for example, Dow, 1993). Once the liquidity preference decreases, the capacity and willingness of financial institutions to expand the credit supply increases. At the same time required banking reserves fall as banking customers transfer their funding from cash to time deposits, banking certificates and so on.

Consequently, there is a reduction of the proportion between monetary liabilities and non-monetary liabilities. The capacity of increasing the credit supply by non-banking financial institutions also increases as agents' confidence allows them to hold non-banking liabilities (debt securities). Therefore, new economic activities as well as activities related to the current financial and real assets (for example, mergers and acquisitions) are financed, reinforcing the dynamism of capital markets. Thus, while positive expectations last, raising asset prices, declining liquidity preference reduces the level of financial prudence of the financial institutions.

17.3 Revisiting the Financial Instability Hypothesis

The present chapter adopts changes to the core of the FIH (see Chapter 1) related to the hypotheses of correspondence between the demand price for investment goods and capital assets prices to determine the investment level and to the FIH in a closed economy (Minsky, 1975). These reformulations can be justified by the rise of financial dominance in the process of capital accumulation and by the existence of higher international capital flow mobility.[4]

First, the process of investment described in the Minskyan 'two prices' (see, for example, Chapters 3 and 4) lacks the fundamental dimension of the 'competition for yield' among assets within a portfolio. Given that economic units have capital restrictions, the available amount of internal and external financing is scarce. Financial conditions are more favourable for the asset with higher expected yield, being a financial asset or an investment good. Therefore, in the process of capital allocation it is necessary to take into account a large range of (financial) assets which is not in the Minskyan 'two prices' model. This makes the process of investment more unstable as the investment should be considered as part of a portfolio.

Secondly, foreign capital has become an important source of financing for investment, increasing financial fragility of domestic agents and hence creating instability in the investment process. This rise in fragility becomes notable when lenders raise the borrowing rates, constrain the available amount of funding and/or cancel the international credit lines, or when the exchange rate changes.[5]

Over the last years, in which the influence of the financial dimension on capital accumulation has become increasingly dominant, there has been an increase in the cash flows coming from balance and portfolio activities relative to the cash flows coming from income activities.[6] This in turn has implied an increasing predominance of speculative and Ponzi financial postures on the aggregate level as the balance and portfolio cash flows have become more relevant to the generation of the total cash flow. So, a highly indebted financial structure characterised by a large proportion of speculative and Ponzi financial postures precedes a financial crisis. A financial crisis is a situation characterised by a fall in assets prices and a generalisation of liquidity and solvency problems among financial institutions and debtors, in which banks find themselves increasingly incapable of raising funds (credit crunch), generating negative effects on the real economy (Minsky, 1986; Akyüz, 1991). According to Gray and Gray (1994), a greater integration among domestic financial markets increases the possibility of financial crisis due to the financial contagion among them.

The fundamental difference between financial and foreign exchange crises is that the former is primarily related to the incapacity of refinancing capital assets positions (either domestic or foreign), while the latter is related to domestic agents' incapacity to refinance their foreign liabilities which, in turn, has a direct effect on the exchange rate. However, the spread of financial liberalisation and integration of domestic financial system in the global economy has increasingly led to a combined or at least intertwined appearance of financial and currency crisis.[7]

17.4 The adapted Financial Instability Hypothesis and the 1997 South Korean financial crisis: from financial globalisation to financial crisis

In this section it is shown that Korea's 1997 financial crisis can be explained using Minsky's FIH.[8] This is done through an analysis of the performance of Korean financial institutions in the 1990s. This performance was fundamental to the rise of financial fragility in the Korean financial system, and consequently to the process of financial instability in the country.[9]

The measures of financial liberalisation implemented during the 1990s caused substantial changes in the Korean financial system (Chang *et al.*, 1998). Deregulation of interest rates on deposits, greater managerial autonomy of banks and lower barriers to entry allowed banks to engage in better assets and liabilities management. This led to a rise in financial innovations, offering new sources of funding to financial institutions. As outlined above, during an economic boom one observes a fall in the ratio of the net worth to total liabilities, as banks – being more confident on monetary returns – raise their liabilities in relation to equity. This fall indicates a rise in financial fragility and emergence of financial instability as banks increase their borrowings and their lending operations.

Furthermore, the increased financial liberalisation allowed banks to raise their foreign liabilities through foreign branches and foreign subsidiaries, raising the capital inflows and potentially foreign exchange exposure of banks. Depending on amount and maturity, this exposure can generate a currency crisis.

The liberalisation of the foreign exchange market was important to the consolidation of financial liberalisation in Korea. This freedom in transacting assets and liabilities denominated in foreign currency had a fundamental impact on the Korean economy during the 1990s as it facilitated the investment and funding of domestic agents, mainly banks, abroad. This in turn was fundamental in raising banks' foreign liabilities and in unfolding the Korean crisis.

17.4.1 South Korean banks' financial fragility during the 1990s: some considerations

South Korea's financial sector was always directly connected to the financing of the economic development. This was evidenced by the high share of claims on the private sector (loans or corporate bonds) in the commercial banks' balance sheets (around 80 per cent of total assets). This characteristic was even more striking with respect to other financial institutions (OFIs)[10] where the claims on the private sector amount to around 90 per cent of their total assets. The importance of the financial sector in the economy can also be measured by credit supply to the private sector as a proportion of GDP. During 1990–1995, this rate was around 55 and 57 per cent and, in the period 1996–1998, the credit rate jumped from 61 to 74 per cent (World Bank, 1999).

As outlined above, in order to understand the causes of the 1997 financial crisis it is necessary to discuss the Korean financial system behaviour during the 1990s through an analysis of commercial banks' and OFI's consolidated balance sheets.[11] The performance of the financial system during the 1990s, especially by commercial banks, can be understood through Minsky. According to the FIH, banks raise their credit supply to the private sector during the economic boom (this was the case of South Korea since the 1980s) and, in search for new sources of funding, increase their liabilities in relation to their equity accounts (net worth). Banks and OFI increased the proportion of their claims to the private sector. So during the boom one can observe a fall in assets held for their liquidity premium as banking reserves once the financial institutions' confidence rises. In this vein, there was a rise in the claims on the private sector from 70 per cent in 1990 to 80 per cent in 1995, in the OFI's balance sheet, a level that remained until 1997. This rise was based on the favourable economic conditions during the 1990s in terms of economic growth. It happened because the good economic environment leads to positive expectation among the economic units and, consequently to the rise in their level of indebtness.

The process of financial liberalisation in Korea allowed the institutions to raise their foreign exchange transactions. On the liabilities side, an increasing share of foreign liabilities in the institutions' balance sheets could be detected. The funding raised through foreign liabilities allowed the financial institutions to raise their loans and securities (foreign or domestic) portfolio and, as the expectations on future returns were favourable, this type of funding continued to increase. This, however, has important implications for financial fragility if foreign liabilities exceed foreign assets.

In summary, the favourable return expectations and institutional changes caused an increase in the foreign assets and foreign liabilities held by financial institutions, mainly after the middle of 1993. On the asset side, there was an increase of foreign assets as a share of total assets from 1.5 to 4 per cent in the middle of 1997. However, the most important development took place on the liabilities side as external financing through loans and bonds issuance became one of the main sources of funding to commercial banks and OFI (including public institutions). As a result, foreign obligations of commercial banks increased from $10 billion (6.3 per cent of the total liabilities) in the early 1990s to $43 billion (12 per cent of the total liabilities) in 1997. The speed at which these liabilities were accumulated accelerated in 1995, as international financial markets showed an increasing confidence in Korean economic performance. In relation to the OFI's liabilities (essentially investments banks), one can observe an enormous increase in foreign liabilities from $6 billion (2.5 per cent of total liabilities) at the beginning of the 1990s to $36 billion (10 per cent of total liabilities) in September 1997. Moreover, the proportion of time deposits in relation to the banks' liabilities remained constant until the 1997 financial crisis. Demand deposits remained relatively constant until 1995 but showed a significant drop afterwards and reached a minimum level of 3.8 per cent in the first quarter of 1998.

On the investment banks' liabilities, it is possible to observe a rise in the quasi-monetary liabilities as a share of total liabilities. Those liabilities were sources of short-term funding used to finance long-term capital assets, being less liquid than demand deposits. The increasing share of this form of financing reflected how speculative financial postures gained share in the system, as the rise in the quasi-monetary liabilities from 42 per cent in 1991 to the level of 52 per cent between 1995 and 1997 (Figure 17.1). This increment was fundamentally related to two factors: first, the low cost of borrowing of foreign funds; second economic unit's state of confidence with regards to the stability of the Korean exchange rate regime, which was based on the belief that domestic capital asset positions measured in foreign currency would not suffer capital loss.[12]

In the context of an open economy, changes in exchange rate and the magnitude of foreign funding to the banking funding (in relation to the domestic sources of funding) have effects similar to those of changes in interest rates and to the domestic sources of funding in a closed economy respectively. The magnitude of those effects depends on portfolio composition of the economic units. The argument is in line with the Minskyan idea that the shortening of liability maturities is one of the main characteristics

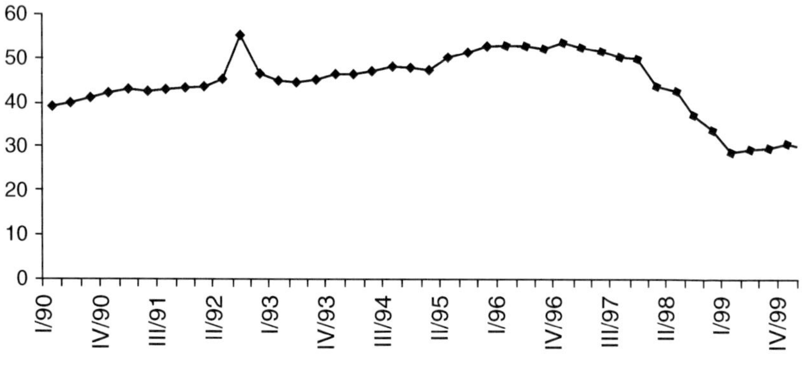

Figure 17.1 Quasi-monetary liabilities (percentage of total liabilities).
Source: IMF, *International Financial Statistics*.

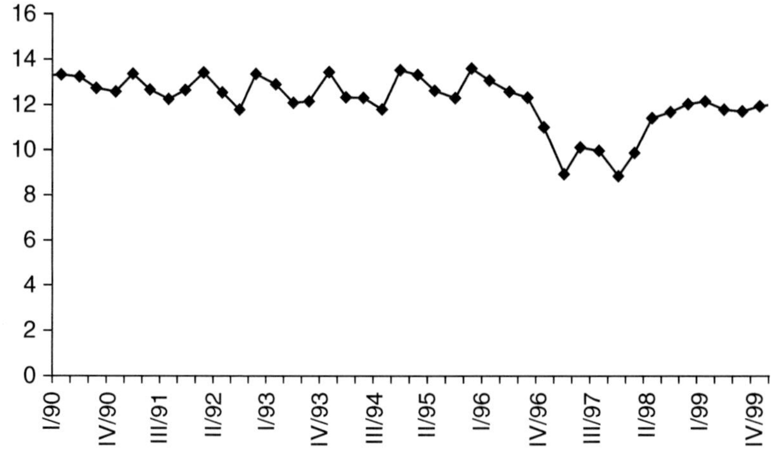

Figure 17.2 Asset liquidity (percentage of liquid assets).
Source: IMF, *International Financial Statistics*.

of business cycle. The high level of short-term foreign liabilities and the impossibility to refinance capital positions were the main causes of Korea's financial and currency crisis. Through the study of amount, maturity and type of foreign liability holder it is shown how a financial crisis turns into a currency crisis.[13]

In addition to an analysis of banks' balance sheets, this chapter presents several financial indicators to show the rise of financial fragility in the Korean financial system during the business cycle. Figure 17.2 shows liquid commercial bank assets (banking reserves, claims on central banks and governments) as a percentage of their assets which, until mid 1995, remained relatively stable. After that they dropped by around 35 per cent. This fall in the safety margins of the Korean banks made them increasingly vulnerable to changes in economic conditions and increased the likelihood that they would find themselves unable to meet their outstanding liabilities.[14]

The rise of banking liabilities is one of the main characteristics of the boom phase of a business cycle, indicating a fall in banks' liquidity preference as new asset positions were increasingly financed by taking on new liabilities. As such, the participation of net worth in total liabilities is considered a fundamental indicator of a possible financial fragility of the system (Minsky, 1986). It shows banks' capacity to meet financial commitments with their own capital. There was a decreasing trend in that participation during the 1990s (Figure 17.3).

The share of demand deposits in the total liabilities is another indicator of financial fragility. Figure 17.4 shows a constant fall since 1991. In the case of the Korean banks, the liabilities' rise was mainly through foreign liabilities.

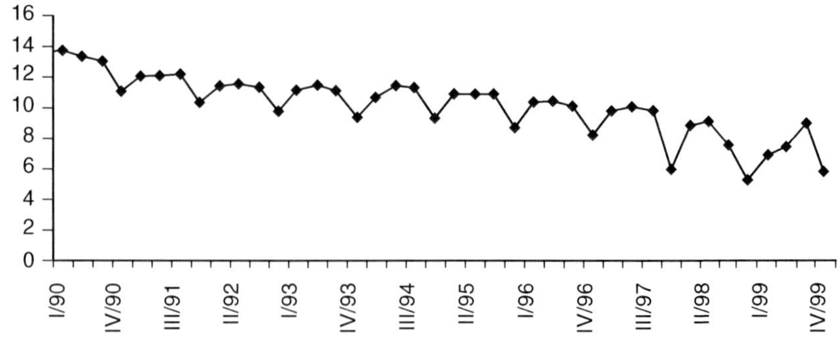

Figure 17.3 Net worth (as percentage of total liabilities).
Source: IMF, *International Financial Statistics*.

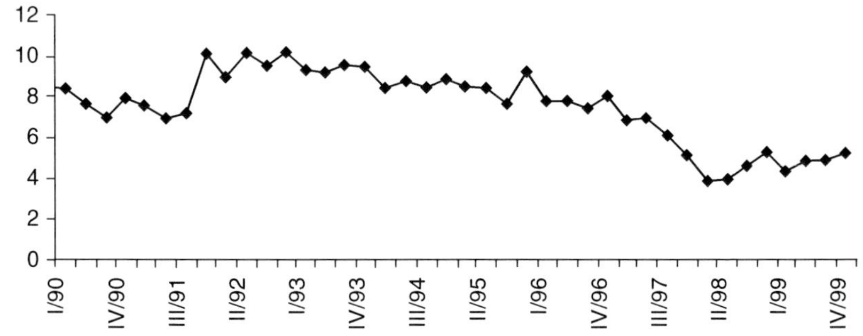

Figure 17.4 Demand deposits (as percentage of total liabilities).
Source: IMF, *International Financial Statistics*.

The share of foreign liabilities in the total liabilities increased from 3.8 per cent in 1994 to 9 per cent in the first quarter of 1998.

17.4.2 Banks' financial fragility and the emergence of Korean financial instability: the question of foreign funding

This sub-section analyses the role of banks' foreign exchange exposure in reinforcing Korea's financial fragility during the 1990s, showing the strong connection between banks' foreign liabilities and total Korean foreign liabilities. This connection in turn, as this chapter argues, was the fundamental cause of the currency crisis.

The evolution of banks' net foreign liabilities showed a period of strong external borrowing starting in 1994 with an increasing trend until the third quarter of 1997 (Figure 17.5). This shortage in the banks' external financing was the trigger for the Korean financial crisis. In other words, it was the lack of external financing in the face of outstanding liabilities that triggered the crisis.

Banks drastically reduced their credit supply to the private sector as they became unable to refinance their foreign liabilities, largely of short-term. In the third quarter of 1997, 59 per cent of foreign liabilities of all Korean financial institutions were of a maturity below 1 year. With the inclusion of overseas branches and subsidiaries, this percentage reached 67 per cent. The financial institutions' external liabilities were equivalent to 42 per cent of total Korean foreign liability. When considering the overseas subsidiaries and branches of Korean banks, this equivalence reached almost 57 per cent of the country's external liabilities (BIS). The speed of expansion of short-term external debt dropped with the Thai crisis. Since then, the perception of foreign investors and domestic financial institutions in relation to the sustainability of their capital assets positions started to deteriorate, given the high proportion of short-term foreign liabilities in total banking liabilities. In the third quarter of 1997, the amount of domestic financial institutions' net foreign liabilities and the ones of overseas branches and subsidiaries of Korean banks ($74 billion) were higher than the total net Korean foreign liabilities ($67 billion). The fundamental role of banks in the process of financial instability in Korea is shown with the net external liabilities drop by $20 billion, with banks being responsible for around $18 billion of this drop (Figure 17.5).

Central for the conversion of fragility into instability – was currency depreciation. But during a crisis it is more important to stress the financial structure than the trigger mechanism in itself. It is the over-leverage of the system that creates the seeds of financial instability. In South Korea, it happened because of the high level of Korean financial institutions' net foreign

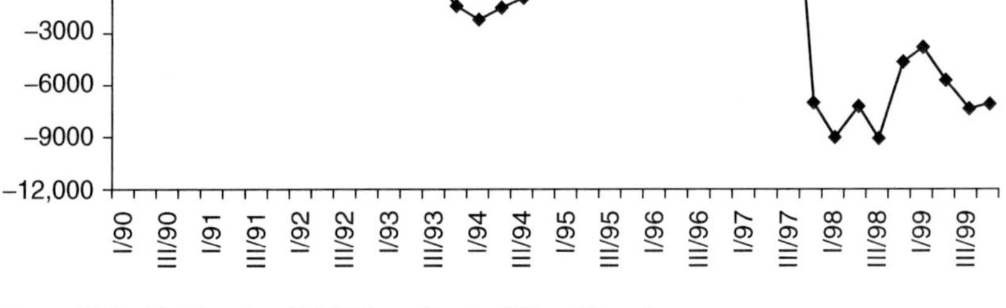

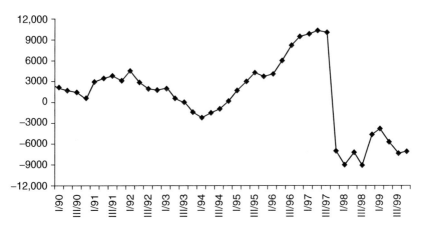

Figure 17.5 Net foreign liabilities – Banks (US millions).
Source: IMF, *International Financial Statistics*.

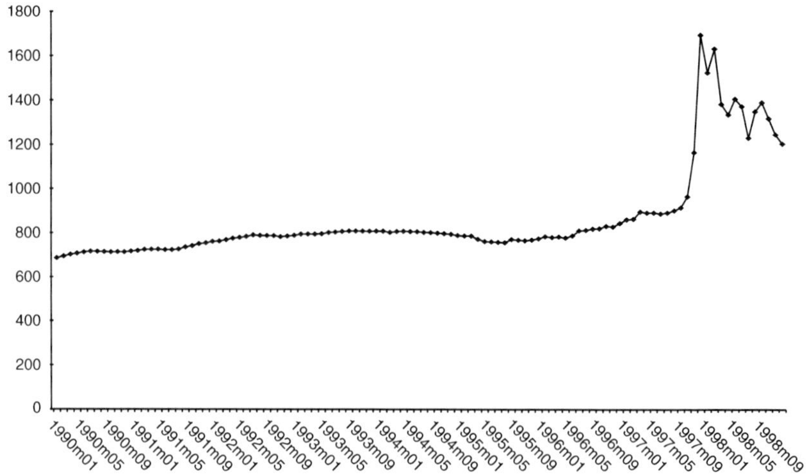

Figure 17.6 Exchange rate – Won/US$ (monthly, end of period).
Source: IMF, *International Financial Statistics*.

liabilities, mainly of the short-term, in relation to international reserves. Then the Korean financial crisis became also a currency crisis.

Financial liberalisation reinforced the relation between banks' performance and business cycle and the rise of external vulnerability to external shocks during the 1990s. In this context, the increase of the stock of portfolio investment and of the short-term capital, which was linked essentially to the banking liabilities, were the main variables to explain the evolution of the financial fragility during the 1990s. The stock of portfolio investment increased from $10 billion in 1993 to $70 billion in 1997.

The exchange rate stability was also important to maintain the increasing capital inflows during the 1990s (Figure 17.6). To a lesser degree the trade balance deficit, mainly between 1995 and 1997, also affected the external vulnerability.

Thus it is possible to affirm that the rise of the external financial vulnerability during the 1990s was closely related to the external capital inflows, mainly of short-term. As foreign borrowing was essentially made by banks, it is possible to establish that the move upward of the Korean external vulnerability is essentially supported by the financial institutions' behaviour during the business cycle of the 1990s.

17.5 Conclusions

The Minskyan theoretical approach is analysed through banks' liquidity preference during the business cycle. This state of preference causes the expansion of credit supply which sustains the economic boom. This phase can be interrupted by changes in the degree of confidence of economic agents. This chapter argues that banks assume a special role, because their liquidity preferences determine the credit supply which, in turn, will be affected by changes in the interest rates or by changes in the exchange rate which affect the sustainability of the financing conditions of their assets positions. In the contraction phase, banks' liquidity preference increases because of the low level of confidence in their profitability perspectives. Therefore, financial institutions prefer to hold more liquid assets with lower return in their portfolio. Consequently there is a contraction in economic activity as banks reduce the credit supply to the private sector. The chapter also sheds light on the Korean crisis in September 2008 where the main holders of short-term foreign liabilities were financial institutions. It is shown that the main causes of the financial crisis in 1997 can be found essentially in the financial institutions' behaviour during the business cycle. The increasing fragility in banks' balance sheets in turn contributed to the outbreak of the financial crisis as a sharp depreciation increased the value of liabilities and external funding for the banks was limited.

Notes

1. This chapter is based on (Painceira, 2003, http://www.sep.org.br/pt/congresso.php?PHPSESSID=15adbb2aef13973fcb29f5daec229999#). I would like to thank Annina Kaltenbrunner for comments. All remaining errors are my responsibility.
2. On those changes, see Minsky (1986, 1994); Chesnais (1996); and Plihon (1995).
3. For a detailed account of the evolution of derivative markets, see Kregel (1998).
4. For more details on the relevance of those changes and their effects on the original model of FIH, see Painceira (2003: Section 17.2).
5. See Kregel (1998) and Arestis and Glickman (2002).
6. About the importance of cash flows in the process of financial instability, see Minsky (1986: Chapter 9).
7. See Chang and Velasco (1999), Corsetti *et al.* (1998), Finger and Schuknecht (1999), and Lindreng *et al.* (1999).
8. Analyses of the East Asian crisis, including the Korean, based on the FIH theory can be found in Kregel (1998) and Arestis and Glickman (2002).
9. Other analytical references to the Korean crisis are Chang *et al.* (1998) and BIS (1998).
10. This aggregate is composed by trust accounts banks (investment banks) and development institutions.
11. For a full understanding of the Korean crisis it would be necessary to analyse the Korean economic and political relations, mainly those among the biggest corporate conglomerate, the Chaebols. This analysis is not part of the chapter.
12. In addition to the lower costs, there was an institutional incentive to the short-term borrowing in relation to the long-term one. On this point, see Chang *et al.* (1998: p. 739).
13. Besides the exchange rate stability, another important factor to attract capital flows was the long period of economic growth in East Asia. This economic performance contributed to the 'strong growth in the asset prices and lead companies

and households, as well banks, to underestimate the overinvestment risk' (BIS, 1999, p. 119). However, following Minsky's ideas, when the state of confidence is favourable and all economic units are very confident in their expectations the underestimation of risk is a rational process.

14. This percentage indicates how the financial institutions are able to deal with unpredictable changes in the cash flows of economic units.

References

Akyüz, Y. (1991), 'Inestabilidad e Incertitumbre en los Mercados Financieros Internacionales', *Boletín del CEMLA*, vol. 37, no. 6.

Arestis, P. and M. Glickman (2002), 'Financial crisis in Southeast Asia: dispelling illusion the Minskyan way', *Cambridge Journal of Economics*, vol. 26.

BIS (1998), 68th Annual Report, Basle.

BIS (1999), 69th Annual Report, Basle.

BIS Statistics on External Indebtedness, various years, Basle.

BIS The Maturity, Sectoral and Nationality Distribution of International Bank Lending, Consolidated Banking Statistics, various years, Basle.

Carvalho, F. C. (1999), 'On Banks' Liquidity Preference', mimeo, IE/UFRJ, Rio de Janeiro.

Chang, H. J., H. J. Park and C. G. Yoo (1998), 'Interpreting the Korean Crisis: financial liberalisation, industrial policy, and corporate governance', *Cambridge Journal Economics*, vol. 22, no. 6.

Chang, R. and A. Velasco (1999), 'Liquidity crises in emerging markets: theory and policy' *NBER Working Paper Series*, n. 7272, Cambridge.

Chesnais, F. (1996), *A Mundialização do Capital. São Paulo.* Editora Xamã. (in Portuguese).

Corsetti, G., P. Pesenti and N. Roubini (1998), 'Paper Tigers? A model of the Asian Crisis', *NBER Working Paper Series*, n. 6783, Cambridge.

Dow, S. (1993), *Money and the Economic Process* (Aldershot: Edward Elgar).

FED of New York (1990), Funding and Liquidity: Recent Changes in Liquidity Management at Commercial Banks and Securities Firms, Staff Study, mimeo.

Finger M. K. and L. Schuknecht (1999), 'Trade, finance and financial crises', *Special Studies*, no. 3 (Geneva: WTO).

Gray, H. P. and M. J. Gray (1994), 'Minskian fragility in the international financial system' in G. Dymsky and R. Pollin (eds) *New Perspectives in Monetary Macroeconomics: Explorations in the Tradition of Hyman P. Minsky* (Michigan: The University of Michigan Press).

IMF (2008), *International Financial Statistics* (Washington, DC).

Kregel, J. (1998), 'Yes, "It" Did Happen Again – A Minsky Crisis Happened in Asia', *Jerome Levy Institute Working Paper*, n. 234.

Kregel, J. (1998a), The Past and Future of Banks, *Quaderni di Ricerche*, n. 21 Bancaria Editrice, mimeo.

Lindreng, C. J., T. J. T. Baliño, C. Enoch, A. M. Gulde, M. Quintyn, and L. Teo (1999), *Financial Sector Crisis and Restructuring: Lessons from Asia*, September (Washington DC: IMF).

Minsky, H. P. (1975), *John Maynard Keynes* (New York: Columbia University Press).

Minsky, H. P. (1982), *Can 'it' Happen Again?, Essays on Instability and Finance* (New York: M. E. Sharp).

Minsky, H. P. (1986), *Stabilizing an Unstable Economy* (New Haven: Yale University Press).
Minsky, H. P. (1994), *'Integração financeira e política monetária'*, in Economia e Sociedade, no. 3, Campinas, Unicamp. (in Portuguese).
Painceira, J. P. (2003), 'The role of banks in the financial crisis of the South Korea in 1997: the financial instability hypothesis approach', *Annals of the VIII Encontro da SEP.* Florianópolis. (in Portuguese).
Plihon, D. (1995), 'The dominance of speculative finance' in *Economia e Sociedade*, no. 5, Campinas, Unicamp. (in Portuguese).
World Bank (1999), *World Development Finance* (Basle).

18
Minsky and Indonesia: Revisiting the Indonesian Crisis by Financial Instability Hypothesis

Yasuyuki Matsumoto

18.1 Introduction

In 2007, the instability and fragility of financial markets due to the US subprime mortgage crisis became tangible. It awoke bankers' and investors' scepticism above underlying credit and liquidity risks and turned them to extreme conservatism in managing their portfolio. They scrambled to liquidate property-related, highly leveraged, complex and/or less transparent financial products. These unwinding activities worsened bankers' and investors' balance sheets through marking down the value of portfolio to the market and forced them to face a shortage of capital. It also broke down mutual credibility among financial institutions. Inter-bank market lost mutual-credibility and liquidity decreased. As a result, the credit default swap (CDS) market collapsed. CDS spreads skyrocketed crushing market values of collateralised debt obligations (CDOs).[1] Central banks pumped huge liquidity into the inter-bank market to prevent commercial banks from rushing into asset sales and withdrawing liquidity. Central bankers were forced to use emergency methods such as accepting securitised products as collaterals for lending and purchasing low-grade corporate papers, in order to sustain the financial system.

This uncertainty led to the breakdown of cash flow and credit chains, the dislocation of liquidity and to de-leveraging on a worldwide scale. A number of leading banks and investors facing fatal cash and capital shortage seek the governmental bail-outs. Finally, the financial fragility and instability caused a gigantic contraction of real economy increasing unemployment and decreasing income.

The scale of the current financial failure is comparable only to the Great Depression of 1929. However, the boom–bust process of the current financial crisis could be observed in previous episodes as well, in which debt played an important role. Capitalists accumulated debts and created complex cash flow chains during the boom periods, but debts can be devastating for the cash flow chains during the bust stages. Hyman Minsky placed debt at the centre of the capitalist economy for his Financial Instability Hypothesis (FIH).

This chapter interprets the FIH by using a financial accounting approach. Secondly, it revisits the 1997–1998 Indonesian financial crises and attempts to find common points with the current financial crisis by focussing on the evolution of the financial structure from the *finance boom* in 1994 to the crisis of 1997.

18.2 An interpretation of Minsky's FIH: the financial accounting approach

The financial accounting framework is used to measure the financial stability of economic units and to aggregate micro financial activities into macro financial structures (Minsky, 1986). First, Minsky analyses the stability of economic units by measuring two margins of safety. The first one is excess cash flow. He considers that the economic unit is stable if its assets can generate cash inflows in excess of cash outflows to fulfil its payment obligations. A stable unit keeps its earnings before interest and tax (EBIT) interest coverage ratio, earnings before interest and tax, plus depreciation and amortisation (EBITDA) interest coverage ratio and debt service cover ratio (DSCR) higher than one. However, as data on debt repayment are difficult to collect, this analysis uses EBIT and EBITDA interest coverage ratios. The second margin of safety is positive net worth or capitalisation. Minsky also considers that the economic unit is stable if the value of its asset exceeds the liability; enterprise value is larger than its debt value (Table 18.1).

Second, Minsky categorises units into three types. Hedge financing units maintain both margins of safety are positive. Speculative financing units keep the first margin of safety positive up to the final payment of its debts for which it needs to liquidate assets and must have positive net worth in order to do so. The stability of a speculative unit depends on the relative size of final payment to net worth. At worst, a speculative financing unit can meet its interest payments but cannot pay down the principal of debts unless liquidating the assets. For a Ponzi financing unit the first margin of safety is negative. Therefore, the unit needs additional debts to finance the negative cash flows. Hence, the second margin of safety also becomes negative.

Third, Minsky categorises the economies into two types, robust financing structure in which hedge units predominate and fragile and unstable financing structure in which speculative and Ponzi units prevail (Table 18.1). Moreover, financial structures necessarily evolve from robust to fragile and unstable in a capitalist economy.

Fourth, Minsky's FIH is built on a closed and advance economy. The theory requires several adjustments in order to apply it to an open developing economy. In particular, the analyses on the margins of safety must include the

Table 18.1 Interpretation of Minsky theory by financial accounting

Minsky's words	Minsky's definition	Interpretation by financial accounting
Hedge financing units	Hedge financing units are 'units whose realized and expected income cash flows are sufficient to meet all payment commitments on the outstanding liability of it' (Minsky, 1986, p. 203).	EBIT interest coverage ratio > 1; EBITDA interest coverage ratio > 1; DSCR > 1; Net worth > 0; The above ratios of this unit are at high level.
Speculative financing units	In speculative financing units, 'balance sheet cash flows from the units will be larger than expected income receipts, so that the only way they can be met is by rolling over (or even increasing) debt' (Minsky, 1986, p. 203). In other words, this unit has enough cash inflows to meet interest payment commitments but not principal repayments (but may be able to pay down part of these commitments) (Minsky, 1991, p. 14).	EBIT interest coverage ratio > 1; EBITDA interest coverage ratio > 1; DSCR > 1 (except for final repayment); Net worth > 0; The above ratios of this unit are lower than those of hedge financing unit; This unit carries a refinancing risk at the payment date of debt obligations.
Ponzi financing units	Ponzi financing units have to increase debt in order to pay debt service, as they do not have sufficient cash inflows to meet even interest payment commitments and cannot help but capitalise interest payments. The increase of debt is accelerated because they have to pay interest on capitalized interest (Minsky, 1986, pp. 207–208).	EBIT interest coverage ratio < 1; EBITDA interest coverage ratio < 1; DSCR < 1; The net worth of this unit becomes negative.
Economy with a robust financing structure	In an economy with a robust financial structure, hedge financing units are dominant (Minsky, 1986, pp. 203–204, 208–210).	Low leverage; Low mismatch of asset-liability duration; High, debt service capacity; High net worth.
Economy with a fragile and unstable financing structure	In an economy with a fragile and unstable financial structure, speculative and Ponzi financing units are dominant (Minsky, 1986, pp. 203–204, 208–210).	High leverage; High mismatch of asset-liability duration; Low-debt service capacity; Low net worth.

nature of debt, such as foreign currency denomination and mobile capital (that is, market-based capital, not relationship-based). Moreover, foreign exchange fluctuation and the availability of hedging tools directly affect the level of leverage and cash outflows. The behaviour of mobile capitals in debt structure can easily push borrowers into insolvency.

Finally, Minsky analysed economic development in the context of evolving financial structures of the capitalist economy in four stages: (i) commercial capitalism with trading activities have a dominant position in the economy and finance serves mainly the provision of short-term working capital by commercial banks and trade/credit unions, easily repaid by cash inflow from sales of inventories. The financial structure is robust; (ii) finance capitalism in which capital-intensive production and investment finance for capital assets dominate and finance requires borrowers to be corporations: founder shareholders and/or financial institutions occupy a dominant position in the ownership (both equity and debt, that is, financial structure) of the corporate sector; (iii) in managerial capitalism the ownership of companies is widely dispersed to individuals: management and ownership are separated and (iv) in money manager capitalism the ownership of companies and even underlying capital assets are more widely distributed. Furthermore, ownership changes into more sophisticated forms, such as mutual funds, pension funds and securitised products (Minsky 1992a). Throughout this development, the financial structure of the economy, including relations between finance and firms, becomes more complex. In the 1990s, excluding Japan, Asian countries, including Indonesia, were at the finance and/or managerial capitalism stage while the United States was at the stage of money manager capitalism.

18.3 Revisiting the Indonesian crisis

Indonesia suffered the deepest economic contraction among all Asian countries after the crisis. As a result, Indonesia fell behind less affected Asian countries, such as China and India, in terms of economic development. This section analyses the evolution into a fragile and unstable financial structure during the finance boom.

18.3.1 The speculative/Ponzi financing unit – the corporate sector

Prior to the 1997–1998 crisis, the country experienced several financial crises due to external debts accumulated by the state and/or banking sectors. However, in the 1990s, the government had maintained macroeconomic stability and prudently controlled public external debt levels. The government had minimised the increase of its external debt under the pressures of international financial institutions. The government expected the private sector to directly access offshore funds for investment. The crisis was caused by an external debt accumulated by the corporate sector, defined as the private non-financial sector (or the private non-bank sector, depending on the availability of data in this work), which obtained, during the finance boom, various types of finance on a huge scale from offshore as well as domestic markets.[2]

The government completed the liberalisation of the capital account in 1970 and also deregulated the domestic financial sector through a series of deregulation packages in the 1980s.[3] In the 1990s, even though government and Central Bank introduced a series of market-based policies and new governance banking procedures in order to prevent overheating, the government intended to actively liberalise the financial environment.[4] The corporate sector, in principle, did not have any significant barriers against accessing both domestic and overseas financial markets for raising funds. Rapid liberalisation of the financial environment led to an expansion of both domestic and external debts in the corporate sector during the 1990s before the crisis (Table 18.2).

Nevertheless, the corporate sector was unable to raise external funds as they had before the boom. A number of offshore banks were still cautious against the corporate sector which did not qualify for international credits prior to the finance boom: even top private companies needed foreign partners' and/or governmental supports to obtain offshore finance. Bank Indonesia and state commercial banks served as intermediaries to access

Table 18.2 Debts by Indonesian corporate sector (billion US dollars, percentage)

Sector	1990	1991	1992	1993	1994	1995	1996	1997
Domestic debt	29.9	35.0	38.0	47.9	58.8	69.7	84.8	58.4
	–	*(16.8)*	*(8.5)*	*(26.1)*	*(22.9)*	*(18.4)*	*(21.8)*	*(–31.2)*
Rupiah	24.2	27.4	29.6	35.6	43.7	51.1	61.8	35.0
	–	*(13.1)*	*(7.8)*	*(20.3)*	*(23.0)*	*(16.9)*	*(21.0)*	*(–43.4)*
Foreign currency	5.7	7.5	8.4	12.3	15.1	18.6	23.0	23.4
	–	*(32.6)*	*(11.2)*	*(46.5)*	*(22.9)*	*(23.0)*	*(23.9)*	*(1.5)*
External debt	12.0	13.2	14.3	15.3	24.6	33.3	42.1	53.6
	–	*(10.2)*	*(8.4)*	*(7.0)*	*(60.7)*	*(35.5)*	*(26.2)*	*(27.4)*
Total debt	41.9	48.2	52.3	63.2	83.4	103.0	126.9	112.0
	–	*(15.0)*	*(8.5)*	*(20.8)*	*(32.0)*	*(23.5)*	*(23.2)*	*(–11.7)*
Foreign currency	17.7	20.7	22.7	27.6	39.7	51.9	65.1	77.0
	–	*(16.9)*	*(9.7)*	*(21.6)*	*(43.8)*	*(30.7)*	*(25.4)*	*(18.3)*
Reliance on external debt (a)	28.6	27.4	27.4	24.2	29.5	32.4	33.2	47.9
Reliance on foreign currency debt (b)	42.1	43.1	43.4	43.7	47.6	50.4	51.3	68.7

Source: Memorandum (by financial advisors) and Bank Indonesia.
() Annual growth.
(a) Reliance on external debt = external debt/total debt.
(b) Reliance on foreign currency debt = foreign currency debt/total debt.

offshore funds for the corporate sector. Debt finance from domestic banks, especially state commercial banks, was the most important funding tool for the corporate sector until the middle of the 1990s. This changed in 1994 when the market for offshore finance suddenly opened to the Indonesian corporate sector. The demand for foreign currency loans increased sharply under the relatively stable crawling peg. Thanks to the cost of borrowing differential between Rupiah and US dollar the corporate sector's external debt jumped by 60.7 per cent in 1994 and grew at an average annual rate of around 40 per cent until the outbreak of the crisis. The corporate sector constantly increased its foreign currency denominated debt from domestic banks. In 1996, it reached $42 billion and the total of foreign exchange denominated debts amounted to $77 billion. This was more than one and a half times as much as the government external debt.

In 1996, the corporate sector's reliance on external debt (including both onshore and offshore) suddenly turned upwards reaching 51.3 per cent: the largest share of funding requirements of the corporate sector was given over to foreign currency debt whose accumulation accelerated. The availability of foreign currency hedging tools, such as currency swaps and forward transactions, was improving but still limited at the time: a substantial part of the foreign currency debt was not hedged. The corporate sector believed in a stable rupiah and introduced non-hedged foreign currency positions into its financial structure.

The excessive reliance on offshore markets and foreign exchange debt made the economy extremely vulnerable to external shocks, such as sudden reversal of capital flows.

Tables 18.3–18.5 show how the accumulation of Indonesia's external debt was driven by the corporate sector. Moreover, the state had limited the growth of its external debt's increase to an average of 5.3 per cent per annum.

Table 18.3 Indonesian external debt 1989–1998 (billion US dollars)

Sector	1989	1990	1991	1992	1993	1994	1995	1996	1997	1998
State	43.2	49.3	50.5	55.8	60.7	66.5	68.3	62.0	63.8	76.3
Government	39.6	45.1	45.7	48.8	52.5	58.6	59.6	55.3	53.9	67.3
Banks	0.4	1.1	1.4	2.5	3.1	2.8	3.9	3.0	5.9	4.8
Non-banks	3.2	3.1	3.4	4.5	5.1	5.1	4.8	3.7	4.0	4.2
Private	8.8	13.5	15.2	17.5	19.9	30.0	39.5	48.2	62.1	69.4
Banks	0.4	1.5	2.0	3.2	4.6	5.4	6.2	6.1	8.5	6.0
Corporate	8.4	12.0	13.2	14.3	15.3	24.6	33.3	42.1	53.6	63.4
Corporate (non-finance)	7.9	11.3	12.4	13.5	14.4	23.2	31.4	39.7	50.2	61.3
Finance	0.5	0.7	0.8	0.8	0.9	1.4	1.9	2.4	3.4	2.1
Total external debt	52.0	62.8	65.7	73.3	80.6	96.5	107.8	110.2	125.9	145.7

Source: Memorandum (by financial advisors) and Bank Indonesia.

Table 18.4 Annual growth of Indonesian external debt (percentage per annum)

Sector	1990	1991	1992	1993	1994	1995	1996	1997	1998
State	14.1	2.4	10.5	8.8	9.6	2.7	−9.2	2.9	19.6
Government	13.9	1.3	6.8	7.6	11.6	1.7	−7.2	−2.5	24.9
Banks	175.0	27.3	78.6	24.0	−9.7	39.3	−23.1	96.7	−18.6
Non-banks	−3.1	9.7	32.4	13.3	0.0	−5.9	−22.9	8.1	5.0
Private	53.4	12.6	15.1	13.7	50.8	31.7	22.0	28.8	11.8
Banks	275.0	33.3	60.0	43.8	17.4	14.8	−1.6	39.3	−29.4
Corporate	42.9	10.0	8.3	7.0	60.8	35.4	26.4	27.3	18.3
Corporate (non-finance)	43.0	9.7	8.9	6.7	61.1	35.3	26.4	26.4	22.1
Finance	40.0	14.3	0.0	12.5	55.6	35.7	26.3	41.7	−38.2
Total external debt	20.8	4.6	11.6	10.0	19.7	11.7	2.2	14.2	15.7

Source: Memorandum (by financial advisors) and Bank Indonesia.

Table 18.5 Share of Indonesian external debt by sector (percentage)

Sector	1989	1990	1991	1992	1993	1994	1995	1996	1997	1998
State	83.1	78.5	76.9	76.1	75.3	68.9	63.4	56.3	50.7	52.4
Government	76.2	71.8	69.6	66.6	65.1	60.7	55.3	50.2	42.8	46.2
Banks	0.8	1.8	2.1	3.4	3.8	2.9	3.6	2.7	4.7	3.3
Non-banks	6.2	4.9	5.2	6.1	6.3	5.3	4.5	3.4	3.2	2.9
Private	16.9	21.5	23.1	23.9	24.7	31.1	36.6	43.7	49.3	47.6
Banks	0.8	2.4	3.0	4.4	5.7	5.6	5.8	5.5	6.8	4.1
Corporate	16.2	19.1	20.1	19.5	19.0	25.5	30.9	38.2	42.6	43.5
Corporate (non-finance)	15.2	18.0	18.9	18.4	17.9	24.0	29.1	36.0	39.9	42.1
Finance	1.0	1.1	1.2	1.1	1.1	1.5	1.8	2.2	2.7	1.4
Total external debt	100.0	100.0	100.0	100.0	100.0	100.0	100.0	100.0	100.0	100.0

Source: Memorandum (by financial advisors) and Bank Indonesia.

Government and state companies, increased their external debt by only 2.7 per cent per annum during the finance boom. The state sector's share of external debt decreased from 78.6 per cent in 1990 to 56.3 per cent in 1996. By contrast, during the 3 years of the finance boom, the private sector's offshore debt dramatically rose from $19.9 billion to $48.2 billion, and the sector's share of total external debt jumped from 24.7 per cent to 43.7 per cent.

The corporate sector drove the external debt throughout the period. The share of this sector in total external debt also doubled from 18 per cent to 36 per cent.

During the 1990s, the state restricted its foreign borrowing while the private sector expanded overseas borrowing at an increasing rate. Capital controls proved to be reasonably successful. Ironically, it was the absence of controls on corporate external borrowing that ultimately destroyed the banking system.

18.3.2 The engine of the corporate sector's financing – offshore syndicated loan

The role of financial products in the process of financial evolution was important to Minsky. In Indonesia, most external finances were obtained from bank lenders rather than portfolio investors. In particular, during the finance boom, the corporate sector aggressively used offshore syndicated loans and leveraged its balance sheet sharply.

Tables 18.6 and 18.7 summarise offshore syndicated loans from 1993 to 1997. In 1993, the private sector had used more offshore syndicated debt than the state sector (number of transactions). Nevertheless, the state sector still had a significant share in terms of dollar amount: banks were major borrowers of offshore syndicated loans (both number and volume of transactions).

Offshore lenders had not accepted a wide range of corporate borrowers at this stage. In 1994, this situation totally changed. Both the number and volume of offshore syndicated loans sharply increased to 143 and $8.1 billion. Private non-bank companies began to access the offshore syndicated

Table 18.6 Offshore syndicated debts for Indonesian borrowers (by the number of transactions)

	State			Private			Total		
	Banks	Non-banks	Total	Banks	Non-banks*	Total	Banks	Non-banks	Total
1993	18	5	23	44	22	66	62	27	89
	20.2	5.6	25.8	49.4	24.7	74.2	69.7	30.3	100.0
1994	14	3	17	43	83	126	57	86	143
	9.8	2.1	11.9	30.1	58.0	88.1	39.9	60.1	100.0
1995	17	10	27	55	136	191	72	146	216
	7.8	4.6	12.4	25.2	62.4	87.6	33.0	67.0	100.0
1996	25	13	38	62	238	300	87	251	338
	7.4	3.8	11.2	18.3	70.4	88.8	25.7	74.3	100.0
1997	15	9	24	45	184	229	60	193	253
	5.9	3.6	9.5	17.8	72.7	90.5	23.7	76.3	100.0
Total	89	40	129	249	663	912	338	703	1,041
	8.5	3.8	12.4	23.9	63.7	87.6	32.5	67.5	100.0

Upper: the number of syndicated debts.
Lower: the share of the sector.
*Including the corporate sector and non-bank finance companies.
Sources: privately collected data and IFR.

Table 18.7 Offshore syndicated debts for Indonesian borrowers (by the value of transactions)

	(US$ million, %)								
	State			Private			Total		
	Banks	Non-banks	Total	Banks	Non-banks	Total	Banks	Non-banks	Total
1993	1,236	820	2,056	2,172	548	2,720	3,408	1,368	4,776
	25.9	17.2	43.0	45.5	11.5	57.0	71.4	28.6	100.0
1994	1,827	228	2,055	2,820	3,245	6,065	4,646	3,473	8,119
	22.5	2.8	25.3	34.7	40.0	74.7	57.2	42.8	100.0
1995	1,820	911	2,731	2,870	10,805	13,675	4,690	11,716	16,406
	11.1	5.6	16.6	17.5	65.9	83.4	28.6	71.4	100.0
1996	2,081	1,352	3,433	3,410	18,034	21,444	5,491	19,386	24,877
	8.4	5.4	13.8	13.7	72.5	86.2	22.1	77.9	100.0
1997	1,330	1,683	3,013	2,231	18,219	20,450	3,561	19,902	23,463
	5.7	7.2	12.8	9.5	77.6	87.2	15.2	84.8	100.0
Total	8,293	4,994	13,287	13,503	50,851	64,354	21,796	55,845	77,641
	10.7	6.4	17.1	17.4	65.5	82.9	28.1	71.9	100.0

Upper: the aggregate value of syndicated debts.
Lower: the share of the sector.
*Including the corporate sector and non-bank finance companies.
Sources: privately collected data and IFR.

debt market and offshore lenders also started accepting the risks associated with the sector.

Offshore fund raising accelerated in 1995 and reached its peak in 1996 and 1997. This situation clearly indicates the finance boom in Indonesia. Offshore syndicated loans for private non-bank borrowers accounted for more than 70 per cent of the total. Indonesia's external debt problem shifted from a state sector problem to that of the private sector and, in particular, that of the corporate sector.

Offshore lenders enthusiastically provided unimaginable foreign currency liquidity to Indonesia's corporate sector and expanded the range of acceptable non-bank borrowers. In addition, average tenors and all-in margins, for both banks and non-banks, improved dramatically during the finance boom (Table 18.8). The first was stretched from 2.1 years in 1993 to 3.4 years in 1997, and the second dropped from 232.11 in 1993 to 191.13 basis points per annum in 1997. For non-bank borrowers, the first increased from 2.1 years in 1993 to 3.5 years in 1997, and the second decreased from 234.27 in 1993 to 207.65 basis points per annum in 1997. Table 18.9 indicates that the above trend is more definite for regular and top-tier credit borrowers in the corporate sector. The average tenors for both regular and top-tier credit borrowers doubled, and the all-in margins for them were also narrowed sharply. The combination of offshore lenders' enthusiasm and Indonesian debtors' strong demand for offshore funds with better terms and conditions built up foreign currency denominated external debts in a huge scale creating an extremely fragile and crises-prone financial structure in Indonesia (Tables 18.8 and 18.9).

Offshore lenders also drove the diversification of borrowers. During the finance boom, new borrowers with higher credit risks such as grandchild subsidiaries of leading business groups, medium and small business groups and real estate companies entered the offshore syndicated debt market aggressively. Table 18.10 indicates that the Indonesian borrowers of offshore

Table 18.8 Average tenors and all-in margins of offshore syndicated debts

(years, basis points per annum)						
	Average tenors			**All-in margins**		
	Banks	**Non-banks**	**All**	**Banks**	**Non-banks**	**All**
1993	2.1	2.1	2.1	165.14	234.27	205.54
1994	2.3	2.6	2.5	155.49	229.80	207.44
1995	2.8	2.9	2.9	126.77	205.17	188.34
1996	3.1	3.0	3.1	115.02	209.04	192.54
1997	2.9	3.5	3.4	110.44	207.65	191.13

Sources: privately collected data and IFR.

Table 18.9 Average tenors and all-in margins of offshore syndicated debts

(years, basis points per annum)						
	Average tenors			**All-in margins**		
	Top ten regular borrowers	**Top-tier credit borrowers**	**All borrowers**	**Top ten regular borrowers**	**Top-tier credit borrowers**	**All borrowers**
1993	1.6	1.9	2.1	222.94	218.33	232.11
1994	2.4	2.7	2.6	212.79	201.58	229.80
1995	2.7	2.8	2.9	202.68	187.46	205.17
1996	2.7	3.2	3.0	198.17	164.67	209.20
1997	3.3	3.7	3.5	193.15	159.93	207.65

Sources: privately collected data and IFR.

Table 18.10 Debtors' concentration in offshore syndicated debts

	Number of transactions					**Funding amount**				
	1993	**1994**	**1995**	**1996**	**1997**	**1993**	**1994**	**1995**	**1996**	**1997**
Top 5	31.8	31.7	26.2	24.7	18.3	42.4	38.3	22.8	29.2	18.0
Top 10	43.9	41.3	38.7	34.3	31.0	50.5	47.4	32.6	39.5	27.7
Top 15	57.6	48.4	47.6	42.3	35.8	56.7	49.2	35.9	46.4	33.0
Top 20	63.6	54.8	53.9	47.3	41.5	63.5	54.7	41.5	49.6	34.9
Top 25	68.2	59.5	59.2	51.3	43.2	68.9	59.6	45.0	51.9	37.6
Top 30	72.7	61.9	62.3	55.0	45.4	70.6	62.0	46.3	54.0	40.9
Top 35	72.7	64.3	63.9	56.7	48.9	71.7	63.9	47.1	55.7	42.5

Sources: privately collected data and IFR.

syndicated debts diversified as the finance boom developed. Tables 18.11 and 18.12 also show that the range of business group borrowers widened during the period. The credit quality of Indonesian debtors was obviously driven down. This situation diversified the contact points between offshore financial markets and the Indonesian economy, and thereby rendered Indonesia's financial structure more complex.

In addition, offshore loans totally differ from domestic bank loans provided under heavily relationship-oriented bank-based financial systems. Offshore loans are money from the market-based financial world, and offshore financiers do not hesitate to make simple judgements based on risk–return calculations. They are mobile capital investors for whom expectation and perception of other investors' opinions play an important role. This causes a sudden reversal of capital flows and contagion to other countries. At the beginning of the Indonesian crisis, offshore lenders' perception

Table 18.11 Offshore syndicated debts for Indonesian business groups

	Business groups	1993	1994	1995	1996	1997	Total
1	Sinar Mas	5	11	19	23	9	67
2	Salim	5	9	9	15	9	47
3	Astra	7	9	9	11	10	46
4	Bakrie	1	4	7	12	10	34
5	Ongko	3	7	6	13	4	33
6	Gajah Tunggal	4	5	6	7	5	27
7	Dharmala+PSP	1	2	5	6	8	22
8	Ciputra+Jaya+Metropolitan	0	1	5	5	7	18
9	Ometraco	2	3	5	4	4	18
10	Napan+Risjad	1	1	3	7	5	17
11	Bank Bali	2	4	4	5	2	17
12	Lippo	2	2	4	4	2	14
13	Modern	2	2	1	7	2	14
14	CP	3	1	3	3	3	13
15	Mulia	0	0	5	5	2	12
16	Niaga	1	2	2	4	3	12
17	Panin	2	3	3	2	2	12
18	Kalbe	0	3	2	2	3	10
19	Argo Mannungal	0	0	4	3	3	10
20	Tirtamas	1	0	1	4	2	8
-	Others	24	57	88	158	134	461
	Total	66	126	191	300	229	912

Sources: privately collected data and IFR.
Notes: Others includes Gunung Sewu, Aneka Kimia Raya, Danamon, Sierad, Raja Garuda Mas, Sungai Budi, Maspion, Sampoerna, Artha Graha, Texmaco, Hadtex, Bukaka, Tigaraksa, Ever Shine, Barito Pacific, Suharto family and others.

Table 18.12 Offshore syndicated debts for Indonesian business groups

(by the funding amount) (US$ million)							
	Business groups	**1993**	**1994**	**1995**	**1996**	**1997**	**Total**
1	Sinar Mas	300	671	1,446	2,008	872	5,296
2	Salim	381	668	662	1,132	1,133	3,977
3	Astra	325	628	538	1,318	602	3,410
4	Gajah Tunggal	117	288	243	951	543	2,142
5	Bakrie	30	70	230	863	537	1,730
6	Ongko	45	190	174	692	121	1,222
7	Dharmala+PSP	26	50	208	488	435	1,207
8	Ciputra+Jaya+ Metropolitan	0	40	261	170	710	1,181

Table 18.12 (Continued)

	(by the funding amount) (US$ million)					
Business groups	**1993**	**1994**	**1995**	**1996**	**1997**	**Total**
9 Ometraco	88	80	355	315	223	1,061
10 Napan+Risjad	60	192	338	537	489	1,616
11 Mulia	0	0	333	510	180	1,023
12 Raja Garuda Mas	0	33	0	290	325	648
13 Sampoerna	96	25	0	150	300	571
14 Aneka Kimia Raya	72	50	48	370	0	540
15 Medco	0	0	75	155	280	510
16 Bank Bali	70	75	108	190	48	490
17 Lippo	31	60	156	154	88	489
18 Kalbe	0	75	125	55	215	470
19 Tirtamas	25	0	175	216	42	458
20 Gudang Garam	60	120	195	82	0	457
- Others	993	2,750	8,006	10,800	13,307	35,856
Total	2,720	6,065	13,675	21,444	20,450	64,354

Sources: privately collected data and IFR.
Notes: Others includes Gunung Sewu, Aneka Kimia Raya, Danamon, Sierad, Raja Garuda Mas, Sungai Budi, Maspion, Sampoerna, Artha Graha, Texmaco, Hadtex, Bukaka, Tigaraksa, Ever Shine, Barito Pacific, Suharto family and others.

suddenly shifted in a negative direction. A number of offshore financiers did not help the financial restructuring of troubled Indonesian borrowers by waiving breaches of covenant provisions but attempted to accelerate debt repayments. This situation put pressure on the borrowers to repay. Finally, it caused a sudden reversal of offshore bank money in a large scale worsening the crisis.

18.3.3 The evolution of the Indonesian corporate sector's financial structure

Tables 18.13 and 18.14 summarise the transition of the corporate sector's financial positions in the 1990s by focusing on Minsky's margins of safety, that is, leverage and debt service capacity. These ratios indicate that the corporate sector steeply leveraged its balance sheet and deteriorated its financial soundness through aggressive debt finance during the 1994–1997 finance booms. The corporate sector shifted itself from hedge to speculative financing unit in less than 4 years.

At the beginning of the 1990s, the corporate sector still maintained a healthy balance sheet and high capacity of debt service payments. The leverage ratio was 0.78; the equity ratio was 56.1 per cent. The ratios of gross/net debt to equity and gross/net debt to EBITDA were 0.48/0.37 and

Table 18.13 Financial ratios of the Indonesian corporate sector

	Unit	1990	1991	1992	1993	1994	1995	1996	1997
Leverage	times	0.78	1.21	1.28	1.23	1.21	1.52	1.84	2.37
Equity	per cent	56.1	45.2	43.8	44.9	45.3	39.7	35.2	29.7
Gross debt to equity	times	0.43	0.83	0.92	0.80	0.82	1.02	1.11	1.71
Net debt to equity	times	0.37	0.77	0.79	0.71	0.69	0.82	0.87	1.42
Gross debt to EBITDA	times	1.78	3.31	3.75	3.18	3.35	3.80	4.35	8.78
Net debt to EBITDA	times	1.54	3.09	3.23	2.82	2.83	3.04	3.39	7.29
Gross debt to CS+APIC	times	0.62	1.22	1.38	1.31	1.25	1.60	1.83	2.67
Net debt to CS+APIC	times	0.53	1.13	1.19	1.16	1.06	1.28	1.42	2.22
Long-term to short-term debt	times	0.43	0.70	1.13	0.99	1.43	1.72	2.12	1.86
Net short-term debt to EBITDA	times	1.01	1.71	1.24	1.24	0.87	0.64	0.43	1.58
Operating profit margin	per cent	11.8	12.3	13.5	15.0	16.3	17.3	16.4	13.8
Net profit margin	per cent	8.2	8.0	8.3	8.8	9.7	10.0	9.6	-4.5
EBITDA margin	per cent	14.2	15.3	17.6	19.3	20.3	22.3	21.8	20.5
Return on assets	per cent	11.2	9.1	8.2	8.7	8.9	8.3	6.8	3.9
Return on equity	per cent	13.9	13.1	11.5	11.5	11.7	12.1	11.2	-4.3
EBIT interest coverage	times	3.32	3.25	2.76	2.97	3.63	2.86	2.00	1.30
EBIT funding cost coverage	times	3.02	2.55	2.30	2.62	3.08	2.36	1.81	0.69
EBITDA interest coverage	times	3.98	4.04	3.59	3.84	4.52	3.69	2.67	1.93
EBITDA funding cost coverage	times	3.63	3.17	2.99	3.39	3.85	3.04	2.41	1.02

Sources: annual reports.

1.78/1.54, respectively. Both the EBIT and EBITDA interest coverage ratios were 3.32 and 3.93 times, respectively. In sum, the corporate sector financed its balance sheet predominantly by equity and had high level of debt service capacity. In Minsky's terms, the corporate sector was hedging financing units with high margins of safety. Taking the relatively sound financial positions of

Table 18.14 The changes of financial ratios of the Indonesian corporate sector

Ratios	1990	1991	1992	1993	1994	1995	1996	1997
Leverage	0.64	0.99	1.05	1.00	0.98	1.24	1.50	1.93
Equity	1.25	1.01	0.97	1.00	1.01	0.88	0.78	0.66
Gross debt to equity	0.54	1.04	1.15	1.00	1.03	1.28	1.39	2.15
Net debt to equity	0.52	1.09	1.12	1.00	0.98	1.15	1.23	2.01
Gross debt to EBITDA	0.56	1.04	1.18	1.00	1.05	1.19	1.37	2.76
Net debt to EBITDA	0.55	1.10	1.15	1.00	1.01	1.08	1.20	2.59
Gross debt to CS+APIC	0.47	0.93	1.05	1.00	0.96	1.22	1.40	2.04
Net debt to CS+APIC	0.46	0.98	1.03	1.00	0.91	1.10	1.23	1.91
Long-term to short-term debt	0.43	0.71	1.14	1.00	1.44	1.74	2.15	1.88
Net short-term debt to EBITDA	0.82	1.39	1.01	1.00	0.70	0.52	0.35	1.28
Operating profit margin	0.79	0.82	0.90	1.00	1.09	1.16	1.10	0.92
Net profit margin	0.93	0.91	0.94	1.00	1.10	1.14	1.09	−0.51
EBITDA margin	0.73	0.79	0.91	1.00	1.05	1.15	1.13	1.06
Return on assets	1.28	1.04	0.95	1.00	1.02	0.95	0.78	0.45
Return on equity	1.21	1.14	1.00	1.00	1.02	1.05	0.98	−0.37
EBIT interest coverage	1.12	1.10	0.93	1.00	1.22	0.96	0.68	0.44
EBIT funding cost coverage	1.15	0.97	0.88	1.00	1.18	0.90	0.69	0.26
EBITDA interest coverage	1.04	1.05	0.94	1.00	1.18	0.96	0.70	0.50
EBITDA funding cost coverage	1.07	0.93	0.88	1.00	1.13	0.90	0.71	0.30

Sources: annual reports.

the state and banking sectors into consideration, Indonesia was an economy with a robust financing structure.

Immediately prior to the finance boom, the corporate sector slightly increased its leverage by using domestic bank funds. Although the corporate sector improved operating profit, net profit and EBITDA margins, the debt service capacity was slightly reduced. Due to the tight money policies introduced in 1992, the corporate sector improved both balance sheet and debt service coverage in 1993. However, the government and central banks did not change the direction of financial liberalisation.

In 1994, the corporate sector entered the finance boom and the era of high leverage. In 1997, the ratios of leverage, gross/net debt to equity and gross/net debt to EBITDA reached 2.37, 1.71/1.42 and 8.78/7.29 times, respectively. The EBIT and EBITDA interest coverage ratios sharply declined to 1.30 and 1.93 times respectively. The corporate sector successfully increased the portion of long-term finance. However, this did not help to improve debt service capacity due to covenant provisions. Even long-term bank loans can be easily converted into short-term claims during currency crises through breach of covenant provisions triggering an acceleration of debt repayment. In Minsky's words, during the finance boom the corporate sector deteriorated its margins of safety and fell into speculative financing unit through the leveraging processes and changed Indonesia as an economy with fragile and unstable financial structure.

18.4 Conclusion

During the finance boom, the Indonesian corporate sector aggressively accumulated external debts. The corporate sector held huge foreign exchange risk and leveraged its balance sheet to an unsustainable level. Offshore financiers' enthusiastic approaches provided a wide range of Indonesian business groups with access to external debt finances. This complicated cross-border cash flow and credit chains between Indonesian economy and offshore markets. In addition, such external loans were unstable, mobile capitals which were mainly financed by market-based offshore banks. The corporate sector, therefore, held a risk of sudden reversals of offshore funds. Following Minsky's FIH, the corporate sector evolved to speculative financing unit during the finance boom and finally escalated to Ponzi financing unit. The corporate sector introduced an unstable, fragile and crisis-prone nature into the Indonesian financial structure. In the current US crisis, both individual and financial sectors have played speculative financing unit roles and finally evolved themselves into Ponzi financing units. In particular, the US individual sector, which aggressively borrowed consumer loans and hybrid housing debts, such as subprime mortgage loans and home equity loans, have formed typical Ponzi financing units.

In the Indonesian corporate sector, business groups were the driving forces to leverage the sector's financial structure with fragile and unstable offshore debts. During the finance boom, Indonesian business groups financed new business opportunities by using third-parties' funds as much as possible. They, furthermore, attempted to cash their existing investments with third parties' funds in order to create liquidity against their illiquid investments. For this purpose, they aggressively absorbed any types of debts. International financiers also provided abundant offshore liquidity to the Indonesian business groups and made them vulnerable against external shocks. In

Minsky's terms, during the finance boom, both Indonesian business groups and offshore financiers enthusiastically co-operated to force the evolution of Indonesia's financial structure from hedge to speculative financing. In the case of the current US crisis, huge liquidity in the financial markets, financiers' greed for profit and individuals' desire for consumption similarly forced the evolution of both finance and individual sectors' financial structures to speculative and Ponzi finances.

Minsky also studied the role of financial products in the process of financial evolution. During the finance boom in Indonesia, offshore syndicated loans were actively used in order to leverage the corporate sector's balance sheet. In the later stage of the finance boom, advanced, risky equity-linked financing tools, such as share finances and exchangeable bonds, were also introduced by Indonesian borrowers. As widely argued, in the United States, securitised notes, hedge funds and other highly leveraged financial products are typical financial tools to have developed extremely unstable and fragile financial structure, which led to the current crisis. Finally, in both the Indonesian and the current financial crises, financiers scrambled to liquidate their investments (that is, the above-mentioned financial products) and thereby the unwinding of complex cash flow and credit chains suddenly happened in a large scale. This eliminated the margins of safety, damaged the financial structures and systems and finally ravaged the real economies in both countries.

As argued in this chapter, Minsky's FIH clarifies the motor force which drove the financial structure and introduced extraordinary fragility and instability into Indonesian economy during the finance boom, which finally led to the crisis. In the boom–bust process, Minsky's key factors, such as debt, cash flow, economic unit, financial product and forward-looking behaviour, determined the fragility and instability of the financial structure. The author of this chapter concludes that Minsky's theory can explain the boom–bust process of most financial crises, including the current crisis.

Notes

1. The underlying portfolio of CDO refers to CDS, and mark-to-market prices of other credit products, such as loan fund, also refer to CDS.
2. Due to the availability of data, the debt figures of the non-bank sector are analysed as those of the corporate sector.
3. Deregulation policies were introduced between 1983 and 1989. In June 1983, bank credit ceilings and most interest rate controls were eliminated. In December 1987, a deregulation package for the investment and capital markets Packet 23 Desember 1987 (PAKDES I) was introduced, in which daily price controls on the Jakarta Stock Exchange were eliminated. In October 1988, the government introduced a major banking reform and deregulation package Paket 27 Oktober 1988 (PAKTO) that eliminated restrictions on the opening of new banks, branches and foreign joint-venture banks. In December 1988, the amendment and supplemental package Paket 20 Desember 1988 (PAKDES II) was introduced allowing foreign

ownership of securities companies. The government refined PAKTO in March 1989 Paket 25 Maret 1989 (PAKMAR) and changed foreign borrowing restrictions on bank and non-bank financial institutions (NBFI) to controls on net open positions.
4. These included liquidity management through control over interest rates on SBI (Sertifikat Bank Indonesia) and discontinuing purchases of SBPU (Surat Berharga Pasar Uang), and 'new risk weighted capital adequacy measures (such as Capital Adequacy Ratio CAR)'. The combination with other contractionary policies, slowed domestic credit growth in 1992 which accelerated again in 1993.

References

Arestis, P. and M. Glickman (2002) 'Financial crisis in Southeast Asia: dispelling illusion the Minskyan way', *Cambridge Journal of Economics*, vol. 26.

Cole, D. C. and B. F. Slade (1996) *Building a Modern Financial System: The Indonesian Experience* (Cambridge: Cambridge University Press).

Matsumoto, Y. (2007) *Financial Fragility and Instability in Indonesia* (London: Routledge).

Minsky, H. P. (1986) *Stabilizing an Unstable Economy*, (New Haven and London: Yale University Press).

Minsky, H. P. (1992a) 'Reconstituting the United States' financial structure: some fundamental issues', *The Jerome Levy Economics Institute of Bard College Working Paper*, no. 69 (New York: Annandale-on-Hudson).

Minsky, H. P. (1992b) 'The capital development of the economy and the structure of financial institutions', *The Jerome Levy Economics Institute of Bard College Working Paper*, no. 72 (New York: Annandale-on-Hudson).

Minsky, H. P. (1992c) 'The FIH', *The Jerome Levy Economics Institute of Bard College Working Paper*, no. 74 (New York: Annandale-on-Hudson).

Minsky, H. P. (1993) 'Finance and stability: the limits of capitalism', *The Jerome Levy Economics Institute of Bard College Working Paper*, no. 93 (New York: Annandale-on-Hudson).

The World Bank, Financial flows and developing countries (various issues), Washington, DC.

The World Bank (1998) Indonesia in crisis: a macroeconomic update, Washington, DC.

The World Bank (1999) Indonesia: from crisis to opportunity, Washington, DC.

Data

Bank Indonesia, Statistik Ekonomi Keuangan Indonesia (Indonesian Financial Statistics), Jakarta.

Bank Indonesia, Report for the financial years (various issues), Jakarta.

Lazard Freres, Lehman Brothers and UBS (then SBC Warburg) (financial advisors), Memorandum: The Republic of Indonesia (various issues), (not public paper).

Thomson Financial, International Financing Review: 1992–1998.

Index